X

Rorschach's Test

III. ADVANCES IN INTERPRETATION

By Dr. Samuel J. Beck

RORSCHACH'S TEST

Rorschach's Test

III. ADVANCES IN INTERPRETATION

By

SAMUEL J. BECK, Ph.D.

*Institute for Psychosomatic and
Psychiatric Research,
Michael Reese Hospital, Chicago.
Departments of Psychology,
University of Chicago and
Northwestern University*

GRUNE & STRATTON

NEW YORK

1952

Library of Congress Catalog Card No. 44–3779

PRINTED AND BOUND IN U.S.A.
FOR GRUNE & STRATTON, INC.

CONTENTS

FOREWORD

The present volume reports and illustrates my advances in interpretive use of the Rorschach test since publication of *Rorschach's Test, Volume II*, in 1945. These advances are in part based on two research projects in which I have been engaged for the past five years. In part they result from continued exposure to clinical method. From these two sources have emerged the fresh insights into the significances of the psychologic operations projected by this particular instrument. The researches have been invaluable in making it possible to build up quantitative data, hitherto unavailable for the Rorschach test. The data have provided spheres of reference essential in any procedure that undertakes to measure. Such compass points are more, not less, essential when the object under scrutiny happens to be the human personality. Each human is, to be sure, a universe in himself. But these universes are as subject to general law as are any of the other countless varieties of universes on which science focuses. To the extent that the data make it possible, therefore, it is necessary to count, and to measure.

The other area of advance, the one more characteristic of the clinical setting, has been of qualitative order. Many observations constantly force themselves in the use of the Rorschach test, observations that cannot be quantitatively defined or arranged in numerical rankings. They recur with a frequency such as to indicate some regularity behind their occurrence, given certain personality conditions. That is, they have validity. They also carry the pitfall of any qualitative judgment, that of becoming subjective. Their value will vary directly, therefore, with each examiner's ability to set up his operational definitions, and to refer each qualitative judgment to such definition. Not to employ these observations, only because they are qualitative, and not to report them, will be to omit technics that do provide very much information about the personality under investigation. The science of personality has not yet made such progress that it can afford to ignore recurring events, the judgments concerning which have, for the present, to be qualitative.

The advances in interpretation are thus both quantitative and qualitative. They are exemplified in seven test records for four patients, either in psychotherapy or in psychoanalysis. All interpretations go into meticulous detail. They report everything that I consider valid, whether in major structure, or finer lineament, for each person, as described by the Rorschach test technic. They trace a picture of the growth in the two boys, the two for whom I have more than one test record each. I also report in detail the non-Rorschach test data, that from the social work and the psychiatric records.

These interpretations are, therefore, a statement of where the Rorschach test, as I use it, is at the present time. The student will note that a great deal of quantitative analysis is possible in the Rorschach test. This is not to say that I am deceiving myself as to whether we have a measure of the whole human personality, in the strictly defined sense of the word "measure." We do have a good test, one that uses a fixed set of stimuli, and that gives results useful to the clinic and to the practitioner. Within a range of error moderate for what it attempts, the test provides dependable diagnostic pictures, and guide-posts for treatment. The test and its claims are now being subjected to some hard thinking and experimental check. As to the value, and some fallacies in these, I make reference in the text (p. 287 ff.). The additional comment is in order that the reports I have seen are classifiable into two groups. One, and the majority, limit themselves to individual test variables. They are procedures only partially applicable to the problem of a whole personality, conceived as a universe of interacting forces. They do not, therefore, add light on the validity of the test; nor aid directly in the scientific investigation of that datum called the human personality. A very small number of students have taken up the challenge which the test is setting up. The issue is being squarely joined. It is from that quarter that I look for hypotheses and a logic that will advance a science of the whole human personality. Whether this will be with the Rorschach, or any other test, will not then matter. Meanwhile, and in absence of research more convincing toward refuting the validities that have emerged, there are still the ten Swiss ink blots.

The two researches to which I refer above are being carried on under grant from the National Institute of Health. Results from these researches have been separately published. More are forthcoming. An inclusive monograph is in preparation. This is my opportunity to acknowledge my deep gratitude for those grants. They alone have made possible the laying of foundations that are *sine qua non* for any scientific endeavor. Secondly, I want to express grateful acknowledgment to Dr. Roy R. Grinker and Dr. Bruno Bettelheim, the Directors, respectively, of the Institute for Psychosomatic and Psychiatric Research in Michael Reese Hospital, and of the Orthogenic School of the University of Chicago. By permitting me to use the files of patients, they enabled me to make my selection of cases as well as to study the pertinent non-Rorschach test data. I am also indebted to Professor William E. Henry of the University of Chicago for his invaluable aid in reading the proofs, a most laborious task in this kind of book. The gratitude that I can least adequately state is that which I owe to my wife. I am not even attempting it. For, with Tennyson (and like projective tests),

... words, like Nature, half reveal
And half conceal the Soul within.

S.J.B.

To

Morris Berick

What is man, that thou shouldst magnify him,
And that thou shouldst set thy mind upon him,
And that thou shouldst visit him every morning,
And try him every moment?

—Job

CHAPTER I

CONCERNING THE PERSONALITY

A. THE FUNCTIONING UNIT

The human personality is a single functioning unit. Any action of any human can be understood as activity of the unit whole, of a living organism, a purpose-moved being, attempting to continue himself in existence, to maintain equilibrium, to feel comfortable. Human actions cannot be fully explained except as actions of the personality as a unit seeking to preserve itself and its comfort.

This is the only concept of personality with which I find it possible to understand any individual. It is a position inductively arrived at from study of clinical data concerning patients with mental disease, paralleling investigations with the Rorschach test. It is an interpretation of the observed data, clinical and Rorschach, which accounts for all these behaviors, whether as part manifestations, or as wholes. The thesis enables us to understand: (a) why the patient has "symptoms," and (b) why he suffers any mental disturbance or illness at all. When enough of the facts are available, i.e., when we have knowledge concerning that whole person, this concept explains also (c) the choice of the symptoms and (d) the choice of the disease.

In the "normal" endeavors of life, it explains an individual's character course. It clarifies the logic of finer traits, and of deeper motives—those which the great novelists and dramatists too beautifully and truthfully light up. This concept of a whole person alone explains all the observed facts. The others do not. There have been many others. In his book on *Personality*, Gordon Allport[1] identifies fully five species of personality definitions other than the psychological. In the psychological, he finds five varieties, aside from his own. Many of these definitions do formulate an inclusive view of the personality, one which provides for many behavior layers. They remain—there are exceptions to which I shall return—additive concepts. They represent fictions or abstracts rather than persons whom anyone has known. "Man, merely as a participant in economic organization, the *homo economicus*, is only a fiction."[1a]

One inclusive set of such fictions has received serious consideration in psychologic literature: Spranger's social, economic, political, religious, aes-

---

[1] ALLPORT, G. W.: Personality: a psychological interpretation, New York: Holt, 1937, p. 29 ff.

[1a] ANGYAL, A.: Foundations for a science of personality, New York: Commonwealth Fund, 1941, p. 184.

1

thetic, theoretical, man. They are fictions in not being descriptions of any actual whole person as he is. One of history's great statesmen was Richelieu; his all-dominating passion was France. Operationally he was political man. But he was, too, *Cardinal* Richelieu. How, then, about the religious man? The example can be endlessly duplicated in historical figures and in the men and women we know at everyday levels.

Great portions of the whole person are usually ignored in human intercourse. It all depends on the biases of those who do the ignoring. These biases represent critical needs. The lawyer nearly always sees the other person as fitting, or not fitting, the legal prescriptions of behavior. Most preachers measure a man by his adhesion to, and support of, certain rituals and codes. The businessman judges his confreres or rivals by production. All these perceive sections of personality. They cannot see the entire, usually because they *will* not to.

In the scientific literature, Gordon Allport strikes the keynote for the principle of independent traits within the personality. He is presenting the case for functional autonomy.

The dynamic psychology proposed here regards adult motives as infinitely varied, and as self-sustaining, *contemporary* systems, (Allport's italics) growing out of antecedent systems, but functionally independent of them. Just as a child gradually repudiates his dependence on his parents, develops a will of his own, becomes self-active and self-determining, and outlives his parents, so it is with motives. Each motive has a definite point of origin which may lie in the hypothetical instincts, or, more likely, in the organic tensions and diffuse irritability described in Chapter IV. Theoretically all adult purposes can be traced back to these seed-forms in infancy. But as the individual matures the bond is broken. The tie is historical, not functional.[2]

This statement completely ignores the data reported by the clinical psychoanalysts. Yet, many of these are reporting findings from intensive studies much more meticulous and intensive than the laboratory psychologist can carry on. A serious psychology of personality cannot shut its eyes to the accumulated work by two generations of painstaking observers. There is cogent evidence, as anyone knows who has studied mentally ill patients, that there are repressed emotions, and that these emotions persist. They are the seed forms which become the feed roots of traits.

One example of what, on the surface, is entirely autonomous functioning is a tic. Muscles twitch in apparently full independence of that individual's current directed behavior. He may be making a speech, or be engaged in a casual conversation. The ear jerks, the corner of the eye quivers. The person, himself, does not know that a part of him is so active. Yet, the tic is something he is doing. He is funneling off affect, displaced affect. His ego had rejected the wish because it was inconsistent with built-in standards. At

---

[2] ALLPORT, *op. cit.*, p. 194.

some juncture, in a painful conflict between opposing trends, the man or woman had adopted this expedient. In new moments of stress, he is again using a tactic that had formerly served him. He needs so to behave, sensitive as he is to the social situation of the moment. The tic projects that desire in him which he must hide, both from his society and from himself. It tells what he is like as a whole.

The functional autonomy principle is being currently challenged in psychology itself, by McClelland.[3] It receives more sympathetic treatment from Murphy. But his critical eye catches some of the weaknesses in it.[4] Irwin cites and summarizes both these writers.[5]

The foundations for my concept of the whole personality are sunk first in the clinical thinking of a man associated not with psychology, nor with the analytic school, but with neurology, whose life-long interest was in the physical substratum for mental life. This is Hughlings Jackson. He alone best speaks for himself. I quote:

> In every insanity there is morbid affection of more or less of the highest cerebral centers or, synonymously, of the highest level of evolution of the cerebral sub-system, or, again synonymously, of the anatomical substrata, or physical basis, of consciousness. There may be discoverable disease destructive of nervous elements, or there may be loss of function from some undiscovered pathological process inferred from symptoms. In every insanity more or less of the highest cerebral centers are out of function, temporarily or permanently, from some pathological process; for my present limited purpose it matters little what that process may be.[6]

He represents his construct by a diagram showing "layers" of the cerebral centers, "A, B, C, D."

> Whilst noting that in this, the first degree of insanity, the layer A is out of function, possibly permanently, we have to keep vividly in mind that the three other layers are intact . . . there is in every insanity (1) negatively, defect of consciousness (loss of some consciousness), and there is (2) the consciousness remaining . . . disease only causes the physical condition corresponding to the negative mental element, defect of consciousness . . . we have not only to take into account the dissolution of one layer A caused by the disease, but the evolution going on in the layers B, C, and D, which no pathological process has touched.[7]

To Jackson, then, a person is always behaving as a whole; whether at his "highest self," in the aura which precedes an epileptic fit, or in the uncon-

[3] McCLELLAND, D. C.: Personality. New York: William Sloane, 1951. See p. 217 and especially p. 403 ff.

[4] MURPHY, G.: Personality. A biosocial approach to origins and structure. New York: Oxford, 1938. See p. 178 ff.

[5] IRWIN, F. W.: Motivation, in: Helson, H. (editor): Theoretical foundations of psychology. New York: Van Nostrand, 1951, p. 221 ff.

[6] JACKSON, H.: Selected writings. London: Hodder, 1932, Vol. II, p. 411.

[7] Ibid., pp. 414–15.

sciousness of the fit itself. This thinking will be found applicable to any clinical picture, and explains any behavior pattern. A low-feebleminded (mental age not above 3) in an institution barely learns to insert two or three of the Seguin blocks into the appropriate recesses in the form board. He has to be helped in many of life's simpler tasks. He needs to be watched, if he is to avoid common hazards. He is, in most instances, passive and easily led, with especially disastrous results to girls so deficient. He is behaving so with his whole available intellectual equipment, and the low drive which that small quantity of intellect generates.

In the intermediate (mental age 4 to 7) and higher (mental age 8 to 10) ranges of deficiency, the clinical facts are that learning can embrace that much larger a field, and be that much faster. The child can engage in fairly complex activities, in the institution. He shows initiative. Some strain at the confining walls; they want to be out on parole. These are functioning with a total structure (in Jacksonian terms) critically different from that in the 2 to 3 year level. The whole neurological equipment makes for another kind of total "cognitive structure." I am here anticipating Kurt Lewin's formulation. It results in a personality organization which is of quite another quality. The final outcome is a totally different adjustment pattern, or effort at one.

The brain tissue equipment, and the functioning potential, are proportionately better as we move from the defective to the normal sections of the intelligence curve. This differential accelerates at the level of any society's leaders, those in the upper two per cent, or uppermost half of one per cent, of the population, psychometrically. Their better brains have not only amassed more information, but they grasp more relations and more complex ones, between the impressions they have admitted. Their more extensive intellectual activity feeds back new urges, in pathways from the cortex to the thalamus, which return as new drive, activating more intellectual searching, and grasp of relations—all in a benign circle. The activity at this, or at any psychometric level, structures into a mental whole, which is to say a personality whole, one that varies significantly from that at any other level. The superior is another person from the average, the average from the inferior. But between two persons with about equivalent brain potential, there are still significant differences in regard to what the whole personality is like. Life's varied experiences make for the variations in personality forms. Culture shapes according to its general mold. Within that mold, the amount and kind of upbringing and education to which each one is exposed, forges the product he finally is. Each will be doing what he does, owing to the chance that he lived where and how he has, and adsorbed the kind, and amount, of information which he has. King Arthur, in *The Connecticut Yankee,* disguised as one of his own varlets could, when the test came, only straighten out and command. He had been reared a king.

The question now is: what about the neuroses and the psychoses? Here, the clinical facts decisively demonstrate the Jacksonian principle. In fact, it was my observations in them that led to this train of reasoning. View the symptoms of any obsessive, hysteric, schizophrenic, depressed, and it is clear that, quoting Jackson, some "layer of the highest cerebral centers is rendered functionless by some pathological process." What we are seeing is the "lower range of evolution" at which the patient is functioning, the "dissolution" of a higher "layer." This is the way the person now is, in consequence of what has happened to him. Whether physical or psychological, this is how he must now see his world: limited, twisted, even bizarre. It is his present top level of total perception. Hence, too, his behavior, cramped, odd, perplexing as it appears. He is reacting logically to the world as he understands—and feels—it.

Any full study of a mentally ill person cannot stop with the symptoms. To do so would be like limiting the scientific investigation of a tree to inspection of its fruit. Obtaining the premorbid and developmental histories are elementary routine in the study of a mental patient. They help explain his present odd perspectives and thinking. The assumption by students of mental disease is that the present psychologic phenomena are end products of old and continuous courses. The facts of regression so demonstrate. The person once again uses patterns he had abandoned in the course of growth. Some have been unused so long they appeared extinct. Unless it is argued that they were born suddenly, *de novo*, they must have been there all the time, and latent. How active? That can be the point of controversy. It depends on one's confidence in the hypothesis of the unconscious.

Here the concepts of Jackson and Freud converge. The behaviors from which Jackson reasons to his dissolution are the same as those which led the psychoanalysts to set up their hypotheses of repression, archaic omnipotence reactions, and the others. The obsessive neurotic represses certain desires. To make that repression good, to keep the feeling pressures encapsuled, he must set up certain defenses. This demands investment of effort and its continued maintenance. Struggle is costly. The person gives up much of his richness and freedom. The overt picture: the strained character, rigid or odd; maladaptive in most of life's crises, major or minor; inefficient at other times. He is not functioning at his level, either intellectually or emotionally. What we see clinically is the new whole person, after the repression has crippled him. Truly crippled. This is the present unit personality. It is not (Jackson) what he could be, minus what he lost by repression. It is another kind of a person. And it is a psychological force which has done the crippling.

In depressions, the whole person is of another kind: sad without cause, and deeply so, infecting those about him; moping over sins that he has not committed, or that are not sins; and, in extreme cases, destroys the guilty person, himself. Like Samson in his blindness, he cuts himself down in destroying his enemies, even the enemies within. The exceedingly painful emotion is, of course, the identifying differential. The visible product is another kind of whole. It has certain elements in common, to be sure, with other mental diseases; with the obsessives, for example. But there are important variances in the psychologic trends, emotional and intellectual, that constitute each whole. And there are differences, therefore, in what each does, which is to say, in what each is.

The schizophrenias, too, are explicable by the same whole person concept. The descriptive statement concerning a schizophrenic is usually one of two (much oversimplifying): (a) the patient lacks contact with reality, or (b) the patient lacks appropriate affect. In either event, he is less than a whole. He is in some phase of dissolution. Yet, he is a whole. The misconstruction of reality, and the indifferent or inappropriate affects, are the behaviors which define the present boundaries of the personality. His sub-ego conduct by usual standards, is the measure of his present ego. This is his central directive.

From the psychodynamic point of view, it is a course the patient has elected as his way of seeking comfort in an irritating, or harsh world; a regressive adjustment. How much is being contributed to the schizophrenic reaction by constitution is an unknown factor. However much that may be in the individual patient, how much his nature and how much his choice, the net total is the same: the separate symptoms make clinical sense only as production of that entire psychologic organism.

The paranoid schizophrenic, Hickey, in O'Neill's *The Iceman Cometh*, murders the wife who had always, and with all affection, forgiven his infidelities and his purblind drunks. The guilt which her forgivings had piled on him finally became unendurably painful. Every organism seeks to avoid pain or remove the cause of it. To see himself as the cause of his guilt was not possible for Hickey. His ego armored him off from that greater pain. He projected. The murder is inescapable logic.

It is with beautiful artistry, incidentally, that the dramatist portrays Hickey's total lack of, which is really to say inappropriate, affect. One senses it from the moment he enters the stage. His cleansed mental state, since he had already committed the murder, and reform campaign, are grotesquely incongruous in the setting of the saloon, with its Skid Row derelicts, all set for a grand spree. Hickey goes on, totally without grasp of their attitudes, without emotional contact, to the moment when, equally affectless, he identifies himself as the murderer to the policeman. With full psychotic logic he had telephoned the police informing them where he would be found. The guilt, projected though it had been, was still his until expiated.

It is all a nice example of schizophrenia, complicated with a paranoid defense. As we approach such a patient entire, we can put the jigsaw puzzle together. What was formerly disorganized and in many pieces is now an intelligible whole. Each piece does have meaning in the framework of the whole, and only in that framework.

In the affective psychoses, some statistical evidence does accent the constitutional factor. Any particular breakdown can be related to a precipitating life event. Whatever the relative contributions from the two causes, the design of the illness is simple. Observe a hypomanic, in his ebullience, or in his violent aggressiveness, and you note a severe imbalance of the two psychologic quanta, the feelings and the judgment. An emotional tempest is destroying reason. The whole person is storm-tossed. The clinical output is the ravings or excitement we call "mania."

If we focus for the moment on the mental diseases incident to brain pathology we are back where we started from on Jackson's neurological ground. To quote again, the patient is "in the strictest sense another person."[8] He has lost the use of some brain tissue. Yet, the new person he now is cannot be described by subtraction. Simple senile dementia illustrates the dissolution. A new set of values now governs. The symptoms as described by Bleuler will be recognized by students familiar with such patients: feelings labile, reaction to trifles (the crotchety grandfather); excessive suggestibility, or stubborness (the droll old lady); the neophobia (things were better in the good old days); picayune pedantry (the finicky great aunt); the endless empty chatter (more likely to be grandma). The intellectual deficits are well known: forgetting; retardation; reduction in more difficult abilities; in instances, perseveration and loss of orientation. In extreme conditions the patient loses interest or withdraws from the world, becomes torpid or too lively to the point of depression or manic state. Delusions or hallucinations may be present. All this is not the former person less some functioning, conditioned on the loss of tissue; it is the person functioning at his present best. None of the above symptoms are functionally autonomous. They are the work of a whole old man or woman. He or she, like the old gray mare, just "ain't what she used to be."

Similarly, we cannot define developing personality in terms of addition. The growing child becomes a new human being as he reaches his several growth stages: someone at 6 that he was not at 2; at 14 that he was not at 6. As the man of 25 he is still someone else; and, again, in "later maturity," whenever that begins. As usual, Shakespeare said it: Jacques' famous seven stages.

In these psychologically well, just as in the ill persons, the particular behavior data again are understandable as functions of character, which implies a unit, and a consistent one. Human relations, through the ages, have

---

[8] *Ibid.*, p. 26.

been maintained on the theory of predictable behavior, and that it is goal-
bound men and women, as such, with whom we are dealing. To grant functional autonomy to traits, as though they are separate units, is to reify them
and de-emphasize the individual. I make this criticism with all hesitancy,
knowing Gordon Allport's profound interest in the individual as such. Yet,
the inconsistency is there.

The ancient observation that the child is father to the man is confirmed
not only by the clinical facts, but those concerning personality generally.
The mental life of the adult at 25 can be traced, feeding on the roots of
habits and emotions that set in at age 2. In mental disease the archaic
thought productions or the content of the hallucinations are too clearly the
release of latencies; a subject in which psychology has long been interested.
The facts are finally that psychologic causation can effect any behavior
manifestations produced by brain pathology. The whole patterns, to be sure,
differ. The organically induced disability must follow in the pathway of the
lesion in the neural structure. Functional disorders are not so bound. Also,
the course differs; when a depression lifts, the patient's torpor lifts. He
regains his former mental vigor. In general paralysis the torpor progresses
and the person regresses to the vegetable point. The thinking of the para-
lytic can be extremely bizarre; in the depressed it is usually narrowly and
excessively accurate. Different psychologic wholes are before us.

The congruence of the Jacksonian and the Freudian concepts has been
formulated by Grinker. He writes that, in the growing child, the

dominance of neural activity and its concomitant psychic activity is present in
newer stages, but since these represent more mature states (physically, neurologi-
cally, and psychologically), they not only add a new quality to the psychic life but
hold older ones in abeyance, to a degree depending upon constitutional and individual
fixations, that is, growing of these older reflex functions.[9]

In mental disease, the Jacksonian shift to the "lower self" is seen by
Grinker as the "disintegration of the higher inhibiting functions, allowing
the lower levels to reassert themselves."[10] Again, in both repression and in
inhibition,

a certain level of activity is abandoned and a positive factor results from or is permitted by the shift of activity from one portion of the nervous system to another.
In the evolutionary (phylogenetic) process and in biological learning (ontogenetic)
the shift is upward. In the devolutionary process of disease, either functional or
morphological, the shift is downward and is termed regressive.[11]

---

[9] GRINKER, R. R.: A comparison of psychological "repression" and neurological
"inhibition." J. Nerv. & Ment. Dis. 89: 765–81, 1939.
[10] *Ibid.*
[11] *Ibid.*

The Jacksonian and the Freudian concepts diverge, for in the one, the causation is physical; in the other it is psychologic. Interpersonal stresses are the core of psychoanalytic theory: ego versus id. Extrapersonal factors, the culture, are the forces which shape the ego and breed superego; the *dramatis personae* are therefore three, ego and superego versus id. Or, in instances, the person has an even tougher battle: ego versus id and superego.[12] In any event, the person is always a balance of stresses, within a field of stresses. Now one force pushes the other back; the ego is holding the controls. The person moves along smoothly. Now the emotions over-run their banks. The great and costly flood is on. The individual is in disruption or panic. This is the ebb and flow of psychologic tensions; habitually stabilized in some; chronically labile in others. They are the events which constitute and issue as the living person we see before us.

All this bridges over to the constructs of an experimental psychologist whose work has centered on psychologic stresses. It demands thinking in terms of a whole psychologic person. His concepts have suggested designs for testing out psychoanalytic principles. They make possible hypotheses with which to understand the workings of the Rorschach test.

Kurt Lewin may not, in view of the nucleus to his method, appear a happy choice for purpose of supporting my argument. His experiments are set up always to investigate a current field of stresses. The results are, therefore, applicable to the present psychologic state only. He is explicit in weighting test results above historical data: "the value of a present test is, from the point of view of methodology, superior to that of an anamnesis."[13] He criticizes, "Psychology has used diagnosis by anamnesis rather excessively particularly in classic psychoanalysis and other clinical approaches to problems of personality."[14] McClelland summarizes,

As an experimentalist he has perhaps contributed more to our knowledge of the psychology of motivation than almost any other person, but as a theorist, his contribution has consisted largely of 'situational' or field analyses of motivated behavior.[15]

Nevertheless, the implications from his theory, and from some of his results, are applicable to personality as historical development. They are essentially hypotheses which explain actions and reactions seen in mental disease. Another writer does, in fact, apply Gestalt thinking to the life course of the individual. This is Angyal whose valuable theoretical book is being strangely neglected in psychology.

---

[12] FENICHEL, O.: The psychoanalytic theory of neurosis. New York: Norton, 1945. See Chapter VI.

[13] LEWIN, K.: Field theory in social science. Selected theoretical papers. Edited by Dorwin Cartwright. New York: Harper, 1951, p. 49.

[14] *Ibid.*, pp. 49–50.

[15] McCLELLAND, *op. cit.*, p. 404.

First, I quote from Lewin. The man best speaks for himself. The citations are from *Field Theory and Social Science*, papers by Lewin, selected and edited by one of his close co-workers, Dorwin Cartwright. Thus, his "field theory emphasized the importance of the fact that any event is a resultant of a multitude of factors." But it is "something more specific," and he exemplifies, showing how changes in certain variables will change a result, and "one can represent these variables as five dimensions of a diagram."[16] He includes stresses within the individual as forces in the field when he says that "the psychological past and the psychological future are simultaneous parts of the psychological field existing at a given time *t*."[17] I place this construction also on his statement that "study of the level of aspiration has given us considerable insight into the effect of the psychological past, (namely of previous success or failure) on the psychological future."[18] He is explicit in accenting the "dynamic aspects of events . . . an analysis which starts with the situation as a whole."[19] I am, of course, citing Lewin selectively, with an eye to Rorschach test operations, using statements in which I recognize not only clinical stresses but also Rorschach test equivalents. Assuming the Rorschach test assumptions are valid, these Lewinian statements can be rewritten in the symbols of the test. For other samples: "The essence of the constructive method is the representation of a single case with the help of a few elements of construction."[20] Again, Lewin states what is almost an axiom in Rorschach test method, when he says "forces leading to change in cognitive structure (are) very similar to, if not identical with, those forces which govern the perceptual fields."[21] In the paragraph following, "the cognitive structure is deeply influenced by the needs of the individual, his valences, values, and hopes."[22] It is a principle we see operating every day in the Rorschach test.

As I interpret Lewin's own data and reasoning, with reference to the field of personality generally, his concepts are applicable to the longer series of events that fashioned the present "life space." In this "life space," he sections an individual's psychologic organization at some moment. He obtains a cross-section of the strains and stresses, the checks and the balances. He sees the applicability of this construct to the historical process in the person, essentially a clinical concept. Thus:

the problems of development and of regression have their scientific place at a particular intersection of historical and dynamic problems. They point on the one hand to

---

[16] LEWIN, *op. cit.*, p. 44.
[17] *Ibid.*, p. 54.
[18] *Ibid.*, p. 55.
[19] *Ibid.*, p. 60.
[20] *Ibid.*, p. 61.
[21] *Ibid.*, p. 83.
[22] *Ibid.*, p. 83.

a unique sequence of experiences, situations, personality structures, and styles of behavior during the history of the individual. On the other hand they point to the dynamics and laws which govern the behavior in any one of these stages and the transition from one stage to another.[23]

There is no reason why Lewin's method could not long-section the personality, representing the historical dynamics. A model from a quite different branch in psychology, but one that might be adapted, is the color pyramid.[24] The difference will be a construction in three dimensions of personality; rather than in two, as in Lewin's present sections. I have played with it for this purpose. It can be done. Lewin's deficit for this kind of construct was that he was not clinically trained. He can think in two dimensions. But his anxiety as experimentalist blocks his moving into the third.

The different styles of behavior existing at different times in the history of an individual cannot be treated as parts of one field of coexisting areas in which one can move about, i.e., not as a life space, because a field is a *dynamic unity existing at one time*.[25]

Yet, life is a time Gestalt. This is the conclusion reached by Angyal. His clinical habit of mind no doubt gives him a perspective lacking to the experimentalist, Lewin. Angyal published his book while Resident Director of Research in Worcester (Massachusetts) State Hospital. This very busy clinical center and fertile ground for psychologic research would have provided an effective setting within which to extend the Gestalt idea to the human being's whole life pattern. The individual is continuous with a larger whole. This is the society or biosphere to the shaping of which each person contributes and which, at the same time, shapes him. Angyal develops this into a concept of "biospheric dynamics." He goes further than Lewin, since he sees any one life moment as resultant of what that individual has experienced before. Life is a time Gestalt.

The life history, beyond giving a historical understanding of personality, gives us also a picture of the person as a temporally extended whole. We have offered a point of view according to which personality is not concentrated in the present but is a whole, the parts of which are distributed along the dimension of time, whereby the person extends into the past and into the future. The hypothetical traces which past experiences leave in the organism are only the means which allow a communication with the past. The dynamically active factors are, however, not these traces but the past experiences as such, which from a temporal distance exert an influence upon the present.[26]

Recapitulating, it is possible to equate two major clinical concepts, those

[23] *Ibid.*, pp. 88–9.
[24] TITCHENER, E. B.: A text-book of psychology. New York: Macmillan, 1924. See p. 63.
[25] LEWIN, *op. cit.*, p. 91, italics mine.
[26] ANGYAL, *op. cit.*, p. 372.

of Jackson and of Freud. In both of these, the fundamental orientation is of
the individual as a functioning unit; this concept is the essence—even if
implicit rather than explicit—of a theory directing a major experimental
school in psychology, Gestalt. The Lewinian data and formulations have
the merits which belong only to an experimental method: they provide
designs for testing out his hypotheses. What he has done, therefore—even
if he may not have believed it—is to set up methods of experimental psychology which serve to investigate the Freudian intrapsychic actions, and
their integrations; or the Jacksonian mental life as evolution or devolution.

The translation of these three sets of concepts into Rorschach's formulations follows readily from the hypotheses as to the significance of the test's
variables. Hence, a personality described in the languages of the three clinical and experimental approaches can also be described by the symbols of
the Rorschach test. I showed something of this equivalence in another publication.[27] The essence of my argument is: the Rorschach test summary of the
response scorings is a cross-section representing the present outcome (Lewin)

TABLE 1

The Significant Ratios in Personality Structure

r F. C−Y	r C−Y. M	r M. W−Z
r F. M	r C−Y. W−Z	
r F. W−Z		

of stresses between the "higher" activities and the "lower" ones (Jackson),
or between ego and id (Freud). This interpretation is inherent in the quantitative ratios obtaining between F+, C − Y, M, W − Z; all in "press"
(Murray) against one another, in one multidimensional set of operations.
The ratios to be obtained are as indicated in table 1.

This still leaves out many of the operations that go into a Rorschach test
interpretation. It does represent the major psychologic tensions that a
Rorschach test examiner holds in mind, forces and counterforces all issuing
as the personality under inspection. This is the *Prägnanz* of Angyal, the
life-space of Lewin. In my earlier paper I wrote, "The Rorschach personality pattern is a combination term. Such forces as those represented by M,
fantasy living; C, affective experience; Z, organizing of complex wholes;
F+, reality testing, all of which are in one general field . . . influence one
another so that the net result is as the square of the field, that dynamic,
obdurate, unpredictable activity we call the human personality."[28]

Writing today, I am willing to omit the word, "unpredictable." How all

[27] BECK, S. J.: Error symbol, and method in the Rorschach test. J. Abnormal &
Social Psychol. **37**: 83–103, 1942.
[28] *Ibid.*

this emerges in the actuality of a test applied in the crucible set up by a clinical situation, the tests and interpretations in this volume attempt to demonstrate. What will emerge in these interpretations—imperfectly enough for I am really stating here the design for a test of personality—is that the patterning out of a whole person requires delineating (a) interaction between certain psychologic stresses, conceived of as impersonal forces; and (b) appraising the roles of these interactions in shaping (or misshaping) the whole. This is to say that the Rorschach test's quantitative measurements and the ratios between them do not directly define the personality. But we cannot define a personality by the Rorschach test without these quantitative measurements. All it is, is the measuring tool. But once a measure is taken, the investigator's next problem is what does the finding mean? What prediction can now be made regarding the object measured? The situation in personality in no wise differs from that in any of the "exact" sciences. Take prediction of weather. It starts with certain readings; the positions of needles on brass discs. Precise numerical data are recorded. What their significance in terms of "fair and warmer" tomorrow, or "much colder, more snow," derives from a relation between the numbers on the discs to which the needles point. Also, much other information. The prediction presupposes (a) understanding the relations, within (b) the framework of weather behavior. The interpretation is in its final emergence always the work of some human brain trained in the particular science. This is true in every science. Medical diagnoses today avail themselves of any number of laboratory measurements. The diagnosis is always an interpretation.

The interrelation of these measures, as total activity of the one patient, is grasped by one trained mind. The interpretation can, of course, be no better than (a) the validity of the individual data in measuring what they say they do; and (b) the tested knowledge as to the meaning of the interrelations. But they can also be no better than the understanding of the mind that does the interpreting. This dictates breadth and depth of experience in the particular field. In the Rorschach test, this requisite experience includes extensively using the test in many patients in the various mental diseases. At the same time unremitting effort must go on at objectifying the Rorschach test components. The symbols must stand for behavior stresses that are really there. Experimental psychology and statistical science have currently been putting these variables under scrutiny. The returns are still coming in. Results are conflicting in respect to some of the test's claims. They have clarified or sharpened the thinking in regard to significance of others. A full evaluation of all the Rorschach test accumulating literature, pro and con, will need to await a separate paper *ad hoc*.

In closing my argument regarding the personality as a whole, I have recourse to, and speculate from, the knowledge available concerning the brain and its functioning. One, is localization. Certain of our mental activities are carried on by certain areas of the brain. Two, is the cortex. The critical, and to me the most significant fact concerning the cortex, is that it is never itself the direct terminus of a receptor nerve. The messages it receives are relayed to it from other centers, lower ones, which may themselves have them relayed, or receive them directly. When these perceptions enter the cortex, they are changed from what they were like at the first point of entry, *via* the incoming nerve impulse. That helps explain why we never, as psychology has long understood, known a percept "pure," whether it is auditory, visual, cutaneous, olfactory, or the others. The percept is changed the moment it becomes one—this goes back at least to William James—changed by "previous experience."

Meanwhile what is the function of the cortex as a unit? I quote here from Sherrington. He refers to

the neopallium, a correlation-mechanism of still more decisive and capital importance, destined in man to exceed in size the total rest of the central nervous system. In man it is the seat of all which is exclusively human in the mind. It is a structure in which are brought together paths from less comprehensive correlating centres, e.g., those of the thalamus. The archipallium correlates recepts from the olfactory distance-receptor with others from the skin, mucous membrane and muscles of the mouth region. The neopallium working on a grander scale brings together recepts from all the various species of receptors, distance-receptors and others alike.

But it is never reached by any receptive nerve immediately; it is reached only through relay-systems which climb to it *via* successive correlating mechanisms. The recept-patterns which enter the neopallium (cerebral cortex) *are therefore always greatly changed* (italics mine) from those furnished to the first receiving stations by the groups of receptor nerves themselves.[29]

That is, the cortex, so far as we at present understand, is the organ which fuses *all* our stored experiences into the attitudes which at any given moment produces our total behavior. It is the seat of that which produces the activities specifically characteristic for each of us, or our personality. The evidence concerning the cerebral cortex, as stated in the literature generally, appears to agree with this formulation as it is in Sherrington. Following his thinking, we have the rationale dictated by the facts of brain architecture which not only (a) explains that organized psychologic phenomenon we call the whole human personality; but also (b) excludes any interpretation other than its constantly integrated functioning as one whole.

The various clinical manifestations are all intelligible and explicable by this rationale. They are those activities specifically characteristic for each person in a mental hospital, those unique sets of behaviors, attitudes and

---

[29] SHERRINGTON, C. S.: Brain, in: Encyclopedia Britannica. Chicago: University of Chicago Press, 1946, vol. 4, pp. 1–8.

emotions which makes each patient so distinct. The neopallium available to each has such and such percepts to correlate; each redolent of its emotional flavor; and for historical reasons in each, has reorganized them into the final visible human product, whether deluded, mentally deficient, or genius. The differing Rorschach test patterns in the various clinical pictures are sections, crude though they are, cutting across these personalities and corresponding to these differing psychologic wholes. This is the logic for the Rorschach test, sound to the extent that it validly differentiates between persons and enables clinical prediction as to any person.

This logic explains too why the whole Rorschach test personality picture cannot be derived by any additive procedure: so much $F+$ and so much M and so much Z and the others. It cannot be stated as:

$$(nF+) + (nM) + (nZ), \text{etc.} = \text{the personality.}$$

The problem is always what does a person operating so as to produce his nF do to his nM; what does nM do to his nZ; and what do the interrelated activities nF, nM, do to nZ and to the interrelation nF, nZ, and to all the other variables, separately, and in interrelation. It is the human neopallium working on the grander scale.

One major function of the Rorschach test I have so far not discussed. This is its job of projecting the ego. The test patterns I have described project the person's life space, his striving within his biosphere, phase of evolution or whatever concept we use. Contributing to the fashionings of a life pattern are the personal values which, up to that moment, the individual has been holding. The social goals he has been perceiving and his ideas about them resident in his cortex form one of the dynamic units which, with others, his neopallium has been organizing into the whole personality. This is that all-important component in the personality, its indispensable servant and central directive, the ego.

B. THE EGO IN THE RORSCHACH TEST

The ego gives to the personality so much of its direction and "color" as to lead, sometimes, to an equating of the ego with the whole personality. From differential Rorschach test patterns, the conclusion is that the ego and the personality do not coincide point for point. The personality is something larger. The ego is an agent, even a tool of the personality. The further, and corollary reasoning is: it is a behavior complex which every human develops. A psychologic organ like any physical structure, it is useful in the adaptive struggle. It is a peculiarly human structure or organ. No infra-human animal, by this understanding of the ego, can have an ego.

The observations that follow grew entirely out of Rorschach test research. Among the varied groups of persons from among whom I was collecting

Rorschach test records, certain individuals could be distinguished from the others along two dimensions. One, they followed some goal which was their central directive in their life pursuits; and they followed it with persistence. They had "character strength." Two, the goals were of a kind that carry social endorsement in varying degrees. The common denominator in both these dimensions is a value concept. The individual has a built-in standard of conduct and a set of personal values all of which are also the values of his society.

These observations first jelled with reference to the superior healthy. They were, as their intellectually more demanding vocations showed, select. But the characterizations also applied to others at more modest levels of endeavor. These vary from the superiors always in respect to the social or prestige value of their goals. They resemble them in many instances in the integration and undeviating aim with which they carry on. It should be noted here that the individuals within the superior group themselves differ from one another in degree of integrated and firmly maintained effort. There is variation of ego firmness at the top levels; and, indeed, the ego can be very firm at any level within the healthy ranges. Meanwhile, I had been constantly studying the several clinical groups, and the data from these support my reasoning. The discriminating Rorschach traits develop as to be expected. The findings make good clinical logic.

In the Rorschach test protocols the common factor that at first emerged as the test's measure of ego was $F+$. More recent experience has indicated that it is not $F+$ alone, but that is the cornerstone. Without a certain minimum $F+$ the ego is insufficient. The basis for this conclusion is empirical $F+$ data obtained in various clinical groups of variant ego growth and strength. The evidence is consistent. The higher the $F+$ per cent, up to a certain optimum, the more mature and better structured the ego. This latter judgment is made from clinical classifications. Thus, the less developed the child's personality, the lower the $F+$ per cent. The more disturbed the patient, the lower the $F+$ per cent. Table 2 shows the facts, synoptically.[30]

Having my hunch concerning $F+$ as measure of ego, a re-reading of Rorschach's theoretical exposition of this test trait proved rewarding. His description will be found in his own monograph.[31] I have quoted it in several publications and do not repeat it here. Assuming that it is correct psychologically, and that it is methodologically controllable, which it is, it provides support for a theory as to a value system forming the principal constituent in the ego.

[30] BECK, S. J.: Rorschach F plus and the ego in treatment. Am. J. Orthopsychiat. **18:** 395–401, 1948.

[31] RORSCHACH, H.: Psychodiagnostik: Methodik und Ergebnisse eines wahrnehmungsdiagnostischen Experiments (ed. 2). Bern and Berlin: Huber, 1932. Transl. by Lemkau, P. and Kronenberg, B. New York: Grune & Stratton (distr.), 1942.

In day-to-day operations, the ego's functioning can now be described as follows. Assuming a healthy adult, the criteria for most of his acts are established. Also, the criteria serve him habitually; he is unaware of them. Or, at the nearest, they are in his "preconscious." As a crude example, no one who reads this, nor any close acquaintance, is likely ever to murder. An established, built-in, automatically functioning steering gear or com-

TABLE 2*—*F+ Trends in Various Personality Groups*
For Healthy, Average Adults, Mean Is 78.25, SD, 10.20

IN NORMAL ADULTS	F + % IS	IN CHILDREN	F + % IS
Superior intelligence....	High	Ages 14–17..............	Average
Average intelligence.....	Average to low	Ages 10–13..............	Average to high
		Ages 6–9................	Average
Inferior intelligence.....	Low, average or lower	Below age 6.............	Average to low
IN THE SCHIZOPHRENIAS	**F + % IS**	**IN FEEBLEMINDED**	**F + % IS**
		Medium deficiency.......	Low to very low
Autistic without emotional distress........	Varies around low average	Severest deficiency......	Exceptionally low
Autistic and emotionally distressed.............	Varies: low average to lower	**IN AFFECTIVE PSYCHOSES**	**F + % IS**
		Manic depressive manic..	Low
		Manic depressive depressed................	Very high
Confused intellectually, distressed emotionally.	Very low	**IN ORGANIC PSYCHOSES**	**F + % IS**
Stuprous................	Bi-modal		Varies downward with degree of involvement
Withdrawn..............	Variable		
Simple.................	Low to very low		

* The present table is altered slightly, conformably to norms derived since the 1948 publication, in which I apply my reasoning about F+ as ego to the question of treatability. To be treatable, a person has, at the least, to be able to see straight. It will be noticed that I use the superior healthy as my criterion group. I decided on them for two reasons, even though they are not representative of the population at large. First, I had accumulated a sample of them such that, as a group, they gave dependable evidence of consistent results. This was so whether judged by the Rorschach test, or by non-Rorschach frames of reference. Second, since this is the personality level out of which the nation's leaders emerge, I arbitrarily decided on this, "the highest," as the standard by which to measure the others. Theirs, the "best" ego, was my frame of reference.

pass sets our courses in such matters. We have certain standards on certain behaviors. Our self-respect directs us. This is the ego.

The steering becomes conscious activity when a new decision needs to be made. The person scrutinizes the situation, compares, appraises in the light of older knowledge. He decides. Two lines of psychologic activity always plot his course. At their point of interaction is his decision. One is the conscious comparing and judging. It is cortical, carried on at the highest centers which mediate consciousness. The other is the older established attitudes as to what we want or do not want to do. This consists of all those integrated values held by each culture, and those more immediate motives, consisting of conscience molded by one's family and parents.

A single example may be in order. *A* drives at 70 miles per hour in a city street. He does this with enough skill to avoid accidents. *B* says this is good driving. But this judgment is grossly inconsistent with the value held by *B*'s community. His judgment concerning *A*'s driving is an F−. His perception is not that of most persons. If he so responds a large percentage of times, his judgments are usually poor. He may be mentally deficient, or hypomanic, deteriorated, schizophrenic, clouded by alcohol, or a twisted psychopath. His ego would be insufficient for long-time adaptation in a present day western city. In the Rorschach test, his F+ per cent may not necessarily be below a certain minimum. That would depend on the whole personality framework. But it would certainly include some very erratic deviations from the norm. Presented with Figure V, he says, "two pressed leaves." He perceives inaccurately. He may and he may not see the very common "bat." If he misses it, he is failing to recognize a very familiar stimulus, one meaningful to most normal adults. In the one instance he misshapes, or is indifferent to the real form; in the other, he just fails to see it. In either, the judgments used by most persons in his group as to accurate-inaccurate are not his. He does not feel the need to conform to community values in his perceptions. This is ego failure. The need to be approved by others is lacking. There can be no ego without an *alter*. A man or woman alone on an island can dispense with the ego and usually does. All of which is not to say that because a person sees Figure V as "a bat," that he really sees a "bat," or that the figure is in the least a bat. Nothing in the Rorschach test is real. Everything in it is a test for seeing the real world as others do.

Certain Rorschach test traits other than F+ provide evidence regarding the ego's work. They are: productivity (R), grasp of relations (W, Z), orderly method (Seq), popular responses (P) and breadth of content. In addition there are the clusters from which the trait patterns are inferred. All these are quantitative data. There are also qualitative observations, correlating with the ego's developmental stage; or the level of its functioning. Such are the language forms, vocabulary, originality in content and the qualifying or rejecting of one's own responses.

Some of these Rorschach test traits offer leads as to the ego's initiative and energy, e.g., W, Z; also, R and content, whether as breadth or originality. Others tell of its integrating success. Such are Sequence, and the defenses. All presuppose the operation of a sense of values. In the integrating mechanisms, it is there, by hypothesis. The most "integrated" persons, in a society, are those who most efficiently pursue their goals. They always have a clear-cut notion of where they are headed for, and they cannot be diverted. A set of values is always charting the ego's direction. In variables such as W, Z, R and breadth content, we see the ego in its reaching role. The person is putting his best foot forward. It is self-extension, whether healthy or symptomatic extension. Implicit is the consciousness of the self and the values with which one identifies. This is ego.

The P response is a special form of F+. In fact, it is F+ at its most concentrated. As such, it provides especially close identification with the norm-setting group. It is a most conscious respect for the formalized values; a surface propriety. Some experienced Rorschach investigator may here ask why do I exclude the M, the C variables, and the Y and V variables from my list of ego operations? They are not, as I understand them, ego operations. They are, in the first instance, work of the emotions. They are representative of those extra-ego resources of the personality which the ego is always manipulating or attempting to manipulate in the interest of the person's welfare. How well it succeeds is a function of its firmness relative to the emotional forces. When the latter are too powerful, values give way. This is ego insufficiency (Fenichel), whether as lag in growth, or loss of it. In the Rorschach test, in such instances, the control and integration traits diminish relatively to the emotion-dictated variables. The latter dominate in the pattern. The specific significance of these test variables, the advances in interpreting them severally, receive exposition in the chapter that follows.

How this total psychologic economy emerges, this balance of ego strains against emotional stresses, and the shape which the personality, as a whole, consequently takes, is the purpose of the cited Rorschach test records to demonstrate.

CHAPTER II

ADVANCES IN INTERPRETATION

A. The Four Tasks

A test that undertakes to test the whole human personality should provide a cross-section of at least three sets of data; and better still, also a fourth. The three are: (a) the psychologic structure; (b) the current functioning; (c) the adaptive solution by the person of his life's problems. The fourth, when available, would uncover something of the psychodynamics preceding the present status. This may sound like reasoning in reverse, since such is the personality that we carve out with the Rorschach test. In fact, it is a hypothesis that follows on Rorschach test observations. But an inspection of the three requisites in my description will show them applicable to findings about human personality by any method of study. In the Rorschach test, the psychologic structure is blueprinted in the quantitative data that project, on the one hand, the intellectual life, and on the other, the emotional or "inner world." Current functioning is depicted in evidence reflecting the ego's operations, both healthy and impaired, and in the quality of the emotional life in all its many facets. The total solution is a description which can usually be translated into one of the clinical diagnostic classifications. The data of the fourth variety are information as to premorbid events. Whether it is the Rorschach test or any other method of investigating the personality, results such as the above report both its anatomy and the live tissues. That is, by any method the results must give us a valid picture of a live human being, one striving in the several dimensions, who feels, thinks and who attempts to maintain his psychologic homeostasis constant.

In the psychologic structure as projected in the quantitative summary of the Rorschach response scorings, the variables may be classified into two broad groups. In the one are principally F+, W − Z, Sequence, Approach, per cent A, P. In the other are the variations of C, of Y, of V and M. In the one group will be recognized the intellectual productions; in the other, the emotional manifestations. Together they tell the present mental equipment. The several quantitative relations between them all give a picture of the stresses being maintained by the several psychologic forces, and so the balance or poise in which the whole is revolving. The content tells something of the cultivation to which the individual has been exposed. It may, although does not always, disclose the personal values which he prosecutes. The structural data are a record of *impersonal* psychologic forces, and the cross-section they give is that of the personality as it has

20

jelled at the time of testing. The content reports something of the *social direction* of the personality. The one tells what the individual is; the other where he has been.

The structural summary is the essence of the Rorschach test personality. It is the first approach to interpretation; but it does not highlight the details of the person's functioning from moment to moment. The high and low tones emerge only in a response-for-response inspection. These tones are significant but their recognition is especially dependent on experience with the test over a broad clinical range. Some factor analysis studies to which the test is currently being subjected are lighting up new nuances as to the meanings of the variables. Scrutiny of the individual responses, and of their technical treatment, i.e., their scorings, is therefore essential toward the interpretation. They are the details which fill in and complete the picture of the personality.

B. The Insufficient Ego

The test discloses these individual responses in the operations of the intellect. They are overtly observable, and so give a first lead as to how well and at what level the ego is responding, or how seriously it is involved. The critical information emerges in the evidence regarding the ego's impairment. That is, we know the ego's functioning from its dysfunction. The test results to be observed are the following. Per cent F+ which really means, amount of F−. This is the traditional F+ technic as published by Rorschach. In addition, I have for some years now been making qualitative judgements as to individual F− associations. These are of two kinds. One refers to the degree of inaccuracy, the amount of deviation from form. The other attempts a distinction between "personal" and "impersonal" F−. It is to be emphasized that all these judgments are subjective. There is no objective measure of distance of any F− from what is "good" form, and norm, perceptually in the test stimuli, i.e., in the respective W, D, or Dd. The experienced Rorschach test investigator is in this respect generally in the position of the clinical practitioner. The more he has seen and validated various phenomena, the more sensitive he is to their significance. The framework of the judgment is thus really a quantitative experience. But each individual judgment is still a subjective one. Examples of "personal," "impersonal" F− are clarified, as they occur in the test records themselves. The personal F− is found more frequently in neurotics and in the healthy. The impersonal F−, in brain damage, in feebleminded and in some schizophrenics. Attention lapse is a probable condition that produces many of these. In schizophrenia both the personal and the impersonal are found.

Thus, F− may be indicating a perception which is inaccurate as a result of failure of self criticism or one in which there is a misshaping of reality as dictated by personal need. The F−, very far from norm, with its bizarre content as very erratic percept, is therefore either (a) a disregard of or indifference to reality; or (b) its distorting. When this inaccuracy is extremely severe it may be the lead to thinking disorder, to confusion, especially when the content is of very unique, or queer quality. When the theme is highly personal, the primitive ego is again emerging. A cluster of such misinterpretations when the Z score is high, and especially when there is also a high percentage of s, is the test's warning to the clinician that the patient is a rather sick paranoid.

F+ may be too high. This, too, is ego insufficiency. It tells of excessive clinging to accuracy, sign of an inner compulsion. More will be said concerning this Rorschach trait in the exposition of the defenses.

A typical approach (Ap) distribution is an excess attention to one of the three variables: W, D, Dd. Surfeit in any of these means a deficit in either or both of the other two. A constricting fixity of the attention is the critical finding. If Dd is exceptionally minute or in a very unusual location, it has additional diagnostic significance either as obsessive-compulsive neurosis or schizophrenia. The judgment on these very unusual Dd responses rests in a quantitative sphere of reference, since the more common Dd have been statistically determined. The list has been published. It follows that any other Dd is a more rare selection than the most rare of the published ones. The range in these is down to 0.1 per cent frequency of selection in the test figure.

The hunch has some strong empirical support that certain major details, D, are preferred by certain kinds of patients. This lead is receiving statistical study not yet ready for publication. The evidence indicates also an avoiding of various details, usually of sexual significance. Of interest in this connection are certain findings with relation to the popular response. Molish[1] has shown certain differences and also similarities between normals, neurotics and schizophrenics in their P associations. To report P a patient must of course first select the necessary stimulus. What the test demonstrates is that there is selective perception, out of a field of stimuli. It is to be recalled that Klopfer[2] has proposed classifying the Dd selection, according to their location on the test figures, e.g., edge Dd, center Dd, and others. Much research is, however, still required in exploring the preferences and their significance in discriminating various personalities.

Excess D is one of my present diagnostic leads to concretistic thought processes. The W, if any, in such records are the "lazy" ones; those that

[1] MOLISH, H. B.: The popular response in Rorschach records of normals, neurotics and schizophrenics. Am. J. Orthopsychiat. **21:** 523–531, 1951.

[2] KLOPFER, B. AND KELLEY, D. M.: The Rorschach technique. New York: World Book Co., 1942.

are essentially equivalent to D. A narrowed interest content usually accompanies. The ego's really heavy loss in this reaction shows up in the lack of the good W and in the insufficient Z. Clinically the findings are projecting a thinking disorder. The patient is not synthesizing as he can, he is inefficient or anergic.

W and Z, when within the known normal range for a person's age group, establish the extent to which he is synthesizing at expectancy. W tells more about his conceptual activity; Z, his grasp of relations between the stimuli in his perceptual field. It reflects adeptness in solving one's problems, although the relationship is by no means one for one. Some persons with very high Z can still be quite inept in solving their day-to-day problems. That other trait, adaptive intelligence (Ap), is also needed.

Ego insufficiency may be disclosed both in inadequate and in excess quantities of either W or of Z. Excess W is related to an exaggerated perception of the self, especially when the quality of the W is inferior. It projects an overall, unanalytic reaction, one likely to be hasty and not discriminating. In more disturbed persons the form quality of the W percept is inaccurate or WF−. In disintegrated condition, the thinking in these W may be "mixed-up," dillapidated. A Z finding in excess of a patient's ability is very rare; it cannot occur as a result of ego insufficiency. Apparent but spurious exceptions are the high Z scores in patients with excessive W's. Nearly all the responses may be W, and this inflates the Z score. But it may be disregarded in these cases as not indicating a vigorous intelligence. The more so the latter since much of the form perception is minus. The quality of the W's is the truer index of the patients' mode of conceptual operation: diffuse and vague rather than energetic.

DW continues to be useful as indicating what Rorschach calls *Konfabulatorische* thinking. His use of this term appears to differ materially from Bleuler's, who describes it at several points as a "memory hallucination."[3] In the Rorschach test it is essentially representative of alogical thinking; but depending on the extent of the total disintegration it may be expression of a tangential thought process.

Sequence (Seq) too continues to retain the function which Rorschach assigned to it, that of gauging orderliness of one's intellectual method. The range is from the over-stiff inflexibility of the neurotically too controlled; through the moderate variability of the healthy; the irregularities of the less seriously disturbed patient; to the confusion and unpredictability of the schizophrenic. Towards solving the problem of a quantitative formula by which to arrive at Seq, I can report no progress.

Animal per cent, when too high relative to expectancy, is now useful in

---

[3] BLEULER, E. P.: Textbook of psychiatry. Transl. by Brill, A. A. New York: Dover, 1951. See p. 106.

uncovering the ego's weaknesses in various ways. A too cautious adaptation and thus a too fearful clinging to most familiar stimuli (see Defenses) raises this percentage. It may also show loss of spontaneity or dullness in responding to the events of one's world. The feebleminded, some organics, the depressed, torpid schizophrenics, all respond with high animal per cent. It is one of the most sensitive of the test's variables in shifting its quantity with the patient's emotional vicissitudes. It thus well demonstrates the principle that psychologic needs can be dynamic in simulating symptoms resulting from pathology of nerve tissue.

When per cent of animals is too low, a nonadaptive inadequacy in knowing one's environmental stimuli is at work. It means that the subject's mind is preoccupied with the very original. But the condition is going beyond the normal limits. Among the clinical groups, I have myself found low A per cent only in schizophrenia, and only in some of them. They are so original that no one is like them. They stand alone. Rorschach reports low A per cent in his "early" epileptics (*frühdemente*) and also in his disordered schizophrenics. The hypomanics range at intermediate levels in their animal per cent. This may cause surprise in view of the high A per cent score regularly observed in the depressed. By straight clinical logic we should infer a low score in the hypomanics. But the two diseases do not, intellectually, produce patterns which are mirror images of each other. My speculation is: in the hypomanic excitement and the consequent breakdown of the ego, the attention flight prevents the developing of the associations of which the patient is capable. The more obvious ones, which in the Rorschach test are animal forms, have the right of way. Yet the lively affect also stimulates richness, and so reduces the number, and hence the per cent, of animal associations. A parallelogram of forces is operating.

One other group that regularly produces a low per cent of animal forms are the healthy adults of superior intelligence. The literature generally is agreed on this finding. But there are critical differences in the records as a whole of these healthy adults as compared with those of schizophrenics. In the healthy adult the percentage is low. In schizophrenics it is *too* low; too low relative to expectancy. That is, in the disease the originality is an imbalance. The person is leaning awry. The whole personality structure as measured by the other test variables and the ego particularly cannot cope constructively with original ideas. These ideas thus represent a deviation, and as can be seen from the themes, a regressed preoccupation with personal needs. In the healthy superior the low animal percentage tells of an originality spread out among diversified interests, such as are understood by others, and can be shared by them.

The popular (P) response has been correctly evaluated as measure of the ability to recognize the most common percepts of one's milieu. It points therefore to conformity in the thought content. Speaking of the healthy superiors, it is of interest that original though they are, they still score well within normal in P. They can be bright, but they know their group's conventions. In fact, they set those conventions. Schizophrenics however score low P; they do not share their communities' thoughts. Their insufficient ego is in regression, judged by the fact that in this variable they rate numerically on a par with younger children, those whose egos are only beginning to grow in respecting the world's properties. Low P is found in some adult neurotics as a rebellion symptom at the conscious level. In some homosexual patients the P is low. But from evidence at hand the distribution of P in a large sample of these persons may be bimodal since in some homosexuals this score is very high. I interpret this as camouflage; a defensive effort to cover up the non-conventional sexuality by being very conventional in everything else. Excessive P is also found in other neurotics as a conscious passivity, a knuckling under—the Uriah Heep complex.

Total scored productivity (R) I am now finding a dependable index to liberated drive. It varies directly with life age and with intelligence. The feebleminded and most patients with brain pathology produce few R. But its range is rather wide in advanced age. In 19 subjects of age 63 to 90 this range was 8 to 62 (unpublished study). R is very sensitive to emotional forces, as is reported below in the test interpretations.

High productivity can betray an ego insufficiency as one manifestation of self-extension. Quality of the associations is in these records not at the level of quantity. Interference with speech has been taking place when, following a very slow time for first response, the patient produces a normal, or higher, number of associations. Or when the inquiry is liberating some new responses while the free association has been chary of them. When these findings go to extremes, the thinking has been blocked.

Such blocking is to be inferred when the time for first response is abnormally slow. This finding too may be reflecting speech stoppage as one aspect of a motor retardation. This, in some patients, shows itself in very slow average time for all associations. When these retardings go to great lengths, either in the average time for all responses, or time for first response, we may be seeing an actual regression in speech functioning, depending on the condition of the record as a whole. The patient is withdrawing to a very early developmental level before he had acquired this distinctly human equipment for mastering his environment.

Fluctuation in time for first response is the Rorschach test expression of unsmooth mental life, ataxic thinking and behavior. But a too smooth tempo still points to insufficiency in the ego. Norms are now available for this behavior in the healthy groups. When the time for first responses is too even, it is the counterpart of clinical inflexibility. Some neurotics and more schizophrenics show this pattern in the test. Fluctuation also takes the form of severe or frequent shifts in F+, F−; sometimes from very good, or P associations, to severe inaccuracies or queer percepts. Many shifts of theme in the content into different categories with little, if any, integrating framework are another way in which the ataxic psyche discloses itself.

Card turning can be another index to the motility and the extent of the ego's control over it. Insufficient control shows up in much, rapid and overtly nervous turning. The patient hardly holds the card in one position long enough to permit a percept to form or to sharpen its boundaries. At the other pole is the very slow turning with long staring at the test figure and without producing associations. It goes with binding of motor functions. More serious, although rare, are the stiff, even ritualistic motions with which some patients turn the cards. This is a rigidity, likely to go with stereotypy. When this is part of a severe enough regression, the ego has retreated to the point where it is nonassertive, failing to take the initiative necessary toward obtaining one's satisfactions.

Some persons never turn the test cards. Their number is small and this pattern is atypical. But it is not serious in itself. I have observed it in the milder neuroses, and even in an occasionally healthy adult, but also in some seriously withdrawn patients. I interpret it as habit binding in the less serious conditions, cramping inhibition in the more serious total involvements. It is not infrequent in adolescents who are very fearful.

When qualifications weight down a record, a deflated ego is speaking. Within the term qualification I include, aside from the usual "looks like," "could be," and the others, a variety of reservations with which some patients hedge their associations: apologetics, self-criticisms, question form of response, negative form of response, self-disparagement. At the attention level, this is over-caution and contracted focusing. More deeply the patient in these instances sees himself as very small, looking down on himself. The affective well-spring is a gloomy one of depression quality. The dynamism is guilt. Total failure to qualify is common only in children at the very youngest ages. In adults, I therefore look on it as a regression. It is a resistance to the test, reflecting a hostile attitude by the patient to his world generally.

Rejection of test cards is looked on by some writers as a form of qualifying, an end stage of this behavior. This is an error. Full rejections are actually more rare than would be inferred from the references to it in the literature. Few depressed, for example, reject a test card. These patients are frustratingly slow and exasperating in their qualifying. But they do see something, and verbalize it eventually. Where rejections do occur is in mental deficiency and in schizophrenia. I therefore look on it again as evidence of speech deficit. In the schizophrenics it is regressive.

Another speech finding is the repeating of the same, one or two or so, phrases with a large percentage of the associations. They become monotonous. Anxious children use them, and also some brain damaged. It is a stiff mannerism. The suggestion in it is that it is another form of stereotypy. As such it can be another caution signal, foreshadowing regression or the inclination thereto.

"Edging" can take many forms aside from that which first gave it its name, squinting at the card edge-wise. Patients will hold the cards in the oddest angles: over their heads, down at their ankles, flat on their palms, at arm's length. The oddity of the behavior, qualitatively judged, is the measure of the degree of likely clinical manifestation. Very much at the hunch level is the suggestion that it is a regression in the motor sphere, corresponding to mannerisms or grimaces. On more substantial ground is the interpretation of edging, strictly so-called, in the obsessive neurotics, in whom Kamman first observed it. In them it reflects the compulsion to impeccable accuracy. They must inspect the situation from every most minute point of view.

Reaction to "accidental stimuli" refers to response to artefacts on the test cards, marks of any kinds or sizes left on them in consequence of use. More frequently it refers to reactions to Dd on the blot figures, but remote from, and by usual standards not related to the portion to which the patient is associating. This is due to attention dysfunction. But it does in instances point to something more serious, involvement of the thinking. Or the details are juxtaposed, but no one else sees the relation which the patient does. His productions result from the happenstance that the stimuli came within his field of vision. At the same time these associations do not have, so far as can be judged, the ego-saving intent of a paranoid misinterpretation. These reactions appear to be truly accidental, brought about by the chance that the stimuli were seen. The position (Po) response was earlier recognized and is the primary form of accidental thinking.[4] It always betrays a disorder in the thought processes or a break in normal logic. All these manifestations are found in disintegrated personality states; usually, not always, schizophrenia.

Related but less serious in clinical significance, because they are found over larger clinical range, are the very frequent shifts of content themes, or the elaborating of them with the irrelevant, or totally unrelated. This too can mean disturbance no worse than at the attention level. But it is the ego's weakening grip over the thinking which emerges in this finding; the patient's ideas bear off into what has nothing to do with the case tra-la.

In perseverations, whether to the stimulus or to the content, we see a nonadaptive stickiness of the attention. The patient cannot rid himself of an older impression. An asthenic ego is functioning, one that has lost its

---

[4] RORSCHACH, *op. cit.*, p. 38.

spark, if ever it had one. It can be the sign of breaks in the efficiency. The absorption in the old stimulus prevents attention to the new, and appropriate one. So it also obstructs the considering of the problem at hand.

Language forms provide sundry leads to the ego's functioning. The quality of the language is, of course, index to the person's verbal facility and so some measure of his intelligence. But this can be deceptive. Bleuler comments, "a good fluent speech, congenital or acquired, often disguises real deep defects of intelligence . . . in such cases one speaks of higher dementia, and persons so afflicted sometimes play a great part in life."[5] Many a Rorschach test record demonstrates this in the almost endless flow of associations given with little observable affect, either pleasurable or painful, and consisting of little more than a droll enumeration of the more inferior percepts that the test elicits. Then too, superior language out of context for the rest of the record is another mark of the patient's need to magnify himself, stemming from a consciousness of inadequacy. In severely disordered or disintegrated patients the language confusions and the perplexing unintelligible productions speak for themselves. Very rarely one can actually characterize the productions in the test as one of Bleuler's "word salads." Not quite so rare is a "klang" response.

The content can tell much about the ego's functioning and dysfunction in a structural sense totally apart from its value in projecting out a patient's personal interests. This follows from the fact that animal content is reckoned as per cent of total productivity. Therefore the fewer animal associations, the more content in other categories. Hence breadth of content varies inversely as number of animal percepts. As a corollary it is to be expected that the fewer animal forms, the more original the record. This statement usually holds, but cannot be made as a prediction since many non-animal responses are not original.

The whole human form was noted by Rorschach, and identified by other students, as going with healthier, mature intelligence. Its absence, or low quantity in an otherwise intelligent individual, is likely to indicate repression of this theme. Hysterics produce fewer humans than others; the inference is that they are repressing painful or conflictual thoughts concerning their relations with others. Preoccupation with a topic, irrespective of its personal significance, tells of a maladaptive reduction of interest in the world. Sometimes this preoccupation discloses a clinging need, sometimes phobic thinking, sometimes autistic satisfactions. Or, with less deleterious results, absorption in one's vocation. The concentration on the one topic is necessarily at the expense of others. The loss to the ego is in narrowing the focus of the person's attention. The hemming-in process progresses to the point of stultifying the thinking. The patient, formerly with a wide range of

---

[5] BLEULER, *op. cit.*, p. 69.

ideas, possessed of individuality, is now unrich. The effect spreads and he is not managing problems which are within his range. A person who should sparkle and act brightly is dull; later phlegmatic; in end stages, torpid. The description fits "organic" and depressed patients. The emotions do in the latter what damage in the brain tissue has done in the former. There are, to be sure, differences in the patterns, clinically and in the Rorschach test.

Content can be a structural index to the degree of the whole person's disintegration. This inference can be made from bizarre content, in some persons to the point of the idiosyncratic. The motifs warrant in some patients the conclusion that the person is engaged in animistic thinking or moved by ideas of cosmic grandiosity; or he is living similar rationalizations which can only flower in a soil of very deep regression to primitive archaic levels.

C. THE DEFENSES

Two major defense strategies will first concern us. They are (a) withdrawals and (b) the self-reinforcing character hardenings. In the one, the patient escapes. In the other, the ego evolves a psychologic armor which makes him impervious to the "slings and arrows of outrageous fortune." This armor serves him on two fronts. It not only fends off "the whips and scorns" from without, but also those frequently more troubling ones from within.

These defense strategies about to be described have been patterned out strictly from Rorschach test behavior. Using Rorschach's assumptions as to significance of the factors in his test, and translating these into clinical significance, the defense patterns emerge. That is, they follow strictly from Rorschach test logic. But they correspond also to clinical logic, the defenses as described by Anna Freud and by Fenichel. Their final proving must rest in correlating the clinical description with the Rorschach test description, patient for patient. To correlate these two methods of investigation has been the task of our two United States Public Health Service researches in schizophrenia. These are being reported separately, together with the extent of the validation.

In addition to the two strategies I name above, the following are also derived from Rorschach's test: projection, a variety of mechanisms which may be classed as more at the level of tactics, certain content motifs and anxiety. Description of these in Rorschach test behavior follows except for anxiety. Exposition of the defense service which it provides will form part of the paragraphs concerning that emotion.

First the self-reinforcing phenomena. In these the ego does something about its psychologic annoyances and threats. It takes the initiative. But the operations are directed upon the personality itself. The person must build a thick outer skin to be strong against the missiles that constantly rain on him from the spaces outer to himself. The outcome as we see them in the test are Pyrrhic victories. The more successful the defenses, the more the mental life is reduced. The person is psychologically ham-strung, intellectually bound, the ability to enjoy one's self, choked off. The more the ego wins, the more the patient loses.

Dd in notable excess is a result of inner compulsion to miss nothing. The ego is obeying a "strange command" (Fenichel) which it is powerless to disobey. Those extremely rare Dd, the unsigned[6] ones, are another Rorschach trait extorted by this command.

The most common distortion of Ap in the compulsive character is in the direction of too much Dd. But there are persons who over-accent D. More rare is the Ap in which the individuals select too many W. Iron hard habits are operating in the D! and Dd! approaches. This can also be reported, although with less assurance, of the W! approach. The W's are likely to be the lazy ones; although in rare instances they include a good dose of the truly difficult ones. In these instances they reflect the superior mind usually in a professional or an academic person. The compulsions in these too direct their attention to Dd. But many of these are elaborations, and do not get into the scoring. The Ap is therefore not necessarily W! (D) Dd! But the trained Rorschach student will not miss the pull to the rare detail.

The Z score in these superior persons is usually high. This is not only because of their intellectual drive, but also, because the command forces them to look for connections. Usually, but again not always. In some it is discrepantly low. The frantic search for the minute, the horror of not being thorough, of overlooking something, actually prevents their grasping relations of which they are capable. Their scoring summary shows a Z total disappointingly inadequate for the rest of the record. But the Z total can be reduced also as a direct consequence of the rigorous reaction pattern, the defense which constricts the functioning along all dimensions of the personality. More of this in a moment.

Sequence in these persons well projects the fixity of their character. Unvaryingly they first take the overall view, interpret the whole. Next they systematically dispose of each major detail. Finally they do a clean-up job on the smaller details. In life they are clad within the fortress of certitude in their proven method and are likely to be insensitive to approaches not fitting within their routine; they are as predictable as the movements of the planets. Some scientists of very high rank answer to this description. Among them are also found those persons securely but narrowly anchored

---

[6] Unsigned, i.e., unnumbered because selected too rarely to require identification as do my usual Dd and all my D, (see p. 22).

to some especial set of values, to one's vocation or to one's political or moral attitudes, intolerant of any deviations.

The obsessive drive to completeness makes for much associational productivity. This is more usual among patients with higher intelligence. It is not infrequent at intermediate and even the inferior ranges. But when chronic enforcement of defensive attitudes has a cramping effect, the result on productivity is the contrary. It is low, judged by expectancy set up by internal evidence in the test as to the patient's productive ability.

F+ per cent in some of these persons is very high, out of balance with the record as a whole. It stands out in especially high relief in records of low productivity since in these the quantities of the other variables are restricted. High F+ per cent means that the patient is engaging in a cautious hold on reality which only means that he has an unremitting grip of watchfulness over himself. It is a defense which channelizes him against any straying from the straight and narrow. But in obeying the neurotic command he is also overthrowing that ballast so necessary to the healthy personality, namely the ability to enjoy life.

High animal per cent usually goes with this kind of self guarding. Content range is restricted. The patient recognizes chiefly the more mundane stimuli. He dare not be tempted by the novel. That is violation of the prohibited. Therein lies searing guilt.

Much qualifying has been observed in patients with the hard outer defensive shells, and with the severe personality constraints. This is one manifestation of their caution. The person is trying to give himself all possible assurance. It "looks like," but he leaves the road open, just in case, "it could also be," and "it reminds me," and so on in the inordinate number of precision alternatives.

In their fearful needs for certainty, individuals will show trends to rejection. Nothing ventured, no wrong committed. This would be a sure defense. But they seldom reject. The fear of not responding is just as cogently threatening.

The urge for completeness shows up in a search dictated by the symmetry of the blots. The patient, having associated to a D or a Dd, finds it necessary to inspect the homologous one on the other side. Sometimes he is satisfied that it is identical with the percept he has just reported. Sometimes he detects differences, even if ever so minute.

When the fixed monotonous phrases (see p. 26) appear within the general framework of a neurotic defense pattern, I take them to be manifestations of inflexible habit. So also is failure to turn the test cards. Or the turning follows a very precise and regular pattern (p. 26).

Lambda high is another test technic uncovering a reinforcement of the outer defenses. The patient is responding excessively to external stimuli in his environment. It is a circumspect focusing on reality. He does this at the cost of inadequate response to his inner world. As a result the experience balance is a coarcted one. The ego's defensive operations are in these cases attacking the personality at its core. In the obsessive reaction patterns, a frequent finding is the ambiequal experience balance, whether coarcted or expanded. For causes on which there has been some speculation, but which are anything but cleared up, the color total balances the total of movement responses. This is found with great regularity in the Rorschach test, not only in the obsessive-compulsive neuroses, but also in the depressed and in the hypomanic. It is to be kept in mind here that some clinical observers look on the affective reaction forms as on a continuum with the obsessive-compulsive patterns.

Discussion of the EB opens up consideration of emotional forces. This leads to exposition of the withdrawal defenses. M and Y are the test symbols which represent the principal withdrawals. M does this in its primary function of autistic living. It is a city of refuge for feelings which the patient cannot, which really means dare not, externalize. The literature on the nature of M is extensive, although largely speculative. Neither the theories nor the facts can be restated here. The depth of withdrawal, the distance to which the person escapes psychologically, can be gauged by three factors: One, is the extent to which the number of M overweights the total quantity of C. Two is the absolute quantity of M taken by itself. Given two EB's in which the M to C proportions are the same, the one with more M points to deeper withdrawal. Three is the individualized quality of the content in the fantasies.

M can be a healthful defense. When it appears in the dark figures it is absorbing the anxiety in imaginative activity. The ego is therefore under less urgency to exercise conscious control. In this cluster of behaviors the fantasy serves similarly to sublimation. To be sure it does not have the same universal and socially constructive value that the artist's sublimation does. But there is in it a value which is general to wishful mental life, that of a biological economy. The human organism lessens in this way the friction and heat attendant on a head-on clash between ego and feelings. It is a measure which the ego takes in order to safeguard the personality's health.

The content in the fantasy can be the lead to certain special, individualized turns which the defenses are taking, the kind of solution to which the patient is looking. Such, for example, are certain destruction and disintegration themes in which the patient is projecting his sense that the world is ending. To cite Fenichel again, it is truly ending; the *patient's* world is ending. Another use of fantasy as defense measure is found in projection, in the clinical sense. This is separately discussed below.

The light-determined associations (Y) are those which indicate withdrawal directly into emotional passivity. They are the index to the painful retirements. See more fully below (p. 37 ff.) in discussion of anxiety. When intense excitement accompanies the withdrawal this is gauged in the color structure nuances. In the color cards, withdrawal from emotional contact is etched out also in the color flights and rejections.

The qualifications are another expression of withdrawal. When they run high, the patient is shrinking his psychologic size, making himself inconspicuous. So he defends against any self-assertive prominence such that he may be struck down for it. The affective quality in these expressions can usually be identified as painful. It is a dour behavior; at times, when the inherent aggression does not conceal itself, a sulking one. Achilles in his tent.

There are withdrawals from social contact without the use of fantasy. The scoring summary in these patients may have little or no M. The patient is not turning to autistic solutions. But the distance which he is setting between himself and his fellows is still apparent in intellectual factors, those that project the ego's overt operations. The P count is low; the patient is not recognizing social standards. Low also is the per cent of animal forms, the measure of that adaptive ability much overlapping with what is projected in P, namely knowing the more common percepts of one's field. But, in some retreats, the animal percentage is high. This apparent contradiction is entirely within clinical logic. The grip on the self so narrows the range of the usual interests that the patient's mind sees proportionately too many of the common objects. His stereotypy prevents his sharing his community's broader ideas. The person with too low an animal percentage is prevented by his individuality. The content of these latter is therefore original. But the number of different content categories is not large. These persons are turning to what sets them apart, not what is of interest to many. In some individuals content is heavily weighted down by some one theme. Sex and anatomy are the two more common ones. The patient is shutting out the world by occupying his mind in the one topic. It is always one of personal determination. There is also a kind of apparent preoccupation with one interest which however has no personal significance. This is the repetition of the same one or two responses to the record. It may be "stone," "tree," "mountain." The animal percentage will therefore be very low. But the patient is anything but original. He shows rather an arid stereotypy, such as found in the feeble-minded and the deteriorated.

D. Projection

In the two defense patterns described, the Rorschach test strategy of the one may be characterized as positive, the other as negative. In the one the ego constructs something, a wall. It does happen that, like the great wall of China, it not only defends but also isolates. Yet a structure it is. In the other, the ego preserves the personality by retiring into an inner citadel. My term "negative" is a misleading one. It carries a connotation of inactivity or of a subtracted activity. Like negative algebraic quantities, this would be purely imaginary. The test is photographing a real activity. Retreat is negative only in the sense of subtracting distance from some point of reference. The action, as all action, is positive. This holds in the first place for the fact of the movement itself. The person, or in the military counterpart, the army in retreat, is going somewhere. It holds also in the consequence, which can be of great anguish, to the object against which the action is directed. The Russian retreat from Moscow held such consequences to Napoleon. The psychologic withdrawals have similar intense and aggressive effects on persons with whom the patient stands in certain relations. With this explanation, I am retaining the word "negative" as the one in English best carrying the sense needed here.

In projection—in the strictly clinical sense—the Rorschach test actions are both of the positive and of the negative varieties. The ego definitely takes the initiative. It is on the offensive. But it does this in an inner theatre of operations. It is withdrawing. Such is the case when the fantasy is a projection (clinically speaking). The patient is solving his ego-unpalatable desires by imagining it is someone else who is possessed by them. Such an expedient is an extreme measure. And projection is just that, extreme and malignant. The fact that the patient turns into his fantasy with it, is evidence of how personally critical it is to him. Fantasy can be an activity very deep in the psyche, at its innermost depth it is dream-living. Strong emotions are turned inward, and there given the right of way. To live something within is to want it very much. To have someone else do it is very much not to want it. So the projection is a radical solution. The patient eats his cake and has it too. But it requires a splitting within his mind between what he daydreams and what is its significance as an adaptive solution. Projections are in this sense paranoid referring to the Greek meaning of the term, mind that runs along side mind within the same person. The mental process goes on with another mental process, along parallel tracks as it were, and each leaves the other to one side.

The recognizing of M which is paranoid projection is still the crucial scientific problem. Most M is not paranoid as most fantasy living is not. The content in the Rorschach test fantasy is the clue and I can offer no fixed rules or criteria. Certain fantasy content I regularly report as leads to be explored for their projection (in the *clinical* sense) significance to the patient. The validation so far rests only in this: some persons with these associations are clinically found as defending by way of paranoid projections. Since "some" does not include "all," it follows that some persons with these associations may not have this trait. This is correct. The lead is not to be construed as a finding. It always requires confirmation by other exploring in the patient. The Rorschach test may strengthen any one lead by more additional evidence in the same test protocol. This consists of either or both, (a) in the content, more themes associated with paranoid behavior; and (b) in the structure, the cluster Z high, per cent F+ low, and s high; which in English is grasp of relations while misconstruing reality and stubbornly adhering to these ideas. When evidence converges from both content and structure, the paranoid picture is the more certain. It warrants looking for delusions to the level of systems. For the specific content themes, see p. 67 ff.

Aggressions are at times projection, but as frequently not. They may be the overt disclosure of an unconscious wish. The patient is only withdrawing with it into his fantasy. He is entirely happy with it in that inner haven and by no means finds it necessary to doubly defend by projecting on to another. But some such associations are paranoid projections. Many are attributed to animals. Caution is in order here that the defense may be a less radical one, a displacement. The likelihood of a projection defense will vary with structural evidence (high Z, low F+, high s) in that test record for paranoid misconstruing.

Whether the test can photograph those subtle mechanisms reported in the psychoanalytic literature, the use of bodily functions as physical models for projecting, is at present questionable. The suggestion has been made that some content, not necessarily of fantasy structure, is such projection. It is within the anatomy category, but of pathological quality. Principal attention is directed to the internal organs, especially digestive; it is also directed to the excretory passages with emphasis on their cathartic functions. An inference is that the patient's thoughts are concerned with cleansing of the person, stemming in turn and more intensely from ideas of cleansing the soul. A paranoid schizophrenia is indicated. The lead to be followed in these associations generally is their value as an index to organized delusions. However, I have seen them in patients with their outer defenses still operative. As one example, a woman of 46, in severe disruption, reactive, liberating paranoid behavior, not psychotic, associates to Figure VII, D 6, the vagina detail: "looks like a bulb, and this is the long part that screws in, . . . a technical bulb, grey metal with long neck, in my Hammond organ" (the musical instrument). This response also exemplifies the hazard in interpreting manifest content directly. Only the patient can trace out its meaning in therapeutic sessions.

Systematic study of the paranoid personality in the Rorschach test still awaits doing.

E. A GROUP OF TACTICS

Dd in some patients are a displacement. Attending to the insignificant relieves the individual from focusing on the more essential issues. He busies himself with the peripheral elements of a problem and so skirts the real trial. The ego saves the individual from tackling a too troubling test head on. Dd is also the test's technic for the isolation mechanism. By perceiving disparate elements of a situation, the patient can prevent the entire from jelling into what may be an organized and meaningful but disconcerting unit. Yet the obsessive is ever driven to get all the facts. This he does in never satisfied measure. Hence the ever more and more Dd but without knitting them into the experience of a larger significant whole. He adds, not organizes. He wants to see everything but shuts himself off from its import. His producing Dd is also a method of undoing. This, in its role of ritual. In properly attending to fine point after fine point we can still the pressure from emotion and so undo what has in it potential for being a troubling eventuality. A large increase in Dd is result in some patients of reaction formation. This is seen following anxiety shock; and as frequently seen after neurotic shock. Frightened, the patient over-reacts by overly much associations, setting up a camouflage of being at ease and actually giving himself reassurance. But the emotion actually scatters the attention to the minute. Or it activates one of the defenses just described, isolation, displacing.

W is in some persons the index to the escape into vague abstractions by speculating. Both the richer W and the weaker ones are utilized. Content is original in these W. But it is an oblique originality redolent of the patient's one-sided personality. It does not strike a responsive chord from others. This kind of production will be found frequently in a "verbalist" setting. The patient is using words as words, incompatible in quality with the inferior quality of the test record as a whole. The words preserve him from contact with his real problems. In more serious conditions, they isolate from reality. This trait is relatively frequent even in milder maladjustments; and in inappropriate intellectualizing which betrays the inferiority consciousness it intends to cover up.

Very high productivity also goes with some of this inferior philosophizing. This finding will be the lead to two other defenses: in (a) the isolation tactic, productivity builds up as a result of the patient's searching out the many small details; or (b) it is another result of the reaction formation above noted, the "paradoxical increase" following anxiety shock. It helps bind the unsettlement.

Other tactics. Digression as dictated by symmetry also requires observing as undoing defense. By attending to one side, and then to the other, the person goes through with a formality which undoes the conflictual or fearful thinking. Part human forms (Hd) sometimes appear to be a displacement. As such it may be an especially important finding, displacing emotions and content on to body parts. The lead from the test may be to a defense against a seriously undesired attitude. The body part is invested with the feeling belonging somewhere else.

Very slow time for first response is one technic by which the patient tries to keep a distance between himself and the painful feelings which are threatening him. The ego is blocking off the affects. Rejection of a test card is the same behavior going to end stage. Intermediate are some trends to rejection in which, however, the patient still produces an association. An intriguing psychologic problem is what happens in the full rejection? Is the patient dispelling the affect? Freeing himself from it? Or does it so overpower him as to prevent his associating rendering him momentarily speechless? If the latter is the fact, a more correct description of this defense tactic is that the affect is blocking off the intellectual life. Hypothalamic influences are at high flood, choking off the activity in the cortex.

It is to be emphasized that the rejections and the blockings are entirely intrapsychic mechanisms. The patient is truly shutting off either affect or intellect, as the case may be. The rejections are not to be mistaken for that conscious refusal to associate or to report an association. These latter are symptoms of hostility. Some paranoids go to the length of rejecting all but one or two test cards. This is, of course, still a defense.

A tactic in connection with shock phenomena is the postponement of affect as delayed shock. The dysfunction induced by Figure II may not set in until Figure III; that induced by IV, not appearing until V. Color shock activated by Figure VIII or IX, may not be evident until Figure X. Rejection by a person of color as a determinant in a response usually reported as color-determined is another isolation technic. It defended the patient against affective experience, pleasurable living, since that is (to this patient) punishable.

Some content directly serves defensively. Such are the phobic themes. The patient binds his deeper fears by centering them on the socially accepted fear sources, e.g., animals. Little Hans is the classic example. This defense is also a displacement. In fact the test frequently uses animals to engage in the hostilities which are undesired by the patient's ego. Anatomy associations are another defense of this variety. By concentrating on his "poor health," the individual has a cause for anxiety which screens his vision from the ego-alien one.

F. ANXIETY

The purpose of anxiety as defense is receiving much exposition in the current psychologic literature. The Rorschach test, because it can contrast anxiety with another defense activity, withdrawal into fantasy, throws fresh light on the nature of both these defenses. Fantasy living is a psychologic tool necessary to the individual as a biological organism. Anxiety is needed by him as a social organism. The one reduces attrition within. It gives the ego some place to go where it will not be in unremitting mortal combat with the emotions. Fantasy is the lubricant that permits the personality wheels to move smoothly. It thus conserves the individual's strength; and it aids him in his struggle to survive. Anxiety effectively slows down or halts the psychologic machinery when the personality is being tempted to behavior not consistent with his society's standards. That person's sensitization to those standards, which is to say his ego, gives the signal to the anxiety, and the brakes screetch. In instances the reaction goes to the point of dead stop; the panic generates paralysis. The anxiety protects the patient from himself.

A word of theory is therefore in order here as to what happens in anxiety shock in the Rorschach test. From the validating clinical conditions and from what is known of the personal dynamics in each patient, my only conclusion is that the person becomes truly anxious. This is to say that when a person manifests shock phenomena while associating to Figure IV, VI, VII, and as the case may be, Figure I or V, he is actually suffering an agitating experience. But this is not to say that he is frightened by the black masses constituting these figures. He is frightened by the thoughts which he holds and has held for a long time. They are urges to erotic or to aggressive acts; urges which horrify the person by reason of the values he holds, or more accurately, hold him. The test figures awaken attitudes that are part of the person. They cannot generate anxiety shock in individuals who are not anxious. It is not the test, but their own wishes that make them anxious. The great service of the instrument is in identifying those who have these wishes.

Of the all-grey-black figures, the fuses that liberate this painful emotion, not all are equally effective. Figures IV, VI and VII are the most effectual. Figure I does arouse the shock phenomenon in many patients. But it can also be innocuous even in persons vulnerable in any of the other four. Figure V is the least traumatic; so much so that when disturbance does develop in it, I look for evidence that it is due to shock delayed from Figure IV, rather than generated by V itself. The evidence in IV is likely to include reaction formations, such as too fast time for first response, significant increase in productivity, tightening of the intellectual grip on the self or on reality. When shock in IV is uncontrolled, its appearance in V is a continuance of that set going in IV unless it can be directly related to anxiety laden motifs in V. Such are the threatening mouths; reclining human figures, especially when of the same sex as the patient; accent on the blackness of "the bat," or making it a "vampire"; or the occasional "serpents" seen in the projections of this test figure. When there is no evidence of shock in Figure IV, or of defense against such shock, its appearance in V is generated by the latter figure.

The most important new diagnostic differentiation I have been attempting in this sphere is that between anxiety as free or as bound. By "free" I am referring to that which strikes the individual suddenly, overcomes, renders him speechless. Overt activity may be arrested. This is the clinical picture. In the Rorschach test certain of the measures through which we regularly identify anxiety shock reach extreme points. These measures follow the patterns I formerly described as the anxiety shock phenomena with small modifications. I now summarize them as follows: time for first response, either very retarded, or impressively fast; productivity, either notably reduced, or significantly increased; form quality, impaired or more rigidly accurate than in the record as a whole. Decrease in Z; a fixed pattern in the Approach; disturbance in Sequence, although this finding is less frequent than I formerly thought; fantasy can become very autistic, providing a lead into the personal source of the conflict, but the finding emerges in relatively few persons; restricted associational content; delay or loss of the popular associations; the x response becomes prominent; sex content emerges; phobic and counterphobic associations or elaborations. Qualifying is very notable, also rejection trend. These reactions have continued to be dependable indicators that anxiety was in process of being mobilized.

The manifestations of free anxiety: the response time for first association will be severely retarded. Productivity is likely to be significantly reduced, can go to the extremes of rejection, especially in Figures VI and IV; more rarely in both. It is a temporary paralysis brought on by the panic. In less acute instances, the patient although giving evidence in his record generally for potential for many and original ideas, will respond in the anxiety-shock figures with only a single, or at the most two associations. Both will be scored F+. But in many instances P is notable by its low quantity. The shock is interfering with the individual's more conformable (adaptive) thinking. The high accuracy is therefore not adaptive behavior. It is rigidity. Hence the content themes will also be stereotyped; there will be high animal percentage, many Hd. Conversely, there will be a sharp narrowing of otherwise original and broad association range. Or, organization activity diminishes sharply to the zero point. In a word, all the signs point to the stoppage of mental activity. The tempo with which it all happens is notably violent.

This is not so in bound anxiety. But what is bound anxiety? Fenichel speaks of the ego harnessing the anxiety. The metaphor is a fortunate one in describing what happens clinically. A hysterical conversion, a psychosomatic illness, an obsessive-compulsive neurosis, they are psychologic loads to which the ego harnesses, or binds, its fears. Dragging this baggage, these *impedimenta*, which is the concretistic and accurate Latin word for baggage, the anxiety is impeded and so prevented from facing its real and most painful source. The person is protected.

In the Rorschach test the binding is projected directly in two kinds of response, and it can be inferred from a third. The two are (a) certain defensive structural operations which I will designate as the "self-reinforcing" variety; and (b) certain content categories. The third variety consists of some clusters of test behavior, complexes which are the test's equivalent for the clinical complexes by which the ego binds the anxiety.

Inspecting first these test clusters: productivity high; organization activity reduced; attention to Dd very high but entirely disregarded by some persons. In this group of Rorschach traits, the patient is immuring the anxiety within an obsessive wall. When the Dd score is high, the lead may be to a ritual-like precision in the behavior pattern.

Self-uncertainty. The manifestations are qualifying to an exaggerated degree; doubting or rejecting one's own associations; criticism of the test figures and especially captious attention to small imperfections in them; absorption in symmetry, usually by comparing the similar details on the opposite laterals of the test figure. All these traits are obsessive-compulsive phenomena. The patient sets up a barrier of doubts around which his energy expends. He binds the anxiety in these doubts and so saves himself from facing his painful, deeper fears.

Ambitendencies emotionally. The experience balance is the core of this reaction. The number of M just about equals the sum of the color weightings. A curious thing that it should work so, in so many obsessive neurotics. It does. For each impulse to express his emotions, the patient has a contrary one and turns inward with them. The "double front" (Fenichel) is mirrored in the test. The experience balance may be expanded (*dilatiert*), or narrowed in (*koartiert*). It is still ambiequal. The double front is an especially dominating condition when percentage of white spaces are above average in quantity. The patient is fighting now his outer contacts, now his inner world. This sets loose all those insufferable self-doubtings that consume these patients so. Ever nullifying each start by the move in the opposite direction, the victim of this neurosis remains spinning in dead center. Always in movement, he arrives nowhere.

The depression reaction and overt anxiety. Experience balance is very much restricted: M at 1 or 0; color sum is at about the same level. R is much reduced; also Z. Time for the first response is slow in most of the figures; average time for all responses, very slow. All these are findings that go with a retarding of mental activity. But per cent of F+ is high, and so betrays the painful selfguarding which is the enemy of free mental life. With this cluster Y will appear, and less frequently so as FY than as YF; now and then it will be Y. The melancholy mood and the passive response to life's cares are here being projected. Another pain-toned reaction is the vista response. But this is not so inevitable. It is a more specific index to the unhappy sense of inferiority, and as such contributes heavily to the entire dysphoric state of mind. As a finishing touch, are the dysphoric motifs in the content, projections from the somber, or oppressive thinking.

All this is a heavy price for the personality to pay. The question is germane: is the defense worth the cost? The answer: the high cost is a measure of the need. By binding at this level the patient staves off what is to him more catastrophic knowledge. Whether or not rightly (by others' standards) he would need to bring very heavy punishment down on his head if he admitted to his consciousness what is acusing him deeply. The more consciously rationalizing mind diverts him from that castigating voice.

The "strong attack is the best defense" strategy. The patient attacks the environment: white space count is very high in an experience balance which in color total is notably greater than the number of M. The human figures may be heavily caricatured or altogether deanimated such as puppets, statues, idols, skeletons or dead bodies, either human or animal. At times they may be decapitated. Question of depersonalizing needs to be raised in such content although the Rorschach test counterpart of this clinical finding is still very much in the hunch stage. The patient frequently displaces the hostility on to animal content. Or he associates with aggression implements.

Test traits are separately used in binding mechanisms in the following ways. R, unexpectedly high as reaction formation. Dd, in high quantity as undoing, but also as displacement of attention from D and from W, i.e., from the more essential fact in the environment. The importance of Dd in the obsessive picture has been noted. A very high F+ per cent in the shading shock figures is a favorite binding tactic; the patient concentrates hard and becomes inflexibly realistic. Rejections and rejection effort are an avoidance of the issue by flight. This is the test's equivalent of the counterphobic flight of the clinician. The patient will in instances verbalize his fear of the threat activating stimulus, or he will express an unpleasant emotion. "Horrid, disgusting, I hate it, gruesome," and the like. Figures IV and VI are among the grey-black ones, those that most frequently receive this treatment. Figures II and IX draw it very heavily.

In the inner living, certain M stances project the patient's inability to make up his mind, whether to cling submissively, or to assert himself. This is the significance in the static M or in those in which the action is both flector and extensor in the same association. The experience balance is usually extratensive in the hysterical reaction pattern with a small quantity of M present. But the latter is not enough to absorb the agitating feelings. These are converted into symptoms typical for this neurosis. Anatomy content may also be present with this structure, and in these cases the entire defensive pattern is as likely to be one of the psychosomatic disorders.

Content which is phobic or dysphoric on the face of it also uncovers the binding expedient. The person is halting at theme points which are dangerous or troublesome enough in their personal values. But by mulling about these he again saves himself from facing more crucial issues. Anatomy motifs render this service. One can complain about poor health and remain in good standing socially. Others are the threatening animals, especially those with large biting mouths, e.g., snake, wolf, lion, tiger, crocodile. Also, the fangs, teeth or claws of these animals. In other instances human figures are explicitly threatening such as giant advancing, witches grasping. Overtly dysphoric: black clouds; storm or variations, e.g., tornado; landscapes denoting the lonesome or isolation (see p. 65 ff.). In some instances the test stimulus is directly translated into mood: "depression."

All this binding of anxiety is a defense against the anxiety. But the anxiety is itself a defense, a mobilizing of affects so as to forestall ego-undesired behavior. By harnessing the emotion, the ego achieves two objectives. For one, it holds the force of the emotion within bounds, prevents intellectual disintegration or even dysfunction. Secondly the ego by this mechanism saves the personality from worse trouble, i.e., from conscious awareness of the real dynamic behind the fear. It prevents the person from facing the first *raison d'être* of his painful affects. The ego mobilizes the personality's resources to prevent behavior undesirable to itself. Binding is therefore a defense against a defense.

G. The Lively Affects

In connection with shock phenomena, I touched, above (p. 37) on the workings of Figures II, III and VIII to X as comparable to those in the gray-black figures. In so doing I inadvertently pointed to some functioning that is similar for the two kinds of stimuli. Both arouse emotions. They have shock value. Nor is the liberation of anxiety limited to the black figures. Color shock also sets anxiety into motion. The important difference between the chromatic test figures, and the gray-blacks, is the nature of the stimulus that generates the shock. In the blacks, a readiness to feel guilty is touched off. The person's thinking irradiates—to fall back on an older psychological term—unpleasant affect, anticipation of the very painful and in instances, of doom.

The further fact is that it is a reaction related to stimuli associated with depression. A guilt thought is activated. The person suffers from something he has done, whether he has done it or not. This is the theory behind "anxiety-shock," or more properly as it is called by some writers, shading shock. In color shock the stimulus has the affective quality within a pleasurable modality. It can arouse impulses that are very exciting. That is it awakens some urge for gratification still to be experienced, a desire. But the shock, the upset, is evidence that the wish is incompatible with ego standards. By the logic of dynamic psychology it was a wish that has been repressed. Whether repressed or not, the essential fact is that the emotion does not concern something which the person has done. It concerns something which he would like to do, but must not. Upbringing and standards command against such behavior. Yet it would result in experience that is very gratifying. It is a temptation. In this important way the anxiety set in motion by color shock differs from that activated by anxiety shock. In the latter, set off by the gray-black figures, the anxiety looks to the past, to something the patient has done. In color shock it looks to the future, to something he wants to do.

The color shock phenomena themselves in the test follow the pattern I have formerly described. A number of investigations have within the past few years focused on the question whether there is a differential reaction to chromatic as compared to nonchromatic test figures. The most recent (at this writing) is that by Siipola, Kuhns and Taylor.[7] They appraise the pitfalls both in designing the appropriate researches, and in drawing conclusions. They sum up their own findings in the cautious statement, "The results, then, are conclusive in showing that an individually oriented technic of measuring color influence is feasible." In any event, Rorschach test records that are differentiated by their color shock yield diagnostic pictures that are differentiable from those without shock. This holds not only for (a) the fact of finding shock at all, but also (b) the degree of shock. The doubts that the experiments on the problem raise are as to what it is conceptually that produces the differentiating reactions. But whatever the underlying process is, the phenomenon has clinical validity. It reliably separates out personality patterns that are unlike one another.

The color shock behavior, in summary, and with modifying observations that are in order in consequence of experience since I published these (in 1945) follow. Time per first response, retarded. Productivity, significantly reduced. Form quality, impaired; a most important finding including far deviations from accuracy. Associational content unique, highly personal. The fantasy, regressive in structure, unique in content to the point of communicating a totally private world; in instances it is of dream quality. Sequence, shift toward the less controlled. P responses, lacking; or appearance is delayed. Organization activity, reduced. Associational breadth narrows. Anatomy, sex, associations emerge; this is consistent with the pattern of releasing unique thinking. The x associations, or trends to them, prominent. Qualifications, rejection trends, prominent. Color avoidance, flight or rejection. Of less frequency than I formerly thought, but still noted in some patients is rejection of test card without any response; this is found principally in Figure IX and in Figure II in that order. Regressive shift of color-determined associations, in the direction of $FC-$, CF or $CF-$, and pure C. Shift in quality, or imaginative richness; $F+$ to $F-$; M to F. The affective ratio, low; below 0.40.

[7] SIIPOLA, E., KUHNS, F. AND TAYLOR, V.: Measurement of the individual's reactions to color in ink blots. J. Personality, **30:** 153–171, 1950.

Lambda index, shifts violently. This is a most important new observation. Computed for the color shock figure alone the index will either significantly decrease going below 0.55, or it will notably increase, rising above 0.85. For critical discrimination, the lambda index needs to be calculated separately for the finding in the shock figures and the comparison then made. The shift can be understood as the patient's response to stress under shock conditions. When the lambda index decreases, the patient is responding to his inner world at the expense of the outer. He is either more responsive to emotion-toned stimuli, lively or painful (increase of C or Y associations). Or he is taking flight in fantasy (increase of M).

The older, known color shock traits are listed above in the approximate order of their effectiveness. Most rare are low affective ratio and rejections. For that reason they are the more significant when found. Two or three color shock findings are about the average number that I look for in any one record. A single one, when in extreme degree, exceedingly slow time for first response, very poor form quality, great increase of Dd, are adequate evidence of shock.

In interpreting findings for color-determined associations, i.e., in the sphere of the lively affects generally, certain new significances are apparent. These are additional to those that have been known, rather than corrections of them. The assumptions as to psychologic significance of color and the variations of this response appear valid as published by Rorschach, and as demonstrated in the studies clinically in applying the test since the *Psychodiagnostik*. Some additional interpretive comments, including elaborations of old ones, follow. Color, C unmodulated; CF. The former in its role of projecting impulsivity and the latter uncovering emotional pressures too little disciplined have the effect of loosening the thinking from its normal moorings. One result is an undirected flight of ideas, irrelevant, sometimes without coherence. Push of personal needs and desires can in instances be detected in the content. But the productions are frequently the very erratic outcome of unbridled temper and the record is therefore dotted with much impersonal F−. These two test behaviors are also the index to a diffuse lability, manifested as the crochety irritability of the chronically neurotic and of those ageing persons in whom this process and consciousness of it are attended by a morose mood. Motor manifestations accompany: much and rapid card turning, restless shifting by the patient in his chair and very rapid language production. With this behavior, and with the C, CF findings, there will cluster some very erratic F−. The over-all conclusion can be drawn that the feelings are playing hob with the ego. The impulsivity and lack of restraint in the C, CF, are accentuated when found in a cluster with many white spaces and only few fantasy responses. The opposition energy turns against the outside world and the person is not equipped to consume it within. The pure color and color-form variables thus continue to be useful in indicating the person's condition of inner unrest; the man or woman is not stabilized emotionally and therefore is unstable in his reactions to life's events.

Abstract qualities derived from the color-toned stimuli characterize persons whose thinking is heavily dominated by the feelings. It takes a very firmly rooted ego to handle such strong emotions. In schizophrenics, in hypomanics and in neurotics the emotion so projected is quite dissociated from directed control. This is most rare, however, when found in neurotics.

When the color-dictated associations all follow one structural nuance, or nearly do, whether this is C, CF or FC, the person is always reacting at about the same emotional tone. A too even, unchanging, affect is dominating him. This is so also when the patient is producing no color associations. His personal tone is a dull one. Insofar as there is a person who is emotionless, that is what a Rorschach test with a zero color finding projects (provided always that it is within a test structure consistent with this indication). At the best, this inability to react to color is the mark of the person insensitive to the world's exhilarating values. Some of these patients engage in color naming or color description, but do so perfunctorily. They lack all real interest in the colors as color.

The total absolute number of color-dictated associations needs to be noted. Statistics are not available as to what makes many or few such responses. On empirical basis, I make my sphere of reference, six or more such associations in a total productivity of forty. The more color-dictated associations, the more the individual is capable of reacting with verve toward, and warm feeling for, his fellow humans. Again, the finding must occur in a cluster which is consistent with the interpretation. This cluster includes FC, a high affective ratio and color total above 5.0 all within a record which is not pathological. Hence the quality of the content in the color associations will add additional discriminating information.

Mood as elation. "Color love" can form one factor in a cluster projecting too much warmth, which is really heat. Total color score will be very high with abundance of both C and CF. By "color love" I include excited expressions, sometimes ecstatic, with which some patients greet the color figures. Color symbolism will also appear as "green" is "spring," the "rose" (of Figure X) is "gaiety," "white" is "purity," "blue" is "truth." Such associating characterizes the superior in his intenser and passionate moments. Orlando and Rosalind in their mutual yearnings in Arden, for example. These persons will name color, and the student will learn to discriminate between the indifferent, perfunctory enumerating by the asocial and the exuberant reaching of the hypomanic or the healthy elated. Affective ratio is above average; when 0.80 or higher, is at once the lead to emotional reaction in high key. In the more egocentric reaction patterns, the individual makes himself the sphere of reference for the judgment on these percepts: "I love this," "it's darling," or "this is awful," "I hate it." This behavior will be more frequently noted in the hypomanic and the lead to be explored is the feeling of omnipotence to which the patient may have regressed. Elaborations, extravagant or lush, will be observed in these patients, also in some with brain damage. I have noted it too in epileptics, but younger ones.

The affective ratio. For the research data from which this factor was derived see the full findings in the normal adult group. It is obtained as a quotient of R in Figures VIII, IX and X divided by R in Figures I to VII inclusive. The mean for a normal adult group was found to be 0.60, SD 0.19. Therefore I use any finding between 0.40 and 0.80 as within normal range. Psychologically I look on the affective ratio as measure of the readiness to quicken to life's pleasurable experiences. Or, when low, to remain inert. When the ratio approaches 0.80, the person is volatile, liable to excitement. When it is 0.40 or lower, he is under-responsive to emotion-toned stimuli. Depending on whether there is other evidence of emotional withdrawal, the low affective ratio may accent in the fact of shallow feelings. This ratio does not necessarily correlate with the absolute number of color associations, or the total color score. Some persons with high affective ratio produce discrepantly few color-dictated associations. The discrepancy is an important finding; the person has the latency for emotional contact, but is not making it. The maladjustment is impeding his capacity for pleasurable response. So we know not only that he is conflicted, or withdrawing, but also that he has the reserves ready to become active, a very important bit of information for the therapist.

Thus a high ratio can point to favorable results, in a pattern otherwise unpromising. Such are some anxiety reactions and the depressions. The finding discloses lively, unused resources. The depression can be understood as a reactive one. The patient should be accessible to directive or encouraging therapy, and depending on the other equipment in the personality, to a deeper treatment technic including that involving a transference relationship. When the affective ratio is high, it may be one of a cluster of variables showing the emotions as dominating the thinking. But excessive flights of ideas will be found, produced by the feelings, without the ratio necessarily being high. It is in some persons high, in others low. When high, the feelings are on the loose. They step up the quantity of production in test cards VIII, IX, X; at the same time that they may significantly vitiate its quality.

A low affective ratio is sometimes found, although it is rare, in Rorschach test structures with C and CF. The number of associations so dictated will be small. They tell of the unpredictable explosions which in some schizophrenics are inappropriate reactions. The patient is otherwise little responsive emotionally. Potential temper outbursts which impair the perceptual accuracy and disorganize the thought processes are here indicated. Such a combination of findings, low affective ratio, emotional lability, appears also in some children in whom there is a lag in emotional maturing; it also appears in many hysterics and in some organics.

Other structural traits in the test need to be noted, traceable to sensitivity to color and so to emotional responsivity. Productivity, as we have seen, may be stepped up. But the quality is inferior. Originals are few, stereotypy high. The other Rorschach test signs of the rich mentality are lacking. The range of content will be wide in some patients. But in them too, the quality will not be commensurable. The originals are unique, rather then spelling cultivation. They are product of the patient's preoccupation with some one topic. They dot an otherwise mediocre set of associations. The entire content has thus an uneven quality. In some of these patients too the quick, jittery change of ideas will be found. When total productivity is low, and is in a cluster including a low affective ratio, few color-dictated associations, the sensitivity to the world's satisfying stimuli is low.

When time for first response or average time for all responses is very fast it may be a clue to quickened emotional sensitivity. The fast time will be especially found in the color cards. It is common in hypomanic conditions. The feeling pressures in these patients permit of no delay or restraint.

Domination over the individual's thinking by intense emotions centered on particular topics will be evident in the test in the content of the color-determined associations. The themes may be out and out pathological or regressive, sick anatomy associations, sexual or anal body portions, food, fire or blood, or other violence motifs. Or they may be of healthier potential, among others, the arts or nature in its pleasurable aspects. How appropriate the patient's emotional response generally is can be judged from the content in this sphere. But I can offer no precise rule whereby to identify those color-dictated associations which are "appropriate." In general, they are more frequently produced and carry pleasant connotations (flower, Christmas tree, or art motifs). The student learns to identify those which are off the beaten path generally, or which play a unique role in the particular test record. Rorschach develops this topic of strong emotions storming within the individual in his posthumous paper.[8]

H. THE PAINFUL AFFECTS

Concerning the vista and the light-determined responses some additional interpretive nuances have been observed. The latter, Y, in its three variations, Y, YF, FY, is the test's counterpart of the emotional passivity, the defense of lying low. The term is thus misleading since it gives the impres-

---

[8] RORSCHACH, H.: *op. cit.*, p. 219 ff.

sion of inactivity. Passivity as a withdrawal is a positive if not an overt act.
It is something that the individual does. The shading determinant identifies
the painful character of the withdrawal. When vista is also present the inferiority consciousness aggravates the pain. It deepens the passivity, and
accents the submissiveness. When the two factors appear, and they usually
do, in depressions and anxieties, they disclose an especially severe passivity
accompanying these conditions. Should they, but especially the shading
element, be prominent in the color cards, the depression is very painful.
These factors become confirming indications that the anxiety is more free
than bound. They add the acrid savor of agitation to the inner unrest which
is being projected by the C and the CF. This, in whatever cards the shading
responses are found. The irritation is the sharper when they are determinants in Figures VIII, IX, X; and most discomposing when C and Y
co-determine an association (the blends). These tell of both pain and excitement in the same reaction. Each overdetermines the other, and the clinical
equivalent is a jumpy uneasiness in which motor phenomena are prominent.

When the shading determinants are very numerous in the black figures
themselves in a record having the structure of a depression, and if the
emphasis is on the shading rather than on the form (YF or pure Y, VF or
pure V), the lead is to either (a) a panic danger when the condition is also
that of a very free anxiety or to (b) a potential for an ultimately stuporous
emotional state.

From all this it follows that shading especially, and also vista are important as mood indicators. They sound the gloom note. Vista as inferiority
feeling may only intensify an unhappiness already set going by anxiety.
But it will add its own especial significance as structural evidence of self-
devaluation and depreciation. In turn these stem from self-castigating ideas.
In back of these is conscience. The state of mind in all these experiences is as
of one in deep trouble. Dame Care sits on the patient's brow.

One cluster of test traits consists of motor signs, much and rapid card
turning, the edging trait and behavior which is directly distinguishing.
Examples of the latter are vigorous manipulating of the test cards, slapping
them down in returning them, even tossing them, or the patient is overactive, in instances rising out of his chair. Here should be noted certain
verbalizings that disclose inner unsettlement: mistrust by the patient of his
accuracy, complaining about his inability to associate and dysphoric content.
The significance of all this as emotional ploughing up is again the more conclusive when in a record whose Y and V complicate the C and CF picture,
and especially when there are shading-determined associations in the color
figures as above described. The clinician's cue is to look for perturbed behavior emerging overtly in a setting of depression.

The cheerful mood and its test indicators have been described above

(p. 45). There are many records in which these pleasure-toned, even elated, and always gratifying color-determined associations appear together with the gloom carriers. They are from persons in whom the pleasurably exciting truly mingles with a painful emotion. Such is the lover's unsatisfied longing, or the wish-gratifying fantasy which attempts to cope with the aching reality. This blend of pangs with happiness is more frequently projected in the test as a unit reaction in certain fantasy associations.

I. THE FANTASY ACTIVITY

The nature of M as emotional response requires emphasis. Rorschach is explicit on this point: "are we dealing with an *experience of movement* (*Erfühlen der Bewegung*) and not only with the perception of a form, which is only secondarily being interpreted as in motion?"[9] Some lines earlier in this context he defines what is not M. He cites as examples, "a duck going into the water," "a dog snapping after a butterfly," "a bird on the wing," "an airplane in flight," "a mountain belching fire." He comments that "in by far the greatest number of instances, these are not M responses. They are form responses, designs following only the form of the picture, and calling it movement is often only a rhetorical dressing up of the response, a *secondary* association."[10]

The M response, then, designates an experience of felt movement. The literature, especially the American, has been disregarding the term "felt." Because M is set opposite over against C in the experience balance, the interpretive significance has been attaching to M as of something opposite to that which is inherent in C, psychologically; namely something opposite to feeling. To be sure the overt identifying character mark of a dominantly M person contributes to this error. He is "calm and collected." But these outwardly calm persons are among the most intense emotionally. The greater literary artists have long known this as their created characters demonstrate. Many historical persons illustrate the point. Among the former, there come to mind Jacques in *As You Like It*, Olav in Undset's *Master of Hestviken*, Ivan in the *Brothers Karamazov*, Conrad's *Lord Jim*. Among the latter, the Cardinal Richelieu; the philosophers Plato, Spinoza; the painter Cézanne; and among American presidents, Lincoln and Woodrow Wilson.

All felt intensely. In the historical characters, we know it from their biographies. In the created persons, the proof is in the feelings which they generate in the reader. They are projections, as all great achievements are, in the men and women who see and hear the dramas, read the poems or novels, gaze at the sculpture, or the architect's structure, or listen to the

---

[9] RORSCHACH, H., *op. cit.*, p. 26 (Rorschach's italics).
[10] *Ibid.*, p. 25–6 (Rorschach's italics).

music. Whatever the nature of the art may be, it is projection not only of its creator, but also of him who enjoys it. That is the essence of universal art. Regarding the historical personages, the evidence is that outwardly self-contained as they were, all were passionately moved toward the particular ends which they pursued.

That is, all were "introversive." The term means simply that they turned their feelings inward. It also means that they had feelings. What differentiates them is the directions which the feelings are taking with reference to the personality. The individual is intro-verting; turning them inward. The feelings are none the less powerful for being contained. In fact, their very containment is responsible for the intensity which so characterizes them.

The M person in the Rorschach test is therefore, and the point bears repetition, one moved by strong feelings. They are feelings which the person holds in. In clinical pictures, and in healthy living, the mental stuff of M emerges as achievement of the new. The individual is converting his emotions. It is "inspired" work.[11] In neurotics, it is daydreaming. In the psychotic the daydreaming degenerates into autistic, dereistic living. In the strong, healthy adult it is sublimation.

With regard to interpretive nuances of M, its use in defense deserves some fresh comment. Its essence as shock absorber has long been understood. It makes for biologic economy to the individual. Affording the feelings free play within, it relieves the ego of the strain incident to preventing its being liberated outwardly. The ego is thus freed for its proper duties of evaluating, integrating and directing. It carries on more smoothly. This is what I understand by Rorschach's statement that M stabilizes the affects.

The M defense is a major strategy depending on (a) the total quantity of M; and (b) the degree of introversion (proportion of M to sum of the color values). The strategy is that of withdrawal into autistic living. In a person who has also broken with reality, this is a lordly retirement into a world where he is master of all he surveys. Incidentally, in evaluating M quantitatively, I judge any number greater than six as "high."[12]

---

[11] I am of course aware of the criticisms in recent literature of Rorschach's hypothesis concerning M as creative activity as well as some of his other assumptions and conclusions. A valuable current survey of these writings is that by M. R. HERTZ (Current problems in Rorschach theory and technique. J. Proj. Techniques 15: 307–338, 1951.)

[12] In using this point of reference, I follow the findings of MOLISH, H. B., MOLISH, E. E. AND THOMAS, C. B.: A Rorschach study of a group of medical students. Psychiat. Quart. 24: 744–774, 1950. The data reported by these writers agree well with my own in superior persons. The many investigators scoring FM or other variations of M may wonder how my rule of seven applies. My suggestion is to follow Rorschach's principle, and I quote: "the rule generally holds that M comes into consideration

M is a favorite technic for projecting (in the clinical sense) paranoid thinking. The rub is to identify that content, M or other, which is paranoid projection. On the difficulties involved, see p. 34.

The stance in the fantasy activity may provide evidence supporting the homosexual lead. Such is the case when the dominant pose is contrary to that which would be expected from the sex of the patient. The critical observation to be made is as to the direction of the activity as extensor or flector; clinging to, or pulling away, from the center; as submissive, or self-assertive; and so as of feminine, or masculine, sexuality in the unconscious. The male patient with clinging, feminine stance or the female, with self-assertive masculine attitude may safely be set down as of homosexual structure psychologically. Within such a framework, fantasy content that is specifically homosexual (p. 67), naturally strengthens the finding.

Flector stance in the M associations will accent other evidence in the test of a passive adjustment. Similarly, extensor M tells that in the unconscious at least the patient is handling himself as a dominating individual. This may only be expressing a wish contrary to the clinical reality. Some M stance is, however, equivocal or static. Unable to turn either to the left or the right, to advance or to retreat, the patient remains fixed, as if bound to a post. Actually he is bound by his ambivalent tendencies, the one neutralizing the other. The technic is a defense, usually against the anxiety.

Some anxious persons exploit the defensive function of M especially well against the anxiety. They produce few or no M in the first three test figures despite the potency of these figures to activate M. Then fantasies will appear in quantity in Figure IV, with two, three, or even four such associations. M responses will continue numerous in the rest of the test. Figure IV sets off anxiety shock and sends the ego flying into the inner world. Once the fantasy has become kinetic, the fairy and eerie shapes flutter freely. Whether it is to be a Pandora's box with shapes unholy, or more Promethean inventions, depends on the whole patient. Also, on the therapist.

M can be valuable as diagnostic differential in both depression and other dysphoric mood conditions. Depressions in which the test draws out two or more M, or even one if it is intensely experienced (p. 56 ff.), are reactive, and to that extent more benign. A patient who, in a moody state can still fantasy, is availing himself of affective resources. This is always a promising finding, even if for the time the patient is using the asset symptomatically. Where there is liveliness, there is hope. The affective quality of the fantasy can be known structurally when the M blends with one of the C or one

---

only then, when human figures are seen; and in addition, frequently, when animals are perceived in anthropomorphic movements (bears, apes)." In the few instances where associations around inanimate objects need to be scored M, the association should meet the criteria I describe below (p. 54).

of the Y nuances. In the former, affect may be pleasing or exciting to the point of painful tension in M.C responses since the feelings in these are so concentrated. When Y blends with M the depressive quality is the more strongly felt. If the ego is in a weak state, the outlook is for agitation.

The diagnostic significance of M in Hd or in Dd associations requires further study. True, these are seen more frequently by persons at immature developmental levels and in patients with ego insufficiency; but the depth of the regression is not necessarily serious. This conclusion follows from a comparison (research not published) of these findings in a normal adult population with those in neurotic and schizophrenic patients. The differences are not statistically significant.

The comment is in order that the "normal" adult sample used in this study is to this extent immature. This surmise can be supported by other of the test findings in that normal group. Assuming that the sample is representative of the average in American life, the test is turning over evidence that immaturity marks the average American, male and female.

Lack of M or a very low quantity of it can be a positive finding if the rest of the record discloses the other assets that go with an M person. An expected trait is not functioning. Whether the patient is repressing it or he is constitutionally lacking it does not for purposes of this interpretation matter. The person does have other resources. Imagination would aid him in exploiting them, and enhance the total richness of the personality structure. Deprived of this ability, he is to that extent dull, stolid. Total adjustment is inferior to what it would be, given creativity.

In depression and severe anxiety the M failure is a direct result of the illness. The patient's mental processes are retarded. The inability to fantasy, assuming there is either clinical or test evidence that the patient is capable of it, measures the degree of inhibition or depression. The absence of M in a withdrawal state tells that the patient is not using autistic living as his refuge.

Content in the M associations. Fantasy in which the actors are animals has a diagnostic value more significant than do many fantasies involving humans. The only real problem in connection with fantasies in animals is that of correctly identifying what is fantasy and what is not. Rorschach's principle above quoted is my sphere of reference. But I have extended it some. His rule that the action must be one within the human repertory is sound. But certain patients have produced associations concerning animals in movement, patients whose condition as a whole clearly dictates scoring these associations M. In each instance it has been an activity not normal for the animal. Two examples: in Figure III, both D 1 together are a "dragon's mouth," and D 3 is a "butterfly being swallowed up by the mouth." I scored D M+ A. The "A" is for the butterfly. The other example is in Figure VIII where D 1 is "an animal stuck in quicksand." D M+ A. My rule is, therefore, score M (a) when the animal's action is normal for a human and (b) when the animal's movement is one obviously not the normal one for him.

The butterfly in the example is being acted upon. The activity is passive, a fairly common variety. Similarly the animal is subject to conditions beyond his control. The problem is different in the association to Figure IV as a whole: "a scorpion—a bird of prey—is ready to leap on you and to sting you." Two movements are here seen: the acting animal and the human being acted on. Yet no part of the stimulus figure is seen as human. I scored W M— H. That is, I interpolated the H. The technical warrant, following the second half of my rule above, is that it is not within the normal behavior of a scorpion to "leap on you." A bird of prey might conceivably do so but is not known to do so. The psychologic importance of the association is in its dream-like phobic content of panic proportion. What the patient is saying is "I am about to be leapt on, to be stung, by a scorpion or a bird of prey." We could interpret the association directly without scoring. This would not be objectionable if we wanted to restrict ourselves to interpreting M only.

The more unique the themes in the fantasy, and the greater the quantity of these, the deeper is the withdrawal and the more autistic the solution of his problems by the patient. He is living his dreams and in what Frank designates his "private world." Magical thinking may be so projected. In some persons in an autistic withdrawal the content will include large nature scenes, with loss of support, or collapse motifs such as stones or rocks or mountains crumbling, large consuming fires, trees fallen or dead, houses in some form of breakup. Some of these are scorable as M. The clinical lead is to "end-of-the-world" fantasies. Some anxious adolescents produce such associations, and the correlative clinical finding is the loss of a parent for purposes of support to the child. The loss may be because of death or illness. It may be actual abandonment or it may be psychologic abandonment. The parent is failing to provide the so much needed warmth of feeling. For the child it is the "end of the world." Fenichel reports this fantasy as one of schizophrenic level. I have found these Rorschach test associations in schizophrenics of all ages. But I had earlier observed it in adolescents without schizophrenia or any detectable danger of this disease. The clinical history in these children confirmed the finding of anxiety centering around the parent, usually of the patient's own sex.

Hostility themes in the fantasy are evidence that to this extent the patient is handling his aggressive impulses by introverting them. When this M is in animal content, the hostility is likely to be a displacing, irrespective of whether it is a paranoid projection. In either event it is a defense mechanism. The projection is simply a more drastic one. Another defense expedient manifest in M are certain philosophical meanderings by means of which some persons avoid the real issues in their conflicts or isolate themselves from worry. Such M are usually very original in content or motion abstracted directly out of the test stimulus. They are very superior productions. But they are discrepancies within the particular test record, the quality of which may be mediocre or worse.

The most ticklish problem in scoring M, the one providing more than usual room for error, is in relation to objects not capable of locomotion. Among these are living things such as plants as well as the totally inanimate. When the action is one normally belonging to humans, there is no problem. Thus the "waving trees" in one of the records in the present volume (p. 102). Another example, "the white resembles a dance of some kind," the white space generally exterior to Figure II. When the movement is specifically characteristic of the object, but the examiner suspects a Rorschach M, there is most room for error. The inquiry needs in those instances to be both more persistent and more cautious. We are at the mercy here of the patient's language indicating that he feels himself into the moving object. The hazard is always present that the examiner is too eagerly crediting an M where in fact there is none. When the doubt is more than a captious one for any M I do not so score but note the trend. One kind of an association I have usually been able to establish in the inquiry as M. These are certain abstract force, or art associations; interpreting the lines of the test figures as music; verbalizing tension or a sense of strain in the lines and explicitly abstracting of motion. There is one good reason why these responses do not frequently give trouble. The simple and fortunate fact is that they come extremely rarely.

The Rorschach concept of M as felt experience, incidentally, receives some support quite adventitiously in a current article, the author and subject of which have no relation to the Rorschach test. The publication is that delightful exposition of psychologic phenomena, *The New Yorker*. The writer, S. N. Behrman. The subject is the art scholar and critic Bernard Berenson. In the particular incident which Behrman is narrating, Berenson is in an art gallery.[13]

He found in a panel of a nearby altarpiece a Church father in a heavily brocaded robe, one hand holding a staff, the other resting on his knee. "See the *weight* of that hand!" Berenson exclaimed. "And the *weight* of that *brocade*! You must feel a muscular reaction if you don't feel it physically, it's mere illustration." The correspondent did indeed feel the two weights.

[13] BEHRMAN, S. N.: Profiles. The days of Duveen. New Yorker. **27**: 36 ff., in No. 36, Oct. 20, 1951.

The art critic, in his own words, and with reference to that very achievement which Rorschach claims to be the work of M, creative art, the art critic is here restating Rorschach's principle. "If you don't feel it physically, it's mere illustration." Rorschach's language: "They are form responses, designs following only the form of the picture."

J. The Levy Movement Scale

Making Rorschach's M his point of departure, D. M. Levy has for some years been experimenting with a series of blot figures of his own. They were constructed and selected especially for their potency in eliciting movement responses. I have used this series from time to time to supplement Rorschach tests in patients without M in their records. In 1948, Zubin and Young[14] published a description of the series together with a number of "scales" according to which they evaluated the responses they obtained.[15] Concerning the scales they say[16]

The Levy Movement Blots consist of finger paintings prepared by spreading the paint on suitable paper, folding the sheet inwardly, and then rubbing the thumb nail over the outside in a studied manner. When the sheet is opened two symmetrical figures appear on each side of the middle crease. In this manner symmetrical figures of various sorts can be produced. After experimenting with this method seven designs were found which elicited variegated responses, and these constitute the present set of cards. Since one of these designs is used in three positions and the first design is repeated at the end, there is a total of ten cards.

The purpose of the Levy Movement Blots is to elicit movement responses of the type expected on the Rorschach ink blots. The cards consist of only one physical determinant: chiaroscuro. Instead of utilizing the rather free directions of the Rorschach Test: "What might this be?," the subject is given specific directions for seeing people in action. Consequently, the Levy Movement Cards may be regarded as a variant of the Rorschach procedure in which the physical determinants have been reduced to one, and the mental set of the subject has been directed towards finding one type of response.

They classify their scales among the following psychologic operations: compliance, movement, interaction, conflict or interference, adient-abient and content. They subclassify the latter into the following headings: animate-inanimate, whole-part, affective value of content, gender of observed figure, sex reference, abstract-concrete, attitude toward reality of response, self estimate of adequacy of response, congruity of response.

[14] Zubin, J. and Young, K. M.: Manual of projective and cognate techniques. Madison: College Typing Co., 1948.

[15] In crediting the work they say, "The scales for evaluating the responses were devised by the senior author and underwent considerable modification under the hand of Dr. Ralph M. Rust, from whose dissertation the results reported in this manual are taken."

[16] Zubin and Young, op. cit.

They have also subgrouped their "movement" scale into several categories, one of which is the "movement energy scale." They calibrate energy in a movement association on an eight-step scale. Their description of these steps follows:

0. No movement; dead figures, statues, etc. Parts of the body pointed out but only as parts—here's a leg, etc.
1. Maintenance of life, but minimal activity for existence.
2. Maintenance of static position but a position that demands more effort or bodily tension than 1.
3. Maintenance of static position involving balance of whole body—small movements of body parts.
4. Active or vigorous movements of parts of the body, which demand more effort or energy expenditure of the body (than the small movements in 3 above).
5. Movement of the whole body, but such that little more than normal exertion for this type of movement is demanded.
6. Faster or more difficult movement.
7. Up and down movement or peculiar horizontal movement (e.g. walking on hands).

They provide 307 illustrative samples distributed among the eight scales.

This is the scale with which I have myself been experimenting. But I have applied it almost entirely to the movement responses in the Rorschach test. Every M in the present volume will be found evaluated also as to the amount of energy indicated, as measured by this Zubin-Young-Rust scale. My purpose in this has been to find some measure of energy invested by the patient in his Rorschach test M associations. My hope has been that this would provide some index as to how intense is the wish in any particular M. So far this hope has not been fulfilled. The principal shortcoming has been that we have no data by which to judge the clinical significance of much or little M energy so measured. I had started with the assumption that much energy, as found by this scale, tells of strongly felt fantasies. But this rule has gone counter to obvious significance in many M responses. Thus in Figure VI, D 2, "a man is impaled on a stick." By the Zubin-Young-Rust scale, I should have to rate it at zero. But it appears to project out a very significant fantasy. Even more compelling is the following produced by a 48 year old woman to Figure VI, D 1, "standing in front of a pedestal, a tall pedestal . . . and on the pedestal a glass tube, and in the tube a man who has been crucified on a cross. Or is it a man, or a fat woman? It is very clear." Still another example, a 42 year old male, in response to Figure IV, "the two projections on the sides look like useless appendages hanging there in an idiot sort of manner . . . the entire figure looks like some horrible monstrosity . . . some helpless looking arms . . . large spaded feet sitting on a sawed-off log . . . there are not enough features to make a face, so I can't say leering."

In all these, the low energy measure gives an inadequate impression of the feeling in the patient's wish or fear, if evidence in the content is the criterion. The content is, to be sure, judged without measuring scale. But even allowing for error incident to subjectivity, the personal significance in the examples cited cannot be ignored. This, whether based in clinical orientation or even by ordinary standards for judging verbal productions. Less troublesome is an objection which has been arising from the opposite point of view, namely, M that measures high in the Levy scale but probably stems from little personal feeling. These are the well known M in Figures III, II, VII, IX and I. So many persons produce them that they are essentially nondiscriminating. I refer here only to those most stereotyped M responses: in Figure III, the men bowing or pulling; in II, the clowns dancing, or holding hands; in VII, the women in some either competitive or conversational relation to each other; in IX, the clowns or witches in behavior conventional for such human forms. When even around the most common themes, the elaboration is personalized, it is discriminating; hence, clinically valuable. In short the number of high energy associations that are stereotyped, and therefore not meaningful, is very small.

Zubin and his co-workers report results of investigations by means of the Levy blots in personality groups as follows: 88 children ages 9 to 13; one study of normals, neurotics, schizophrenics and psychopathic personalities; a comparison of 30 normals, 50 neurotics, 51 schizophrenics; and another investigation in 27 mental hospital patients of which 12 were topectomized. They report findings in various of their scales, but not for the movement energy scale.

In interpreting the energy scale I have after some trial and error settled down to a procedure in which I both take the energy measure, and evaluate the content. The possible combinations are: (a) energy measure is high (4 or more), theme meaning, significant; (b) energy measure high, theme not significant; (c) energy measure low (3 or less), theme significant; (d) energy measure low, theme not significant.

The interpretive lead is clear in (a) and (d) where the two kinds of observations converge. In (c) I take my clue from the content and interpret as vigorously felt fantasy, one which has a strong hold on the patient. It is in respect to (b) that there is most room for uncertainty. When the fantasy is of the stereotyped kind noted above, I disregard it for purposes of gauging the energy loading. In all other instances I make the assumption that high energy rating discloses relatively high feeling investment in the wish or the fear.

K. THE EXPERIENCE BALANCE

An element of the mystic has attached to this concept of Rorschach's. It is a unique concept, not only in the field of personality, but in all psy-

chology. In this uniqueness lies the difficulty. Other test technics have not
envisaged this perspective of personality, and hence have not directed
thinking to such an idea. Rorschach states the nucleus of its meaning in a
sentence to the effect that the *Erlebnistypus* tells not how the person
actually lives at any given moment but how he *could* experience. The mystic
element derives from his use of the word *Erlebnis*. It is one of those strong
German words that can be indefinite in its meaning and hence opens up
paths to suggestion. So it can have different meanings to different investigators. Rorschach delimits it by using, in contrast, the term *lebt*. "How the
person actually lives" is a function of mental operations other than those
that issue as the experience balance. The ego, especially in its defensive role,
is the deciding force. When effecting a neurosis or a depression it drastically
cuts down the individual's ability to experience (*erleben*). The nub of the
matter is in Rorschach's identifying as "experience" that which, in more
familiar language, is called the "inner resources" of the individual. In
writings about the histories of culture, or of an era in civilization, the term
used is "spiritual life." These are the resources that are converted into the
art achievements of a people, their religion or their science. They are products of strong emotions, of high intellectual grasp, at the level of creative
imagination. These are the two psychologic sources from which the experience balance is fashioned: feeling pressures and fantasy living, C and M.
But few individuals or peoples live anywhere near the potentials of their
spiritual resources. Harsh realities or ego insufficiencies, the neuroses, set
crippling limits on those potentials. Hence, "The psychologic apparatus
through which the individual experiences is a much broader, more extensive
one, than the equipment with which he lives."

All this should take the experience balance out of the realm of mystery
in which it has so consistently been enveloped. It is just one more personality factor or, rather, cluster of two factors, the workings of which
make sense only within the setting of a personality as a whole. A broad,
restricted, ambiequal, extratensive, introversive experience balance—each
is a mental activity of the organ of mind, the brain. How much of it can be
effective depends on the whole person who produces it. What he does with it,
i.e., with his inner living, depends on what he is as a unit personality. The
contrast between ability and achievement is an old story, whether in psychology or in the broader literature. Says Browning:

> What hand and brain went ever pair'd?
> What heart alike conceived and dared?
> What act proved all its thought had been?
> What will but felt the fleshly screen?

Technical uses of the experience balance in interpretation, some of which
have formerly been published, are as follows. Ambiequality in the obsessive-

compulsive defenses. It is a remarkable fact that so large a percentage of these persons produce a mathematically even or nearly even balance of the number of M responses with the total of color values. The urge of the feelings inward or outward is offset by an urge in the opposite direction. The ego must always be neutralizing wish fulfilling activities, whether in the imagination, or in the world at large. The adaptive purpose of this behavior is, of course, defensive. To this kind of neurotic, any satisfying of a wish is punishable. The neutralizing operation prevents the carrying out a desired activity, and so saves from punishment.

A coarcted experience balance is another outcome of a defense effort. It results from rigid hold by a patient on himself. Here is destructive work of the ego. It wins control and stabilizes the individual. It does this at the expense of pleasurable living within one's imagination or in the outer world. Carried to an extreme as it is in many anxieties and depressions, it is the stability of death.

The constricted experience balance is likely to form one finding in a cluster which characterizes patients intellectually resistant to change (see also concerning approach, sequence, symmetry, description). Life-long habits of doing things in accordance with certain routines make them obdurate to thoughts of departing from them. Underneath is a fear of deviation, the fear which originally turned them to immutable patterns. These persons, of highest intelligence though they may be, do not learn. They are not good treatment prospects.

A passive-apprehensive mood also constricts the experience balance. When at the 0-0 level, the mood may be that of deepest depression, or even of stupor degree. This experience balance too will be one finding in a cluster (restricted content, shading responses, high animal per cent, high per cent F+).

The extratensive experience balance when in a neurotic reaction pattern, leads to one of two indications. In a hysteric structure, it dictates searching for a conversion symptom. This is the more likely when the patient associates with many anatomy associations, especially if they are obviously pathologic. Secondly, and more frequently it is the test's indicator of psychosomatic illness. In these latter patients, F+ is high enough to indicate a very alert ego, and at the same time pressure of affects is very strong, usually as C and CF. The ego is holding the fort with determination against feelings which are investing the personality powerfully. Neither force gives way. The inner cushioning of fantasy is not available. The pathology develops directly in the soma.

Attack on the environment used as defensive expedient against one's anxiety will have its Rorschach test equivalent in an extratensive experience balance with s and hostility content (pp. 41, 65). The fight reaction in such instances does not serve the aggressive impulses as such. It drains off the painfully pressing inner forces. In these conditions it serves essentially biological needs. It is thus a form of sublimation, but destructive sublimation. Some children in their maladaptive externalizing of aggressions are thus dissipating their unbearable tensions.

In the introversive experience balance, the essential fact is that fantasy is dominating the inner world. As such it simply projects the known functions of M (p. 49 ff.). More specifically the introversive balance is a measure of the extent to which autistic living occupies the mental life. This is gauged in the amount to which M outbalances the C total. Additional evidence is found in the structure of M as sound or regressive and in the content as unique. The more there is of the latter, the more daydreaming in the patient or solving one's needs autistically. It follows that when a defensive withdrawal is marked also by an introversive experience balance the contraction is not merely intellectual; it is a retreat into autistic living.

An introversive balance can be critically informative in patients who clinically are misleading by reason of their overtly quiet or sober mood. The patient may look depressed; actually he is anything but. He has only "stabilized" his feelings by introverting them. He is preventing their outward expression. The test, by the technic of the M associations, rules out depression or establishes the condition as a reactive one.

These are among the diagnostic values which I am finding in the experience balance. All this may seem to be de-emphasizing it. It is so only to the extent of removing from it the aura of the strange in which Rorschach's exposition has left it. It has been his concept most perplexing to the psychological world. Actually it is only another cluster of psychologic traits. Cutting across, as it does, so much of the emotional life, it is still that "broader, more extensive structure," which Rorschach describes.

L. THE WHITE SPACE

For measurement technic I now use per cent of total instead of absolute number of white space responses as formerly. My reasons for the change are as follows. Rorschach's principle is that more than one white space response is suspect. But there are white spaces and white spaces. There are the three large spaces in Figures II, VII, IX. These are the only three statistically found to be D. The Dds are numerous. Then again some associations are primarily or exclusively responses to the white space, whether Ds or Dds. "A building" (Ds 5 in Figure II); "a bay" (Ds 6 in Figure VII); "an urn" (Ds 8 in Figure IX). Many responses that are scored s are primarily to the blot stimulus, with the Ds or Dds as only a secondary attraction or altogether incidental. "Mountains, with a lake" (Figure II); "island, with water" (Figure VII); various landscapes elaborated with sky (Figure IX). Samples of Dds: the "glowering eye" or "snarling mouth" of D 7 or D 8 in Figure X. In many responses in which standard technic dictated scoring s, what has been suspect is whether the reaction is psychologically s, i.e., opposition. Enough doubt developed to dictate discounting for the size of the white space perceived, and for its weight in the total percept. Secondly, at least one published factor analysis study[17] shows per cent s to be correlating higher with total productivity than does the absolute number of s. Third, no statistics have been available to me providing a frame of reference whereby to appraise any particular per cent of white space. I now have these statistics, (as yet unpublished) obtained from my normal population sample. The findings are as in Table 3. Any s percentage of 10.0 or more I therefore look upon as significantly high.

In interpretation, when a significantly high percentage of s clusters with an ambiequal experience balance, it highlights the obsessive-compulsive condition as more aggravated. The patient is fighting both his world and his unconscious needs. To attack such needs is to attack one's strongly felt inner wishes. This generates doubting, and to doubt one's deep wishes is to doubt one's self, a most painful state of mind. The cluster is thus found in persons suffering endless self-distrust and perplexity that goes with a picture of compulsive thinking.

When white space percentage is high in an extratensive experience balance, the person is having difficulty in controlling his impulses. There is a trend to discharge in immature, undisciplined pattern. Aggressions find their way out in ways likely to be unpleasant to others in contact with the individual. Among those persons who defend themselves from their inner fears by attacking the environment (p. 41), many will fill in the extratensive experience balance cluster with a high white space score.

Tenacity as a form of stubborness is among the traits which high white space percentage projects. This is the more so when the s percept is a reversal of figure and ground. Quantity of s is, in fact, some measure of the persistence with which the patient is likely to hold to a course whether it is a good one for the personality or bad. Thus the many s found in most paranoids are the stickiness of these patients to their ideas. It effects that recalcitrance with which, come the hell and high water of any logic, they cling to their delusions.

Contrarily, a low percentage of space responses or total lack of them in a test record confirms findings of passivity. It may be a lead to suggestibility. S is low or 0 in most depressions. It is passivity carried to its ultimate.

---

[17] WITTENBORN, J. R.: Level of mental health as a factor in the implications of Rorschach scores. J. Consult. Psychol. 14: 469–472, 1950.

M. The Content

The associational content makes two major contributions to the projection of the personality. One is structural; the other is in the significance of the themes to the patient. Its value as structural index is clear-cut in animal forms, and this has been known since publication of the *Psychodiagnostik*. The higher the per cent of animals, the more inert the individual intellectually. A similar diagnostic value also noted by Rorschach obtains in the whole human percept, and in the ratio of whole to part humans (H: and Hd). The former goes with liberated intelligence. The latter tells of a functional restriction effected by anxiety. The ratio between the two is a measure of the individual's mental freedom or his inhibition. Still another known structural value of content has been as finding of broad or narrow interests. I judge this by the number of categories in which the content distributes, counting all the categories other than the three most frequent ones, i.e., H (with Hd), A (with Ad) and anatomy. But the especial elaboration of H content usually projects interest beyond normal range, e.g., a Hindu priest, a deep sea diver, a bride with her attendants. The range in any one record is measure also of the person's spread of intellectual effort. It tells of his reading and cultivation to which he has been subjected, if not where he has actually been. Whether or not he has translated this curiosity, or opportunity, into achievement productive in the world at large, only the findings for his personality as a whole can tell.

Narrow content projects the person whose vision is channelized, horizon lowered. There are blinders on his perceptual apparatus. The extreme of this condition responds to the test with 100 per cent animal forms. While rare, such records are produced. The patient may be of limited endowment originally, or with brain damage; or the mental reduction may be neurotically induced. The outward result is the same, the person has no verve. The spark-plugs are not firing.

The narrowing is in some patients a symptom of thinking dysfunction; manipulating ideas at simpler, rather than at conceptual levels. In the conflict conditions, this tells of a loss to the person rather than his constitutional insufficiency. The patient is handling his life's affairs at levels inferior to his capacity. The inhibition and loss are results of a defense. In his clinical behavior, the patient is unfree, anergic.

Overemphasis on one topic is one form of narrowness; in rare instances, the record is essentially monotopical. The theme usually stems from an obviously special concern of the patient. In any event, it does not strike a chord familiar to the examiner, or impress him as likely to elicit such from others. The excluding of the more usual topics elicited by the test is one index of a maladaptively inadequate turning to reality. In the monotopical record, the patient may be shutting out all normal interests from his mind.

But the restriction may be caused not so much by an absorption in some-thing, as by inability to strike out independently, and to take initiative in reaching for the new and different. The patient perseverates around one theme, irrespective of whether or not it holds personal value to him. This finding is likely to go with others that add up to suggestibility. The person too readily yields to such thoughts as happen to strike him. He is a bit of chaff in the intellectual winds. It is ego insufficiency to the point of total lack of ego. When the perseverated topic can be judged as of personal deter-mination, it is lead to the conflict source. The ego is none the less weak or suggestible. But the motif is something on which the patient has fixed owing to some event in his life, rather than it being something accidental. The outlook is somewhat better than with the former finding, as it always is when there is personal motivation. While there is ego, there is hope.

But the content which dominates the thinking may be very individual-ized, unique. If the person is sufficiently disordered, the dominating theme may be the lead to his delusional ideas or to the hallucinatory percepts. In relatively intact but neurotic conditions, such highly original thinking is a defense; a withdrawal by the person into his own little acre. Without M, the withdrawal is at least not into autistic fantasy. The patient is simply insulating himself off from social contacts.

But the content may be more than simply unique. It sometimes is ex-travagant. Figure X for example is seen by a young male schizophrenic as an elaborate heavenly scene in which he and his bride are being joined in the presence of angelic attendants. Another example, a middle aged female schizophrenic, in Figure VII, sees the "Rock of Gibraltar, you follow up the coast on the left, the extreme top is where Cousin Tom was wrecked by Theodore Roosevelt"; and in Figure VIII, "Peary and Cook shaking hands. . . . Cook claimed me as his daughter and that started the big law suit." The recourse to deeply regressed, infantile thinking for purposes of self-gratifying is clear in these examples. Less elaborate, although with simi-lar florid quality, are the percepts of some persons with brain pathology.

The relation between content and emotional pressures is manifest in rapid changes of theme. Ideas push, one past the other, in no apparent relation one to the other. The patient elaborates, whether with or without relevance, and usually with little central direction. Some of the bizarre or very personal, including paranoid thinking so comes to expression. The strong feelings that animate the individual, whether as longing or as hatred, are breaking out.

This exposition has related so far to content as structural finding. As such it is impersonal. It tells how the organism operates, and only inci-dentally what it is that drives him on. The patterns described can be found with different specific themes. What the personal source of the patient's distress, the focus of his conflict, the nature of his yearning, can be answered only if we know the significance of the content to him personally. Here, however, arises a major difficulty in Rorschach test interpretation. The same content can have such different meaning to different persons; and various persons express the conflicts that are common to human life in such different imagery. Are there any stable guide lines, therefore, by which content in the test can be interpreted dependably? And to what extent?

The present situation, not only with reference to the Rorschach test, but in the field of free association as a whole, leaves very much to be desired. We must start with the condition that there are as yet within the psychologic sciences no systematically established laws as to the meanings of particular content themes. There is a large literature, principally contributed by the psychoanalysts, in which content is being interpreted. Certain themes appear with a sufficient frequency to be a safe lead toward constancy in meaning. The clinical logic for the patient's producing them, while varying in cogency, supports the interpretation. The assumptions which the writers make as to personal meanings, make sense in many, but by no means all the publications, in the light of the whole clinical pattern reported. In the field of psychology proper, Murray's test has sparked numerous investigations, searching for meaning of content. These provide some desirable statistical data. Thus there are two broad sources as starting points.

Thirdly, when content is specific or original enough it has a special meaning long understood in everyday speech. The significance clinically is likely to be of more surface than deep quality. But it carries the weight of extensive validation. One cannot discard the accumulated backlog of "common sense" even in scientific psychology.

Finally, I noted above that published reports are convincing by reason of a particular content's fitting into each separate whole personality picture. But experience makes it equally clear that personal meaning is not a constant. Any one theme, critical dynamic though it may be in Patient X, may not have the same force in Patient A. It follows that any association must be judged not with reference to any general meaning, but with reference to its meaning in the particular record in which we find it.

My present procedure in interpreting content is therefore to draw on three resources: (a) clinical sophistication, my own, and that in the available publications; (b) the usual judgments of everyday life; (c) the logic or sense which any interpretation makes in the framework of the whole personality. As general orienting frame of reference, I utilize Murray's principle that the content communicates *needs*. The more individualized a theme, the more certainly it discloses uniquely personal psychologic needs in that patient. They may be so individualized as to be no longer intelligible even to the long experienced psychiatrist. The patient is talking in what Campbell calls his "private idiom." His is the language of schizophrenea. He is a one-man greek letter society with a secret language, the meaning of which (still according to Campbell) can be known only when we know his code. Which is to say, we need to know the premises by which that schizophrenic is reasoning.

A large factor of ignorance, and therefore an important element of surmise, must at the best obtain in respect to meaning of content. Certain theme groups do to be sure more dependably light up the personal dynamics. But in all instances I look on the theme as lead, not as finding. It is an arrow directing the investigator or therapist to a personality area which he is to explore directly in the patient. And he may as well start with the knowledge that the lead has about a fifty-fifty chance of being a false one. But since any one topic does not have the same significance in different patients, failure of a lead in one person does not vitiate its potential clinical value in another.

A list of some theme groups and their interpretive applications, follows:

Aggression, hostility. In defense against anxiety, this content supports structural findings of handling one's apprehensions by attacking the environment. Also, the person is one usually ready to fight, beyond the call of the social circumstance. It is a maladaptive trait.

Anatomy. This is one theme in which some patients are so preoccupied as to virtually exclude other interests. They restrict their attention to it. When the association is of more pathologic flavor, dealing with internal bodily functions, especially sexual, digestive or eliminatory, the thinking is more malignant. As "organ speech" it may project hypochondriasis. When found in neuroses with hysteric features, the lead may be to a conversion symptom. When in a neurosis marked by a determined ego, strong feeling pressures, but without fantasy, the anatomy emphasis warrants looking for psychosomatic stress. But neither in these conditions nor in the hysterias, does the content of the anatomy necessarily give a clue to the particular organ involved. The Rorschach test is not as specific as that, excepting in very rare instances.

Animisms. This is a product of, and therefore diagnostic index to, seriously regressed thinking.

Architecture. The theme is a lead to the person's perceiving himself as incomplete. But the response structure has to be V. The theme is one of several within a larger group generically stemming from feelings of inferiority. When present, it fills in indications from other sources in the test of self-devaluation.

Birth processes and related topics. The possible relation to a birth, or rebirth fantasy needs to be explored. As such it may stem from the patient's effort, even if of regressive order, at rebuilding himself.

Breasts. A possible lead to oral reunion fantasying may be involved. I have had reason to suspect such significance in this association, in patients either schizophrenic, or flirting with schizophrenia. Confidence in the interpretation will vary with the amount of oral content in the record and how regressive the intellectual life and the fantasy.

Cosmic themes. World reconstruction ideas may be in the patient's mind. Again it will depend on how regressed the structure, how unique or distorted the content generally, how autistic the fantasy.

Destruction motifs. Whether in the fantasy or at more intellectual levels these can be of much significance. Exploring for "the end of everything" ideas is indicated. It can be the test's equivalent of Bleuler's dereistic thinking. It is a defense, and a drastic one; a withdrawal, and a very painful one.

Oral. The intake, satisfying motifs are to be distinguished from the threatening, dangerous ones. The former naturally accent the gratifying, dependency wishes. They include not only mouths and lips, as eating, sucking or kissing, but also food and drink topics. In severe enough regressions the yearning for oral reunion may be being expressed. The threatening oral themes which include not only large open mouths, teeth, but more frequently animals known to be threatening with their mouths, are leads as to be expected to phobic states. These frequently are defenses against deeper anxieties.

Philosophical. These productions too are a defense. They envelop the patient in a vague aura of intellectualization which screens him from contact with life's real issues.

Phobic. All such needs to be evaluated for its defense quality. Whether amounting to obsessional thinking, as much does, will depend again on whether the personality structure follows an obsessional pattern. The association will in instances be accompanied by expressions of repulsiveness directed at the test card itself. This is a counterphobic flight; the defense against the defense.

Religious. The patient is trying to stabilize his too acutely painful feelings by turning to that age old solace, religion. The stresses, tensions, fears have been too much. It is a protective measure. The ego is looking to the interest of the psychologic organism as a whole. It saves the pieces before they break off as such.

Sex. This is another theme which, like anatomy, and even more frequently so, may take up the patient's entire thoughts, waking and sleeping. The psychologic need may be more intensive than in anatomy, in the measure that the sex hunger can be all possessing and deforming of a personality. Accent on the theme will be a clue to the likelihood that the patient may be "acting out" his or her disrupting sexual needs. Also the total absence of such content in a record, the structure of which points to disturbance on this ground, is actually a clue to the topic's importance. The individual is too obviously excluding it.

Vocational. This is still another topic group, themes in which absorb nearly all the mental energy in some persons. The absorption too is a defensive device, something for the person to cling to. It provides the safety and comfort that go with the familiar. In some vocations it reinforces an otherwise weak ego since it enhances prestige. But the price of safety is a limited horizon. Rorschach calls this personality the *Fachsimpel*.

Two theme categories require special comment. They are topics stemming from paranoid thinking and those uncovering homosexual urges.

The Rorschach test literature on paranoid content is scant. This probably follows from the failures so far to establish any paranoid whole personality structure. It takes on protean shapes. Introversive, extratensive, coarcted dilated, highly realistic, grossly inaccurate, excessively conventional, asocial and the other Rorschach patterns can all be found in persons clinically with or suspected of paranoid traits. Hence the pressing need for systematically studying this important human defense expedient (p. 35). Certain content themes, whatever the structure, are found regularly in persons with the clinical symptoms. A small sample of these follows:

The staring or listening H or Hd associations; essentially all "eyes," especially if scorable as M; veiled, heavily robed or otherwise covered humans; the Devil; facial expressions of meanness or hostility, especially when in persons of the same sex as the patient.

Content themes specifically significant of both paranoid and homosexual thinking as obtained by the test are reported by Lindner.[18] They are included among forty-three responses which he has isolated and lists as diagnostically discriminating, or pointing to psychologic dynamics. Lindner has been focusing especially on content, and so provides one sphere of reference for studying this variable.

The identifying of homosexual thinking in the test can be done with slightly more confidence than paranoid projection. The literature, is to be sure, a little larger. A valuable recent paper is that by Fromm and Elonen.[19] In my own experience, the manifest content may consist of confusion of the sexual characters in the same human percept. Or, the patient ascribes feminine qualities to figures usually seen as males, e.g., D 1 in Figure III; or masculine features to details usually seen as feminine, e.g., D 3 or D 4 in

---

[18] LINDNER, R. M.: The content analysis in the Rorschach protocol, in: ABT, L. E. AND BELLAK, L. (Editors): Projective psychology. Clinical approaches to the total personality. New York: Knopf, 1950, pp. 75–90.

[19] FROMM, E. O. AND ELONEN, A. S.: The use of projective techniques in the study of a case of female homosexuality. J. Proj. Techniques 15: 307–338, 1951.

Figure I. Most commonly, two humans of the same sex are seen in a relation normally of heterosexual variety such as lying down or kissing. But the males of Figure III, or the dancing girls of Figure VII reversed are entirely in normal range. The mythological figures, e.g., the Pans, Satyrs, are to be followed-up as stemming from probably homosexual interest. From more primitive personality layers are animals in which either a sexual or anal role or detail is accented.

Having scrutinized the content, the investigator is in a position to evaluate the likely social consequences of the patient's structure. He can know now what direction the person is likely to take. The feelings may seek outlet as aggression, in erotic gratification, or be translated into socially constructive endeavor. They may turn inward into autistic living. The content may tell us what wishes the patient is manipulating in his imagination, what he fears, or it may tell us the more creative ideas into which he can transmute his emotions. What is the source of the painful emotions? What is the conflict focus? Or what is the topic around which the lively affects play? Are they egocentric? Symptomatic? Or more appropriate to a social setting, and cheerful? Not many Rorschach test records answer all these questions. Some, only very few; in more, they give only traces of answers. Yet much can be obtained from content in many records. And what is found has its place in the logic of the structural findings. How all these data interweave into the woof and texture of the personality, the reports that follow attempt to demonstrate.

CHAPTER III

AN ADOLESCENT BOY IN PSYCHOTHERAPY

A. THE TREATMENT BEGINS. THE FIRST TEST

The two Rorschach tests here evaluated were administered almost exactly at the beginning and end of the extensive therapy which this patient was undergoing. Duncan was just under 16 years old when he came for treatment to the outpatient clinic, Department of Psychiatry, in Michael Reese Hospital. The referral reason as seen by himself, and told by him to the referring agency: he is in conflict with his mother, and wants to be placed away from home. Lean as is the time available in an outpatient clinic for intensive therapy, and almost nonexistent for psychoanalysis, Duncan's psychologic drama achieved his being taken on for one treatment interview each week. The psychiatrist soon requested a Rorschach test, and this was administered within a month after therapy commenced.

The first test protocol,[1] with the scorings and response summary follow.

RESPONSE RECORD

Figure I (5″)

'This is rather a gloomy card (because of the contrasting shades of black and gray and the grotesqueness of it), you might say it suggests—

1. D M.Y+ H
4.0

'Witches (D 2), witches are suggested in this' (seem to be 'fighting over the beheaded female).

2. D M+ H

'Also a beheaded female' (D 4; Dd 27 is 'the belt buckle'; 'skirt' is different shade).

3. W F+ A P
1.0

'At first glance I should have told you that this was a bat. I don't believe there is anything else. ∨∧ I don't think so.'

Figure II (62″)

'This appears rather, I'd say, queer

---

[1] This record, and an interpretation were published in 1945 in BECK, S. J.: Rorschach's test. II. A variety of personality pictures. New York: Grune & Stratton, 1945. See p. 167 ff.

... I don't know exactly what it suggests.

4. D FV+ Ls

'Oh yes, it might be rugged mountains (lines on D 1).

5. Dd F− Ls, Na

'Or a wavy sea, not too wavy (lines on D 1). I don't think there's anything else—no, I don't think so.'

Figure III (2″)

6. D M+ H P
   4.0

'This appears, you might say grotesque.... It looks like a couple of queer figures, very dignified, humorous in their dignity (they toss heads back) bowing to each other or having a stately tug of war (D 1).

'Do I tell what the different blots represent?

7. Ds F+ Fi

'I think the center dim blot looks like a fire, and—

8. D F+ Hh

'The two objects that the figures appear to be holding look like kettles (D 4 are 'kettles'; D 8 with white interspace is 'the fire'). That's all.'

Figure IV (17″)

9. W M.Y+ H
   2.0

'This seems to remind one of the sort of devil in the Fantasia picture (W). He seems to be peering down at something and there is a sort of murky blackness (a cloudlike blackness) around and the two hooklike objects at his sides appear to be his hands, with which he seems to be trying to grasp something.

'May I reverse it and tell you everything?

10. Ds FY− A
    5.0

∨ 'Reversed it appears like a very upright wolf (D 1; head, ears, general shape) silhouetted against light rather than dark—

11. D F+ A

'While the hooklike objects which be-

12. D F+ A

fore resembled hands, resemble snakes (D 4)—

'Or vultures' (because of 'long necks'). 'I don't think there is anything else.'

Figure V (5″)

13. D M− A
14. D F+ A

15. D F+ A

16. D M+ H

'This looks like a fallen cow (D 4), or ostrich' (because D 1 'looks like chicken leg, and it is feathery).

'A rabbit (D 7), holding it up in the middle. There doesn't appear to be much of a design, as in the others, due to the different shades (just murky blackness, not many different shades).

∨ 'Reversed it looks like a man standing on his head (D 7; D 2 as arms, D 3 as legs). I don't think there is anything else.'

Figure VI (39″)

17. D F+ Ay

'This has a very nice shape, its irregularity is very pretty.

'Reminds me of an Indian totem pole (D 3, with D 7 as head of totem pole).

∨ 'I guess there is nothing else. ∧ I don't think there is anything else.'

Figure VII (7″)

18. D M+ H P
    3.0

19. D F+ Oj, Pr

20. D YF+ Cl

'This looks like various impish figures (D 1; also D 3 look a little like it) with only faces, gazing impudently at each other.

'There is a rather absurd feather-like object on there (D 5), on the back of their heads.

'The lowermost pair of figures look like large billowy cumulus clouds (D 4 because of color . . . lightness), more off to a distance.

21. Dds FV Na

'It appears that the sun is setting much farther away' (tiny space above D 6; 'it's a round white spot'). 'I don't think there is anything else.'

Figure VIII (19″)

'This is quite colorful in comparison to the others.

22. D C Art, Fd

'The pink and orange on the bottom remind me of an ice cream cone ad' (D 2; color only).

23. D M− A

'While the red figures at the side look like sleek dancing pigs' (D 1; attitude or pose indicates movement).

24. D F+ An P

'The figure at top and center looks like an internal view of a human' (skeleton and ribs; D 3 with Dd 21 as esophagus).

25. D CF+ Ls

'The bluish color in the center (D 5) looks like a bird's-eye view of a pounding surf' (D 5; 'waves and foam'; color, form). 'I don't think there is anything else.

26. D M− A
3.0

'The top figure (D 4) is like a giant panorama of slim wolves leaping up at nothing in particular; and they are one, like a huge bundle' (each Dd 31 is tail, forelegs, and head, as in a bundle, and 'they converge on one another').

Figure IX (13″)

27. D M+ H P
4.5

'The orange figure, the pair of orange figures at the sides, at the top, once again remind me of a pair of witches (D 3; making faces at each other, grimacing) coming out of some sort of—

28. D F− Na
2.5

'Mysterious vapor' (D 1, shape; no color).

29. D F+ Na

'What do you call those things? Oh, yes, the long figure, going up and down, reminds me of an oil geyser, if that's correct' (D 5; 'seems to be going up and curving back down; has a gray-green color, but it is not the particular color,' i.e., of oil).

30. D C.T Cl

'And the green-blue blots look like a very warm summer day, but rather moist due to their overheavy color' (D 1; color chiefly, shape 'a little').

31. D F— A

'The couple of red figures at the bottom remind me of some fish we studied in school' (D 10; 'has the eye, the shape, and the body').

32. Ds F— Ad

'The very large white figure reminds me of the head of an octopus' (only head, no legs seen—Ds 8, with Dds 23 as eyes).

Figure X (9″)

33. D F+ A

'The blue figures at the sides (D 1) do look like octopuses, only very queer ones, since they have arms coming out of their arms.

34. D F+ Art

'The blue and green figures at the bottom look like some very priceless idol' (D 10; 'reminds me of something I've seen').

35. D M.Y+ H
4.0

'The two dark figures at the top look like huge staring hooded men' (D 8; shape; blackness suggested 'hooded'). 'Altogether it represents quite a picture of contrasting colors.

36. D FC— A

'The little green figures remind me of parrots' (D 12; form, color).

37. D C Bl

'And the reddish color reminds me— makes me think of what our blood might look like minus the contact of air' (D 9; color).

38. D FV+ Ls
4.0

'It also reminds me of two huge overhanging cliffs (D 9) joined together—

39. D F+ Ar

'by a very dainty bridge' (D 6; 'rather a natural bridge').

'I don't think there is anything else.'

RESPONSE SUMMARY

R total 39

W	2	M	8 (3−)	H	8	F+%	78	
D	35 (s 3)	M.Y	3	A	12	A%	33	
Dd	2 (s 1)	C	2	Ad	1	P	5	
	—	C.T	1	An	1	S	4	
	39	CF	1	Ar	1	S%	10.4	
		FC−	1	Art	2			
		YF	1	Ay	1			
		FY−	1	Bl	1			
		FV	3	Cl	2			
		F+	14	Fi	1			
		F−	4	Hh	1	T/R	52.3″	
			—	Ls	4	T/first R	17.8″	
			39	Na	3			
Z	37.0			Oj	1	Af r	0.86	
Ap	(W) D! (Dd)				—	L	0.46	
Seq	chiefly	EB 11/6			39			
	methodical							

INTERPRETATION

The mood-chord which characterizes this record is announced in its first words, "a gloomy card."

Duncan gives here the key to his prevailing affect: a vague apprehension. Ultimately this leads to the central source of his unhappiness, a conflict concerning which he could not be even dimly aware, until many hours of psychotherapy had raised it to consciousness.

He projects more of this feeling tone in his descriptive "the contrasting shades of black or gray," and in the critical comment "the grotesqueness of it." He strikes this note heavily in Figure IV, "murky blackness, . . . cloud-like blackness." He continues the complaint in V: "the murky blackness." Of significance is his pleasurable reaction to the usually unpleasant, black mass making up Figure VI: "This has a very nice shape . . . its irregularity is very pretty." The meaning of the inverting of this usual affective preference is one of two. Either one, it highlights Duncan's mood as especially attuned to the somber aspect of this test figure. He is *Il Pensoroso*, declaiming, "Hence vain deluding joys," and "Hail divinest Melancholy." Or, two, he is defending against the oppressive sense by emphasizing; an undoing technic. And so the pattern goes in Figures I and in IV through VII, the darks have their hold on him reflecting his down-hearted brooding and a fear-laden state of mind.

In these comments, intertones in any Rorschach test protocol, Duncan is only corroborating a trait prominently projected in the structure. The diffuse, shading-determined (Y) responses are numerous norms for a proto-col of under 40 associations. The anxious passivity of which they speak lies heavily on this adolescent boy. In R 20, scored YF, the shading nuance is the primary determinant. In R 10, FY—, the form perception is inaccu-rate; the mood is painful enough to disturb the intellectual control. Doubly acute is the distress set going by R 1, 9, and 35. Each of these blends with M; is bound in with some unconscious fantasy experience. The M is in its own right a strongly felt reaction.[2] The fusion with the Y reinforces the significance of each beyond what it would mean standing by itself. The cluster of the two does more than summate them. It makes for a state of tension with a new quality peculiarly its own. The strength of the uncon-scious motivation, makes the ache in the depressing mood moments more poignant. The poignancy of the mood intensifies the longing, or fear, repre-sented in the M. The gloomy affect is thus lived not only intensely, but also deeply. Duncan is in these reactions living the essence of Y as described by Oberholzer in his exposition of this Rorschach test trait.[3] It is *Die Angst vor der Angst.* An adolescent suffers more acutely just as he craves and enjoys more vehemently.

So heavy a mood can only mean *anxiety*. The influence of this emotion is apparent in all the massive gray-black figures. In Figure I, the low lambda index shows Duncan inadequately regarding external stimuli. He has turned extensively to his inner world. The sequence is inverted. The P response is delayed. His opening association is that intensely experi-enced one in which communication out of the unconscious blends with the structurally dysphoric, M.Y. The themes in 2 out of 3 responses expose troubled thoughts (discussed more at length, below, p. 84). In Figure IV we find all these trends, the more accented. The first response again fuses painful mood determinant with fantasy, M.Y. In all four responses, the themes are phobic or threatening. Duncan fails altogether to perceive the P form, the most conventional association to this figure. Form perception is erratic once (R 10); as two psychologic trends converge to plow up the personality (see p. 90). It all tells of the ego functioning insufficiently. The theory concerning Figure IV is that it arouses father imagery. The lead as to Duncan: thoughts in him that center about his father are a focus of anxiety, a threat to him. The further reasoning is that Duncan actually fears not his father but himself. Or rather, he fears the thoughts which are his in relation to his father. This is the theory regarding any of the "shocks" induced by the test. They are real upsets, produced by real anxieties. Yet it is not the test figures that do the shocking. They are after

[2] RORSCHACH, H., *op. cit.,* p. 68 ff.
[3] OBERHOLZER, E.: in: DuBois, C.: The people of Alor. Minneapolis: University of Minnesota Press, 1944, Chap. 22, pp. 588–640.

all, and before all, just ink blots. The ideas which they set going are the
source of the emotion (cf. p. 38). To quote the ever quotable Khayyám,
"I myself am heaven and hell." I cannot respond with anxiety unless there
is anxiety in me.

The shock effect persists and shows some worsening in Figure V. Duncan
opens with a fantasy which is of regressive structure and deep significance
in content. He turns to fantasy a second time in which he again communicates an important personal need. In R 13–14 he does some unique elaborating. To cap it all, he fails to produce the P percept; not only the easiest
of all the P's, but actually the most frequent of all associations to the test.
He overtly verbalizes an inadequacy though he projects it on to the test
card, "there doesn't appear to be much of a design . . ." So, in Figure V
Duncan's intellectual life goes off course and he gives rein to his imagination. An emotion is stirring.

The effect is different but no less decisive in Figure VI. Duncan goes in
it to the extreme of 100 per cent accuracy. This is rigidity; it costs him all
other mental productivity. The figure limits him to a single association. His
time for it is the slowest, except for the traumatic Figure II. This is the
behavior of blocking although the confusion that attends on full blocking
is not here in evidence. The reaction is, therefore, a sharp reflex in which
the patient becomes stiff as the proverbial poker. In Figure VI the usual
shock stimulus, the one that calls out the defensive anxiety, is the phallus-
like detail (D 2). Less frequently it is the vulva form (D 12). Which of these
it is, or whether the figure started some other thought against which Duncan's ego recoils, cannot be known from the fact of shock alone. This is
structural pattern, impersonal.

In Figure VII Duncan's trends are mixed. He does approach recovery
in it but only partially. Productivity goes up; the first association is a P.
Duncan acts more comfortably in Figure VII. But here too the lambda
index is low; in only one association does he respond exclusively via the
intellectual sphere. In fact, a low lambda index is Duncan's pattern in all
the massive dark cards. His ratio actually is 0.46 for the protocol as a whole;
the mean for ages 14 to 17 is 64.50; SD 15.40. Under influence of these black
masses he tends to block out external stimuli. He perceives with and responds to inner receptors. Still in Figure VII, the "mother" figure, he manifests the fewest anxiety shock effects. It is the least traumatic of these 5
gray-black ones. The test findings here offer a lead of critical importance.
They bring into question the apparent reason for the referral, namely a
struggle between mother and son. The struggle with the mother now develops out as a possible screen for a more essential cause of the gloom. As
such it throws a new light on the trauma in Figure IV, the "father" card.

As a whole Duncan's anxiety is more bound than free. The rigidity trends in Figures I and VI are a binding activity. The emotion does get away from him in Figure IV and continues free in V. It has the better of the ego to this extent, yet never with noticeable disruption. Where the onset is acutest, the very slow initial time of Figure VI, the counter reaction is also sharpest; it is a reflex. It is not a beneficient defense going to excess as it does and freezing the mental life. It does serve the purpose; it securely ties down the anxiety.

The lively affects. Duncan's subdued disposition, deep and extensive as it is, still cannot suppress his exciting and his pleasurable emotions. He is not, to be sure, as liberated in this sphere as he is in his fantasy living. But the feelings do express themselves. Duncan does reach out to his environment.

The 3 unmodulated color responses (C) first hold our attention. They represent reactions of primitive force. They may tell of rage, the condition of being "beside oneself," or similar unrestrained discharge. The Rorschach test variables report the genus of a reaction; they are not specific to the point of identifying the finer nuances of character. The epileptic and the manic both respond with C. So also do some neurotics who are, however, more characterized by CF which in turn they share with natures attuned to the artistic. Developmentally, three C may represent an emotionally ungrown condition. It is a tension which lays greatest strain on the ego.

In any event, Duncan emotionally is highly volatile. He does give some evidence of effort at growth in the one CF, and the one FC responses. In both of these, form perception is entering into his total reaction and modifying his feeling-dominated responses. But in CF it is still in subjection to feelings more than it is sympathetic understanding of the outside world; it is a labile, sensitive reaction. In the FC his ego is mastering the feelings. But it is doing so only with difficulty and not with full success. The scoring is FC—. Erratic thinking, disclosed in the minus element, betrays the affects as still shaking the ego's control. In all the color-determined responses we see, therefore, pressure of emotion such as to express itself in disregard of the ego. The outlook in the majority of the instances is for a breakaway by the emotions.

The total weighting of color values, 6.0, in a record with R 39 indicates a high average quantity of emotional reactivity in liberation. This is an asset which needs to be reconverted, from emerging principally as the C, CF of now, to CF, FC. The goal representing the optimum condition will be an FC quantity higher than that of CF. The activity *must* be so reconverted if the patient is to learn to use this important asset to his advantage. At the present time Duncan is in readiness to externalize, to discharge his feelings without adequate pondering by the ego. This can make for maladaptive discharge.

The balance of F+ relative to total weighted color score is, however, promise that he will restrain this discharge. Duncan's respect for reality is high. In fact the ego is exerting strong effort. This involves strain, wastes energy, and the cost is high with a loss to the total function. But all conflict whether intrapersonal or other pays this price of waste and loss.

For all this pressure that is manifest Duncan still has some unused assets emotionally. The affective ratio is high: 18 responses in Figures VIII to X, 21 in Figures I to VII. The ratio is 0.86, and compares with the mean of 0.60, SD 0.14 in the adolescents. This is a readiness in our patient to reach, to be in social contact, to communicate with the emotions. He confirms this partially in his absolute number of 5 color-determined associations. Statistics are not at hand, but empirically this can be judged as at least average. It holds promise of some rise in his spirits given the appropriate turn in life's events. He has the wherewithal which can dissipate his gloom. Yet certain other qualitative signs of warm reaction, lively spontaneity are lacking. They are the expressions of pleasure in color-toned stimuli and in content which is pleasurably toned. Only twice does he strike lively sparks, and both times they are pale sparks. One is his introductory phrase for Figure VIII. The other, his nearest approach to spontaneity, is the comment following R 35. The promise remains mainly promise. The pensive mood lasts. It will be noted too that Duncan produces no color response in either Figure II or III.

The content in this sphere has an element of originality in all but one instance (R 36). The associations offer leads, therefore, to topics by which Duncan's feelings are more strongly awakened.

In R 22, the "ad" is a differentiating feature. The "ice cream" topic is found frequently enough in adults, especially in reaction to this particular detail. It may be set down as an immaturity within the normal range. R 25 is a picture of nature on a grand scale, forceful, possibly pleasurable. Its particular meaning to this patient is, however, not known from the Rorschach record alone. In R 30, what starts out as a possibly pleasurable association, actually develops into a discomfort motif. The anatomy response in R 37 is of pathological quality frequent in acute neurotic conditions. A symptomatic worry over health can be inferred from it. One other judgment that may now be made, therefore, is that when Duncan's strong feelings are activated they revolve around motifs which are very individualized and unhealthy to the character.

Color shock. In Figure II, where this can first occur, it is clear-cut and acute. The patient's reaction to it is one of defensive rejection; the response time is slow enough to indicate blocking. Associational productivity is below his own average for the 10 figures. He deviates in the approach type in inadequate D or W relative to Dd. No entirely ego-controlled association is found; no F+ uninfluenced by another determinant. The F+ per cent for this figure is actually zero; perceptual dysfunction. The lambda index is low; relatively inadequate response to outer stimuli as Duncan responds to inner ones. At the moment, in Figure II, these inner stimuli derive from inferiority feelings with their unsatisfying mood loading.

Duncan recovers himself in Figure III. An important sequel, this, to Figure II, as evidence that the ego can regain balance following the impact of the color shock. Signs of the recovery are the excessively fast response time, the most normal association with which he opens the reactions to this test card and the full, in fact excessive, intellectual control. This perfect control, together with the almost instant initial response times are over-reactions both. This may look like strength; it is really a reflex action, and as such, a vulnerable trait. Yet the pattern in the card does uncover a reserve of strength. The information is of critical value to the therapist. To get Duncan to requisition on this reserve, such will be the course in mapping out the therapy. The boy has the resources. Can they be called out and directed so as to give him the satisfactions which will impel him to call on even more of his strength in a benign spiral?

The emotions take over at once in Figure VIII, in which the first association is an unmodulated color response with its particularized content note. The first form perception is erratic, F− (R 23). More minus behavior is found in R 26. Lambda is again low. Contamination in content, and deep regression structurally in R 23; this process is on again in R 26 with its very personal thinking. To the extent that the M in these responses are true M in Rorschach's sense, the patient is communicating dream material. It becomes obvious that exciting stimuli have a liquescing effect on the personality. They loosen the ego's repressing hold.

In Figure IX the color shock persists. The F+ per cent is low by the usual standards for the normal adolescent; and more so with reference to the patient's F+ score for the test as a whole. The one color response is still without tempering by the ego. Nonstructural but characteristic color shyness is the use in R 27 of color for identifying the detail without its determining the associational content. The term "color-shy" is Rorschach's, "*Farben-scheu.*" The uneasiness is reflected in another behavioral indication, his difficulty in verbalizing the "oil geyser," (R 29) a percept well within the repertoire. The content throughout the figure, original as it is, discloses the emotional loading, and there is a tinge of preoccupation with the strange, "mysterious vapor" (R 28).

Certain elements of strength are, nevertheless, evident in Figure IX. The very first response is, in structure, of the healthiest: a good M, a human association, Z activity, and a P. Nor do we see in Figure IX any of the deeper regressions of Figure VIII. The ego is here once more demonstrating its ability to regain balance.

In Figure X recovery is achieved but not fully. Time for the first response

is fast by the standard which the patient himself sets. Productivity is high.
Accuracy is as high as it can be, 100 per cent F+. He scored at this level
too in Figure III. But 100 per cent F+ is higher than the optimum. The
most efficient and adaptive persons do not distinguish themselves by perfect accuracy. The patient shows here a snap-back from the letdown in
Figures IX and VIII: again a reflex self-correction, but like so many reflexes an overcorrection.

Duncan shows improvement also in the emotional sphere. In the FC
response he is making an effort at mastery over the affects; a striving for
some emotional rapport. The struggle is not without its cost; the FC is
FC—.

The ego's vulnerability is, to be sure, manifest in still other ways. For
one thing, P failure in a figure which offers ample opportunity for P association. Lambda is again low, well below the limits in the adolescent range.
The reaction pattern in Figure X includes in fact all the inner living activities: M, C, Y, V. The shading determinant is especially rare in the color
figures and Duncan shows in it how ready he is to feel unhappy.

One other response in this sphere arrests special interest. This is the C.T
blend (R 30). Its importance is structural. In it, Duncan is abstracting out,
from a color stimulus, an experience in another sense modality, the tactual.
"Moist." What the personal meaning is to Duncan, we cannot know from
the association alone. What it does tell us is that he can feel very vehemently. All abstractions from C or M project intense feelings. The response,
therefore, throws that much additional light on the intensity with which
this adolescent boy is now living his other experiences, and the conflict
projected in the test record.

In all, the findings in this sphere of the lively affects are favorable. Duncan
responds to them. He possesses unused reserves. He is vulnerable, but the
ego holds its own against the feeling pressures. Thus both in his emotions,
and in his ego, he brings assets which the therapist can help him to reinvest
in the effort to be well.

The fantasy life. A major question now: how is the patient handling the
excitement potential, the labile activity represented in the C, and the CF?

In the Rorschach test, the fate of the personality possessed by strong
feelings is settled by the action of three other character components;
those projected in the variables F, Y and M.

The third of these, M, opens to view that most important sphere of an
individual's inner life, his wishful living. It communicates needs of which
he is unaware. At the same time it tells of capacity for turning inwardly
with the emotions. It becomes thus a biological economy along two directions. One, it offers the emotions a theater of action other—and less dangerous—than the outer environment. So it saves him from executing his will

where it may boomerang. This is an economy to the individual as a social being. Secondly, M frequently diverts the affective energy from turning upon the person himself with the accompanying distresses taking the form of psychosomatic disease. M is the stuff of imagination. The point has been adequately treated in the literature beginning with Rorschach. But imagination can be a gift of Icarus, carrying the wings of the owner too close to the warming sun, singeing them and their binding wax; as a result he falls to his destruction into the deep sea—of psychosis. How healthfully the individual uses this gift is judged by (a) the other Rorschach test findings as always; what kind of a person is using the fantasy? It is also judged by (b) certain aspects of the M.

First the total quantity. Eleven M are a high quantity, although it can be found in a well-balanced adult of higher intelligence. But our patient is not an adult. The quantity is found in many adolescents, usually not well-balanced ones. Eleven M are high for Duncan's quantitative productivity. He is using up too large a portion of his mental life in the imagination. For the not too much above average response total of 39 it is a luxury he cannot afford.

Secondly, the intensity of the fantasy experience, as measured by the Levy concept of movement energy (p. 55 ff.). Rating Duncan's M responses in the order in which he produced them:

R	Degree of Movement
1	6
2	0
6	4
9	4
13	2
16	7
18	3
23	5
26	7
27	6
35	3

From these evaluations it would follow that this boy's wishes are intensely experienced four times: R 1, 16, 26, 27; they are at about the mean, or moderately above in three instances, R 6, 9, 23. In the other four, energy is mediocre to low, including one zero. The weight of the evidence is for a strongly felt wish experience and domination by it. An inconsistency is found as one sets the measured energy side by side with the content in the same fantasy response, in R 13. It is among the low energy fantasies by the

Levy scale. Yet there are reasons for believing that this boy is here communicating a strong attitude, a displacing. The cow is a large female animal; and the patient's relation to his mother is one of the important dynamics in this personality struggle. It was the overt reason for referral to the psychiatric clinic. Low energy rating would, therefore, in this instance not be communicating a weakly felt wish. This problem receives attention again below, in connection with a similar discrepancy in Duncan's second test (p. 121).

Structure in Duncan's fantasy, in terms of good or poor forms seen in movement (M+, M−) is predominantly as in the normal, but with notable exceptions. Of the 11 M, 8 are plus. The imagination feels the censoring eye of the ego, and its productions in these 8 fantasies. They are such as are experienced by many people in their waking moments, and can be utilized by others, each for his own particular wish-fulfillment. In 3 of these 8 M, the form is P, (R 6, 18, 27). These do not differentiate this patient. M which are also P disclose what may be considered only a commonplace, community-shared, fancy. They do not project any specifically personal unconscious experience, excepting when the association carries also some additional, very unique, elaboration.

Duncan provides additional evidence that he will keep his fantasying safely in check. This is in the ego-fantasy balance; the quantity of M relative to that of F+. The amount of accurate form perception in this record is promise that, much though he uses his imagination, his sense of reality will operate alongside it. The ego will keep an eye on the imaginative activity; there is no danger of run-away autistic living.

Yet there will be individual such experiences. At the opposite extreme from the M which are also P, are the M−, especially when the content in them is some animal. In the M− the patient is in regression. Unconscious urges are coming to expression, powerful enough to break through the ego's defenses. The responses: 13, 23, 26. Not only is the perception in these 3 unclear, but the animal content is a safe disguise of what must have personally critical meaning. Hence the disguise. Dreams are being experimentally educed in these M. The ego uses this tactic in the Rorschach test as in life. The content requires, of course, further exploring for special significance. What humans do these animals represent? The test is here providing critical leads to conflict foci in the personality. They are being inspected in detail below.

One other structural factor still requires scrutiny: the extensor-flector stances, as described by Rorschach.[4] In the stances he takes, Duncan does not follow a consistent line. In R 6 he is definitely flector; in R 2 altogether

---

[4] RORSCHACH, H., *op. cit.*, p. 30.

passive. The actor in R 2 is not only not acting but being acted upon. In R 1, as in some others, he is equivocal; there is aggressive content, while the direction of the action is centripetal. Actual experience shows that in very few M do persons take one of the two stances as sharply defined as Rorschach describes them. This is so in the present record. Following are the positions which Duncan takes in his other M: R 9, flector, but with phobic-aggressive ideas; R 13, very flector; R 16, static, i.e., neither flector nor extensor; R 18, centripetal-static; R 23, an extensor trend; R 26 vigorously extensor; R 27, centripetal-static; R 35, centripetal-static.

It is definitely easier for Duncan to turn to the center line; to look for a support to which to cling. Such an attitude, unconscious though it is, cannot be palatable to a masculine ego. The test projects here one of the problems which this adolescent boy's ego needs to handle. Yet R 26 is also evidence of an inner urge to the contrary, against the need for clinging and submission. In it is the seed of the struggle for independence. Numerous aggression motifs are more flashes of dissatisfaction with the dependent role. This is a favorable sign prognostically, since it points to a most valuable therapeutic reserve. It is a trait of which the firm ego will avail itself. The two findings together, conscious ego strength and unconscious urge to self-assertion, are promise that the psychiatrist's investment of his time will yield returns. Under clinic conditions, which necessitate a very thin spreading out of psychotherapy, such information is of decisive value.

The quality of the fantasies as pleasurable or painful can sometimes be judged directly in the thought content. The judgment is subjective. Nor can it ever be assumed that some ideas "obviously" painful or pleasurable to most judges do not actually carry the contrary affect to some particular patient under study. Yet, with these cautions in mind, it is helpful toward personality evaluation to appraise the feeling-tone of the fantasies as painful or pleasurable, judging by the familiar value standards.

Structure does in instances provide supporting objective evidence. This is in the blends. An M may blend with one of the color nuances or with a light variation, Y. In the former, the fantasies are likely to be exciting, of self-gratifying quality. The mutual reinforcement of M and Y has already engaged our attention (pp. 48, 51). They record inner living that is agitating, painful. Duncan responds 3 times with M.Y, in R 1, 9, 35. The themes in each of these would be set down as painful. Content and structure here corroborate each other. For the other fantasies I judge the affect entirely from the ideation as follows: pleasurable, R 6, 18, 23, 26; painful, R 2, 27; uncertain, R 13, 16.

We turn now to the thought content in the fantasies and examine it for leads as to the patient's particular wishes or fears.

R 1 and R 2: aggressive competition between two; a "female" is the prize,

and there is decapitation of this female. Who are the two "witches?" What
is the displacement? And so, what has been repressed? The "beheaded
female" is perceived in a maternal formed detail (Fig. I, D 4). An obvious
surmise is the patient's hostility to his mother. It is a surmise or a lead
which the patient will need to confirm in the therapeutic sessions. Autistic
thinking is communicated in both these associations; autistic, but not regressive. Other subjects within normal ranges will produce similar material
which communicates these persons' own idiosyncratic needs.

R 6. In this fantasy, which is a P, the patient is sharing a very common
whimsy, accenting somewhat the condescension, and so displaying a bit of
a superior, critical air. Whether he "prettifies" these masculine figures is
too much a matter of surmise. He does show some contempt attitude. In
male patients this is a hostility in which is cloaked the homosexual interest.
As Duncan associates here, it is only the thinnest kind of lead. But he does
accent the supercilious, "very dignified, humorous in their dignity," enough
for us not to ignore.

R 9. The "devil" is original here; although phobic and repulsive figures,
human or animal, are frequent in reaction to this figure. Individualized are
(a) "peering," a projection (in the clinical sense) and so a defense against
his own need to engage in the peering; (b) the vague "hook-like" objects,
a kind of phobic-aggression content which is common in IV; (c) accent on
the black, discussed above (p. 74).

The association has thus elements of the autistic. The "Devil" I am currently relating to paranoid thinking. The "peering" motif supports this
interpretation.

R 13. Original and autistic in content; one of the structurally regressive
responses, the more so since the actor is animal. On the assumption that I
am technically accurate in scoring this response as M, the animal is a sub-
stitute for some other thought. It is a repression. The question has already
been raised, is the person intended the mother? (Compare R 2.) The patient
will have to confirm this conjecture. The recurrence of the lead is internal
support from the test directly.

R 16. The human in inverted position I have found only in patients with
highly unique thought content. The empirical evidence is, therefore, that
this is an autistic M. Again the test here sets up a question which the patient will, in the course of therapy, answer. Whom is he seeing upside down?
The guess that it is the father has support in what we know clinically. But
what exactly is Duncan thinking in seeing that person as "standing on his
head?" It is certainly a figure of speech, a rhetorical form, and that is something which the unconscious regularly shares with poetry.

R 18. Another P, but with nuances that disclose the patient's own personality idiom, "impish," "gazing impudently." He manifests here some of
that patronizing superiority we saw in R 6. Any interpretation of this as

significant would be contradicted by the fact that this response is definitely a community fantasy. In these amusing, competitive "impish figures," Duncan is reproducing one of the four most common M in the test. One fly does appear here in our Rorschach ointment; Figure VII is the "mother" figure. Since Duncan is in a mother-son conflict, the fantasy here should be crucially autistic; it should be communicative. But it is not. Either the test is letting us down or it is not the conflict with the mother which is the nucleus of Duncan's struggle. The test has already offered this lead once before in the anxiety shock pattern (above, p. 76).

R 23. The pose in which he sees these "pigs" would have to be anthropomorphic. Also, pigs do not dance. Here then is a true M in animal content; it is also a far departure in form accuracy. It is the dream's indifference to reality as the patient achieves in it what Freud has called the primitive narcissism of dream work. The association has in it something of the sardonic. The therapist will naturally be curious as to who are the dancing pigs. Both content and structure, therefore, point to this as a significant fantasy. What the personal meaning to the patient, is unknown not only to the examiner, but also to the patient at present.

R 26. Very original in several themes: panorama, slim wolves, the one bundle; and a possible ironic, futility motif, in their leaping "at nothing." The question may be raised, is this a true M? Is it anthropomorphic action? Or simply a recalled memory picture of an activity which is usual for the animal? As such alone it would not be M (Rorschach's criterion). But there is too much in this association which goes beyond any animal activity. A wolf can leap up; but the panorama in which Duncan has them "converge on one another" is that creation of the new which is Rorschach's M. What the personal meaning to the patient, it is the therapy's task to unravel. The response comes from deep sources in the personality; the M structure tells that. The real thinking is repressed since it can only emerge in disguise. It carries the emotional power of a real need since it forces its way past the ego; we know this from the very fact that it emerges. The minus element tells that the pressure is strong enough to break through the ego's usual adherence to accuracy. This reasoning also holds for R 13 and R 23.

R 27. Another P following the usual antics which these details in Figure IX elicit. In itself, therefore, this is another community fantasy. But it takes an original turn, scored in R 28. Here it becomes autistic. The significance, unknown.

R 35. More commonly seen as obstreperous little animals; rarely human; occasionally, gnomes or similar mythical figures. A phobic element, with paranoid flavor; "huge, hooded, staring." The quarrel motif is frequent here. But patient stresses it in to a degree betraying personal involvement. Duncan's unconscious harbors resentment. He projects it on to others.

One other quantitative relation of M to C is Rorschach's *Erlebnistypus*,

or the experience balance, EB. We will only note here that Duncan is now
in a decidedly introversive adjustment. A fuller discussion of the experience
balance is being saved for below, in the discussion of the total picture.

In all, Duncan possesses a talent in this sphere: the high quantity, usually sound structure, frequently rich imagery. But he is in a neurotic conflict as we know from the color shock pattern. This is a condition of ego
insufficiency (Fenichel). He is not holding on to values such that he is
converting this rich inner world into creative results. His ego can now only
turn to it as a resource in its need; a refuge into which to retire and find
relief from its stresses. This is an unfruitful use of this resource.

Duncan's disposition toward the morose is further irritated and its effect
worsened by *feelings of inferiority*. Projected in the vista response, V, his
total of 3 is high average for adolescents. More tellingly, the content in
them speaks: "rugged mountains" (R 4); "the far away setting sun"
(R 21); "huge overhanging cliffs" (R 38). The themes are heights, distance
and the difficult terrain.

The sun is a general father symbol. Does it have that specific significance
to Duncan? Again the test protocol asks a question which it does not answer. But, as will be seen from the clinical facts, in this percept Duncan
is reporting a most poignant percept relative to himself and the suffering
related thereto: the psychologic distance between himself and his father,
and his consequent self-undervaluation. It is an acrid tasting pill for any
boy. The finding fits in with the others already noted that the father is the
focal dynamic in Duncan's neurosis. It throws new light on the deep gloom
which so pervades the boy's psyche. It raises the question whether this
gloom is emanation from guilt, taken on himself by Duncan in trying to
understand this depressing relationship. The intensity of the mood is deep
enough to be a guilt product.

The "dainty bridge" (R 39) is a sharp contrast to the huge cliffs. Is this
a displacing from himself? If so, he defends against the implication in the
"natural bridge" (of the inquiry), which connotes a heavy solidity.

The "rugged mountains" (R 4) carries a theme present also in R 38, that
of difficult terrain and the sense of "hard going." It is a topic too frequently
present in persons impressed by the difficulties between themselves and
their goals, not to be significant of an attitude characteristic of them.

In all, 3 vista responses represent a not excessive amount of inferiority
consciousness. Nor does their structure in Duncan take on the deeply cutting intensity found in some patients. In none of the vista determined associations does the V variable take precedence over the F. He produces no
pure V. The inference is that this trait is not of so acute a degree as to indicate roots deep in earliest layers of the character structure. Duncan
acquired the trait relatively late in his childhood development, and as reac-

tion to unpalatable life's circumstances. These feelings are symptom, rather than in the character.

A trait in this patient with important consequences in fashioning the neurosis and in coloring the mood is his *resistiveness*. It is very frequently found in the Rorschach test together with feelings of inferiority, against which it is a defensive reaction. Duncan manifests it in a higher quantity than demanded by his inadequacy consciousness. His white space count of 4 compares with the adolescent mean of 2.08 (SD 2.12). The indication is the same when measured by percentage of white spaces in the total productivity. (Mean in adolescents is 4.9 per cent, SD 4.6.) Duncan's white space per cent is 10.3; or just above the first SD above the mean. Taken in itself this high white space score would indicate an important factor in the character structure, the pertinacity with which this individual sticks to his point of view. Generically the white spaces are opposition behavior, the fighting stance. The salient question always is how is this opposition being used? The observed directions are: against the outer world, against the person's own conscious thinking, and against his inner fantasy living. In an introversive person such as Duncan the fight is against this inner life. The social history material, some of the psychiatrist's notes and some of the content in the Rorschach test record shows him in an open struggle with his mother. This is an undesirable attitude, one not consistent with ego standards. It generates conflict. This struggle against her is hardly being carried on in the unconscious. In fact it is overt. His opposition must, therefore, be directed against some other attitude which he holds in the unconscious. This is the important clue recurring in this Rorschach test configuration. The struggle with the mother is not the most dynamic one in the neurosis. There is another person and related attitude against which the ego is in strife. Reasoning from psychopathology generally leads again to a hypothesis already set up at several points above.

Duncan's own attitude to his father is what he is fighting hardest. This fight generates the anxiety. The ego is mobilizing this painful defense against the punishable ideas that he is harboring against the father. The Rorschach test directly projects thus an opposition between deep needs in this personality. His ego cannot bear urges that are of the very essence of his personality. Hence the heavy-hearted mood of guilt quality. But, in turning the battle inward, Duncan renders himself a valuable service. The expedient is a biologic economy. It prevents the opposition trait from taking another, undesirable course: socially disturbing overt behavior; a hysteric symptom; or psychosomatic assaults.

The defenses. Duncan's defensive operations are visible in much qualifying, and questioning as to procedure, a cautious approach. In Figure III, the language includes "this appears," "you might say," "looks like." He

spect to both is that there is no quantitative criterion for them. One must fall back on experience, with the recognition that a subjective factor resides therein. Experience is clear in any event that the personal need of the patient is dynamic in producing some of the F−. It follows that these errors are likely to be emotion-laden; hence the perceptual distortion. Exposition of the "impersonal error" is a concept I first heard discussed by Macfie Campbell, in his clinical teaching at the Boston Psychopathic Hospital. From the patients in whom this impersonal error, as Campbell identified it, occurred clinically, the inference is in order that they are inaccuracies consequent on attention dysfunction, such as due to simple lapse of ego control. This in turn may be due to one of three factors: distractibility stemming from inadequate self-disciplining; overpowering of the ego by the emotional flood; or brain tissue insufficiency, whether due to clouding by toxins, or to damage. But any particular impersonal F−, whatever the condition that permitted it, is presumed not to carry personal significance to that patient. It is not misshaping of reality dictated by personal interests. These latter distortions are the personal F−. The responses in the present protocol, exemplifying the two kinds of errors, follow.

Probably personal F−: R 10, an oral, phobic animal. R 28, "mysterious." R 13, R 23, R 26. As M these are *ipso facto* motivated from within. The M element shows how intimately personal the association is. See concerning these (above, p. 83 ff.).

In R 10 another structural factor enters, Y. It tells of a mood that can well help break down control. But mood as such is impersonal. In R 10 it fuses with the personal need to effect the F−.

Probably impersonal F−: R 5, R 36. No personal reason behind the distortion is obvious and none can be found from what is known about the patient out of clinical or any non-Rorschach sources (but, concerning R 5, see below in exposition of content). In both these percepts the interpretation is that there has been momentarily a sheer suspension of the ego's functioning. The attention either was in flight or otherwise failed. In R 36, a structural factor, also impersonal, the emotional quickening reflected in the color element is present. It may have initiated the lapse in attention or may simply be aggravating it.

Borderline instances: R 31. In itself the "fish" would present no basis for personal F− interpretation. But the association reaches back to an old school memory with which would be bound a larger complex of memories. An older ego state may be in process of reawakening. The error would thus be personal.

R 32. "Octopus" is original to this detail. Its phobic connotation was noted above (p. 88). This is altogether at the hunch level. In absence of more evidence for personal implications, the F− must be judged impersonal.

So far as concerns the degree of error, this appears wider than usual in three associations: R 13, R 23, R 31—the cow, the pig and the fish. But these departures are only moderately wide and not the bizarre misinterpretations which patients in severe mental disorder can produce. Duncan does not distort his world, nor does he permit himself any very vague percepts.

The attention. The approach type (*Erfassungstypus*) is the main line of evidence. The observed ranges are from excessive selection of the W or D, reflecting an unvaried, not discriminating or analytic attention, to an over-selection of Dd, work of distractibility, flightiness, and amounting, in extreme instances, to a splintered attention. When we find the latter, many of the Dd are extremely minute, rare, peculiar. Some may never be selected a second time in the experience of the same examiner. Whether the excess is in W, D, or Dd, the psychologic significance is the same, an inferior adaptation. In the present patient the ego does show an insufficiency in this factor. This is in the excess selection of the large detail, D; a too narrow grooving of the attention to the obvious. But he does no scattering to the minute.

Attention lapses can be detected in the inaccurate, unclear perception emerging as impersonal F−. The two other signs of maladaptive attention are flow of unrelated content and the very opposite, preoccupation with a single interest. Our patient shows nothing of either.

Duncan's thinking is coherent throughout. The nearest approaches to insufficient ego activity are in R 14, in R 23 and in R 26. In R 14 he thinks tangentially using the happenstance that something is "like a chicken leg," and "feathery" to conclude to the "ostrich." This is *non sequitur* logic. In R 23 and R 26 the animals are engaged in human activity. In Rorschach test language this is contaminatory thinking. Clinically it is primitive, archaic, and so regressive. As fantasies, however, these are not conscious thought productions. The F+ per cent for the record as a whole is high enough to promise that these regressions will be kept where they belong, in the unconscious.

In his sequence, when it can be known, Duncan projects a too even regularity. This would mean a fixed logical procedure. Carried to an extreme, it becomes the application of the same thinking procedure to all problems, inflexibility, nonadaptive. Judgment on Duncan's Seq is, however, in this first test seriously qualified by the fact that he uses only one variable, D, in five of the test cards, (III, V, VIII, IX, X). In these, no sequence judgment can therefore be made. It is mildly irregular in one of the others (I). His accenting the D in his Ap, screens whatever logical method may be his. It certainly prevents a disordered Seq. And such may be one of the very dynamics behind the D! approach, which is a defensive device. It prevents untidy method.

recovery, he shows himself stiff, too lacking in resilience to regain his balance when thrown into disequilibrium. An important psychotherapeutic objective here indicated is to loosen his constancy of response pattern enabling him to "give" better with the winds of emotion and so be sturdier in shock moments, more tough. Varying but strong. "Old Hickory," the name given by his soldiers to Andrew Jackson, well identifies this character trait. He was one of our strongest presidents who could bend when necessary, but only to straighten back with deadly force. Yielding but tough.

The experience balance (*Erlebnistypus*) also highlights an insufficient resilience. Duncan is clearly introversive. He is responding now to trying moments by turning into a private world of self-satisfying mental operations. Also, he sticks strongly to his present mental set. This makes change the harder. Introversive, but not introvert. Rorschach draws a distinction with a difference between these two conditions. Duncan does give expression to his feelings. Also he manifests more potential for reaching for warmth than is materializing into such at present (p. 78). There is an urge for its emerging impulsively, irritably. The picture emotionally is principally one of unrest. Overtly also he uses apparent control. Actually he is neutralizing the strong feelings by way of his passivity and his anxious mood. But mainly he internalizes it in his fantasy living. That is, there is conscious control and seeming delay of the impulses, but the waters are quiet on the surface only. Such is the significance of the introversive balance. From this total configuration we must expect that this adolescent boy deals with his aggressive and his erotic needs in part by sheer repression, and in part by internalizing the feelings into a wish-fulfilling, daydreaming activity.

The content. A theme that recurs has a woman as its central character. This is the case in R 1, 2, 27, and is surmised, but requires proof, in R 13. In two of the associations, the women are witches; in another, in a maternal detail, she is a "beheaded female" (R 2). The attitude is not a flattering one. These four associations are of fantasy structure; the patient keeps their significance away from his conscious thinking. The interpretation is that he holds the unflattering attitude toward his mother. The "mother" is an inference from general knowledge in psychodynamics of personality. She is not found in the Rorschach test content itself. This is where we stand at present with content. Leads are what it offers.

Certain deductions based on the known operations in personality are in order. The investigator who extends himself beyond this general knowledge or interprets on inadequate evidence in the particular record does so at the peril of serious error in the personality he draws out of that test protocol. In R 19 Duncan belittles at a more conscious level; the structure is of simple form. He does not in this instance identify the sex of the human figure;

but a sound foundation of experience here comes to our aid. The "object" of R 19 when perceived for what the patient does now, is invariably a feminine adornment; and the "figures" (R 18) to which he attaches the "absurd feather-like object" are in the "mother" card, and statistically the most commonly seen female heads in the test. His antipathy is against women.

Duncan discloses his attitude toward men three times, in R 6, 16 and 35. All three are fantasy-determined. In R 6 he is superior and facetious. In R 16 the position in which he sets the man is not complimentary, but the significance to Duncan is not known to us. The phobic element stands out in R 35, and the "hooded" theme has several possibilities that require clarifying. In three associations, all in the fantasy sphere, all probable displacements, he does not commit himself as to the sex. The "wolves" of R 26 have a male connotation; in the dancing pigs, we are offered no lead at all. In R 18, even though the statistical warrant is that he has perceived a female form, most significance still attaches to his having left these figures asexual. Taken with the fact that his view of women in his fantasy is not to their credit, the question is opened up of a homosexual interest being activated. His unconscious, where his real persona is located, dislikes persons of the opposite sex. This trail is a very faint one and requires much confirming in direct exploring with the patient; at the same time it cannot be overlooked.

Regarding Duncan's present sex interests, charged as they would be with an adolescent's instinctual urges, the content of this record is silent. In R 29 the geyser may have phallic significance and Duncan does correct himself in more than normal quantity in this association. However the interpretation of phallic significance is entirely conjectural. The arresting fact is the total absence of any association overtly resembling sexual imagery, male or female. Nor can this be laid to sensitivity in the presence of an examiner of the opposite sex; the examiner was male. Duncan's control over this thinking at conscious level appears complete. This does not indicate more than normal inhibition in this patient if findings in a normal adult group is a gauge. The 157 S's in that normal adult sample reported only 4 sex percepts, or a mean sex association score of 0.03. Duncan is thus following an established cultural pattern in his verbal behavior on this subject.

A third major and recurring theme uncovers phobic thinking. Two of these (R 10, 12) are at the more conscious level (F responses). The "wolf" appears twice (R 10, 26), and any repetition of a motif especially when it is original, always projects some personal interest. In the "snakes," which become "vultures," he stresses in the fear already agitated in him in R 9, since he identifies these animals with the details seen in that fantasy as "hook-like . . . hands . . . trying to grasp." A phobic note in fantasy R 35,

aware of the attitude, appears to be saying, "Am I really like this?" For the moment Duncan is convinced that he is of this stamp, and hence his mood. It is his ego's judgment unacceptable to the ego.

The clarifying to Duncan of this conflict becomes a major objective in the treatment effort. Successful, it will explain the mood and the anxiety. Once the boy grasps the relationship between his wishes, the ego's resistance to them and the resulting oppressive mood, the other therapeutic objectives may be expected to follow. These are relaxing of the defensive attitudes, softening of the tense emotional state, constructive use of the fantasy.

The outlook for treatment from this Rorschach test record: a potential handicap is the introversive balance. The rich fantasy asset is paradoxically a liability. It permits the patient to fly inward. There he can evade the therapist and he can avoid facing any conscious thinking unpalatable to the ego. But Duncan's total of expressed feelings, his potential for freer emotional response to the world and to make warm effective contact with it, are adequate for transference. The assets include an above average intelligence evident in the breadth of interest. The high fantasy quantity is also promise that the patient will communicate critical inner material. The total experience balance is such as to indicate an inner resilience, Rorschach's *dilatierte Erlebnistypus*. Most important of all the ego has strength. From this the wish to be well can be inferred. Hence it may be expected that Duncan will mobilize his resources so as to (a) obtain the insight he needs, (b) clarify a goal and (c) integrate his efforts toward reaching it.

B. The Second Test. Differential Measures

Between the first and second Rorschach tests, a period of two years and four months elapsed. Duncan's age was changing therefore from $15\frac{11}{12}$ to $18\frac{3}{12}$ years. He was growing from about the middle stage of adolescence into its closing phase; he was entering adulthood. In this interim he was receiving regular psychotherapy excepting for the interruptions in the summer months. Duncan was at this point preparing to enter the military service. As the psychiatrist was drawing the treatment to a close he requested a second test. The protocol follows.

RESPONSE RECORD

Figure I (17″)

1. D F+ Hd   'Looks like a headless woman' (D 4).
2. D F+ Ad   'I see twin heads of wolves' (D 8; not sure).
3. D FV.Y+ Cl   ∨ > ∨ < ∨ ∧ > ∧ < 'Sort of like clouds and cumulus clouds' (D 2 bil-

lowy; shape, round; and shading; and has depth).

4. D M+ A

∧ 'Looks like a dancing bear; twin dancing bears (with amusement) like something out of Fantasia' (D 2).

5. D M+ Hd

∨>∧∨ 'And looks like twin heads on opposite sides; singing . . .' (D 6 and Dd 23; are notes; they drew it).

6. Ws F+ Rc
1.0

'The whole thing looks like a head' (hobgoblin; Dds 30 are eyes; Dds 29 are nostrils; as on Jack O'Lantern).

7. Dd F Ad

∨ 'Also a Saint Bernard dog; I can concoct a Saint Bernard dog.—
'I guess that's about all.'

Figure II (30″)

8. D F− A
3.0

∨ 'Look like two birds at the same water hole' (D 1; Dd of D 4 is 'water, trying to fly and to drink; also, had their beaks caught in a ring, and trying to get out').

9. D Y.V Na

'And that looks like what I imagine would be lava—from a bird's eye view —a covered landscape' (because of shading; 'pools of lava welling up in spots').

10. Dd F+ A

'A couple of laughing baboons; twins' (Dd 31; profile only). ∨>∨>∧>∨ (Studies sundry Dd).

11. Dds M− H My
3.0

∧ 'Looks like I can see three laughing ghosts with their heads above the others. They're a cheerful lot; they look awfully small from here' (Dd 25; and Dds are 'mouths').

Figure III (19″)

12. D M+ H P
4.0

'Looks like two very comical figures having a tug of war, and neither one's going to win either' (because the objects, D 4, are so big, and they are not going to like it).

13. D F+ Mu

∨∧ 'They each seem to have very battered banjos' (D 2).

4.5

33. D M+ H
3.0

mid; not the kind Egyptians had . . .
(W) what some kind of animals make—
'Or people make; some kind of structure, getting up on one another' (as in
gymnastic exercise; D 2 supports D 1;
and D 1 attaches to D 5). 'Looks good
∨ enough to eat.'

Figure IX (20″)

34. D M+ H P
35. D FC+ A
2.5

36. D F+ Hd P
37. D C Ls

38. D FV— Ls
2.5

'An old man, playing a horn (D3).
'Two pink elephants (D 10) looking
at one another very closely' (much
amusement; eyes are very close and
they're looking at each other).
> 'Head of Teddy Roosevelt' (D 4).
'The green spot (D 1) looks like
water' (because of color as on a summer's day with land).
'At the front part—in the foreground
of the picture (D 2, a reefer . . .I guess
because of gray beachland').

Figure X (30″)

39. D M— Bt
4.5

40. D F+ Ad P
41. D FC+ A

42. D F+ Oj

43. Dd M+ H

44. D F— Na
4.0

45. D F+ A
4.0

'If trees ever become alive at night,
this is what they would look like (especially D 1; waving at each other,
waving and laughing at each other').
'A rabbit's head (D 5)—
'And looks like a couple of green
snakes (D 4 . . . green, pearly eyes and
shape').
'Looks like a pendulum,' (D 3 . . .
swinging back and forth).
'I see what looks like Pappy Yokum
laughing (Dd 31; laughing, mouth wide
open.') ∨ < ∨ > ∧ > ∧
'I can imagine a caterpillar sort of
weaving a cocoon around himself' (D
12).
'And I see what I imagine to be . . .
a sort of an expression on their faces . . .
looks like playful female dogs (D 6 . . .

one female is playful; one, male, is angry.) Or very angry male dogs.

'I see what I imagine would be a bird's eye view of a city.'

RESPONSE SUMMARY

R total 45

W	4 (s 1)	M	13 (2−)	H	8	F+%	83		
D	34	C	2	Hd	5	A%	42		
Dd	7 (s 1)	FC	2	A	12	P	7		
	———	Y.V	1	Ad	7	s	2		
	45	FY	1	An	1	s%	4.4		
		FV.Y	1	Aq	1	T/R	61.3″		
		FV−	1	Ay	1	T/IR	17.8″		
		F+	19	Bt	1				
		F−	4	Cl	1	L	0.53		
Z	49.0	F	1	Fd	1	Af r	0.61		
Ap	(W) D Dd!		———	Ls	2				
Seq	Irregular trend		45	Mu	1				
	moderate	EB	13/4	Na	2				
				Oj	1				
				Rc	1				
					—				
					45				

INTERPRETATION

The defenses. In a second Rorschach test, following on any extended treatment, the new state of the defenses is of especial interest. Are they tight, showing symptoms of rigidity? If so, is the patient in a state of mobilization, but not yet attaining insight? Not relaxing into easy self-confidence? Such was the condition of Eddie (Chapter VI), as projected in his second test, but not in his third. Are the defenses too loose? Are they noticeable chiefly by their absence? The treatment may be passing through such a phase, as a prerequisite to refashioning the personality as a whole. Somewhere in between, of course, is the optimum.

Duncan's defenses in his second test show signs of stiffness, in instances exacerbated as compared with his condition as he started treatment. The ego is alerted, as it were; has posted sentinels on the outer perimeter. He has somewhat built up his inner citadel. At the same time, he has retained weaknesses both in his inner living, and in his peripheral behavior. On the whole, his present defensive pattern represents progress. But some of the tactics still add up to a net loss.

Intellectually, he is eschewing perceptual inaccuracies more than formerly. In his now larger total of responses (45 as compared with 39 in the

In per cent, he now rates at the very minimum of the first standard deviation below his group's mean; while the 5.1 per cent was actually slightly
above that minimum in the adolescents. Relative to his total mental activity, Duncan is thus not showing more intellectual initiative. He is not
directing his attention more to the larger units of his presented world. The
ego still holds back; if anything, more than formerly. He is handicapping
himself in the competition with the adults who now form his world.

Z: 49.0 as compared with the 37.0 of the first test. He scores one of his
biggest gains in this trait. Higher intellectual achievement is within his
scope, and the ego has brought it into play. This index measures the ability
to see relations which others miss. Duncan's present score not only takes
him beyond the first SD above the mean of adults; he actually reaches the
seventy-eighth percentile in the second SD (for the adults, the mean is
22.48, SD 14.91). He can handle problems now requiring intelligence close
to the most superior. In his first test he scored at just above the adolescents'

TABLE 4—*Ap Calculated Only from Adult Norms*

	R	EXPECT	ACTUAL	AP
Rorschach I.....	39	W, 7 D, 28 Dd, 4	W, 2 D, 35 Dd, 2	(W) D! (Dd)
Rorschach II....	45	W, 8 D, 32 Dd, 4	W, 4 D, 34 Dd, 7	(W) D Dd!

mean (28.9, SD 23.0). The latency of high ability inferred from findings
in the earlier test is being substantiated.

The treatment and the interim personality maturation are bringing into
function an ability which Duncan had been inadequately applying.

Approach, Ap. The expectancies, the actual findings, and the Ap as
identified in the two tests, are given in table 4. The reasons for using the
adult sphere of reference in calculating any Ap are stated below (p. 256).
However, standards are available for children's groups. In the adolescents
the normal expectancy for their average productivity of 41, is W, 5; D, 30;
Dd, 6. By this sphere of reference, the expectancies for Duncan's R of 39
would be W 5, D 29, Dd 5. The actual findings of W 2, D 35, Dd 2, thus
give him again an Ap of (W) D! (Dd). They confirm the findings based on
adult norms and substantiate the general rule.

A more liberalized and, hence, more adaptive handling of his problems
is disclosed in Duncan's present Ap as compared with that when he entered
treatment. In his perceptual attention he is now breaking down the relative
preference which the D's formerly enjoyed. He is breaking up his larger
stimuli so as to perceive their smaller constituents. Actually, he is doing
this with overemphasis—not excessive—on the Dd. But the fault really
is progress as compared with the former accent on D. The overattention to

Dd is, to be sure, one feature of the obsessive tactics. But it is in the light of these sharpened defensive attitudes that the more relaxed Ap especially represents progress. The tightening defense would disclose itself in a heightened D! approach as a channelizing of the perceptions and narrowing the attention to the concrete. Duncan's course has been in the contrary direction. The therapy has aided him toward some of the fruits of a more alert ego attention to the nicer point, but also with self-assurance such that he does not adopt a crippling inflexibility.

Sequence. (Seq.) This was described under defenses. Comparison of the two Seqs is not very meaningful, since the one in the first test lacks the variation needful for diagnostic significance. In its presently projecting a dominantly stiff attitude, it shows Duncan's ego operating insufficiently and at a disadvantage.

Turning to Duncan's inner living, M. Total now is 13; of these, 2 M−. In his first test, total is 11. But of these, 3 are M−; 3 others are blends M.Y. In both instances, Duncan's M scores are much higher than the ranges in his two groups. (Adults, mean 3.50; SD, 3.24. Adolescents, mean, 3.04; SD 2.70.) The increase by two M in the second Rorschach test is only a moderate change in these large totals. Slightly more meaningful is the decline by one in M− : that much less fantasy of regressive structure, and to that extent, the ego is less off-guard. The big change is in his entirely giving up the M.Y blends. The intensifying of the innermost dream thought into an actively painful experience is no longer in evidence. Those perturbing reactions Duncan is now capable of thrusting well down, out of reach of conscious awareness.

The fantasy life in the second test is analyzed response by response, below.

An important comparison with findings in the first is the even heavier overbalancing by the fantasy over externalized emotions. EB is now 13/4; it was formerly 11/6. Duncan has become more introversive. This is a significant alteration in structure; more so in the light of the harder defenses. The ego is more consciously alert. Duncan is also using more "escapist" living. This is a measure of the extent to which the treatment has not been completed. The ego is not self-sufficient; yet, for this second record as a whole, Duncan shows enough strength from which to conclude that, had not his call to military services intervened, the treatment could have progressed to his greater liberation and fuller independence in achieving a mature goal.

The externalized emotions, C. The change to 2 C, in the present test, from 3 C, is a real difference. The mean for true C in adolescents is 0.33, SD 0.62; in adults, 0.60; SD 0.92. A decline of only one in this category is, therefore, significant. Duncan is now less impulsive. Conversely, the ego is relatively better able to hold the primitive discharges under restraint.

treme in this trait that uncovers an anxious restriction. It is another finding which shows the ego unable to overcome its difficulties. The treatment needed to go on.

This question is in order: is the total lack of Hd an undesirable finding from the viewpoint of mental health? The adolescents' mean Hd is 4.16, SD 3.98. With reference to this high quantity, the investigators[6] say: "Does the greater number of Hd responses characteristic for the children at each developmental stage reflect the operation of inhibitory processes? Or are such findings to be anticipated as part of normal development in children?" The writers do not answer the question. What we know is that Hd is, in the literature, universally suspect. In his first Rorschach test, Duncan was healthier in this behavior than his group. The treatment has effected inhibition. (See, in this connection, the similar phase through which Eddie went, as projected in the second of his three Rorschach tests, p. 241). The conclusion is, again, that the interruption in Duncan's treatment has been premature.

The A per cent (A and Ad together) has risen to 42, from the 32 of the first test. His present score is very close to the mean 46.45 for the adults, SD 13.12. His adolescent score compared with a mean of 48.85, SD 14.0. Since this Rorschach test trait varies inversely as liberated intelligence, the course between the two tests is again toward impoverishment. Not only is the shift higher absolutely but it now places Duncan at mediocrity. Formerly, within the second SD below the mean A per cent, he rated superior. One interpretation: the ego is trammeled. Another interpretation: it is the leveling-off process entering on adulthood. Duncan is settling into more mundane, more adaptive thinking habits.

The anatomy topic (An) appears only once in each test. The content is almost exactly the same, and in reaction to the same stimulus (Figure VIII, D 3). A trend to pathologic elaboration in the first test is lost by the time of the second, as is also the more malignant "blood minus the contact of air" (R 37, first test). Duncan can now, and does, give up some sick thinking. The therapy has aborted a trend that could have grown into hypochondriasis.

F+ per cent. The present 82 is moderately above the adult mean of 79.25, SD 10.20. It is a small rise over the former 78, which compares with the adolescent 70.95, SD 9.20. Actually, the shift is somewhat more meaningful than it appears from these figures. In sigma units, Duncan now places only 0.24 above the mean, compared with 0.77 in the first test. When the treatment started, he was among those of his age group paying stricter attention to reality than do those among whom he finds himself at present. The dif-

---

[6] THETFORD, W. N., MOLISH, H. B. AND BECK, S. J.: Developmental aspects of personality structure in normal children. J. Proj. Techniques. **15**: 58–78, 1951.

ference is not significant. But, so measured, the patient shows up as more like the average of his fellows in the care with which he watches his perceptions. The ego, close though his defenses can be, is relaxed enough so that Duncan is not much more tense than other grownups in the process of arriving at his judgments. If anything, we may expect him now to observe his world with an efficient calm, comparing favorably with the average adult. Here again the beneficial effect of the treatment is to be principally credited. How much is also due to maturation? The answer must be postponed until the nature-nurture question has been finally answered.

The P response. The absolute shift has been to the present 7 P from the former 5. The adult mean is 6.79, SD 2.41; adolescents, 6.75, SD 1.64. In recognizing social canons and in thinking conventionally, Duncan had room to grow when he took his first test; his rating was then scraping bottom for the average. He has grown to expectancy for his adult group. He will respect the usual proprieties.

Lambda. In this, an improvement in absolute quantity; none as measured by his groups' variabilities. In his present test, lambda 53 per cent compares to 46 per cent in the first test. Mean and SD in the adults are 70.17 and 13.71; in adolescents 64.50 and 15.40. In both instances he is below his group means by a significant distance, 1.20 and 1.24 sigma respectively. Duncan is seriously under-responding to outside stimuli, because he is seriously over-responding to the inner; chiefly to M, to fantasy production. In this respect he has not altered with time or with treatment.

These three findings, F+, P and lambda measure aspects of a patient's response to the objective world. In the fourth column of the response summary certain other scores are found: the white space count and percentage; speed of response data; fluctuation of time per first response; and fluctuation of productivity from card to card.

The white spaces, s. The count is reduced by half in his present test, 2 s, as compared with 4. The results for the two age groups approximate each other: adults, mean 1.90, SD 2.14; adolescents, mean 2.08, SD 2.12. In his first test, Duncan rated significantly above his age mates' average; he was among the stubborn. The interval's passing sees him at the mid-point of his now older fellows, neither too much in opposition, nor lacking it. He has enough to promise an average show of determination. Whether the treatment has done it, or the maturing process, he is now more mellow.

Estimating s on a percentage basis, (s/R), the scores are 10.3 in the first Rorschach test; 4.4 for the second. Statistics for my normal sample (see table 3) show a mean per cent of 5.87, SD 4.70; for adolescents, mean 4.9, SD 4.6.

Time data. Average time for all responses was 61.3 seconds in the present test; 52.3 seconds in the earlier one. Group statistics are not available.

pigs." His very fast response time now takes on a new significance, that of a defense against the anxiety. This kind of paradoxical good performance is frequent in persons defending against the upset. It usually takes the form of an increase in quantity. The patient whistles to keep up his courage. When this is so, the anxiety betrays itself in one of the immediately following figures, the delayed shock.

This is the development in Figure V. Initial response time is slow. Productivity is low. Arresting is the failure of the P response, statistically the most frequent one in the test. There is a falling off from the best approach and an imbalance in it, since D is lacking. The patient turns the card very much, motor evidence of the ego's dislodging; and he verbalizes his sense of weakness, "I can partly make it out, not completely." A behavioral note by the examiner is consistent with these structural findings, "studies D, and Dd; he appears bogged down."

Delay of shock is the ability to delay a decision under painful circumstances. Duncan shows more of this ability in maintaining a better hold on himself in Figure V than in VI. Even under stress, and while sensitive to the inner threats, he consistently manages to stave off the evil moment. Figure VI proves, however, to be a severe trial. The agitation betrays itself in loosening some very autistic thinking, R 24, "lazy gorillas . . . half drunk." He turns the card inordinately. The P response is again missing. He uses an F+ uninfluenced by emotional response only once. His 50 per cent of accuracy is well below his high standard for his entire record. One of his rare breaches in Seq is found. Figure VI is obviously interfering with Duncan's handling of his objective world.

Yet there is a sharp difference in the anxiety shock now induced by this figure compared with what it did to Duncan in his first test. He now produces four responses against one formerly. Time for the first response is very fast; it was one of his slowest in the first test. The quality is now richer, even if autistic. Duncan is showing a remission from the fear state into which this figure threw him at the beginning of the treatment. Figure VI is distinctive by the prominence in it of a phallus-form detail. The conclusion is that the psychotherapy has succeeded in freeing Duncan from the apprehension which ideas of male genitality formerly excited in him. What we do not know from the sheer fact of the anxiety shock and its remission—since in themselves they are neutral events, structural changes—is what is the personal, conflictual need that penis imagery aroused? Experience with this figure is that it is traumatic to males sensitive over homosexuality. But it also stirs heterosexual interests in both men and women, especially in adolescent and younger adult years. The test here opens the two leads requiring further exploration. The absence in the test record of evidence for homosexuality as the prevailing dynamic points to Duncan's stirring heterosexual needs as the more likely cause of the anxiety, when he was not yet sixteen. From which it follows that this thinking no longer arouses the ego to organize a defense. The topic is not now a source of guilt. The possible homosexual question is, however, not a closed one. Deep in Duncan's unconscious world such interests appear to be stirring. They are discussed in exposition of the fantasy material.

Since the question of heterosexuality is raised, especial importance attaches to what Duncan does in Figure VII. This is the conspicuous "mother" figure with its prominent middle-aged women's profiles, its vagina-form detail and the harbor-like protecting inner space. If the ego here suffers any twinge of "wrong" thinking or wishing, it does not show it. If anything, Duncan over-defends: the perfect accuracy, the correct sequence. But an over-reaction is both symptom of the startle, and of the ability to control one's self. The patient provides more direct evidence of insufficiency in the near P failure; the "elves" (R 25) is a marginal P. It is, also, avoiding of the appropriate maternal face, caricaturing it, calling it something unreal.

The lambda index, while not lower in this figure than at Duncan's own, regularly low rating, shows it evoking inner stimuli, two M. As he excessively attends to these, he relatively neglects the outer. In one of these M, he provides information as to the personal value of this inner stimulus, the "dancing figures" (R 26). This is one of the possible homosexual motifs, with the attendant anxiety (see below, p. 123). Should R 26 stem in heterosexual interests, it is quite a healthy fancy in a young man of eighteen, and this feminine test figure is achieving the purpose intended in it by Rorschach. It is waking normal needs in Duncan.

But the figure can also stir him into acute restlessness. At R 28, he turns the card 22 times! This is an inordinate quantity by any observed standards, and the highest in this patient who, throughout, engages in much turning. The association is setting off much motility which tells of feeling pressures. But R 28 is in response to D 3, the one detail in this test figure most frequently seen as a male and, usually, an unattractive one. The content is "lion," the male of the animal, a fearful animal, and, as "King of Beasts," an authority-carrying one. How much of this significance entered into Duncan's psychologic experience is again something we cannot know from the test protocol alone. The fact is this patient is thrown into extraordinary restlessness when perceiving this detail as a "lion." Assuming the hunch proves correct, there is displacing of affect centering in the father. Duncan is confirming here what had been recurrently inferred in the first test, his father is the more important need object, and for that same reason, the anxiety source. He is the nucleus of Duncan's neurosis.

The mother is not to be disregarded as a factor. But the reactions to her

nonintellectual living. Duncan dallies in primitive gratifying experiences, in daydream activity and succumbs to a consciousness of being "less." One of the compensations is a rich fancy emerging out of the unconscious. Yet the ego refuses to let go of standards.The perceived forms remain plus, the thinking realistic. This obstinate self-control is manifest also in the 100 per cent D! Ap, an unyielding procedure which, of course, has its price in the unvarying way he adapts to his world generally (see below, p. 127).

The final test of poise under shock is provided by Figure X. Judged by productivity alone, the patient does regain his balance. But there is much other evidence to the contrary. His opening response is retarded; it is one of the two slowest in the ten cards; structurally it is about as deep a regression as he manifests anywhere. There is a highly peculiar quality to the associations. The sequence shows one of his few deviations although it is an irregularity such as found within normal range. In the light of the severe structural regression in the "trees . . . alive" (R 39), the conclusion is that persistent impact breaks him down. He can take just so much shock, after which he regresses. It is regression within neurotic level to be sure. But to this extent the ego shows up as insufficient to hold under the strain. However, there is no disruption. Duncan's defense lines bend; they do not break. The fact is he follows his initial dream-type association with a P association. Approach again becomes D! He does take hold. In all, a young man rather more than normally amenable to feeling surges, but the ego stays in the fight.

The content in the emotion-toned associations: the "ice-cream" in R 31 is a gratifying food theme; a recreational topic appears in R 35; and the exhilaration motif in R 37. But in R 41 another trait emerges, the emphasis is on "eyes." He has also seen eyes in R 35 and at several points in the record. There is seed here of what, in a weaker, or a weakened, ego can take on a paranoid flavor, i.e., suspicion.

The fantasy. However strong the patient's feelings can be, there is little danger of their forcing their way outward as disturbing behavior. Duncan can, and does, internalize his feelings. The high quantity of fantasy associations, M, give that assurance. Thirteen such reactions is at the upper end of the range of a superior, imaginative group. Rorschach's interpretation here would be that the young man is of very superior intelligence. A *non sequitur* in Rorschach's reasoning led him to such interpretation. While superiors do show much M, there are persons with much M who are not superior. Further, not all superiors produce many M although the probabilities favor their so doing. What M does show is that a personality talent possessed by the particular individual is ready to flower. The personality has grown. Given favorable climate, the psychologic enzymes, the person should bear fruit in terms of creative production.

As to the structural quality of our Duncan's M: 11 of the 13 are of plus form, i.e., of structure in which the patient had regard for reality. Of these, three are scored P. A fly in the ointment are the M—; even one is suspect. Fantasy in which the perceived form is distorted, is the stuff that dreams are made of. In Rorschach test records, it is produced by persons whose inner living regresses deeply. The content in such associations usually supports this indication, and it does in the present record, "the laughing ghosts," "trees waving at each other" (R 11, R 39).

Regression as M in animal content (A) is found in this record twice with the compelling implication from these two that a third, not scored M, is also one. The two are "the dancing bear," (R 4) and "the lazy half drunk, gorillas" (R 24). In R 4, he relates the dancing animals to a motion picture, Fantasia. Such responses I have always treated as M, on the theoretical grounds of the equivalence of M to art productions (see especially Fürrer).[7] In the "lazy half drunk gorillas" the M judgment is warranted by the fact that the animal is anthropoid, and engages in an activity which, whimsy though the association is, is only all too human. The third probable animal M is the "two birds . . . fighting . . . at the water hole" (R 8). I scored this F in compliance with Rorschach's canon that the activity in an M must be within the physical repertoire of the human animal. And while humans have been known to fight, they do not do so in the manner of birds. There are, however, grounds for calling this response M. One is the certain M in the other animal associations. The authority for this is the practice in Zürich generally, and Oberholzer's, to score doubtful responses M when the patient is an "M person." Secondly, the theme in this R 8, too, unmistakably points to a probable major dynamic in our young man's neurosis. On this, more below (evaluation of content).

That atypical kind of fantasy living, which is scored as M in Dd or in Hd, is found four times in this record: R 5, 11, 14, 43. At least one of these, R 11, and possibly one other, R 14, stem from deep layers in this patient's personality. R 43 is characterized by empathy. Children more easily accept activity of a part-human. But many were produced also by our normal adult sample, enough to indicate that these response structures do not statistically differentiate the normals from the neurotics or from schizophrenics. What the psychologic significance of M in Hd or Dd is for the present not known to me. Its meaning, therefore, requires systematic study. My hunch is that certain particular themes will cluster around these M.

Another line of evidence, how many of the normal fantasies, those which are frequently produced by healthy adults—the M that are also P—does our patient not experience? He does respond with the "good" M in Figures

[7] Fürrer, A.: Über die Bedeutung der "B" in Rorschachschen Versuch. Imago 11: 362–65, 1925.

III, VII and IX. He misses the ones in Figure II and in Figure I. His imagination lives a high percentage, not all, the fantasies most familiar to the inner world of his fellows. The finding is a net asset.

The stance. The importance of stance has been elucidated by Rorschach.[8] In brief, the indications in the extensor-flector groupings are those of independence-submission, at a deeper psychological level, masculine-feminine. As leads to treatability they have the value of correlating with more favorable prognosis for the extensor, less favorable for flector.

In the present test protocol, two of the M are clearly extensor, the "tug of war" in R 12 and the "dancing trees" in R 39. Two are clearly flector, the "god" whose "wind was knocked out of him" in R 16 and the "drunken gorillas" R 24. In the other M the inner pose is as follows: R 4, not decisive, extensor trend; R 5, no trend; R 11, extensor trend; R 14, flector trend; R 25, centripetal-static; R 26, not decisive, probably extensor; R 33, extensor trend, not fully developed, but marked; R 34, centripetal; R 43, no trend.

The evidence as to the inner pose taken by our patient is, therefore, that he is now *not* more flector-passive-submissive than he is extensor-independent. If anything, he is now accenting the extensor; trying to be self-assertive masculine. In his first test, the prevailing attitude was the flector, clinging (above, p. 82 ff.). The therapy's effectiveness is being disclosed in this favorable trend emerging in the important sphere of the unconscious.

The Levy Scale (see p. 55 ff.). Following is my table of evaluations for the M energy in the present test record:

R	Degree of Movement
4	6
5	3
11	4
12	6
14	2
16	0
24	2
25	3
26	7
33	7
34	3
39	7
43	3

Of the 13 movement responses, 5 are weighted "6" or "7." I interpret

---

[8] RORSCHACH, H., *op. cit.*, p. 30; also p. 217 ff.

this as indicating moments of vigorous wish-fulfilling activity. Yet, in 6 of the M, the weighting is "3" or lower, projecting no more than "maintenance of a static position involving balance of whole body . . . small movement of body parts," which, in the Zubin-Young manual,[9] identifies the "3" rating. In one of these, I am actually rating "0," an M with "no movement" (R 16). This apparently self-contradictory category, M with "no movement," is entirely sound. Such status can represent a true Rorschach M psychologically.

It does happen that this one fantasy, R 16, puts the greatest strain on the validity of my interpretation. Since my rating for it is 0, the interpretation would be that Duncan is only blandly experiencing the latent wish he is here communicating. But the stimulus for this response is the "father" figure. And Duncan has "the wind knocked out of him." This aggression against the father is certainly a personally critical wish. Presumably it projects something he feels intensely. This would hardly deserve a zero rating. This is the kind of discrepancy between theme, as reflecting a strenuous feeling, and low energy rating by the Levy scale, which occurs frequently. Another probable instance in the present record is R 24. Hence my general interpretive procedure is as described above (p. 57).

Altogether, in some of his imaginings, Duncan is relatively mild-mannered. These wishes do not strenuously agitate him. Also, he goes to extremes. Clearly, however, we are without lead as to the psychologic significance of the differential ratings. A research need is, therefore, that of quantifying the Rorschach M by the Levy scale, and so establish a frame of reference clinically for differentiating distributions. For the present, I judge the Levy scale information as other than that provided by Rorschach's evaluations. That there are differences in the *amount* of feeling with which each wish experience is charged, is certain. The Levy scale renders the service of providing an experimental approach toward quantifying these differences.

The content in the fantasy. "In this," quoting Rorschach, "we see what the person's life is. *Was gelebt ist.* I am purposely not saying what he experiences, *erlebt,* in order not to foster the impression that the patient is aware of the nature of this experience. M is the compelling, the what and how of one's living."[10] In a paragraph that follows, he states his well known interpretation of M; it "brings to the light of day the essentially unconscious affairs—those that must stand in the closest relation with that which we are in the habit of calling the unconscious."[11]

In the present record, this compelling inner living is projected in: R 4, a

[9] ZUBIN, J. AND YOUNG, K. M., *op. cit.*
[10] RORSCHACH, H., *op. cit.*, p. 219.
[11] *Ibid.*

recreational theme, whimsical, pleasurable. A probable displacement, since this detail, when movement, is almost invariably human.

R 5. Again, highly pleasurable with elation mood trend. The recurrence of the "twins" motif will be noted.

R 11. The happy mood tone continues. Original in content, and autistic; regressive in structure. This is an M from deep personality layers. A question of depersonalizing needs to be raised: who are the people whom the patient is making into ghosts? Also, there is ambivalence in seeing them in the unghostly act of laughing. In this, he is defending against the apprehensive theme; a counterphobic device?

R 12. The test's potential for eliciting personalized themes in very commonplace forms is here demonstrated. The patient introduces original content in a popular structure. His ironic "and neither one's going to win, either," may well be communicating an accurate conviction concerning his own struggle and futility related to frustration thinking, which emerges in the inquiry. The important question is who are the competitors? This is one of the fantasies with a high energy rating. The hypothesis shapes up; the eternal conflict with the parent of the same sex is being projected. R 16 supports this reasoning. Pieces of the puzzle which make up a personality are here being yielded up by the test. How accurately we are putting them together the validating data will tell.

R 14. Relaxation is the central motif; it is a note which the fantasy has already struck repeatedly (R 4, R 5, R 11). It is important to the patient. An easy-going attitude is now Duncan's. It is a clear change as compared with that in the first Rorschach test.

R 16. The "god" theme in the "father" figure. Religions have long associated god with the father. Duncan thus manifests a well known and deeply felt attitude. But his hostility is also all too clear in the caricaturing and in the complete discomfiture of the massive male form (and see above, p. 121).

R 24. An obvious displacing. The question again, who are the latent humans behind the manifest "gorillas?" The only lead from the test technic directly is that these details when seen as humans are males owing to their massive profiles. The content being as unique as it is, the response is a "must" for tracing in the patient.

R 25. The "inquisitive" theme is the original touch and may be the important communication. In "elves" the playful mood continues. The form is a borderline popular, and to that extent this M is a nondifferentiating one.

R 26. Emphasis on the lack of a limb may be the "compelling" (Rorschach) which is coming out of the unconscious. Also, the figures remain asexual. The lead which requires exploring is discussed below. Still cheerful in tone; also, "twin" again. The M is, however, a very common one in form.

R 33. Very original and of especial value in a young male as projecting interest in vigorous athletic efforts. But the support motif is also present; and "getting up on one another" requires investigating.

R 34. A popular and common M. The "old man" is somewhat less frequent than the "witches"; but by no means original. The horn blowing picture is also frequent, but its oral theme cannot be ignored.

R 39. Out and out dream quality, as an M in which the actors are trees; and hence also, animism. Again, the pleasure motif is present. This is one of those flashes from deep sources telling *was gelebt ist*. What it means is a problem for therapist and patient to work out together.

R 43. The specific association is entirely original. Whether any identification is intended in the caricaturing which is the nucleus of this percept, is the psychologic problem. "Pappy Yokum" now being something of a popular character of North American culture, his specific significance to the patient may be minor. Again, the lighter mood dominates.

Two responses not scored M are the "laughing baboons" of R 10 and the "elephants . . . looking at each other" R 35. In both, the activity is of human variety; more so in the "laughing." I do not score M because the associations do not completely exclude Rorschach's criterion of not being "memory reproductions"[12] of activities usual to the animals. Translated into clinical terms, the conviction is lacking that Duncan is here projecting some intimate wish. Should I be in error in scoring these not M, the error has the consequence of disregarding important inner living in both these associations. In the "laughing baboon" it would be a hostile caricaturing, and displacement. The "elephant . . . looking . . . close" may be clue to paranoid trend, also displaced. In an animal whose form is so unlike a human's, the fantasy, if fantasy it be, is a much heavier screening of the personal need; this in turn would be evidence that the innerly absorbed emotion is much more forceful.

A consistent content trend in Duncan's M is an avoidance of the human form or of issues raised by humans. The actors are animals in R 4, 24, and trees in R 39. They are deprived of life in R 11; are suprahuman but still nonhuman in R 16; and not identified as to content in R 12, "figures." This is the term also in R 26. But in it, he amputates the figures, "seem to be short a leg: and arms, each; only one leg and arm, apiece." This is carrying the attitude much further. He is defending against sexuality. But "figure" is asexual. So far, Duncan does not tell whether it is the female or the male as sexual object which he is warding off. R 33 offers a clearer lead: the fantasy of contact with other bodies that would be essentially naked. Gymnastics most frequently denotes male participants, not necessarily, to be sure. But the likelihood now is that it is a homosexual trend which is stirring in Duncan. He is still avoiding the issue, however, in not naming the sex;

---
[12] *Ibid.*, p. 26.

they are "people." Most unique is the comment which immediately follows, "good enough to eat," the implications in which must be sought along more than one path.

Repression of critical needs, in his relations with others, and of the issues raised by these relations, is what the test is here structuring out. The themes are bringing to light personal foci of the conflict, thinking which the ego finds unpalatable. Whatever they are, they are well submerged in the unconscious life. To redirect the energy in them, to sublimate this inner living into outer, satisfying achievements, this is the problem before Duncan's ego. To get Duncan to perceive this objective is the problem now facing his therapist.

I have saved for the last that most troubling response, R 8. The struggle in it is a grave one, "the birds at the same waterhole ... fighting to see who drinks first." The question as to its fantasy structure has already been raised (p. 119). The content, reasoning from general knowledge of psychodynamics, offers strong temptation to call it M. But to do so would be to reason in a circle. To wit, the content communicates unconscious mental life, hence score M, which communicates unconscious mental life. The test must stand on the validity of its technic. Is the response operationally M? Does it obey the rule whereby other associations are scored M? It does not. Should my criterion for M be erroneous and if this response is fantasy it is the more meaningful in the attempt to repress it in animal content. It becomes altogether a dream. As such, it uncovers one of Duncan's acutest repressions. The identity of the antagonists is very important; an even more critical issue is, what is the real stake represented by the "waterhole?"

The opposition trait. The quantitative data for s, white spaces, shows Duncan at just about average. A normal amount of determination is to be expected of him; its significance lies mainly in the direction which his opposition will take, i.e., in its being part of the cluster s with $M > C$. The introversive whole structure tells that the patient is taking a stand as against his own inner world. How determined this attitude is, is measured in the number of the spaces, in their size, and in whether they are the primarily perceived details, or only incidental to a solid detail. Both of Duncan's space responses are to Dds, and secondary to black stimuli. He is now relatively complacent about his fantasies. At the same time, he need not worry about their running away from him in autistic solutions as we saw from the F+/M balance. His grip on reality is too solid. Again, the therapy has effected a more peaceful inner and total condition.

The ego. (a) *The insufficiency.* This is negative, rather than positive. There are a few instances of positive dysfunction, such as distortion of form perception, flight of attention or thinking peculiarities. The losses mainly are, however, those consequent on the constricting defenses. Duncan does not adequately engage in conceptual thinking. From his Z score, we know that he can grasp more larger wholes than he does. The Ap indicates an expectancy of larger conceptual grasp, (W 8 to 9). His score of 4 means that the ego is here suffering a major loss. W is a test finding by which the ego shows self-extension. Duncan heads in the contrary direction.

He does permit himself some perceptual lapses, the personal F— of R 8, 18, 38, 44. The needs of the personality are here the determinants of the inaccuracy. The "owl's head" of R 22 may be an impersonal error; if so, it would indicate a more severe lapse of concentration, and momentary ego-weakness. But see concerning this response below (p. 129). In one instance the patient manifests one serious perceptual disorder. This is in the "colored feathers" of R 23. In this all gray figure, it is color-distortion. This is Duncan's most severe slip in the test record; it occurs in an anxiety-inducing figure. Language use slightly out of context appears once, in R 7. The word "concoct" is more tangential than appropriate. Its use here has the tinge of the verbalist. Motor evidence of the ego's inadequate grip is available in the very much turning of the test cards. This will be noted in Figures I, II, III, IV; and very much in Figures V, VI, VII. It is most notable in anxiety figures. According to examiner's observations, the turning was slow, i.e., of a deliberate systematic variety stemming from a cautious procedure. Yet there is variation in the amount of the turning, i.e., an uneven tempo in going from task to task. It confirms the evidence in the fluctuation of the initial response time. Duncan discloses these ups and downs of inner pressure, of restlessness, which he does not fully master.

Episodically a sterility of thought content prevails: in Figures I, IV, V, VI, in the high percentage of animal and part animal percepts, together with part humans (A, Ad, Hd). These three categories form 75 per cent of the total productivity in the four figures. Rather high, too, is the per cent of animal associations for the record as a whole. The score 42 is near the mean (46.45) of the average adult sample. In view of Duncan's potential for breadth and his superior intellectual grasp (Z) this animal per cent score is discrepantly high. The optimum for him would be between 20 and 30 per cent. A too great readiness to accent and abide by the easiest percept is here projected. In a person showing Duncan's capacity for originality and his imagination, this is extensive impoverishment. He is stereotyped, commonplace, though he can be differentiated, fresh. He is narrowing in his intellectual horizon. He betrays a limiting influence on his selective attention, also in his emphasis on the major detail (D) in Figures I, III and VI through X. This is a price which he is paying for the safety which his defenses are affording him, a functional arrest of ability.

One other present weakness in Duncan is in his perception of himself.

He is devaluating himself. The lead to this trait is the much qualifying of his associations. The behavior usually is found in one cluster with painful moods. Duncan has these. Both mood and devaluation stem from guilt because of which the ego has to abase itself. It is a universal consequence of conflict between standards and deed, or the urge to certain deeds. The treatment needs, of course, to help the patient develop insight on this point.

The ego. (b) *Assets and total present adjustment.* The assets which Duncan's ego could, but only insufficiently does mobilize in the adjustive effort, include his intelligence of a superior caliber and the imaginative life. Proof of his intelligence is his total associational productivity, his facility in grasping relations between the data of his world, and the broad range of ideas which he has absorbed. The imaginative activity, free, even prodigal as he is with it, is only contributory evidence (see above, p. 118). His response total (R), we have seen, now ranks him among the very productive. From Rorschach on, students of the test have observed a relation between quantity of associations and liberated intelligence. Those who give, must have it to give. But they must be free of the binding inhibitions. The significance of Duncan's present score puts him into superior ranking (see above, p. 105). But he also significantly exceeds the most superior subsample in this whole normal population sample. The mean for this highest sub-group, the subexecutives in the normal adult sample is 28.6, SD 15.7. Duncan's R of 48 is thus well among those in the second standard deviation above the mean. As measured by this index he cannot only hold his own among these subexecutives in this large industrial organization, but he can excel the higher two-thirds among these leaders.

In range of themes, Duncan shows himself capable of an intellectual buoyancy. He produces originals which he could have acquired only with active curiosity. They are signs of an interest beyond the limits of the usual routine. He manifests these either directly in the ideas or in the language usage in R 3, 7, 8, 16, 25, 29, 32, 42.

In relation to his world's realities, Duncan does not regard objective stimuli with the fullness observed in the normal range. The low lambda index so shows. He is diverted from his outer world by his excessive response to inner stimuli. The large quantity of fantasy living requisitions by far the largest portion of this response with, however, the exciting and the painful emotions contributing their share. However, when the patient does attend to the real world he construes it accurately at that high level which his caution brings about. At the same time, in the quantitative relation between M, and F+ per cent, he provides assurance against the danger of subsiding into a dereistic daydreaming fantasy. The ego is acting as a check upon the fantasy. As above noted, the patient has his counter-defense against the fantasy withdrawal defense.

One other index to the relations with the outside world is afforded by the seven P, or popular response. At the level of outer, observable behavior, the patient can be adaptive, conventional. He knows what the proper behavior is, and from the entire personality structure, one may conclude that this proper behavior will be forthcoming.

Overlapping with P but not identical in psychologic significance is A per cent. It gauges a person's ability to recognize the most familiar stimuli of his environment. The animal form score within normal range fills in the evidence of adaptive intelligence. As we have seen, Duncan does not rank at the optimum A per cent. His high score reflects a deficit, since A per cent varies inversely as liberated intelligence. This index overlaps again with D or selective attention to the most obvious presentations in our environment. The adaptive, practical person is likely to score within normal range, tending to high, both in D and in per cent A. Duncan does just this.

Within a framework of a tight defense this finding may be foreshadowing an unfavorable development. He will stabilize as an adult into a person resisting change, and one who tries to fit the world into his own established thought and action patterns. This is, of course, a nonadaptive pattern psychologically.

But the affective findings do include a promise that Duncan can be influenced. His responding with some color-toned associations means that he is emotionally resilient. He responds to outside feeling arousing stimuli. One of these is the therapist. When the latter comes in the course of the therapy to take on the significance of a parent, transference is taking place. The color-determined responses become thus, in the language of the test, the raw psychologic ore transmuted into the transference. Duncan has more of this than he uses, since his affective ratio of 0.61 is a normal quantity, but four color-responses is low. The unused amount is reserve, another asset, an emotional one, which he can exploit in his adjustive effort. But its structure at times exposes Duncan to danger of impulsive outbreaks. Against this hazard his protection are the conscious defense, the passive emotional withdrawal and the introversion of his wishes.

Viewed through Rorschach's *Erlebnistypus*, Duncan presents an outside which is quiet, an unruffled surface. The heavy introversive balance conceals the troubling, at times, stormy currents within. At the same time, this experience balance tells that Duncan will cling to his attitudes, his loves and hates, with little wavering. Rorschach devotes many pages in describing the person whose number of M clearly exceeds his sum C. That is, he who is as innerly intense as he is overtly quiet. In the treatment, however, this adjustment becomes a liability. The patient sticks to a position which prevents his gaining insight. The ego may prefer the path of dalliance, fantasy living, to facing the realities about the self. A rich inner world can be a psychologic weapon cutting in the wrong direction. When this is the case, the problem of therapy has its especial difficulties.

The course and the outcome will be decided by that cluster of psychologic activities which is larger than, and different from, any of the personality's component activities. Chief among these is the set of values which the individual holds; and with these, the system of psychologic stresses which go to make him up as a whole; a system such that he can prosecute those values to success or failure as the case may be. But prosecute them he will. This is the ego mobilizing the person as a whole.

It becomes the task of the test to appraise the stamina of the ego in the light of the tasks being imposed on it, by all the stresses that make up the person. That is, some judgment must be risked as to the kind and depth of treatment; and some prediction as to outcome. We return to this, following the scrutiny of associational content so far not inspected. Additional leads to the personal dynamics, as treatment assets, may be here uncovered.

The content. The principal recurring theme is twins, or *two*, whether or not in some relation. This will be found in R 2, 4, 5, 10, 14, 15, 18, 19, 24, 25, 26, 35. Any recurrence of a theme, whether or not unusual, is evidence of personal meaning to the patient. So much as here found can only mean it is preoccupying him very much. It is thinking that requires thorough exploring. Who are the two? Duncan and his mother? Father and mother? Duncan and his sister? And some friend? The answer must be left to the therapeutic sessions to bring to light.

Of sexual ideas, Duncan produces nothing overt. But in R 45 he does verbalize a thinly screened sex association. A frustration motif is added in seeing the one "male" dog as "angry." In displacing the theme on to animals, and finally perceiving the pair as of the same sex, he opens up a lead to a homosexual interest.

His most original elaboration is on a cocoon theme, in R 44. This motif is relatively frequent in growing children. The hypothesis is that it communicates an interest in the young, in the mother and in reproduction.

Another of Duncan's frequently recurring percepts is "eyes" or "looking." Systematic investigation of the significance of eyes in the Rorschach test is still much needed. My interpretation, on empirical grounds, is that it stems from an attitude of alert caution which, under condition of ego regression, can become a suspiciousness on the way to paranoid reaction. The percept is found in R 6, 16, 25, 28, 35 and 41.

Phobic motifs appear in R 2, 6 and 28. Two of these involve oral threatening animals, the "wolves" (R 2) being more common to our culture than the "lion" (R 28). The significance of the "St. Bernard dog," (R 7) here arouses curiosity. It is original. Its connotation is generally benign. Its meaning to Duncan?

Orality of other kinds next arrests our attention. It emerges as a food or drink association found three times, and in much and varied activity in which the mouth is the principal organ. See R 8, 18, 33; R 5, 10, 11, 14, 24, 34, 43. In sheer quantity this theme is exceeded only by the "twins" topic. The oral activities are in these instances of a pleasurable, satisfying quality. The connection with oral dependency is the clue to be passed on to the psychiatrist.

Three associations include content that must communicate personal interests: R 1, 22 and 42. In R 1, the "headless woman" will recall the "beheaded female" of the first Rorschach test. But it is now not an M response; it has lost the intensity of feeling with which the patient formerly charged this image. The effect of the treatment will here be noted. The "owl" of R 22 raises the question of symbolism. This bird does have a symbolic connotation in some cultures and in literature. R 42 calls attention to itself by sheer reason of its originality. But again the test only raises a question here.

Another theme that recurs centers around recreational topics in R 6, 19, and 20. The "dance" appears also as a fantasy association (R 26). The relaxation chord is a frequent one in the fantasy generally. Here, at more conscious level, the patient adds to that evidence. The topics may also be uncovering the specific interests to be exploited and so project an asset directly.

Summarizing the personality which was Duncan's as he was taking this second test, and also as therapy was being terminated:

The ego's functioning shows improvement. The impersonal F− are lacking. The color distortion (Figure VI), a thinking deviation is however something new. The total number of F− is the same; this is a gain in view of the increase in F+. The selective perception (Ap) is better distributed since Duncan now pays attention to the fine points (Dd) which he formerly disregarded. A new finding is the card turning, a motor symptom in which the ego discloses itself as not controlling the inner pressures. Thus, improvement is only variable. The person is still in tension.

A most serious condition was the devaluation of the self with a weakening of the morale. The signs of this are now minimal. The therapy has aided in mobilizing Duncan's self confidence.

The defenses continue, although he has shifted some of his tactics. He now has less recourse to apologetics. Yet, he has hardened his outer armor. The essential finding is the persisting need for defense. The therapy has not yet relieved him of the inner command to maintain an alert guard as against his world.

The quantity of fantasy-dictated responses is higher in the second Rorschach test than in the first, but about the same for the more released entire mental life (R). With relation to color-dictated association, or to externalizing of the feelings, the balance has gone in the direction of the fantasy activity. He is a little more introversive. This has happened too with relation to the regard for accuracy (F+). But this is less serious since Duncan maintains his capacity to see accurately at high level. The essential finding is that, for all the experience of these past three years, he must still withdraw inwardly.

Some fantasy of regressive quality still emerges, both in the structure and in the content (p. 82 ff.). He still uses this talent for daydreaming solutions as necessary. In stance he is now more extensor, a healthy trend. The content shows Duncan now consistently striking notes of relaxation, or of recreational activities. In all, the net effect from the treatment in this important sphere has been favorable.

In respect to externalized emotional life small but decisive changes are detectable. Trends to outburst persist. The most notable change has been in the affective ratio, from .86 to .61. It is now well within normal. The color shock pattern now follows only a moderately improved course. The ego affect balance is still a delicate, easily upset one, but he can reach to his world healthfully (p. 117).

In his total adaption Duncan uses some of his resources more efficiently; but he can be insufficient. Mental life is more released (R); and higher mental processes also function more freely (Z W). But the absolute total of W remains low. His new freedom does not yet enable him to see wholes at his potential. Duncan's attitude toward the world has become less resistant (s). Perhaps this reflects too the complacence projected in the fantasy life. But it also confirms the persistence of the passive-anxious mood; and as evidence of less determination than formerly, it may represent a loss. There is gain however, and it lies in his not so strenuously fighting his innermost self (see p. 111). The therapy has eased the conflict stress; but the question must be asked, has it done so at the expense of softening the starch in his whole personality? The capacity to come close to his everyday world has risen at the strictly conventional level (P). Significant is the increased readiness to find the easy percept (animal per cent), which also fits in with the findings of an intellectually adaptive pattern. Since perception is slightly more accurate, and is sound, the core of the ego continues hard. It has become in fact, too hard for adaptive adjustments (D! Seq.). In this is reflected the incomplete phase at which the therapy had to stop.

The theme, woman, that dominated the first Rorschach test is now notably absent. The sole remnant is the "headless" woman of R 1. Gone are the "witches" and the "fallen cow." Duncan's hostility to his mother is abating. She is not so much on his mind as formerly. But concerning men, new thoughts are emerging both in fantasy and at more conscious level. Also he opens up with new themes, e.g., twins, eyes (see p. 128; also p. 121 ff.). The therapy has liberated interests not previously communicated; interests which may be psychotherapeutic avenues or be critically significant in disclosing pathologic trends hitherto repressed. The treatment experience has taken the force out of the phobic thinking. Nor is there anything in the second Rorschach test record of the painful anatomy or related associations earlier activated. Concerning his erotic trends he still says essentially nothing. The censor remains on duty. On the other hand, he does verbalize certain constructive motifs which can be utilized for his healthful directing. In some of its details, the associational content generally discloses, therefore, very real progress in Duncan toward better mental health. It supports the structural findings. Duncan is more composed and much more ready to face his new and most difficult life test, namely the army service. If he is not much less conflicted than formerly he certainly is more easy in his inner attitudes.

Finally, what about the persistent melancholy undertone? It can only mean that the conflict and the attendant pain are still on. The second Rorshach test shows the stage at which Duncan has arrived. He has made progress, but he is still at some distance from the goal. It discloses an equipment that can understand in an emotional sense, and an ego that can "take it." Could the treatment have been protracted, Duncan would have achieved a fuller understanding. More of that thick mood would have been distilled off.

D. The Clinical Notes

The first two notes of the psychiatrist are revealing of the psychologic drama to unfold.

A bright clean-cut boy. Discusses rationally and calmly the propositions connected with his wish to be separated from his mother; then shows real affect albeit masked when the father and his "desertion" of the family come into the discussion. I talk with him about this, demonstrate it and raise the question as to its cause. I leave with him the thought for germination that his wish to leave home has some affinity to his feelings about his father and the latter's leaving home. He seems to "get" the point. Will return for another interview.

He came twelve days later. The psychiatrist's note:

Feels that we were somewhat off the point last time, that he knows that he was coming to see me for the purpose of deciding what kind of home he should have, while we turned our attention to why he wanted to leave home at all. In my discussion with him today, I was able to show him that the fact that he had a positive relationship with his mother and his father up to a certain age, which then was replaced by the hostile attitudes which he now possesses, signifies that there must be a reason for this change. He has not shaken off his positive attitudes, they are simply submerged. It is the existence of these submerged attitudes which is productive of conflict, which make it necessary to question the real validity of his wish to leave home. At the close of the interview he tells me, after I have expressed my doubts as to whether he is ready to accept the advisability of investigating further, that he is already convinced, that I do not have to convince him of that. Then he raises the question about time, special arrangements so that he will not have to miss homework, etc. These are obvious defenses and I treat them as such. He accepts the next appointment.

That is, as the treatment begins, Duncan has certain wants centering around his home and parents; he also has need to oppose those wants. The lines of conflict are clearly drawn within the psyche of this not yet 16 year old. The history of the events that lead up to treatment follows:

The original referral letters state that patient is in conflict with his mother and requests placement. He is now living with his mother and sister. The parents are divorced and the father remarried. Although the father supports the family he is not in contact with them. The patient's attitude toward placement appears to mingle apathy with urgency. According to the letter, "he indicates no real preference in the matter, wanting only to be placed in the shortest time possible." He accepts the suggestion to discuss the matter with the psychiatrist before placement. He had first talked about it some six months previously, but now has no doubt about this wish. The mother too discussed placement for six months past. The solution had originally been proposed by another psychiatrist.

The mother herself had been a patient in the psychiatric clinic of Michael Reese Hospital because she was "nervous" and showed rigidity in modifying her behavior.

When the father left home both children preferred to remain with the mother. At that time she wanted to place the sister rather than the patient whom she preferred. She was proud of his abilities and performances. He is reported brighter than the sister.

The father openly disliked the boy, was cruel to him; he in turn is hostile to the father. The latter left the home five and a half years prior to Duncan's beginning of the present treatment. The boy's expressed attitude at the time was: he had no father; he was "ashamed" when other children asked who his father is. "My mother is a good mother," but "father doesn't care for us at all."

The sister is three years older. Patient is in the high half of the second grade in high school.

Physical history: a note in the hospital chart when the boy was not quite eleven reads, "mother claims she can't give the child the obesity diet on her present income." This is a clue to a long history of illness. He is subject to colds; there has been a mastoidectomy, left ear. Birth and early developmental history, normal. While obese, he is of normal stature. Genitalia: testes and penis are very small.

The positive physical findings (at age 10½): overweight 33 pounds for his size and age. The teeth need attention. There is a history of hypogonadism in the family. The mother and sister are also obese. Question is raised whether the personality disturbance may be connected with a Froelich syndrome. The pediatric service recommends dental care and special dietetic advice.

The further story in the clinical notes: the mother does not cooperate in providing the recommended diet. Patient is getting the necessary dental care. A note, by the pediatrician, dated seventeen months later, indicates that the boy has been well, grew as expected, held down his weight. The genitalia grew, but there is a varicocele. While the diagnosis is "definitely Froelich type," and "would probably benefit by some glandular therapy" still "there is no evidence of marked hypogenitalism." A month later the BMR is found at the low limit of the normal. Pediatrician's comment: "no glandular therapy recommended." Through the next five months the child's history shows a healthy course. At this time (he is just under 12), "no secondary sexual characters. Moderate girdle fat, genitalia, testes, normal. Teeth pegged." Three months later the pediatrician's check-up note reads, frequent colds. Otherwise developed quite well. Child is big and sturdy, not especially obese. Genitalia good size but no hair. Seems intelligent, nice disposition. Mother seems very antagonistic and unsympathetic. No glandular therapy advised."

This satisfactory physical development is maintained as we see six months later:

Fewer colds. Lost 3½ pounds weight in past six months. Intelligent. Adheres to diet as well as possible. Child is husky and has a large frame. Both his parents are built short and stocky. Pubic and axillary hair beginning to appear. Both testes descended. Penis normal. Left varicocele. Believe obesity is constitutional. No indication for further therapy other than diet. Refer to surgeon for varicocele.

The history reports that "a neighbor boy pulled his (patient's) scrotum when he was 3 years old." After this there had been pain and swelling of the scrotum for a week. Hence surgery is now indicated. But a left otitis is also found, and the boy is referred to ENT. A note in this department reports a temperature of 103 degrees; advises against surgery at present. It is not until eleven months later that we find him about to go through this experience. The mother takes a directing role. She "wants him to be operated now since school is over." He is, in fact, operated within a month; and "feeling well." At this point social service reports that "some plan whereby patient could receive care out of the home is indicated." The mother does not seem able to assume his care after the discharge; this is a situation of long standing. Soon after the patient is referred to psychiatry. The notes of the first two interviews have been reported.

Additional history: up to about the time his father left, and as a small child, Duncan ate well. It was only following one of his illnesses that he became a fussy eater. He has had difficulty with his ears, having them lanced several times. The mother is apprehensive over his health, regarding him as needing constant attention. He is very intelligent, quite sensitive to the home situation and anxious for some change. He resents the constant "hollering" of his mother, the fighting and scratching by his sister and most of all his father's lack of attachment for him. He gets along well at school and it is the worker's impression that in a different home situation he would do very well. The boy points out that he is not happy, he has bad dreams including night terrors, is afraid of being in the house alone, but has no fear of the outdoors.

The patient sleeps on a daybed in the dining room although previously he and his sister occupied separate beds in the same room. He would go into her bed because "he was afraid." Mother raises the question of sex play. His behavior in school has not attracted any attention. His scholastic achievement is reported as good.

Duncan came to psychiatry for the first time about six weeks following the surgery. As seen in the second note the patient was already on the defense against the contact. He agreed to another appointment, but the next three notes, each a week apart, follow the monotonous formula: patient failed . . . patient failed . . . patient failed. Then he came, about half an hour late, for an appointment which the clinic had cancelled. He "thought that maybe it would be okay to see Doctor X." Another appointment was given him and, "patient failed."

The agency takes over at this point, and it is almost exactly a year after the first interview with the psychiatrist that the patient enters on a treatment program in which he comes regularly, once a week, with very occasional longer intervals due to real illness. From this point on, therefore, and for twenty-nine months he is, excepting for the breaks during two summers, under consistent psychotherapy in a total of fifty-eight interviews. The first Rorschach record was obtained one month after the fourth of these treatment sessions.

The psychologic course from this point was as follows:[13]

Convinced now that there was something to our original interviews. I do not allow him to feel that I am fully confident of his convictions. Make it clear to him that I am still keenly aware of his ambivalent feelings about the mother, regarding his assertion that he has no feelings and wants to get out of the home. Tells me that one of the boys at the Home, a European refugee whom I had sent there, had been instrumental in giving insight into the nature of the position and problems, and would like to do something about them. My technic with him is not to commit myself to the notion that would lead him to believe that I am convinced of the finality of his present position. However, I do tell him that I will take up the matter of seeing him placed in a foster home at the present time while we go on with treatment. He accepts another appointment.

Role of B, whom I saw in getting this boy into treatment becomes more and more apparent. Strong identification with this boy who labeled the patient as having an inferiority complex. Unconsciously patient clicked his heels and bowed in the European way B used to do. I called this to his attention and said that he acquired the habit from B. This was after the interview. The interview itself is rather complicated and the exchange evolves in the direction of exposing to some inspection the expecta-

---

[13] In the text I reproduce the psychiatrist's notes verbatim. In the interspersed comments I call attention in passing to relevant behavior (Rorschach and clinical). A fuller comparison will be found below, p. 145.

tion of aggression from me. He feels uneasy under the staring of my eyes and feels compelled to submit to it and not to flinch away from it and his own feelings of antagonism to others. I am able to point out in connection with this, his acquiescent submissiveness to B, his mother and to me.

Continue with difficult work of attempting to get to this boy, who presents such a different picture from the one he did sometime ago when I originally saw him. There is a passive acquiescence which I am unable to get at in any tangible way. I felt it necessary and advisable to obtain a Rorschach on this case.

The clinical findings include, thus, an ambivalent attitude toward the mother. Is the anxiety we see in the Rorschach test a defense against Duncan's attitude toward his mother? Or is it an apprehension as to what will happen to him if he breaks the tie with his one remaining parent? Ample cause for this fear is provided by the acute flare-up in the mother-son conflict. This is now a bitter one, in the open. Thus:

Just as the boy came in, a telephone call arrived for him from his mother. Turned to me to inform me that she wanted an interview with me. Told him that she would have to arrange that with the Clinic Manager. Afterwards in the consulting room he kept saying that I would find that his mother would do nothing but drool, that I would get nowhere with her, etc. I asked him why that was. He implied that he thought she was crazy. Told of having recently been forced to barricade himself in his room against the threat by his mother to kill him with a knife. Felt that she was capable of it, felt that he was capable of killing her at a moment when he was violently angry at her. Went on to indicate other things in the home situation which were pretty much as bad as the above. I asked him why he had in these weeks of conversation with me not brought this up before and his comment was "I didn't think you would be interested in these things." Then I asked him what he thought I would be interested in. He replied, "I thought you were interested in things I didn't know about." I burst into real, as well as technical, laughter at this comment and we discuss the uses of this attitude in really keeping himself away from the important facts.

This comment relative to "keeping himself away from the important facts" provides the key, as will be seen below, to the real nature of patient's fears. According to a note that follows, the mother "has left home, practically deserted him," and the psychiatrist continues:

Today we discuss his excessively objective, unaffected manner of relating himself here to me and discuss its implications for avoiding emotional involvements in the things that really might be concerned in his reasons for coming here. It is still an up-hill climb working against resistances which may be possibly defending this boy against profoundly threatening affects.

How acute the tension, becomes clear the following week:

Mention of his fear brings tears—fear of my touching sore spot. This becomes clear from reference to B who told him I'd said he (B) had a superiority complex. Then tells of father calling on him (not seen since age of 6) at temporary foster home; and he didn't like it—had a superior attitude—ashamed, father thought it was okay. I indicate sore point may be his superior defense versus the realities of his life.

The father here makes his first entry on the stage. The note that follows, concentrated as it is, throws as concentrated a light on the essential structures in Duncan's personality:

Comes with two notebooks, obviously diaries, a copy of homework analyzing *Macbeth* in which he shows cynical acceptance of murder as a human tendency which most humans are too lacking in courage to carry out, a note passed in class cynically referring to the state of the world. Reports again and again that he is not sure that I will understand what is in the diary. Will be glad to explain it to me. All of this in a mirage of confusion of main issues, namely, that he is interposing his views of intellectuality etc. between me and himself as a means of avoiding coming to grips with what he really knows he must come to grips with. In the upshot he leaves the two notebooks with me for further perusal while in the meanwhile he has told me how disappointed he was to see his father last Sunday and how he protested against father's effort to bring him into contact with paternal family (father is remarried). Patient seems to pull back from all of this and from obvious fondness of his father for him, about which I comment to him.

Three facts stand out: the father is fond of the patient; the father has remarried; the patient has recourse to intellectuality as an expedient for avoiding real issues. This same defense is obvious again in:

Immediately brings up the notebooks which he gave me last time which contained snatches of his diary stuck here and there in various school notebooks. Wants to know if I have read them all and of course I have not and I attempt to deal not with the content of the notes but with his use of them as again a kind of a shield and a foil between us by means of which he can deal with me. At several points in the interview I strike a spark in the form of tears when I try to get a little bit closer to this boy's real affects but nothing materializes. I suspect that I shall have to proceed rather cautiously on the basis of the signs presented by the intense necessity to defend himself against his real affects.

At this Duncan fails an appointment. The therapist decides to be provocative and he writes as follows:

Dear Duncan:
    I was not surprised that you absented yourself from your recent appointment with me since I had the feeling when you left the last time that you were quite upset. I think there are very important reasons for this reaction which it would be very important for you to realize the nature of. I believe we may now be in a position to really work toward that result. I am, therefore, enclosing an appointment for your return next Friday and hope that you will find yourself able to keep it.

A week later the treatment is beginning to have its catalytic effect on the hitherto solid and resistive mass presented by the boy. We see too that inferiority feelings form a deep character trait.

Today he starts dangling before me again the promise of his future communicativeness and finally winds up by starting to tell me something and no, maybe he'll tell me next week or the week after. I go into a form of angry outburst against this dangling technic and in the course of the interview, during which he mobilizes the only real feeling I have ever seen in him, demonstrate to me how he has been coyly playing with me, that behind his ("hebephrenic") smile with which he masks all of his circumlocutions has been hiding an attitude of superiority toward me. That his depreciated attitude toward teacher, school, foster parents—toward all sundry— is a part of this same superiority which he exhibits toward me and which he proves to himself by being able to keep the matter at arm's length so successfully for so long. All of this is a defense against some really important feelings of inadequacy *vis a vis* his mother. I remind him how in the very first interviews I had with him a year ago he left the treatment because I fostered his leaving his mother. Somehow this was connected with the relative status of his mother and the father, the latter being among the depreciated ones.

This technic brings results the following week, even though Duncan is not yet willing to come to grips with his real feelings. But he does shed light on the deeper source of the unhappiness, the importance of the father. In that person's absence the home did not have much in it for the son. This is the real basis for the apparent wish to leave the mother:

Apparently the reaction induced last week resulted in sleeplessness and depression; "a maze" as he puts it. He partly expended his depression on a friend whom he now wishes to refer to me for treatment. I discuss with him how by so doing he was avoiding coming to grips with his feelings with me. He wants to know then, "what about feelings"—what is their purpose, what good are they—trying again to enveigle me into an intellectual discussion which I avoid. It is clear enough that he is filibustering and he recognizes this. It develops as the interview progresses that he has the notion that with his father he does not have to put on the "phony" intellectual facade—that his father is natural—maybe his father really loved him while his mother only had "emotion." In response to this I let him read my initial case note to show him the importance of his father in the picture. I say to him, "when your father left there didn't seem to be much left home for you to stay for." His response is, "did my father mean as much as that to me?" He recognizes this as different from the "importance" of his mother. A breach has been made in the narcissistic defense.

In the next interview:

He discusses his better relationship with his father and I agree to advise his placement at the . . . Institute for the sake of freeing him from too intense contacts with personalities whom he tends to depreciate.

After two more psychotherapeutic interviews, treatment is interrupted by illness in the patient. It is resumed a month after his entering the institution.

Looks pale and drawn. Isolated self from the boys at Institute with superior, ivory tower attitude. Has called them "degenerates."
We discuss this need for isolation in terms of fear of measuring himself versus others. He admits fear of physical contact.

The ups and downs of the conflict and the preparing of the patient for insight is the story reported in the interviews following:

Tells of a visit to his father with his two boy friends, C and B. More kindly attitude toward his father. Told his friends in a conversation that he trusted nobody and me least of all. Nevertheless he keeps coming back. Question of distrust of me is discussed with him in terms of the transference implications. It is soon obvious that the attitude is not to be taken at its face value. He looks pale and wan and evidently is undergoing much internal stress.

I should be seeing this boy more often but time does not at the moment permit.

A week later:

Weekly interviews continue with this boy. Coming more and more into the open with evidence to indicate a chronic depression in which he lives. The feeling of isolation from others, etc. Last week he discussed with me problems of masturbation which have evidently been preoccupying him for some time but with which he has just come out. I conducted the interview along informative, reassuring lines which he evidently required at the time.

Two weeks later:

Today he comes in with a cold and obvious depression. In the background is the fact that after seeing me last time he confessed to a girl whom he has been treating as a boy about the masturbation which he had already revealed to me. She gave him a confidence. Then he began to treat her as a girl. Then something happened and things didn't go well. Spoke also of his mother today for the first time, of how he thought that she was nothing but a semi-prostitute. How she used to come out of the bathroom naked to sit between himself and his sister, etc. Looks very badly, etc.

Comment: I am dealing with a very difficult character neurosis with depressive trends in this adolescent boy and there may be complications before it is over.

Three weeks later:

He realizes that I am right about his depressive reactions. Today he realizes something about the nature of his intellectual defense as a means of protecting him and making him feel more secure.

Four weeks later:

He was happy until last Wednesday, happier than he had ever been. Opened the interview by asking whether we were making any progress and I discuss with him how the last three or four interviews seem to have. The bubble of his good feelings was pricked when on Wednesday the teacher commented that those who act snobbish and superior must be sure to remember that there is inadequacy and feeling of inferiority beneath. This touched off again what we had just recently discussed, namely, the feeling that his mother had made him feel worthless. She had depreciated him and we discuss this as basis for how he also had the feeling that I depreciated him and made him feel worthless. Bringing this into the open last week had brought him close to the feeling of resentment which he had against those who made him feel worthless and depreciated. It was this emergence of his resentment which enabled him to feel better, etc. His appointment has been changed to Friday so that he asks if he is going to be encountering his friend, C. I tell him that he will and he says he doesn't like that and I tell him that it will be useful to find out why.

Five weeks later:

Today we discussed his rivalry which comes into the clear about sharing me with another patient, C. Formerly they had different days, now they see each other. Furthermore, I am able to point out his tendency to act out toward one of the supervisors in the home as a displacement from his mother.

There is a four week interval:

Working on the problem of his need to show others that he has a special relationship to me; he himself comes out with the problem of his wish for a special relationship with the mother in connection with this. I discuss with him today the acting out of this attitude in his showing off to C that he sees me in my private office.

A week later:

Today he opens up the interview with a sarcastic comment about my seeing him in my special office as a special privilege again. Comes out that he felt that I saw him last time in the clinic as a punishment for having played his special privilege up to my other patient who is his acquaintance. I indicate to him that this is his own inference. The question of how long he has been coming to me comes up in connection with a discussion of how he has from the beginning sustained an attitude of control in the whole relationship to me. I point out to him that the only time he felt threatened with the loss of control was the time he felt I talked strongly to him about holding out on me so provocatively. At that time he had been extremely frightened. He acknowledged this. Following this there was a pause. Opens with pauses between thoughts as part of his control and then he begins to talk about his mother. She blows hot and cold. How she was the one who drove his father from the house. Wonders if she was the real king-pin in the house. Wonders if he has any positive attitudes towards her, and in response to my acknowledgement that there might be, also accedes to the possibility that some part of his so-called positive attitude may be really expectant attitudes. In connection with the latter, the question of her blowing hot and blowing cold, and of finally disappointment comes up.

I am able to show him how today, after discussing the major type of his defense, he finally is able to bring into the situation something other than his power with me. This was made possible by the fact that he spoke of his mother as not being interested in anything except her own relationship with him and his sister. That she never cared about anything in their lives outside of her relationship with them. I am able to show him that in the transference situation to me he has taken the position toward me that his mother did toward him and his sister in the above respect and he gets the point. It has been a question of tit for tat in which I have been the scapegoat.

There are the beginnings then of a normally pleasurable affective reaching out to the mother.

Three weeks later:

Open spontaneous outburst of talk about making a rebellious gesture (at the Institute and with mother) then afterward unable to enjoy the fruits of his rebellion and feeling guilty and afraid of what would happen. Then becomes silent; needs to think over what he had the impulse to say.

A week later:

Silence continues today. Evidently attempting to provoke me.

This silent resistance persists:

A period of sulking which we discussed in anger. At the end of the period he says maybe he is angry because I told him last week that he felt superior to his friend, whom I also see.

The week following:

Today his sulking continues. Finally I am able to bring out that together with his reaction of anger to my pointing out his feelings of superiority to his friend and co-patient, he reacted to my not permitting him to talk with another patient whom he encountered on the ward outside of my office. He knew this patient from the . . . Institute as a species high-hatting him. Today he encounters the same patient and because she is so much better herself I permit him to talk to her.

A week later uncovers the still disruptive effect of the mother:

Chocolate soda together by psychiatrist and patient. He has felt different ever since I brought up the matter of his feeling superior to C. Tells of being in mother's neighborhood with C last week, and of running pell-mell to avoid an encounter with her when he saw her.

One other note before treatment was suspended for the summer:

Today in this final interview for the season it becomes explicitly clear how much this boy has been chewing over the matter of his relationship to me since it was complicated by sharing it with his friend, C. He spent the period talking entirely of his gradually drifting away from C for various rationalized reasons, knowing only in the end that it had to do with his competitiveness with C in the present relationship.

The story is resumed in September. The first note:

Had a rather successful summer. Enjoyed farm camp very much and speaks depreciatively of city people and city life since his return. Talks about his difficulties with the . . . . Institute anent enforcement of certain training which he does not believe in. I discuss with him his provocative intellectualization attitude on this point.

He fails the next week, but it turns out to have been for legitimate medical reasons. The treatment continues the weeks following:

He came in some minutes late and advised me that he had had to stay away last time because he had been compelled to keep a medical appointment to have a diptheria toxoid injection. Laughed over the fact that the person who had insisted on his keeping his last appointment had said well, after all, the doctor who gives these shots doesn't get paid very much for them and he knew that my time was quite valuable, etc. Nevertheless he seemed to take pleasure in the situation. Spent the time talking about the mutual interacting of himself and C, and I had the occasion to point out to him that no matter what he and C exchange with each other, he will have to realize that each of them comes to me as an individual and not in terms of their mutual acting.

The next week:

More of the narcissistic problem anent his reaction to my being late.

Two weeks later:

Comes in with a dirty face. Speaks of his disillusionment in his father but it turns out that this is a transference disillusionment and that he and his friend who is also in treatment with me seem to be in the midst of working out on each other their transference relationship with me.

Two weeks later:

I am more and more coming around to holding myself out as an ego ideal for this boy. He seems to be taking it.

Two weeks later:

Patient is glum and angry looking and blocks, and is silent. I comment that he looks as if he might be either mad, or sad, or angry. His reply is maybe all of them, and he remains silent again. It finally develops after much activity on my part that he was upset by my referring to the friend whom he told me about last week, in rather ordinary terms, as regards the latter's sexual activity. The patient had commented that this boy looked to him all shot and from what he had on other occasions told me of this boy, I was led to infer that the patient was thinking that his friend was "all shot" because of excessive sexual activity. He had admitted at that time that my guess about his opinion was correct. But the upshot had been disillusionment in me because he had thought that I and others whom he admired were disdainful or scornful of sexuality and here I was talking quite calmly and commonly about it.

Three weeks later:

He has nothing to talk about. Confused by the fact that he has nothing to confuse him at the moment excepting a vague wondering as to what next. Talk with him in terms of this being in a normal state of expectancy for an adolescent, etc., and I broach a prospect of interruption, the exact time to be stated by himself.

A week later:

Today he comes in with definite reactions against my suggested interruption. He points out what I have to admit is an actual mistake on my part, that in my discussion of the need for interruption I placed a value on his intellectualization which I had originally depreciated. I tell him that he has scored a point there. Feels that he is not ready to interrupt as yet and under the circumstances I let him make the decision to continue.

Changes in the patient's relations with the other boy, who has loomed so importantly, now take place. Understanding into the mechanics of his hostility also comes at this time; and with it, the dysphoric mood:

He has continued in the last two interviews with the problem of his relationship to C, from whom he has broken away, and me. And today again it comes out in a short interview, which external pressure has made necessary, that he somehow is diverting his hostile feelings toward me on to C. He told me explicitly that he was waiting to see whether what I had previously said about dealing fairly with each of them was really true. Likely it seems that what he wants to know is whether I am going to side with him or C in their current differences.

Four weeks later:

Depressed. It develops after much work on my part that his gloominess is connected with C. Thinks he ought to quit his job. Thinks even that he ought to quit coming here which I connect with his feeling about his job. Admits finally maybe he feels guilty toward C although he feels relieved not to be subjected to C's moods of criticism. Anger followed by apology.

An interval of four months without treatment, not explained, follows. Then:

Today he comes in and says he is going to quit the treatment and he is going to do this because continuing to come here only serves to remind him about former things that he would rather forget. I suggest that he is finally arriving at the essence of what pyschotherapy means, namely, to be reminded of things that one would rather forget or has forgotten and see their implications. However, he is determined to quit and it develops that this has something to do with the fact that C is going to a farm this summer. To the patient that means that he is losing something that he has gotten out of his last summer's experience on the farm.

I point out to him that the impulse is delusionally determined and has to do with what he is discovering for himself about his self-centeredness. He seems to be dominated by feeling that if C gets anything, no matter what it is, it is something taken away from him (the patient) even though it has never been his. I leave him with this thought, tell him that the hour will be kept open for him for the next two weeks and ask him to call me and let me know what his feeling and decision is.

It is followed (a month later) by:

Today he came in with a long face of guilt, and at first it develops that he feels that he thought I was angry at him. Connected with feelings of guilt because he wants to treat me as if I belong to him in the first place and he didn't want to share me out like a phosphate soda, etc. Finally I asked him when he received the first copy of a magazine, a year's subscription which I gave him as a graduation present. It turns out that he received it the day before yesterday. Before that he received an announcement that he was receiving it as a gift from me. It impressed him like the names of donors to charity which are plastered high wide and handsome all over the . . . . Institute and I burst into laughter. I say that he really didn't feel any guilt at all but only depreciation of me that I was trying to make myself seem big at his expense. I

interrupt the interview at this point and he gets the point. I tell him that I hope some-
day he will be able to say what he really thinks without regard to what others think of
it. This is the last interview for the present. I tell him that I will see him in September.

Once again the treatment is interrupted. Another summer. The next note
is in the fall. The intervals between treatments are now longer (sometimes
two or three weeks, sometimes a month). A series of significant notes:

Upset and going all around Robinson's barn before finally getting to anger because
of last week's cancellation. Will see next week.

Three weeks later:

Today, *a propos* the fact that he mailed C a book of stamps which B left for C
some time ago when he went to the army, and *a propos* C's prompt response to the
cool cover note which the patient had attached to the stamps, we are able to go over
again the matter of arrogance and his contempt for C. It is possible to bring in for
comparison the similar attitudes toward his father who together with C admire and
so ennobled the patient in their eyes; and how his response of contempt to both of them
was conditioned by his incapacity for assuming the obligations of the ability they visit
on him.

Five weeks later:

He has been feeling like "Uncle Harry" for the past two weeks. "Uncle Harry"
refers to a play which he saw some time ago, about a meek, sweet individual who
planned the perfect crime in the murder of his two sisters. I was unable to use his
preoccupation with Uncle Harry to demonstrate to him that on the basis of the plot
of the play, he thinks himself to be sweet and nice like "Uncle Harry." He entertained
some murderous thoughts and for the same reasons, namely that expectations in
attachments were so enormous that they were doomed to disappointment, and being
doomed to disappointment were doomed to producing his own excuses for the murderous anger. I tie this in to the relationship to his mother whom he refused to leave
three years ago when I first pointed out to him the envy of the sister's better relationship to me.

Four weeks later:

Comes in today. Not terminally euphoric but spontaneous and open in his manner.
Tells me that after much inner turmoil he had called C to find that C was not in. He
had thought over his relationship with C and seemed to him that he felt that C was
dependent on him, needed him and rebelled against the possible implications of this
as regards the demands on him. He also told me that he had objected to going to visit
C's friends, the D's one time because, on the other hand, he now realized he had not
wanted to be the orphan in the party. He has not wanted to be the one who was
getting something from C as a hand-out. His relationship to C had been too much
determined by these problems of who got what and who gave what and who needed
what. That no relationship can be sustained on this basis. Had also decided that he
should not only have been able to share what he had with C but he should have been
able to share what C had to share with him.

Tells me of a letter which he received from B in which B treated him curtly after a difference of opinion on political matters in a previous exchange of letters. Had written a long letter in reply to this rebuff, didn't know whether to send this letter or not. He felt that B had no right to expect him to agree with everything for the sake of their relationship; felt that no more than he had expected from B complete agreement with him, no more should B expect differently from the patient. In the end he decides to rewrite the letter so it is not so emotional but to tell B exactly what he thinks. Ends on the note of expressing feeling that relationships have to be mutual, of a give and take attitude on the basis of something which is of mutual interest.

He agrees to take a repeat Rorschach. Asks if he may write me and I agree. I suggest to him that he call me when he receives his orders.

One week later:

The boy called me yesterday to advise me that he had been notified to report for induction on the twentieth of this month. He seemed in good spirits, asked if he could come in to see me again for a final time. Saw him today.

He is buoyant, open in his manner. Says immediately that he doesn't want to talk about the army, has other things to talk about.

He finally reached C on the phone. Tried to convey to C that he wasn't angry, that C wasn't the cause of anything that he felt. "I told him the entire story and would he accept my apologies?" C seemed surprised. He talked at great length to the patient, in fact monopolized a two hour conversation, told the patient that he tried to reach him. "I wanted to tell him just how I felt and I couldn't; he told me what happened to him. He kept talking, couldn't get a word in edgewise. I wanted to say something. When I asked if I could see him, he changed the subject. It happened twice. Said he'd call back. I wasn't sure if he felt obligated because I had called him. Wasn't sure whether he felt he owed me something."

I comment to him that he is not responsible for the way C feels, only responsible for how he feels. The patient says that he was surprised to find out how many interests and activities C had had, how many friends he had. "It made me feel funny." I said to him that perhaps this was a hangover of the old attitude when he thought that C needed him more than he needed C. Patient recognizes this.

The patient wrote a letter to C to supplement the telephone conversation in which he felt he had inadequately expressed himself. "I told him I wasn't doing this because of any obligation to him but because I felt that we could be friends, that we had something in common. Told him that if all he felt toward me was obligation, I wouldn't want to resume our acquaintance." The patient obviously wants to know my opinion of all of this and I tell him that it strikes me that this is all to the good, that he seems to be coming straight with himself. I further said to him that I thought it was important that today he didn't want to talk to me only about himself (and the army) but that he preferred to talk about himself in relation to someone else.

Patient bursts into laughter and says, "I'll have to join the morale division." He asks my advice as to whether he needs to take any further steps with regard to Q and I tell him that it seems to me that it is Q's turn next. Patient says, "that's what I was worried about, whether I had done everything I really ought to do."

Then he goes on to speak of having made friends with a colored boy who worked in the library with him and to say, "the next time I go down on the south side I won't have to fear it as if it were the jungle." This is with reference to the terror with which he found himself overcome when walking through the Negro district some years ago and which he had told me about in the past. I suggest to him that perhaps this pair of thoughts has to do with his recognition of what was the situation in the past when so much of his own fear was the outcome of his own hostility. Now he is friendly and no longer has to be afraid. He gets the point.

He seems to be waiting for something and I tell him about the outcome of the Rorschach examination, that it confirms what he already knew, and what I knew from our experience that there had been a definite inside change. He says, "thank you." And I reply that this really is not an occasion for thanks, that this was he and not me, to which he responds with a simple "okay!" He rises from his chair smiling in a friendly grinning way and with his hand extended and while we are shaking hands he says, "I'll send you a cigar from Tokyo."

This is the denouement. In good spirits, buoyant, and with apparent insight, some of his fears conquered, clinically he has made real progress. It is during this phase that he took the second Rorschach test. Then he left for military service.

E. Test and Clinical Findings in Perspective

The ego against something; Duncan does not know what except that it is painful. This is the set of stresses which make up this adolescent boy's personality as he enters on the treatment. An excessively alert ego is conscious of something unpalatable, struggling against it. The emotion is painful enough to generate depression (p. 75). The related gloom picture dominates the first Rorschach test; is prominent in the second. From the first moment in the first test cards Duncan is impressed by the black (p. 74). He projects the mood structurally (p. 75 ff.). The content repeatedly carries a tone of unhappiness.

Defenses are a major structure in this personality, and the treatment early collides head on with this well established trait. The therapist's questioning and leading start insight germinating in Duncan. Rather, a fear of insight (the second clinical note, p. 131). Duncan resists; he fails appointments. He keeps himself from important facts (p. 135). One effect in the Rorschach test is the discrepantly low quantity of W. Duncan does not want to perceive a whole field. He has the intelligence whereby to do so (Z). But he limits himself in the relations that he grasps.

The ego is fighting also on a second front against the volatile affects. This is clearly portrayed in the test (p. 78 ff.). There is less evidence of this in the clinical notes. The test here has an efficacy which can elude the clinician. A patient is likely to be on his "good behavior" in the interview. The test penetrates this cover. In one clinical note, however, Duncan confirms the finding: anger in which he is capable of killing his mother (p. 135). This is the clue too to Duncan's need for passivity and in part for anxiety. They are necessary to fence him in against this very anger potential. The test cluster is in fact complete: impulsive urges, countered by passivity, held in rigid check by the strong self-control. The painful emotion, as super-ego product, is strengthening the ego in its struggle over the anger. But the ego needs also to defend itself against the pain in the dysphoric mood. This is the other front on which it is fighting. All this derives from the test findings. Clinically, the reported depression provides the necessary proof that the superego is in the fight.

The anxiety as found in the test is bound (p. 116). While the psychiatrist does not so formulate it, his description of Duncan would justify so characterizing it. At no time does he report any panicky onset or other evidence that Duncan is being overwhelmed by fear.

The inferiority feelings reported by the test (p. 86) are amply confirmed by the clinical facts. The physical history is one to have induced such an attitude (obesity, many colds, mastoid operation; p. 132). Small penis and testes (p. 132) are organ inferiority *par excellence*. The psychological story accentuates this need for self-depreciation: placement in an institution of a boy without a home is an acrid pill in his life experience; this is the darkness in his Rorschach test record. His vista associations are perceptions of distance, of smallness, of objective hard to attain. Clinically the inferiority attitude is known by Duncan's symptomatic reactions: his superiority pose toward all and sundry; the other boys are degenerates; returning from the farm he depreciates city folks (p. 140 ff.). The clinical data accent the inferiority trait heavily; for the comparable test findings see p. 116. One important point of disagreement: the clinical notes report the mother as the cause of Duncan's inferiority feelings (p. 137). This is a relation which the test does not detect. The test logic shows the father to be the probable, more unconscious, source both of this feeling in Duncan, and of the boy's depressing mood (p. 97).

The conflicted condition in this patient is too clear, by both technics, to require much comment. The psychiatrist uses the term "internal stress" (p. 138). At one point he is actually alarmed for Duncan (p. 138). The color shocks in both Rorschach tests clearly describe a neurotic structure which, of course, means conflict. The therapist, to be sure, accents the intensity of the conflict and the stresses more. The painful affects are projected in the test although I do not in my report relate them to the conflict as such as fully as the test data warrant.

The fantasy living is profuse in the test; it does not emerge in the clinical notes. But this is strictly a Rorschach test technic. To find it clinically would require specific investigation in school, or in patient's vocation. The history obtained in this case was not such as to bring such abilities to light if Duncan did give behavioral evidence of it. The introversive structure described by the test does, as I interpret the clinical data, appear to be confirmed: an overtly quiet, indrawn boy.

This introversion is in fact, as one reads the clinical notes, a handicap in the therapy. It frequently operates so in other persons. But it need not be an insuperable obstacle. It took this therapist more than three years to bring Duncan where we see him finally. The patient may use the fantasy to withdraw from the therapist and from his own ego. But it also represents assets, ingredients to be exploited in the treatment effort (p. 98). There are of course other assets, especially those in the affective sphere (p. 98), and the reserve strength in the ego (p. 130), which the psychiatrist so effectively utilized in Duncan.

The content. The mother is a dominating figure in the first test (p. 94). She also holds the spotlight in the clinical notes. So far there is agreement. But in the second Rorschach test, she recedes into the background (p. 130). Clinically she receives constant emphasis throughout. My hunch is that the test is anticipating what would ultimately have been emerging clinically. It is its function to do this. Similarly with the many other very original motifs. Duncan produces these not only in the form responses, but also in the fantasy and in the affect-toned associations, i.e., those in which he expresses what he feels and lives most intensely. The test in these is by-passing Duncan's ego. It is projecting as on a screen that which the ego prevents the patient from himself perceiving or communicating to the therapist. Hence they do not yet appear clinically. But they are too individualized not to be significant for this person. Had the therapy continued it is likely their meaning would have emerged.

The extent to which the therapy succeeded in mobilizing Duncan's resources and the integrating them emerges especially in the findings for the second test compared with those in the first (p. 147 ff.). There are smiles all around as he bids adieu to the psychiatrist. He will send a cigar from Tokyo (p. 145). The ending looks like a happy one. It is, in so far as limited treatment can make it such. He feels better, enjoys life more, yet the ego is only a little more sufficient. The conflict is still on, although less tense. Underneath there still courses the melancholy undertone. The structure in the second Rorschach test indicates that the mark left on him emotionally is a lasting one.

CHAPTER IV

ACUTE ANXIETY IN A SUCCESSFUL MAN

A. THE TEST. ANALYSIS IS INDICATED

A successful businessman, Fisher had long been suffering from severe anxiety and related symptoms. At one time they were acute enough to necessitate hospitalization. He obtained no relief and finally presented himself for psychoanalysis. The psychiatrist requested a Rorschach test and this was administered just before the beginning of therapy. Fisher was at this time 35 years old. The test protocol with summary of response scorings follows:

RESPONSE RECORD

Figure I (9″)

1. W F+ A P
   1.0

2. D FY+ An

'Looks as though it could be a bat, Doctor' (W). (Is there anything else?)

'This way here . . . could be an x-ray. This would be lower extremities of a person; this, the leg—and the pelvic bones' (D 4, form and shading).

3. D F+ A, Art

'Could be the eagle of the United States government (W, except D 8).

4. Ds F+ Ge
   3.5

'Could resemble a map of a country with water around it' (D 2; all the white is water).

5. Dd M− H

'This is someone lying (Dd 22, and adjacent) on his stomach; and might be the rectum' (patient does not recall).

6. D F+ Ad

'Claws on a lobster (D 1).

7. Dd F+ Ge
   6.0

'In connection with the map . . . it may be that the dots could be islands and water (Dd 23).

8. D F− Vo

'Anvil in a work-shop (D 8).

9. D F+ Hd

'Could be a face with the nose, and (D 9), and this part here would be a beast—a water buffalo . . . some kind of animal' (could not find).

10. Dd F+ Aq

'Like a shield . . . a crest' (Dd 24).

148

Figure II (5″)

11. D F+ A P

'Looks like two little Scotty dogs (D 1).

12. D F+ Hd, Sex

'A woman with her legs spread out or something' (D 3, form; cheeks, i.e. buttocks only).

13. D F− Hd, Sex

'Head of a penis (D 4)

14. D F+ A

'and also looks like two cows (D 1).

15. D F− Ls

'Also could be two islands (D 1)

16. Ds FV+ Ls
    4.5

'with a lake in the center' (Ds 5, as inland lake).

17. D C.V Na

'Resembles lava coming out of volcano . . . hot' (D 1 . . . color and is like hot earth).

18. Ds F+ Ar

'Could be the dome on top of building—the white (D 3 with Ds 5).

19. D F+ A

'A small animal with head cut off' (D 1, form only; head missing at the upper part).

Figure III (5″)

20. D F+ An

'That looks like something anatomical (D 8; pelvis).

21. D F+ Cg P

'Could be bowtie (D 3, form).

22. D F+ A

'These resemble fowl or something (D 11). Reminds me of the lower extremity—lower anatomy of a human being (D 8).

23. D F+ Hd

'These things could be limbs of a person (D 5) the leg part; and the lower part might be the leg of a fowl or chicken (D 5); this part here—the fowl, when the taxidermist. . . .

24. D C Bl

'The red ink could be blood spots (D 2 and D 3).

25. Dd F− A

'A couple of owls or something (Dd 22, form; and inner Dd are eyes). I guess I got that one, Doctor.'

Figure IV (4″)

26. W F+ A P
    2.0

'Might be a bear rug on a floor.

27. D F+ Hd, Sex   'Could be a vagina (D 3).

28. D F− Ad   'That might be the head of a deer in rear view (D 1).

29. W FY+ A
2.0   'Could also resemble a bat (W; form and shading).

30. D F− Ad   'This would be a mounted deer like in my basement (D 4 are legs of the deer).

31. D Y Art   'These two shades are a drawing in charcoal to show the different shadows.

32. D F+ A   'A polar bear, out from the water; on an icy day (D 2, form; his mouth is open).

33. D F+ Ge   'The eastern coast of the United States—Maine (D 2), Cape Cod, Florida (lateral, including D 4).

34. Dd VF+ Ls   'This part here, you stand on a ridge and see the tops of the mountains in the distance (Dd in lateral).

'Looks like a nanny goat, sitting on his legs, have a rear view (D 1).

35. D F+ A   'Would be an eagle—the wings spread out' (lower half).

Figure V (3″)

36. W F+ A P
1.0   'This definitely looks like a bat (W).

37. D F+ A   'The lower end is a rabbit (D 2).

38. D F+ Ad P   'The legs of a chicken (D 1).

39. D F+ Adx
2.5   'A rabbit, with wings on it.

40. D F− Ad   'These two together would be frog legs (D 10).

41. D YF− Cg   'Also could be a piece of fur, out of something. (W, except D 8, and D 9; form and shading.) That's all I see in this one, doctor.'

Figure VI (6″)

42. D F+ Hh   'This reminds me of a piece of carpet (D 1).

43. D F+ Ay   'The top part is an Indian totem pole.

44. D F+ Na

    'Could be a floating iceberg (D 4; form only); and this part looks like a war-tank or something;

45. D FV+ Ls
    2.5

    'and this, lowlands out in the country and a straight road in the center (D 10),

46. D Y Ls

    'and gravel (Dd 23) piles on each side (D 1, because of shading). Of course it is an ink-blot (and patient is apologetic).

47. D F+ Bt

    'This part reminds me of a cactus (D 6) growing on the road.

48. Dd F+ Ad
49. D F− A
    2.5

    'Whiskers on a cat (Dd 26).
    'Lions rubbing noses or having their nose together (D 4). That's about all I can see in this one, Doctor.'

Figure VII (14″)

50. D F+ Hd, Sex

    'A woman with legs spread apart (D 6).

51. D F− Fd

    'The fore-quarter of a pig, skinned and dressed (D 3).

52. D F+ Ad
53. Ds F+ Ls

    'Cats' tails (D 5).
    'Also reminds me of an island in the ocean (D 3; white is water; and has shape of island).

54. D F− Fd

    'And this could be the hind-quarter of a pig or lamb (D 1; form).

55. Ds F+ Ls

    'The inside could be inland water of the island.

56. D F+ A

    'A Scotty dog with a great big head, ears (D 2; at Dd 28). Quarters of meat (D 1).

57. D Y Cl
    2.5
58. Dd M.V H

    'Some island and clouds behind it. Lots of clouds (D 11; are white).
    'These two look like they could be two people in the distance (Dd 27).

59. D F+ A

    'Animal, a butterfly, could be body, wings (D 4).

60. D F− Ad

    'The head of a baboon, or could be monkey (D 1), nose out.'

Figure VIII (8″)

61. D CF+ An

'That looks like an x-ray, would be the various colors determining, part of the anatomy, that is . . .

62. D F+ An P

'Vertebra, backbone (D 3).

63. D F+ A P

'Head of an animal; an animal, with a rodent's head, beaver, rat (D 1).

64. Dds F− Im
    4.0

'Something with machinery, drill-press coming through it (Dd 29 and Dds 32).

65. Ds F− Hh
    4.0

'A lamp, and the white being the shade of it (D 4 and Ds 3).

66. Dd F− A

'A duck or goose with the head turned the other way (Dd 26).

67. D FC+ Fe, Vo

'This part here reminds me, forms, like we use in the window, make two-tone garments in it (D 2).

68. Dds F− Hd

'Look like teeth (Dds in D 3).

69. D F− Im

'Look like a bow and arrow (D 4).

70. D CF+ Fe

'The top part, a chubby woman's coat (D 7, color and form).

71. D F+ Bt

'A leaf, some sort, of a tree (D 5); the trunk is small and leaf large, a large-leafy tree, doctor. That's about all.'

Figure IX (23″)

72. Dd F+ Adx

'These two—like eyes on an animal of some kind (Dd of D 2).

73. D F+ Adx

'The two things are like legs of a crab (D 7).

74. D M+ H P
    4.5

'A man with a big hat, like in a fable (D 3) as though brownies, blowing, kidding, laughing.

75. Dd F− Im

'Could be a straight saw with a handle on it (Dd 26).

76. Dd F Ad

'Like the head of a bull or cow (Dd of D 1, with Dd of D 2 at junction with D 3).

77. D C Bt

'Could be a big green tree (D 1, color). Looks like a polly's head—a head of a parrot—with beak sticking out.

78. D F— A   'The red part could be a large insect
                           (D 6).

79. D F+ Ad   'This part in here could be an ani-
                           mal's head, could be a cow (D 2).

80. Dd F+ Hd, An   'An x-ray of the fingers, toes (Dd
                           21; form); eyes could be as on the other
                           side.

81. Dds F— An   'Two things, resemble the pelvic
                           bone, (Dd 23, and the holes). Looks
                           like a wood-carving head, of a pre-
                           historic man, an Indian, with nose
                           sticking out (cannot find).

82. D CF+ Bt   'Top of flower, could be orchid (D 6,
                           color, and form). A little character, a
                           little man of kid days (D 3, like Santa
                           Claus, hat—soldiers, blowing; perse-
                           veration of R 74).

83. D C.V Cl   'Could be clouds in the distance
                           (color; upper part of Dd of D 5, look-
                           ing into the horizon).

84. D CF.Y+ Fi, Hh   'Might be gloaming candles—a very
                           soft light (D 5, straight; and the color).

85. D F+ Im   'This part here, a sharp pointed (D
                           5) instrument, could make a hole in a
                           piece of wood.

86. D F+ Hd P   'A prehistoric man with tongue stick-
                           ing out (D 4).

87. D F— Ge   'Seems to be shaped like a country,
                           France (D 1).

88. Dd F— An   'These two things could be sores, per-
                           haps (darker Dd of D 10), as if im-
                           bedded in skin. That's got me on that
                           one.'

Figure X (10")

89. D FY+ An   'This part reminds me of anatomy—
                           could be anatomy with vertebra, back-
                           bone (D 11; form and shading).

90. D F+ A   'Two squirrels (D 8; an object stick-
    4.0   ing out from the head in a bull fight
                           they stick something in to irritate).

91. D F+ Fd, Vo   'A wish bone (D 3); also brass balls

in front of a pawn shop; an ordinary ink blot.

92. D F+ A P   'A scorpion (D 1).

93. D F+ A   'A crab or lobster (D 7).

94. D F− Ge   'Reminds me of an island, in the ocean (D 13) Jamaica could be.

95. D F+ Ad P   'A head, a rabbit (D 5).

96. D F− Hd, Sex   'and these two look like penises (D 4); and

97. Dd F− Ar   'like rounding of stairways as you get to the bottom (lower half of D 4).

98. D F+ An   'Also reminds me of anatomy, the pelvic bone (D 6).

99. D F+ Ad, Rc   'Mounted horns of a ram (D 4).

100. Dd F+ Bt   'Could be roots of a tree (projections from D 1). Animal image the Old Romans used to use, prehistoric men, carved out of rocks.

101. Dd F− Hd   'A finger, real thin, of an ill person (Dd, projecting from D 1).

102. D F+ A, Art   'These two remind me of two lions in front of Art Institute (D 2).

103. D FC+ A, Hh   'Remind me of dog, a little animal, sleeping in front (D 13; form and color) of a fireplace, very colorful I'd say. (Much card turning here.)

104. D CF+ An, Bl   'Could be human flesh, bleeding (D 9).

105. D F+ Fd   'Two pieces of fowl, chicken (D 6). One standing on the other one's head.
4.0   Looks like a spider (D 1, after much covering it).

106. D F− Fe   'Reminds me of combs ladies used to wear (D 10).

107. D C Art   'And they all naturally remind me, of school. Used to have water coloring on a piece of paper (D 2; as in grade school; color).

108. D F+ A, Bt   'Looks like two animals pushing their
4.0   antlers (D 11) against a tree stump.

109. D F− Ay   'Looks like a stick the Indian medicine men used to carry around.

110. D C Na   'Looks like lava, out of a volcano (D 9; color; hot).

111. Dd F+ Adx   'Like part of a snake' (D 4, head of one).

RESPONSE SUMMARY

R total 111

W	4	M	2	H	3	F+	69
D	87 (s, 6)	M.V	1	Hd	11 (Sex 2)	A%	36
Dd	20 (s, 3)	C	4	A	25	P	12
	—	C.V	2	Ad	16 (x 4)	s	9
	111	CF	4	An	9	s%	8
Z	54.5	CF.Y	1	Aq	1	T/IR	8.8
Ap	D Dd!!	FC	2	Ar	2	T/R	21.5
Seq	Moderately	Y	3	Art	2	Af r	0.85
	irregular	YF−	1	Ay	2	L	0.76
		FY	3	Bl	1		
		VF	1	Bt	5		
		FV	2	Cg	2		
		F+	57	Cl	2		
		F−	27	Fd	4		
		F	1	Fe	3		
			—	Fi	1		
			111	Ge	5		
		EB	3/15	Hh	2		
				Im	4		
				Ls	7		
				Na	3		
				Vo	1		
					—		
					111		

INTERPRETATION

An ego insufficiency and a partially successful attempt to compensate. This is the overtly manifest picture which this Rorschach test presents: in the ego's losses and in the defenses. Underneath, the conflict consists of pressure of heterosexual needs forbidden by a stiff ego. The resultant anxiety is deeply centralized, bound. Feelings of inferiority, also deep, aggravate this complex.

The ego's losses. In by far the greatest number of this man's 111 responses the content is very matter-of-fact, ordinary. The bats, dogs, unspecified animals, or parts of animals, an occasional rabbit, an occasional eagle. These most common forms recur; a desert of unexciting percepts. When this patient, Fisher, shows flashes of originality, as he does here and there, these only highlight the aridity of his mental production generally. The extremely high total productivity would also lead to expect a more differentiated set of interests. There is, then, a reduction of intellectual verve, of spontaneity.

A narrowing of the attention is another aspect of this reduction. Fisher sees the concrete, the practical in his field of vision; he also sees the minute. But he has suffered a loss in abstracting capacity. He produces only 4 whole responses; the expectancy is 21. (Normal Ap for R 111 is: W 21; D 79; Dd 11.) So seriously low a finding in a man who gives many signs of an above average intelligence, means that some personality forces are interfering with his conceptual thinking. For the loss in W he compensates by focusing too much on D, with 87 such responses; and even more so, relative to expectancy, on Dd, 20. It may be added that 87 D is a high number in any record. In itself it identifies the person whose perception habitually lights on the immediately important. Fisher's excess attention to the minute is a defensive operation brought on by his neurotic needs, discussed more fully below (p. 159 ff.). In turning to these, the ego betrays its inadequacy not only in the large number Fisher selects, but also in the rarity of some. Such are the Dd in R 34, 76, 88, 100; the outer white spaces in R 4, 53, as well as the smaller white spaces in R 64, 68.

A limitation on the patient's intellectual horizon is apparent also in his perceiving portions where most people see larger wholes. Such is R 3 (an example of Klopfer's cut-off W). In Figure II he never achieves the W, although three times associating to both large black masses in R 11, 14, 15. In R 41 he again restricts himself to a part where a whole is usually included. In the same Figure (V) he manifests acutely the interference with his grasping the larger view. This is in R 37 and R 39. A rabbit form, with wings on (as in a masquerade), to the whole figure, is not uncommon. This man can see the rabbit and he can see the wings. He can add them together. But he does not achieve the W. Another way in which Fisher shows the blinders on his vision is in the x response, and in the numerous trends to x. Examples in R 2, 23, 56, 59, 60, 63, 72, 73, 76, 79, 86, 111.

Behind this perceptual restriction there lies an unwholesome attitude toward the self, an under-evaluation. Fisher shows this in the resignation formulas with which he sometimes terminates his associating—Figures III, V, VI, VIII, IX. In these too the "doctor" title recurs. Here he is addressing himself to the examiner submissively, "I guess I got that one, doctor." This self-uncertainty is reflected also in an occasional redundant or incomplete description, such as that following R 23. More cogently the patient demonstrates this in an apologetic attitude following R 46. The language pattern, however, goes to another extreme: no qualifying at all; or an almost unvarying introductory formula, "looks like," "could be," "resembles," and the like. In this clipped and regular phrase, he is engaging in some of that stiff behavior which we saw in his narrowed content. The much qualifying is one way in which patients show submissive regard for their environment. In turn, this discloses the apprehension and the self-uncertainty. Fisher's more than normal regard for the outside world will be noted again in a quantitative finding, the lambda index (below, p. 177).

Another motor finding betraying the ego's inadequate mastery is the card turning. This does not follow any regular pattern, but appears to come and go in spurts. Here is an unsmooth behavior. Fisher shows this also in the uneven total associational productivity among the ten test cards; a fluctuation of 3.22, compared with mean 1.35 SD 0.89 in the normals, a shifting tempo in the mental life, and evidence of the ebb and flow of feelings. On the other hand, this patient's fluctuation of time for first response (5.67) is well below the average in normals, 23.36; SD, 18.75. He usually follows a routine. But he can be unpredictable; which, as we shall see, is fully confirmed in the emotional sphere (p. 167 ff.).

In his perception of the objective world, Fisher is frequently inaccurate. The number of F— responses, 27, is large. But relative to the large productivity it is not serious. The F+ per cent is within normal range. One quantitative observation throws some light on the cause of his errors. The patient scores 19 of his 27 F— in the four figures that are most traumatic to him: VII, with its "mother" and female genital imagery, and in the three all-color figures (see p. 163; 169). The ego becomes a frail reed under certain emotional stresses.

Also disclosing the influences of the emotions, but of qualitative kind, are the F— which are personal. The following appear safely so judged: the "penis" in R 13; the "head of a deer" in R 28, established by R 30, in which patient perseverates to the deer head theme, and overtly verbalizes the personal significance. R 51 and its probable perseveration in R 54 as food motifs, are presumed to be personal. The setting in which these appear provides additional evidence of inner commotion. R 51 follows the obviously conflictual and evaded percept of a woman in a sexual position. R 54 follows an "island" association, a theme which this patient accents. It stems from a painful mood. Both these inaccuracies are far from norm, disclosing a considerable loosening of the ego's moorings. The "machinery . . . drill press" of R 64 is extremely original and must be of significance unique to the patient, probably symbolic. Similar are the "anvils in a work shop" of R 8, and the "straight saw with handle" of R 75. All of these have in common an apparent interest in a vocation, or possibly avocation, other than Fisher's actual occupation. Whether they tell of some surface dissatisfaction or yearning, or are a lead to some deeper, repressed interest, only the psychoanalytic sessions can establish.

More validated experience is available for judging the F— personal in

R 65 "a lamp," as home memory; the "teeth," R 68; the "bow and arrow"
of R 69. The sex interest is strong enough to disturb accuracy in R 81,
the "pelvic bone," and again in R 96, "the penises." In R 106 the inaccuracy
is considerable as the patient perceives a strictly feminine article of personal
adornment. The "sores" of R 88 is a type of response I have seen only in
very sick neurotics; a distressing disturbance appears to produce this distorted F−. A similar unhappy thought deforms the percept in R 101, "a
finger of an ill person."

The rating "F−, personal" is made with less confidence in the following.
R 15, R 94, "islands" and the isolation topic. There is other evidence in
the test of the sense of isolation, and Fisher here sees details not as others
do, but as his mood dictates. In R 25, 49, 60, personal needs, enough to
blur the contours of the selected stimuli, may be inferred; phobic in R 25;
erotic in 49; caricaturing, hostile in 60. For the personal influence in R 41
see below (p. 181). The "stairways as you get to the bottom" of R 97 is
another of those originals which, on empirical basis, is assumed to stem
out of personal psychologic sources with resulting disregard of the correct
form. One may easily surmise symbolism here. But the proof would have
to be forthcoming from the patient.

F− is impersonal in 5 responses. This is a high finding in a neurosis,
but within the framework of very high productivity, not serious. The departure from norm can be very far in 2 of these, R 40 and R 66. Fisher
loses control here sufficiently to amount to momentary regression. As impersonal disturbance of perception there are declines, even if fleeting, to
what Hughlings Jackson identifies as lower levels of evolution. They show
how badly the ego can be dislodged owing to the man's generally tense
condition. The other 3 associations rated "impersonal" are R 78, 87, and
109. For none of these 5 responses is there any internal evidence in the
Rorschach test indicating a personal cause behind the perceptual distortion.
This record was obtained under strictly "blind" conditions. If there are
any life factors in the patient producing the F−, the test does not disclose
them. The analyst may recognize personal elements in some of these 5
"impersonal" responses. The psychologist evaluating this Rorschach must,
therefore, risk some loss of accuracy; but the risk is necessary in the effort
at objectivity.

In the thinking, Fisher's disturbance is relatively minor. His ego fore-
stalls any serious impairment of this activity. Three instances of perseveration are noted. This behavior betrays the ego's insufficiency in two ways.
One, continuing in the grip of an earlier thought or stimulus, the patient
is unable to respond appropriately to the stimulus at hand. Two, in so
permitting himself to be directed by an earlier thought or stimulus, he
manifests Bleuler's *aboulia*, a weakness in the thought processes, one mak-

ing for suggestibility in patients with less stamina than Fisher has. The perseverations will be found following R 34, the "nanny goat" from the "deer" in R 28; the "pig" R 54, from R 51; following R 82, the "little character" and the rest of the elaboration of R 74.

There is much of the "psychopathology of everyday life" in Fisher: slips in accuracy, forgettings, blocking, fluctuation of attention and of smoothness. These are manifestations, overt in the test's technic, of the tensions within, between opposing forces. Part and parcel of all this are the patient's defenses. To these we now turn.

The defenses. As noted above (p. 156), Fisher's very high number of associations stands in sharp contrast with the commonplace content in so many of them, and with his restricting his attention so much to D and to Dd. The approach to his environmental stimuli should show a more even distribution of attention to W, D, Dd. While his total score in solving difficult intellectual problems is within the range of the superior, he misses too many opportunities to engage in this activity (Z). He should liberate much more fantasy (M). We should look for more "good" originals in his associational content. The inference emerges that the high productivity is an expression not of a liberated, superior intelligence, but that it is a symptom. Fisher has drive, high drive. But it is canalized. It emerges only as obsessive fullness found so regularly in the test in anxious persons. The conjecture is in order that it is also a reaction formation; owing to destructive feelings of inferiority, the patient would like to withdraw intellectually, and does the contrary. The patient is engaged in a counter offensive against his anxiety. The high associational productivity is his effort at undoing it.

The excess attention to the minute has been recognized by many students, beginning with Rorschach himself, as an obsessive-compulsive operation. Current research permits the reasoning that narrowing of the attention to any of the three major variables in the approach type (Ap), is such a defense operation (p. 30).

This is especially so when the patient does this, as Fisher does, in a cluster of high total productivity together with low conceptual thinking (W). The cluster appears to be the Rorschach test counterpart of the isolation defense. The person observes everything, but separates these constituent variables one from the other. He feels the inner command to add everything into the picture which he reports; but he remains at the addition level. He must identify innumerable D and Dd. But the same inexorable command prevents his seeing them in their unitary relationship. Hence Fisher's recurring failures to grasp difficult relations (Z). The next surmise from the test findings to the clinician is that the patient dares not see certain relations.

Emphasis on the small detail is also a displacing mechanism. By concentrating on the minor, he diverts his attention from the important matter.

Support of this reasoning with reference to the present patient is available in the way he distributes his turning to the Dd. Sixteen of his 20 Dd are found in four of the test cards: I, VIII, IX and X. That is, in an anxiety shock, and in three color shock figures. As he becomes agitated, whether by superego threat or by his reaching for some outer pleasure giving stimulus, he attempts to undo the disturbing emotion by displacing the focus of interest on to a peripheral matter.

Outer defenses of armor-like quality are discernible in the test. One indication is in the pattern of F+ response. In each of test Figures I, III, V, VI, the per cent F+ is above the per cent for the record as a whole, which is 69. For these four figures it is: .87, .80, .80, .83. Fisher is approaching the rigidity level in them with only one F− in each. In Figure II, although suffering color shock (see below, p. 168), he maintained form accuracy at .71 or slightly above his general level for the test. Similarly in Figure VII in which anxiety shock is hard (p. 163), F+ remains at test level. Yet he can be vulnerable in the all color cards (p. 169). The vulnerability throws the period of accuracy into high relief. He can keep himself and his grasp on reality under stringent control.

Of character hardening quality is also the impoverished content, a sticking to the mundane, and taking refuge in the familiar. He follows thus old, established habits of mind. These serve as a sanctuary guaranteeing him safety. But at the same time they insulate him from learning the new, and from relaxing into pleasurable living. This conscious state of alert and resultant warping of the character is evident also in other findings. Among these is the excessive qualifying which appears periodically, an occasional redundancy, or precision alternative as in R 23, R 63. Another is his time for first response. His mean for the ten test cards is 8.8 seconds. This compares with 27.98 which is the mean of the means for the first response for all ten cards scored by our normal adult sample.[1] As to the meaning of very fast time per first response in adults, we do not have validated information. That it is a coverup for apprehension is likely. The surmise is in order, further, that it represents the consciously "efficient" behavior of the

---

[1] BECK, S. J., RABIN, A. I., THIESSEN, W. G., MOLISH, H. B. AND THETFORD, W. N.: The normal personality as projected in the Rorschach test. J. Psychol. **30**: 241–298, 1950. See p. 273 of this report for the table showing means, standard deviations, and ranges of first response times in the ten figures as found in the normal sample. In this study it was deemed not advisable to lump together all the first response times for all members of this population sample and obtain one average. I obtained the figure 27.98 by simply adding the means for the ten test cards and dividing by 10. The mean of these means is a usable sphere of reference by which to judge the average first response time in any one patient. A comparison of the time per first response in any one card in our patient, with the standard deviations, and the ranges in the normal sample will show that this patient is always among the fastest.

"man of action." In a person suffering (as we shall see below, p. 166 ff.) as much as Fisher does from feelings of inferiority, the high speed of response may well be a reaction formation defense, more than overcoming the drag which inferiority feelings effect.

Inspection of the response summary will show that Fisher sees parts of the human body much more frequently than he sees the entire as evidenced by Hd, 11; H, 3. While some of these body part associations disclose an overt sexual interest, the relatively very large number of them raises the question of a displacing of the anxiety on to them. This is a lead which would require following through clinically. The displacing defense appears with more certainty in a number of other associations, although again as leads only, requiring confirmation. These are: R 14, 76, 79; a "cow" for a human female, and the suggestion of uncomplimentary reference, screened. The uncertainty as to sex, "bull or cow" (R 76), supports the conjecture that some sexual significance is present. In the "lions rubbing noses" the surmise of erotic interest has been noted (p. 158). In R 71 "a tree, the trunk is small," while displacing may be inferred, a deeper symbolism is more likely. The defense by way of symbolism is to be considered also in R 64, "the drill press"; in R 85, the "sharp pointed instrument"; the "ram's horns" in R 99; the "dome on top of the building" in R 18; and the "stairways" of R 97.

Certain other defense mechanisms are in evidence. Fisher frequently evades or avoids certain themes, usually sexual. Such is the circumlocution in R 2 and in R 20 much perseverated following R 22. The verbalist evasion is especially notable in the latter; the association is called out by a detail frequently seen as pelvis, sometimes as pubis. The detail calling out R 2 is most commonly seen as a buxom, maternal woman. Fisher avoids this same theme by a similar device in R 81 and 98. In R 12 he admits the sexual interest to consciousness; but here too he suppresses the interest in the anus, speaking of it only in the inquiry, and evasively, "the cheeks." In another association, R 5, the "rectum" appears especially critical since the patient blocks on it altogether in the inquiry; he does not recall it. He forgets another response, on the face of it less significant, the "beast"; following R 9. This does have in it the element of the phobic. The forgetting would, therefore, be another defense tactic against the fear. A defense against the pain in the defense.

Among other tactics, the "baboon" of R 60 in response to the usually somewhat aging female profile detail, has the caricature savor with the related hostility which would center around a woman. In a perseveration following R 82, of R 74, he makes the man "a little character . . . a little man," and also unreal, "as though brownies." The problem is whether this is depersonalizing. The identification of this type of defense in the Rorschach test is still on a very tentative basis. Fisher apparently associates to his own vocation in R 67, and possibly again in R 70. Responses specifically recalling one's occupation are more rare than one might expect (except for the anatomical diagrams seen by physicians). To the extent that he is recalling his own, this patient is manifesting some of his character hardening defense, the clinging to fixed habits. One other manifestation of his urge toward thoroughness is the much turning of test cards. He does this periodically and systematically in a cautious inspection of the presented objects with which he must deal.

One kind of defense which this patient does not use is withdrawal into fantasy. However he may insulate himself from the outside world, he does not retreat into autistic living. The number of his fantasy dictated associations is small by any standard; hence especially so in the light of his very high productivity. So restricted an expression of wishful living in itself points to a defense against bringing these very wishes to the light of day. This side of Fisher's character is discussed more fully below in the exposition of his fantasy life.

The anxiety. The first figure generates initial shock. Sequence is irregular; the approach accents the statistically infrequent detail; the time for first response is one of the three slow ones. In Figures IV and V the anxiety shock is reflected only in the heightened percentage of animal associations. This goes to 60 in Figure IV, and to 83 in Figure V. It is a sterility of content at the level of mental deficiency. But this man is anything but mentally defective. The threat which these massive blacks set up induce a momentary dullness. Although functional, it results in the same poverty of thought that we see in those of very low intelligence. This pattern is itself a defense against the painful quality in the anxiety. The patient permits himself to recognize only the most familiar forms. He sets up his wall against that wide world represented by differentiated content. At the same time, and even more important, he shuts off any intimately threatening thoughts. These thoughts relate to the father and caution the ego; so much follows from the reaction to Figure IV.

The lowered productivity in Figure V is evidence of the aggravating of the anxiety. The ego is insufficiently resilient under its shocks and withdraws intellectually. In Figures VI and VII the trends are mixed. In VI, the content broadens with what is for this patient originality. He increases his productivity in VI, and this accelerates in VII. So far, the conclusion is in order that the ego can liberate itself from the anxiety's deleterious influence. Fisher can and does counter attack. He has backbone.

However, both in Figures VI and VII he fails to associate with the P response. This loss in conventional intellectual reaction is the more striking in a man who, for his record as a whole, goes to excess in these percepts. His total of 12 P is significantly above the usual P score of 7 or 8, so found irrespective of total productivity. Any anxiety shock in Figure VI raises the question as to what has been the role of the phallic formed D 2. In a male the next question is to what extent has this detail activated his latent homosexuality? And how much is the anxiety the ego's defense against the socially unapproved desire? Yet, except for his failing in the P association, Fisher's showing in Figure VI is relatively strong. Unless confirmed by further evidence in the test this lead as to homosexuality can only be held in reserve.

The structural unsettlement is more extensive in VII, the figure with the two clear-cut adult women's profiles, and in the lower center, the equally clear female genital, sometimes seen as anus and buttocks. Time for first response is the slowest so far, and except for the color-shocking Figure IX, the slowest for the ten test cards. Fisher's first percept in this figure is crudely heterosexual, with avoidance. "A woman with legs spread apart." The reasoning is in order that he sees the vulva and anxiety sets in. Also it keeps him agitated in the rest of the figure. His second association, R 51, is a far departure from accuracy; the content in it, food, is regressive. He reiterates this theme three times, and in at least one instance (following R 56) this is a perseveration, i.e., it blocks more appropriate perception. The F+ per cent breaks as compared with the findings in the four test figures immediately preceding.

The anxiety in VII sets going a disruptive reaction from which the patient recovers only in the final test figure. The structural determinant in one of the associations is an unmixed shading response, Y; and the patient dwells on the threat motif, "clouds behind it. Lots of clouds" (R 57). Bound in with this association is an isolation theme which appears twice more in this figure, R 53 and R 55. Finally, the failure of the P association is most noteworthy. In VII the P rating is earned by the one seen as human face, almost always a woman's. It is probably (statistics not available) the first detail selected by most persons. Fisher does not select it until after he has given four other responses. The conclusion is warranted that he avoids the one, a selective avoidance.[2] When he does see meaning in this detail, it is the erroneous percept, and unique "hindquarter of a pig." He returns to the detail again, after five intervening responses, and this time he sees "the head of a baboon . . . or monkey." It is clear that he either (a) avoids this woman's profile; or (b) he sees it one time as meat (food) and the other time as an animal in which the human is caricatured. In the latter there is a displacing of hostility on to an animal form. The former appears to be too many steps away from indicating the true significance to the patient, and no interpretation can be hazarded from the Rorschach test alone.

The evidence builds up that Figure VII is a key figure in setting off the

---

[2] The subject of selective perception, and its complement, selective avoidance, have been separately studied by MOLISH, H. B., *loc. cit.*

anxiety and the consequent neurosis. This centers in the vulva. Whether
the other three valences in this test figure, women generally, the mother,
the security need, are also operative in this neurosis, and how much, is a
question which at this stage can only be asked. The effectiveness of the
anxiety in this figure, its mastery over the man after he has so long kept
his defensive armor whole, point to the convergence of more than one need
especially since these are so inter-related. This much is certain from the
Rorschach test associations: (a) the patient perceives a vagina-formed detail; (b) he consciously recognizes the female genital but avoids naming it
openly (R 50); (c) anxiety develops and is very disturbing. It follows that
(d) the ego is alerted to something which the patient senses as a danger;
from this it follows that (e) he is motivated by some value prohibiting his
attraction to the vagina. In brief, he wants the vagina, fears for himself
because he wants it, and had repressed the wish. This is the anxiety setup.
The ink blot detail is recall stimulus which sets the psychologic cluster in
motion.

Is the anxiety free or bound? The fact is, as found in the Rorschach test,
that no one's anxiety is all free, or all bound. One or the other of these
patterns is more prominent with elements of the other usually detectable.
In the present test record we find a cluster consisting of high total productivity, high quantity of Dd, and relatively less Z. By "seeing everything"
(the high associational total) in the objective stimuli presented to him, he
is restraining his own apprehensive thinking from coming to consciousness.
To the extent that he accents the minute (Dd) and misses significant relations (Z), he is avoiding the essential. In this way he binds his anxiety. The
cluster is such as is found in persons with obsessive-compulsive thinking.
Evidence for a bound anxiety is the fact too that in none of the gray-black
test figures is the shock violently sudden. Rather he shows, as we have seen,
a disposition toward bringing psychological defenses into play. However,
the initial onslaught of the test jars the defenses (Figure I). Distinctly
female imagery, as we have just seen, disrupts them completely. We will
see too that startling events from the outside also disrupt them. That is,
given enough emotional pressure, the binding liquefies; the anxiety is liberated. One other set of structural findings points to a free anxiety. This is
the large number of Y and V dictated associations. The former is essence
of a mood factor, i.e., of one effect which follows from it.

The mood. The evidence for discomforting, painful mood experience is:
Fisher early utilizes diffuse shading in determining an association (R 2); he
does not fail to utilize it in any of the shaded cards; and he is even impressed
by it twice in color cards (IX, X). The nuances in these determinants show
heavy saturation by the shading element, three pure Y responses, one YF
and three FY. In addition, one blend. This is disproportionately high em-

phasis on the Y element rather than the F; on the mood influence, rather than the form perception. Normal expectancy, when the Y response occurs at all, is for absence of the unmodulated Y association, and for emphasis on, or restriction to FY. The patient's total of Y associations is very high, eight. Normal adult mean is 1.96; SD 2.22. In the blend, with a color determinant (R 84), he projects a mixed emotion, that fusion of the happy and the sad, which structurally is intense. In sum, Fisher is very sensitive to the apprehension and discomfort activating stimuli, readily reacts to them, and is strongly moved when he does.

Content converges with structure at one point in this record to give a lead to the source of this troubled mood. This is the series of associations in R 44, R 45, R 46: a floating iceberg, lowlands out in the country, gravel piles. The motifs of the cold and the lonesome will be recognized; the significance of the "gravel piles" is not known. The structure begins with a simple F+ response (R 44); here the patient appears able to defend against the sensitivity to the shading, since the kind of scene he sees is frequent and almost always as a reflection. But the structure immediately progresses to a vista (R 45), a sub-group among the shading determined associations, and it culminates in the indefinite, formless shading of R 46. He follows immediately with an apologetic afterthought which is essentially a denial of the preceding associations: "Of course it is an ink blot."

The isolation theme is present again in R 57, also a formless Y. A threat chord (clouds) is added in. Content in the other gray-black associations: R 2, avoiding a woman's form and the related sexual interest betray the apprehension on this point. The shading which helps the patient see a "bat" in R 29 is usually not a determinant for this percept in Figure IV, and the suggestion of the phobic is raised. The art percept in R 31 may be a pleasurable response; but the formless "charcoal" tone and the verbalized "shadows" uncover a dysphoric quality mingling in with the pleasurable. This pleasure-pain blend stands out sharply in R 84, the response which finds Fisher using both color and shading, and in the "gloaming candles . . . a very soft light," this patient is actually permitting himself a romantic moment, one such as might be aroused by Schumann's *Träumerei*. But it is a moment in which the dominant state of mind is one of passivity. In the final Y determined response, the topic is one related to concern with health, "anatomy" (R 89).

Passivity is implicit in all these mood findings. Such is the empirically observed significance of the gray-black determinant. It tells a story which is the exact opposite of that told by the color determinants. The latter characterizes the out-reaching individual; the Y response, the contracting-withdrawing one. The considerable qualifying in which Fisher engages reflects a self-doubting which is sharp in the apology in Figure VI. These verbal expressions support the structural evidence for passivity. The next, and essential question is why does this man's adaptive struggle dictate his having recourse to passivity? The answer may be forthcoming in the synoptic evaluation of the personality as a whole.

The inferiority feelings. These are a major dynamic in Fisher's neurosis. They are one source of the painful mood experience which they certainly aggravate, as they do also the anxiety. The quantity of responses stemming from inferiority feelings is high, 6, and compares with a normal adult mean of 1.84; SD 2.05. The high productivity in the whole record need not be considered in evaluating the V variable, since it is found independent of associational total. This productive total in Fisher is not only very high by any standard, but also discrepantly so for the quality of his record. It is itself thus, in part, a compensation for the feelings of inferiority.

The nuances of these feelings: in the two of the responses, R 17 and R 83, the V is uninfluenced by an F. The inferiority feeling is all-mastering, enough so to shut out any regard for form, i.e., any stabilizing by the intellect. In another, R 34, the scoring is VF; the inferiority feeling dominates over the intellectual factor. In R 17 and R 83 the vista determinant blends with a primitively strong feeling (C.V), and in R 58 it does this with a fantasy association (M.V).

The content in the vista-dictated responses, i.e., the thinking in Fisher related to the sense of inferiority: R 16, isolation; R 17, "volcano . . . hot" communicates a complex of factors not to be unraveled without more associating from the patient. There is, however, a height element present also. R 18 cannot here be scored V. But inquiry concerning the "top of a building" association, which is a frequent one, has led to the general conclusion that this is a vista response. Rorschach has published its significance as stemming from the sense of inner incompletion. The relation of R 45 to the sense of the lonesome in Fisher has already been discussed, above (p. 165). The "straight road in the center" is a fairly frequent percept here as is also the "country" motif. But, as above noted, the association is one of a series, with some original content of which the meaning to the patient is not now known.

It is the distance theme which most recurs, with the indication that a sense of being far from something is deeply troubling to Fisher. This motif appears in R 34, complicated by the difficulty note, "you stand on a ridge, and see the tops of the mountains . . . in the distance." In R 58 the "two people in the distance" directly communicates some important personal dynamism, involving as it does, thinking about humans. The Dd and the M show further how important this association is to this man, since other psychologic forces (the selective attention to a small portion of the ink blot, and the use of fantasy) converge with inferiority feeling in producing it.

The "clouds in the distance . . . looking into the horizon" (R 83), is one of those blends in which the consciousness of the far away is intensified by excitement (C.V) and thereby made the more painful.

Much unrest is to be inferred from this considerable quantity of inferiority feeling, and its intensity. Together with the high quantity of dysphoric mood, it becomes a distressing restlessness. The total number of associations determined in part by Y or V is fourteen. This is very high. We will see below (p. 178) that Fisher goes beyond normal range in blocking out internal stimuli. But he cannot block out the internal responses represented by Y and by V. It follows that the inferiority feelings contribute to and deepen the pain in the anxiety. It is as though the inferiority feelings are saying to him, "you are too inadequate to deserve the satisfactions which you crave." At the same time it is these very cravings, repressed by the ego, which are the starting point for the anxiety. The inferiority feelings can only embitter this already dour emotion.

The externalized feelings. This man possesses the raw psychologic material wherewith to live out strong emotions. His thirteen color determined responses is high enough to be converted into excitement, and even moments of elation. The affective ratio of 0.85 is more than one SD beyond the normal range (mean 0.60; SD 0.19). He is responsive thus to stimuli that arouse the feelings, and can be carried away by them in gratifying living. There is potential in him for cheerful, self-satisfying experience. Yet in none of the color cards does he verbalize any pleasure in their exciting tones. Persons with elation trends do. He betrays thus a constraint on his cheer potential, one laid on him by the apprehensive mood. Yet the pressure of the feelings is only too apparent, and not only in the color-determined associations. Such is his very fast time per first response, 8.8 seconds (see above, p. 160). This average of 8.8 seconds is for all ten figures. If we eliminate the time per first response in Figures VII and IX, his two shock figures, the average for the remaining eight is 6.37, extremely fast, and disclosing the urge to respond immediately on being presented with the stimulus. The high productivity is another sign of the push within, and we will see in some of the content what are the personal desires behind this push. The card turning is a motor emergence of this drive.

The powerful quality of Fisher's emotions is projected in the nuances of the color associations. Out of the 13, 11 are scored either C, or CF. For the normal adult example, the mean pure C score, with blends, is 0.60, SD 0.92. Vigorous feelings dominate him. Sudden, momentarily unmastered explosions. Of the 11, 6 are pure C, unmodulated by any form element. Emotions of primitive force, undisciplined by appreciation of the world's values are in the saddle. The ego does not here participate.

When the ego does take a hand in any ego-affect trait cluster, in the

majority of instances it exerts less control than do the affects. This is the
structural significance of the 5 CF (normal mean 1.44; SD 1.77); typically
the growing child's stage of emotional development, when he is already
much acquainted with a world's realities, but still responds more freely to
his feelings. In an adult they are the hypersensitive, testy, labile character
traits. Quick, impetuous, irritable reactions are to be expected.

To a smaller degree Fisher does subject his affects to the judgments
of the ego and live with regard for others. He does respond with FC. But
he does so only two times in all his color determined (normal mean, 1.36;
SD 1.21) associations. Only seldom does he really appreciate the other
person's point of view with his emotions. In the majority of instances, his
character requires gratifications of the quality enjoyed by the young child,
and even the infant. In respect to certain enjoyments he has remained
fixated entirely at a very young level.

The ascendance of the affects within the framework of a defense system
which is being well maintained, makes up the neurotic condition. The identifying Rorschach test feature of the neurotic reaction pattern is color
shock. In Figure II the patient is vulnerable to feelings, both exciting and
dysphoric.

In the C.V association neither of the indicated emotions is diluted by
form perception. On the other hand, as a blend, each aggravates the basic
quality of the other: the excitement in the C is intensified; the discomfort
in the V is deepened. One more C.V association, and probably a third (see
p. 166 ff.), is a high quantity, even for the entire test record. The shock has
agitated out some unsatisfying feelings of inferiority. Two crude sex responses, one of which is especially redolent of a fixated interest, are more
evidence of the relaxing controls. Intellectually, however, he maintains his
guard: F+ per cent is near that in the record as a whole; and approach is
rigid, exclusively D. The two Hd with H lacking, also betray ego stiffness,
especially in a figure which so frequently stimulates whole human percepts.
They are a limitation on the perceptual horizon. The ego's losses, resultant
from the shock, show up not as disruption of control, but as its tightening
up with consequent impoverishment.

The destructive consequences to the intellectual life are carried further
in Figure III. Grasp of difficult relations (Z) is reduced to zero; this is the
only test card in which this ability fails the patient. Productivity declines
sharply. Continued powerful affective force is apparent in the undiluted
C response. Yet again there is no disruption. Selective perception in fact
now becomes more adaptive (Ap employs both D and Dd) and conscious
attention to accuracy goes up. The effect of the color shock thus persists.

Fisher continues on the alert. The whole reaction pattern to the figure still discloses an ego insufficiency, that term by which Fenichel so aptly characterizes the condition central to both psychosis and neurosis.

The neurotic shock sets in drastically in Figure VIII. The two Rorschach test indexes most sensitive to disturbances in the intellect's calm are sequence and F+ per cent, orderliness of procedure, and accuracy in perception. In Figure VIII sequence becomes notably irregular. Per cent F+ breaks to .37, significantly below the findings for the record as a whole, and for any one other of the test cards. The sudden presenting of the multicolored stimulus and the excitement it induces, has for the moment broken through the defenses. Two of the F−, R 66 and R 69, are very far from norm, very erratic perception.

The force of the shock accelerates in Figure IX. Time for first response is the patient's slowest, notably out of line with his time in any of the other test figures, and nearly three times as slow as the average for the ten figures. Sequence approaches the "confused" category. Fisher actually attends first to a Dd, a rare finding, and he intersperses Dd unpredictably with his D percepts. As one consequence, the approach shows an imbalance of attention to Dd. The six time selection of rare details is the highest for any of the ten test cards. Three of these are extremely rare, R 72, 76, 88. Either blocking or impersonal overcoming by the affects is to be observed twice: regarding the "polly's head . . . with beak sticking out," following R 77; and the "wood carving . . . prehistoric man . . . nose sticking out" following R 81. The patient was unable to find either of these in the inquiry. Emotions continue to be powerful structurally: two CF and two pure C, of which one is again a C.V blend (see above concerning this blend in Figure II). The content includes "an x-ray" (R 80), unique for this figure; it uncovers anxiety thinking and this goes to the point of the pathological in R 88, "sores . . . as if imbedded in the skin." The color shock in Figure IX is thus deeply unsettling. Given a sufficiently disquieting stimulus, Fisher's ego can become badly dislodged for all its armor-like defenses.

The shock effect subsides in Figure X. In this recovery Fisher nicely follows the pattern used by those neurotics, including "sick" neurotics, who, however serious their discomfiture, possess a stabilizing reserve. The ego regains its balance. This is one finding which makes them a better treatment gamble. The recovery by the present patient in Figure X is apparent in his time for the first reponse now at just about the speed of his average for the ten figures; in the shifting of the sequence back to the "irregular" level, and a notable improvement therefore as compared with the disorderly method in Figure IX; and in the shift in relative attention to major and minor detail (Ap) toward a more normal quantitative balance. The selected

Dd are not as minute as those in which the patient fixes in Figure IX. Some are still more rare than those found within normal range, in R 97, and R 101. Retreat from the emotional surgings set going by Figure IX is noted in the relatively smaller quantity of color determined responses in X; 4 out of 17 in Figure IX; 4 out of 23 in Figure X. But the structure of the color associations in Figure X does not warrant the conclusion that there has been much quieting of the affectivity. Two pure C, one CF and one FC can only mean a little less emotional reactivity. The recovery is not complete. The direction of the personality is still subject to non-ego forces. Hence also the two more than normal rare details which claim his attention; the defensive belittling of the figure following R 91, "an ordinary ink blot"; and starting the associations to this figure with "anatomy" content and with shading determinant, the latter being very rare in a color figure. The uneasiness and the shakiness are still on. They are not serious, the F+ per cent in this figure being within normal range. Yet he does score 16 of his 27 F− in the three color figures. They are the most traumatic to him.

High productivity comes to 40 responses in Figures IX and X. Even after allowing for the stimulating value of the color, this is a very high quantity. Increase of productivity frequently takes place under shock conditions. It is an over-reaction defense. Fisher is talking much and hard to cover up his excitement.

Two other sets of findings highlight the color shock. One is the distribution of the Dd. Of the 20 rare details in this record, 13 are found in Figures VIII, IX, X. The excess emphasis on the niceties and on the finer details of life do not form Fisher's everyday approach. It takes shock to shake Fisher loose from the hard and fast riveting of his attention on to the most essential and the practical. His character is primarily that of a D person. The other finding is the distribution of the white spaces, s. Six of the 9 white spaces selections are in figures with color in them: II, VIII, IX. Of the other 3 space responses, 2 are in Figure VII which very much agitates this man, and the other one is in Figure I. The white space being the index to the opposition-aggression trait, we see here the arousing potency of shock and especially color. Yet there are no such responses in X. Fisher has let down in his readiness for aggression, the neurotic shock having subsided.

Concerning content in the affect-dictated associations, Rorschach makes the point that it stems out of the deepest, unconscious needs of the personality. I quote at length. I want only to emphasize first that a reading of this paper, and of the *Psychodiagnostik* on the determinants color and movement, C and M, makes the following clear: that although C is index to an emotional press outward, it is inextricably woven into a wish within; and that although M reports some wish within, it is as inextricably bound with some powerful feeling which at one time pressed for externalizing, but could not achieve this. The factor of strong affect, deeply involving the person is common to both C and M. The passage from Rorschach-Oberholzer follows:[3]

> If someone produces a considerable series of true color responses and therefore evidence of impulsive affects; and if, as content in these responses fire and blood are constantly recurring, then we must agree that within his personality strong feelings are related to fire and blood, and that fire and blood have some relation with his strong affects. It makes a difference, too, whether one sees the red spot on a test card as an open wound, or sees it as rose leaves, a bit of syrup, or a slice of ham. But the question as to how much the content of such association resides in the conscious, how much in the unconscious can only be determined in the individual and appropriate cases. Such a case is the politician already mentioned, a builder of worlds. Ever and again he associated concerning chaos, the interior of the earth, with color determinants. For movement responses he reproduced "giant gods." We concluded he himself wants to rebuild the earth anew. Yet this is only the manifest content. The latent significance is something else. For, his gigantic gods appear in an extraordinary posture: the indicated movement results in their simulating the foetal position. Accordingly the interior of the earth can signify something quite different, perhaps the womb. This is to say that the color responses reach far more deeply into the personality complexes that may at first appear. It is to say that the self-centered, feeling-toned reactions have their well-springs in the most primitive emotional experiences. The content of the color-determinant associations has therefore a value somewhat similar to that of the manifest dream content the relation of which to the latent meaning can be ascertained only by way of dream analysis.

Inspecting now the content in Fisher's color-determinant associations to see what in him is imbedded in strong feelings: R 17, "lava out of a volcano ... like hot earth"; R 110, the "lava ... volcano" theme recurs.

The feelings around both of these responses are primitively strong. Both are all C. As chance would have it the content is similar to that in the patient whom Rorschach cites, "interior of the earth" material. Can we, therefore, now make far reaching conclusions as to this patient's innermost, affect-toned needs? No doubt Rorschach could; and Oberholzer can. Perhaps too other psychoanalysts who use the test themselves can undertake such interpretation with a minimal risk. The psychologist trained to observe objective data, operationally verifiable must, in the absence of validated results as to latent meaning of Rorschach test content, be satisfied with the leads, offered structurally—C or other—derived.

R 83. "Cloud" is frequently a percept stemming from a sense of threat. It is here structured similarly to R 17, and so borrows halo as an association strongly emotion-toned.

Three responses, R 24, 61, 104, are concerned with "blood," "anatomy" and in the third instance "could be human flesh, bleeding ... as if taken out

---

[3] RORSCHACH, H. AND OBERHOLZER, E.: Zur Auswertung des Formdeutversuchs. Ztschr. f.d. ges. Neurol. u. Psychiat. **82**: 240–74, 1923; transl., J. Nerv. & Ment. Dis. **60**: 225–48, 359–79, 1924; in: Rorschach, H., *op. cit.* p. 219 ff. All references in the present volume to this paper are to the reprint appearing in the *Psychodiagnostik*.

of a person." The latter communicates the individualized and pathological to a severe degree. This theme was noted also in the non-color but personal F— scores of R 88. This recurring emphasis supports Rorschach's contention concerning the color response as reaching into the "well-springs in the most primitive emotional experience." But the Rorschach test, in its present stage of development, cannot be called upon to unravel the latent meaning. Still quoting Rorschach this "can be ascertained only by way of dream analysis."

R 107. The memory goes back to childhood years, "school . . . water-coloring on a piece of paper."

R 103. A picture of home comfort, "a dog, and a little animal, sleeping in front of a fireplace." The scoring here is one of Fisher's only two FC. His respect for accuracy overcomes the emotional pressure, and the structure is such as is characteristically found with social rapport.

R 82. "Top of flower . . . orchid." Evidence is building up from Rorschach test experience that the orchid is a female genital symbol.

R 84. "Gloaming candles . . . very soft light." A romantic motif. Whether this is more related to the affect surrounding the "orchid," to that around the peaceful "fireplace" scene, or to the feelings awakened by the recall of the school years, only analysis of the patient can establish.

R 67 and R 70 show emotions quickening to imagery which Fisher associates with his vocation. He openly verbalizes this in "forms we use in the window, make two-tone garments"; and I am inferring this interest in a "chubby woman's dress."

The fantasy life. Turning inward into a fantasy living is very difficult for Fisher. His 3 M are, in his total of 111 associations, a bare vestige of this activity. After his one fantasy (R 5) in Figure I, he does not score another until R 58 in Figure VII. This is a long stretch to go without any wishful work of the imagination. Creativity is very meager; and the mental life through this stretch unrich, barren. He ranks quite at the mean, 3.50, of the average adult, SD 3.24.

Furthermore the M in R 58 is so scored with some reservations. The evidence is lacking in the inquiry, but usual practice with this type of response favors M.

The quantity of energy which this patient invests in inner living is exceedingly small as measured by Levy's Movement Energy Scale (p. 55 ff.). The ratings are:

R	Degree of Movement
5	1
58	1
74	3

In brief, Fisher wastes little time or effort on imagination. He has plenty of mental energy, but he turns it to exploiting the palpable world, as he showed in the distribution of his attention (Ap; D! see p. 159) and as he will again (lambda index, p. 177).

Yet there is evidence that all these three fantasies mean much to him. Subjectively judged, two of them are vividly perceived; and the third, R 58, is a blend with V, with inferiority feeling. When he does generate an M, when he does permit himself this luxury, it meets Rorschach's criterion of being a strongly felt experience.

In his first movement response, R 5, he sees "some one lying . . . on his stomach . . . it might be the rectum." A regressed sexual interest is here disclosed. The rectum is a rare percept in this detail; the labia, not infrequent. In the pronoun "his" he tells the sex of the person whom he perceived; and a glance at the detail selected, in the test figure itself, will show that the "rectum" of the prone "some one" must be prominently exposed. This fantasy, therefore, is activating homosexual excitement, together with more archaic sex interest. The ego is suppressing the wish, since in the inquiry the patient rejects the association; he does not recall it. The structure, consisting both of the M— and the Dd, confirms the importance of the fantasy, and of its conflictual quality to the patient. The minus element as a departure in perception is evidence of emotion disturbing the control. In the Dd attention has focused on the rare in order to see what he does. Depending on the severity in the condition as a whole, I have been interpreting M— as evidence of dream or daydream living. In the present patient it would be at the less severe or daydream living. Is this fantasy pleasurable? Or painful? His rejecting it indicates conflict with ego standards that he does hold, and hence that it is disagreeable to him. But his engaging in the fantasy shows its attraction to him. The net pleasure that he gets out of it would depend, therefore, on the entire personality attitude. We may reason that to the extent that it does give him pleasure it is a reflection of his regressive and maladjusted sexual phase. Or, put the other way around, the amount of pleasure he gets from this association is one measure of his regressed or fixated phase.

R 58. "Two people in the distance." This is the blend with V coming after 52 responses without any M. When Fisher finally does experience a fantasy, it is dictated equally by feelings of inferiority. Distance is of the essence of this feeling; human beings are very far away from him. The interweaving of this unsatisfying emotion with the inner living can only mean that it is the more bitter. The sense of psychologic separation from others must, therefore, be one cause of acute unhappiness.

R 74. Fisher's most enriched fantasy, and probably the richest response in the test record. "A man with a big hat . . . like in a fable . . . brownies kidding, laughing" and after ten intervening associations, he perseverates to it, "A little character . . . a little man of kid days . . . Santa Claus hat . . . soldiers blowing." Mythology in the content, with very pleasurable connotation, along two directions, "the playful brownies" and the beneficent "Santa Claus figure." The brownies as little people may yield some significant association in the clinical investigation, as may also the Santa Claus percept which is even more original here. The oral activity with its expulsive direction will also be noted. This movement response is the patient's most energetic one, and including as it does, a truly social activity, "kidding, laughing," it projects at least this much wishful reaching to the world.

Question of M needs to be raised in one other response, R 49. "Lions rubbing noses . . . or having their noses together." Rorschach would describe this as "F tending to M" and would score it F until convinced that it was a true M, and then only so score it.[4] As a simple memory reproduction of commonly observed animal behavior, it would be without affective loading, and so simply F. No unconscious wish is implicit in these responses, and no investment of feeling. On the other hand, as evasion or displacing of erotic interests it may well be M, i.e., fantasy, and even repressed and hence more significant. In the Klopfer technic the scoring would be FM. This assumes the M, or fantasy experience which still has to be proven in this instance. Hence I follow Rorschach's procedure of scoring F, and noting the possible M trend.

The direction of the movement with relation to the center line is not definite. In R 5 the prone posture must be construed as more flector than extensor; in R 58 the people are entirely inactive, and no judgement can be made. In R 74 movement is centripetal. In so far as this scanty evidence can be evaluated, the conclusion from it would be that this patient is not, in the little imagination that he does use, striving to free himself from his present neurotic adjustment. The ego gets no help innerly, even if only in a fantasy, toward breaking up the present reaction pattern.

This case naturally raises the question why does this man use the fantasy so rarely? Why does he invest so little energy in this activity? In view of the content in his first fantasy, R 5, and his resistence to it, the hypothesis is in order that he is repressing desires which are his deepest wants, and also are not up to the standard of the conscious ego. He is isolating himself from these affect-laden wishes. Yet the question of constitutional potential for fantasy activity needs also to be raised. It is one that is not being touched by students of the Rorschach test, or other projective technics, and of other methods utilizing free associations, including psychoanalysis.

---

[4] RORSCHACH, H., *op. cit.*, p. 216.

The present record does warrant asking whether there is genetic endow-ment favorable toward a fantasy, imaginative living.

The opposition trait and determination. The white space quantity which measures this trait is high in Fisher, a total of 9. The finding promises that he is likely to be stubbornly set in his present reaction pattern. It also promises a goodly measure of oppositional activity. The finding compares with a mean of 1.90 white spaces in the normal adult sample; SD 2.14. Inspecting the separate white space responses (s), 4 will be found in com-bination with solid portions of the ink blot, D or Dd, which were first selected. These are in R 4, 53, 64, 81. The s received attention and were in-cluded in the percept only secondarily. Discounting for these 4 in the pres-ent record, still leaves it with 5 sure white space reactions. This is within the second standard deviation, above the mean of the average sample. Also 3 of his s are to statistically major details; R 16 and R 18 to the large inner white space of Figure II; and R 55 to the great gulf within Figure VII. The per cent s, 9/111 is 8.1. This is moderately above the average in the normal adult sample (mean 5.87; SD 4.70, table 3, p. 96). By either reckoning Fisher possesses a trait of considerable determination and stub-bornness.

What does he oppose? Against what does he set himself? The answer according to Rorschach test theory is found in his *Erlebnistypus*, or balance of extratensive as against introversive trends in the whole personality. Fisher is decidedly extratensive. His total (weighted) of color reactions heavily outbalances the number of his movement responses: EB, 3/15. The answer from this cluster—high s, with EB of C total notably greater than M total—is that the environment is the object of his opposition. More significant, the high C quantity and especially its structure, uninhibited discharges, can with this much s be bad news. The passions will rage. Hence again, the ego's need for armor is not so much to fend off missiles from without, but to contain those within. As to whom in the environment or what he is fighting, we are at the mercy so far as the Rorschach test goes, of surmise. From the low total of whole human responses, we know that he does avoid the human form; this would be defensive avoidance. On general clinical grounds the reasoning would be that the defense points to an anxiety, which in turn points to a hostility. These are the threads which we can follow from the test findings. But who the specific target of the an-tagonism is, we do not know.

The notable quantity of s is a symptomatic defense against V, a fre-quently found cluster. The accent on the opposition trait is the patient's neurotic reaction to his sense of inferiority. Also, it was noted (above, p. 70) that the white spaces are concentrated in shock figures. It takes the pressure of disturbing feelings to activate his resistiveness. Does he then hold this trait under submergence except when he is under emotional stress? Does it require the challenge of inner irritation to call out his fight reaction? These two suggestions do emerge from the test pattern. But the s total leads to the judgment that anxiety or excitement only quicken, a trait which is constantly in operation and active. Finally, the passivity trait in this man is now psychodynamically understood in the light of the opposition against the environment. The passivity and the anxiety which is always present in it are his countermoves against his urge to take up arms. Since his fantasy living is very inadequate and he cannot introvert his urge to oppose he needs the passivity all the more. But the sense of passivity is unpalatable to the ego, which calls out counter-measures in the form of new stubbornness and opposition, again requiring anxiety defenses, and so on in the endless vicious circle.

The total adjustment. In the background of these stresses, anxiety, excitement, defenses, and need to resist, the total functioning of this man in his world etches out as follows.

With his average to moderately above average intelligence, he extends himself well, and makes the most of his abilities (higher intellectual achievement, Z, in the range of the superior; the very high total productivity; and occasional originals in this content). These go with drive. This success is in the everyday practical world (attention focuses on the obvious, Ap; D!; frequent perception of the familiar, A per cent). Fisher reaches into this busy world with determination (the white spaces, s), energized by vigorous feelings (the color response pattern). Within the restricted range of his endeavor (Ap and the limitation on the originality), his adaptation must be very efficient (high Z score, successful defenses and absence of any severe disruption intellectually).

A streak of passivity courses through the character (shading-determined responses, Y; much qualifying). But the character armor defense warrants the conjecture that the ego has converted the submissiveness to self-discipline. Also, the drive and the adaptive pattern more than compensate for this weakness. The passivity remains latent. He does manifest an overconventionality (popular responses, P, 12 which is well above average; mean of the normal adult sample is 6.79, SD is 2.41). This is a surface conformity which in a weaker person, or in a sicker one, e.g., depressed, would take the outer manifestation of excess compliance to the environment, a social passivity. Fisher's whole personality structure being what it is, we should expect this trait to serve him well in his practical relations to his world, as an astute regard for the day's fashions.

His interests generally remain narrow by comparison to persons functioning in the higher sectors of the population, and certainly by comparison to healthy individuals who associate in such high quantity. A touch of breadth he does show here and there in some original and superior responses (see content below p. 181). He does have ideas, and aspirations perhaps, beyond the narrow sphere of his vocation. Affectively he could reach out with warmth, since he has emotional assets. Right now he is expending these more in egocentric than allocentric behavior. The potential is high; he can "let go." Under therapeutic molding these self-gratifying feelings can convert into emotional understanding of the other person. In fact he does at times so use his feelings now (FC responses).

The relation to the outside world is in all respects that of a person predominantly attuned to reality. In his regard for external stimuli he scores well within average: lambda index, 77 per cent; (mean for the average adult sample is 70.17, SD 13.71). He employs conventional canons, as we have just noted, at well above average level. His adaptive perception was also noted in his recognition of the most familiar forms, A per cent, 37 (mean for the normal adult sample, 46.5, SD 13.62). In his most critical index, accuracy of perception, he shows the resultant of a parallelogram of forces; F+ per cent 69 (mean for the normal adult sample, 79.25, SD 10.20). Fisher's score is characteristically within the range of persons under neurotic stress, in the high sixties and the low seventies. The emotions disturb the control and lower the accuracy. The ego, alerted, sets up defenses. Very few neurotics break below sixty in their F+ per cent. Pushed back, and pushed back again by the affects, the ego appears to dig in stubbornly at a certain point in its hold on reality, a "last white line" beyond which it will not budge. The F+ 60 per cent point appears to be that white line.

Fisher is likely to resist change, to try to shape his world so that it fits into his already fixed and well set mold. His armor-like defenses show this, as does his relatively unrich associational content. In the intellectual structure, there is a narrowing of the perceptual attention (D!) at the expense of conceptual thinking (W). Rigidity, possibly a fixity of tempo, habitually ingrained, etches out in another finding, i.e., in the amount of fluctuation in time for first response from one test figure to the next. Little is known about this index and its psychologic significance. Evidence on hand does indicate that it is related to the flexibility wherewith the individual engages in his activities in life as he goes from one task to another. This patient's fluctuation is extremely small (p. 157). The interpretation is that he has suffered loss in psychologic flexibility. Rigidity as a brittle condition is likely to be thrown into high relief by its opposite, an excessive swing when that develops owing to a severe enough impact. Fisher dramatically demonstrates this in his pattern. For Figures I through VI the fluctuations are, respectively, 4, 0, 1, 1, 3 seconds; then they oscillate in 8, 6, 15, 13 seconds. The last four figures account for 42 out of the total of 51 seconds of fluctuation. The maternal and female genital imagery of Figure VII and the color shock in the last three figures are of course here operating.

The reasoning with reference to psychological significance of time for first response is brought into question by another finding inconsistent with it. This is the fluctuation of associational productivity from test card to test card. The evidence at hand also dictates interpreting this as indicating the smoothness wherewith a person moves from task to task. Yet Fisher's mean fluctuation in associational total, 3.22, is clearly greater than the mean of the average adult sample (p. 157). This finding would indicate then a more than normally unsmooth shifting from activity to activity. Is this finding necessarily inconsistent psychologically with the strictness shown in the small fluctuation of time for first response? We know that the patient is innerly restless and the ataxic productivity would be one of its manifestations. Then too it is two color figures, IX and X, which contribute disproportionally to the magnitude of the fluctuation in productivity, a total of 12 or 41 per cent out of the entire 29. It need hardly be added here that both these indexes, fluctuation in time per first responses and in productivity, and the correlations between them, will need to be watched and studied.

Still one other observation bears on Fisher's inadequate adaptivity to changes in his environment, and to the shocks which these entail to him. It will be noted that his two test figures in which associational productivity is lowest are III and V. Each of these follows a shock figure. The patient here fails to recover his balance. It is another instance of defective homeostasis in the ego.

Finally the inelastic condition shows up in the quantity of fantasy living, low to the point of being nearly lacking. We saw how little energy Fisher invests in the few fantasies which he does permit himself. A very unimaginative person thus, and to this degree non-resilient, unable to put himself in the place of others. Again a deficit which must reduce his psychologic suppleness and so prevent his using his abilities creatively.

A corrective is available to Fisher against all this stiffness. His very liberated affectivity can make for resilience and pliability. But at present the nuances of the emotional life are those of impulsivity and quick irritability. The great excess of extratensive release over fantasy living would result, in fact, in poor control over, and inadequate delay of, outer behavior. His inner set is to react unstably. Hence the surface and ego controls must be very good. This inner condition consists also of a troubling and disconcerting unrest. Inspection of the 26 instances in which he responds to inner stimuli shows that 14 are reactions in whole or in part to shading (Y) or to (V). Passivity-apprehension or feelings of inferiority are being stirred up. In 13 a color is the determinant in whole or in part. The inner stimulus is excitement. In all a general disquiet in the picture as a whole; a man worried, uneasy, impatient. Too much card turning discloses more of this unstable poise. The ego has had to forge the armor defense so that Fisher can constrain and channelize his urges.

Some of the psychodynamics appear in the content themes. Animosity is a motif in enough of the associations to indicate that this urge is fermenting underneath. There is much evidence of regressed or archaic sexual needs. In a neurotic and brittle personality the aggressive and erotic thinking here becoming manifest will, if converted into acts, be maladaptive.

The content. Preoccupation with, or at least heavy accent on, three interests is reflected in the numerous responses concerning them. These are sex, the isolation-cold theme and anatomy. They provide leads as to Fisher's thinking when he gets into his anxious-depressive moods. They also tell something about the psychodynamics in the neurosis. Concentration appears also in certain other themes, but to a lesser degree.

Female sexual associations appear 7 times; in R 2, 12, 20; following R 22; in R 27, 50, 81. The thinking is sometimes partly evaded, e.g., "pelvis," "pelvic bones," "lower anatomy of a human being"; or it becomes overt, explicit, e.g., "woman with her legs spread out . . . cheeks . . . buttocks," "vagina." Male sexual imagery 3 times in R 5, 13, 96. Twice it is the "penis" without any inhibition. The other (R 5) is the fantasy around the "rectum," the probable homosexual idea (see above p. 173). From the great preponderance of female imagery, and the recurring defensive attitude about it, disclosing a conflict, the conclusion is drawn that in so far as the neurosis is on a sexual basis, it is heterosexual. But a homosexual component is also present.

In this connection, the recurrence of the "cow" theme requires exploring. It will be found in R 14, 76, 79. As a large female animal it raises the question of a displaced sexual interest with possibly the element of depreciation. This may be noted also in his specifying the female of the animal, after some avoidance, in R 23, "leg of a fowl, or chicken." In R 76, he equates the two sexes in the animal percept, "a bull or cow." There is much warrant for looking on the blending of the sexes as a homosexual projection. In R 90 the association centers around the punishment which a bull would take "in a bull fight." In R 99 he sees "mounted horns of a ram," an animal known to be a male sexual symbol in ancient cultures. One other response within this group is the "lions rubbing noses," of R 49.

The isolation-cold theme, taken together with ideas of the lonely or distant, occupy Fisher's mind to a great extent; there is a total of 14 such responses. The test here brings to light some of the actual ruminations that accompany Fisher's dysphoric mood structure. Insularity thinking is especially frequent. It is found in R 4, R 7, R 15; is accented in R 53 and R 94, "in the open"; it combines with the "cloud" theme in R 57. In two other associations the insularity is twofold, R 16, and R 55; inland lakes within islands; water surrounded by land, which is in turn surrounded by water.

Two landscape scenes accent the lonely; two others, the distant. The former are R 34, "ridge, tops of mountains," and "lowlands out in the country," R 45. The latter, R 57-8, are "people," "clouds," "distance." Possibly of similar significance is the "cactus growing on the road," R 47, a desert plant with loneness connotation. Whether it has this meaning to Fisher is something he himself would have to establish.

The sense of cold is very vivid in Fisher's two associations on this topic, R 32 and R 44. Both depict scenes suggesting arctic desolation: "a polar bear out from the water, on an icy day" and "a floating iceberg."

The morose attitude takes the form of concern with body parts reflected in the anatomy and related associations. They are found in R 61, 80, 88, 89, 101, 104. The idea of sickness is explicit in R 101, "a finger, real thin . . . of an ill person." This kind of thinking is clearly pathological in R 88 and R 104. "Could be sores . . . as if imbedded in the skin." "Could be human flesh, bleeding . . . as if taken out of a person." Both of these are characteristic of very sick neurotics.

Injury thinking goes to an extreme with displacement in R 19, "a small animal with head cut off." One aggression weapon appears, "a bow and arrow," R 69; it may be of some significance that this follows immediately on a "teeth" association, R 68. Several animal associations have in them the flavor of the phobic, a surmise which must have confirmation in the patient. Such are the "beasts . . . buffalo," following R 9; "owls . . . eyes," R 25; "scorpion," R 92. The "eagle" will be found twice, R 3 and R 35. It may, however, be more of a power symbol, "eagle of the United States government." The recurrence of "eyes" has been observed as related both to apprehension and to suspicion ideas.

Nature as grand force is twice a theme, in R 17 and in R 110. "Lava coming out of a volcano . . . hot . . . like hot earth." Is there world destruction in this? World reconstruction? The quotation from Rorschach and the other discussion of this response will be recalled (p. 171). The dynamic relations between this train of thinking and feelings of inferiority is known. It is, therefore, probably no chance matter that one of these associations is immediately followed by an architectural theme which in Rorschach's exposition discloses feelings of insufficiency, "the dome on top of a building" (R 18).

The significance of Fisher's two oral responses needs exploring. The "mouth open" of the polar bear in R 32 appears more related to the attacking motif of the "teeth" (R 68). But the "prehistoric man with tongue sticking out" (R 86)? Conjecture leads here to some erotic need. And is the prehistoric man Fisher himself? Mouth associations necessarily call attention to the food percepts, R 51, and the probable perseveration in R 54, and again, R 105. Accent in the first two of these is on meat in what would be large sections, and raw. Thus, "fore-quarter of a pig, skinned and dressed," and "hind-quarter of a pig or lamb." In the third he still sees meat, but at a more cultured level, "two pieces of fowl . . . chicken."

Household themes must bear an important value to Fisher. They recur frequently. Their significance may be at a more surface level, the interests in the comforts of home. But they need to be explored as possibly stemming from an older dependency need. They will be found in R 42, "a piece of carpet"; "a lamp, and the shade," R 65; the "candles" of R 84; the "fire-place" picture of R 103. The patient does recall his own pleasant home in R 30, "a mounted deer like in my basement"; on the other hand, what may be a nostalgic memory from early years becomes active in R 107, the "school" association. Possibly related to all this is the strictly feminine article of adornment, R 106, "combs that ladies used to wear." Of similar interest may be "piece of fur . . . cut out of something," in R 41. But here conjecture also leads to a possible vocational interest. The patient explicitly states this in R 67, "forms like we use in the window." Whether the "chubby woman's coat," (R 70) stems from this or from a deeper interest is not manifest from the test alone.

The personal meaning to the patient remains latent, or too much at the level of surmise, in thirteen responses. These include United States eagle of R 3; "anvils in a work shop," R 8; "a shield . . . crest," R 10; "gravel piles," R 46; "machinery . . . drill press coming through it"; "a tree, the trunk is small," R 71; a "straight saw with handle on it," R 75; "the top of a flower . . . it could be an orchid," R 82; the gloaming candles of R 84; "a sharp pointed instrument, it could make a hole in a piece of wood," R 85; "a rounding of stairways as you get to the bottom," R 97; "roots of a tree," R 100; "a stick the Indian medicine man use to carry around with him," R 109. The symbolism looks thick in several of these. But it will take the usual methods of psychoanalysis to bring the latent material to the fore.

In a very few instances only does Fisher show himself capable of breaking through the confines of his narrow interests. Examples of breadth characterizing the superior person's are: "a drawing in charcoal," R 31; "a wood carving head of a prehistoric man, an Indian," following R 81; "animal image the old Romans used to use, prehistoric men . . . out of rocks," following R 100; "two lions in front of the Art Institute," R 102. In terms of the many and different categories into which his associations group, Fisher gives an appearance of breadth. This is to be expected as incidental to the

large number of responses. But he demonstrates no really startling originality. Even his differentiated content is of commonplace variety.

His three big preoccupations shape his horizon. These are, as we have
seen, his concern with health, loneliness, sex. They dominate his thought content, and so effect a narrowing of his mental contacts with the world at
large. This pattern is one facet of an excessively concrete habit of mind.
So firmly is this hemming-in pattern molded into this personality, it appears
in so many spheres, as to indicate that it is long established and perma-
nent.

Treatment assets. A vigorous, ego; drive. These are the prime requisites.
No person can be treated beyond his willingness, and that takes ego. Emotional fluidity is Fisher's even if too much, too labile. But this is the psychologic stuff that becomes converted into a transference attitude. In his
ability to reach affectively, even if as yet in small amount, Fisher is developing toward emotional contact and understanding. His intelligence is adequate. He can achieve insight. Moreover, he even extends himself in making
the most of his abilities. This is promise that he can do so in the therapeutic
program when he begins to penetrate to the values involved.

The critical question is, can he develop the insight essential toward breaking up his neurosis? Can he turn his ability to be realistic so as to bring
into clear focus the conflicting forces within him? Will he be willing to see
how his conflicting needs are defeating himself and his psychologic equilibrium? The psychiatrist has the job on his hands of breaking through a tough
outer psychologic skin. Fisher in his present state of mind will ward off any
information that will crack his defenses. He has too long been safe behind
his fortress. Any glimpse of the free world beyond is too agitating. But it
is light from this world that the treatment will be letting in. From what we
know of patients with similar Rorschach tests, when they go into treatment, there are very many bad moments. Hence the outlook is for a long
process.

Among the deficits: the very small quantity of fantasy living is inadequate opening up of deep unconscious thinking. But these must be communicated to the psychiatrist; the patient's ego must also face them. Another
disadvantage is the narrowed range of interests. It makes for inadequate
elasticity.

In all, however, the man is strong enough within the acre which he has
measured out as his own. He engages vigorously in a social endeavor, even
if symptomatic needs are central to his goal. The logic of these Rorschach
test findings is, therefore, that treatment effort is dictated. It will need to
be psychoanalysis, since the involvement is too deep to be touched by more
surface approaches. It is likely to be a trial and error course. From these

test findings one cannot commit himself as to how long and how rocky the course will be.

B. The Psychiatrist's Evaluation. Stress and Progress

G. F. is a 37 year old male born in the United States of immigrant Jewish parents. About five years before coming to treatment he attended a dance at which the political boss of the neighborhood was scheduled to appear. The patient entered the hall late and searched out a woman who seemed to be the "big shot's" wife. He danced with her several times and soon found out that she was not important but only a local storekeeper. He took her home in his car and had sexual relations with her in spite of the fact that she was an extremely unattractive woman. The next day he "remembered" that her face was scarred and disfigured and became panicky. Thus began his overt and serious neurosis.

He searched out people who knew the woman to make inquiries about her and incessantly asked about every detail of her life. One day he asked his father if he knew Mrs. W and why she was scarred. The father told him it was because she had the "dread disease." The patient urinated in fright and at once sought genital examination and a blood Wassermann. Both were negative. But over and over he submitted to examinations searching for signs of syphilis. At outbreaks of anxiety during the years he ran to doctors for examination of every organ imagining he had syphilis, cancer, insanity and all sorts of serious diseases. Any symptom or the slightest pain provoked anxiety and necessitated a medical examination. He went to many doctors, and he pleaded with each to tell him truthfully that his trouble was not serious. No day was free from severe anxiety and gradually more symptoms appeared. Finally he was hospitalized in a psychiatric unit for several weeks and carried in treatment afterward by a psychiatrist with supportive therapy for about a year with no benefit, but rather aggravation of symptoms. He then began psychoanalytic therapy.

His symptoms could at that time be enumerated as follows:

(a) Severe free anxiety at the slightest hint of physical disturbance or the slightest indication of loss of esteem, rejection, or frustration in the human environment.

(b) Marked feelings of inferiority dating from early life when his father called him "lumple" or "fool" most of the time. Associated with this was much insecurity and a constant desire to please and appease everyone, especially if he thought they were angry at him.

(c) The slightest tinge of anger within him would make him panicky, hysterical and supplicating for forgiveness from people who were unaware of his anger.

(d) A constant compulsion to have sexual relations with dirty prostitutes in perverse manners of all sorts, in locations and situations which were dangerous for him. This was followed by guilt and search for reassurance that he had not contracted a disease. He had intercourse with many women, daily, although in initiating the act he was not sexually stimulated. He also liked to have women exhibit themselves and have homosexual relations in front of him.

(e) A compulsion to remember faces of friends and acquaintances, which he promptly forgot and then had to search them out to view their faces. Often he photographed them for reference.

(f) A conviction that he would go insane.

(g) Severe guilt feelings resulting in his feeling that any accusation against him was justified.

The patient is an only child and has never had any other siblings. Nor was the mother ever pregnant again. The mother was described as a short, stocky, foreign-born woman who spoke only broken English and used a great many favorite German expressions to comment on ordinary life situations. Her aphorisms dominated her verbalizations. She was poorly educated and seemed to have little knowledge of anything but her immediate, small world. Her thoughts were dominated by superstitions and she lived a sort of primitive, magical life, full of rituals and prohibitions. She was constantly suspicious that people were against her, would deprive her of what little privileges she needed and steal her few possessions. Her accusations that the laundry stole the shirts, that the neighbors tapped her electric wires were later found out to be conscious deceptions by which she could claim reductions in her bills or restitution from the tradesmen. She performed her household duties badly and the small apartment was dirty and disorderly. They lived in a state of abject poverty with old, worn and torn clothes. Aside from a few beds and chairs they had little furniture. In fact, the living room contained only a couch.

The mother gave the patient all her attention and interest, smothering him with her entire affection and treating him like a baby. She washed and bathed him until he was an adolescent and he remembers that even at the age of 19 she would take his socks off at night when he came home. She instilled great fears in him against his early developed violent temper tantrums. Dire things would happen to him. The mother was in abject fear of the father, but played a passive role with him. She apparently enjoyed sexual relations, for she would very frequently leave the room in which she slept with the patient to go to the father's separate room with the excuse that she had to "rub Poppa's leg." The patient had suspicions that other things occurred and often followed the mother and listened at the door.

Very early the mother developed an interest of a seductive nature in the patient's genitals which continued for some time. She would wash him and pay particular attention to his penis, often kissing it with great satisfaction and called him endearingly by a name which is dialect for "little penis." She conspired with the patient to fool the tyrannical father. When he refused to permit new clothes to be bought for the boy she would buy them anyway, but the patient would not wear them at home. He would dress in his old clothes, go to a neighbor, change to his new suit and go to school, reversing the process before returning home. Later in life the mother outlived the father and was well taken care of by the patient as he became financially comfortable. She lived alone since she was on bad terms with most of her relatives due to the fact that they had badly mistreated her as a girl. Some of her brothers had beaten her severely. During the course of the patient's analysis the mother developed pulmonary symptoms which were found to be due to a metastatic carcinoma of the breast. She died after a period of considerable invalidism.

The father was a highly intelligent, violently aggressive man who did as little work as possible all his life. He was considered the "king of the coffee houses" where he played cards all day long. He was a sort of reference book of information which he had acquired in his youth. He was also a very strong man, having been a soccer player of considerable note. From time to time he would try some business venture, but neglect his store and go into bankruptcy, fleeing from collectors and forcing his wife to borrow money wherever she could. He was always in debt and refused to spend for the basic elements of living. He called his son a fool and would permit no independence. He demanded complete and absolute obedience and hardly a day went by that he did not beat up the child. When the father approached home after a hard day's play in the coffee house his wife and son would cringe with fear. He would immediately find fault with everything and start throwing his fists around. Disobedience on the part of the patient was a signal for attack not only on him but his wife. He beat her unmercifully and kicked her, often in the genitals. His reputation as a bad man continued so that at times the patient had difficulty when he was discovered to be his father's son. The father died about three years before the patient started his analysis.

The family lived in a German neighborhood in Chicago. The patient went to grade school and after finishing did not continue, but worked as an assistant butcher. He learned the trade and became extremely efficient so that his services were desired by many employers, whom he cheated whenever he could. His intelligence was far greater than shown by his performance in school and at business. Although born in this country and educated in the public schools he still maintained a bowery-type of accent. He worked as a butcher for most of his early life, once or twice attempting to open his own business without success. He tried to play soccer as a hobby, but was not good enough to play with a strong team.

In his early twenties, he met a young woman who was the daughter of a wealthy department store owner. He deliberately chose her because of her money, although he later felt that he loved her. The in-laws set up great opposition, but the marriage was consummated and the patient was sullenly accepted in the family. He worked for his father-in-law, who recapitulated his own father's attitude. Nothing the patient did was right and he was constantly being reprimanded and criticized. No matter what success he had in buying or selling, it was not enough. The patient was constantly in a state of turmoil, beset with inexpressible rage and having to appease the tyrannical father-in-law constantly. He was depreciated in public and insulted on every occasion. However, his financial status immediately became excellent and he was able to live in luxury with cars, a beautiful home and domestic servants. The father-in-law died about five years ago and the patient and his brother-in-law took over the business. Since the brother-in-law was a lawyer who had no business experience, the actual running of the store devolved upon the patient who succeeded in developing the business to an extent never achieved by his father-in-law. His mother-in-law, however, constantly irritated him by derogatory comparisons with the father-in-law.

The patient's wife is an extremely efficient woman and very intelligent. They had three children, one of whom died several years ago of leukemia. His remaining children are healthy and beautiful and constitute his chief interest at home.

His wife is a placid person who he knows had sexual affairs before marriage. Sexual relations with her do not satisfy him and they are, therefore, infrequent. His chief complaint is a body odor and a vaginal discharge. Often after relations he masturbates and during intercourse he often inserts his finger in her rectum and fantasies that she is one of his prostitute friends. Among his sexual fantasies are dogs licking at women's vaginas, cunnilingus and other oral pictures. As a child he masturbated in his clothes and often ejaculated on his own abdomen.

A few years ago he seduced a virginal employee, M, a neurotic frigid, middle aged woman who seemed to love him. She permitted his various oral perversions but each relationship was accompanied by much guilt. Eventually he broke off but fears constantly that she is angry at him for "ruining" her life. He constantly appeases her, becomes angry at her and then pleads for forgiveness. In fact he evokes her anger by talking to her about what he has done and then pleads for forgiveness. This compulsion to repeat such a pattern is acted out daily.

The analysis began with much free anxiety about his guilt and he con-

stantly sought for reassurance. He acted like a little boy pleading for forgiveness and expecting severe punishment. His guilt was always projected
to M and what he had done to her; or to his mother who was then still
alive. He took any interpretation as criticism, upon which he would writhe
and often kneel before the therapist to plead for forgiveness. The first transference vacillated between that of a father type with fear of punishment
and a mother type with traps set for expressions of love and sympathy.
His compulsive seizure of every word, in order to involve it intellectually
in his doubts, and his incessant need for verbal reassurance, could only be
dealt with by almost complete silence on the part of the therapist. Only
crucial and succinct interpretation could be given. The patient took these
day after day with intellectual grasp, forgetting and needing repetition of
the material until suddenly with great affect he would "understand" and
"feel" what had been interpreted for weeks or months. Patience was necessary, for he eventually gave way to understanding.

To the surface manifestations of passivity, inferiority and need for acceptance he reacted episodically by an aggressive defense against being
overpowered. He envied and tried to be as "good" as the therapist but
gradually fell back to a passive need for acceptance. This was partly a feminine wish toward the therapist, with receptive infantile trends permeating
the whole structure.

Considerable time was spent in analyzing the maternal "magical" aspect
of his superego which he finally ejected as he realized his anger at his mother
and could feel his hatred for her. During this phase moderate depressive
elements were lived through but no suicidal tendencies were expressed in
action or in his unconscious material. The depressive elements reached no
great depth despite the total absence of fantasy retreat. Most of his dreams,
even, were sentences, often not fully formed, or consisting of one or two
words. He recounted few dreams of action. During these he would project
his need for punishment on distorted sentences taken out of context from
some article guaranteeing him punishment in the form of "incurable neurosis." Actually his life pattern was that of a successful extremely practical
businessman who could drive a shrewd bargain.

Underneath his passivity and secondary inferiority feeling there lay a
violent, volcanic hostility with essentially oral components. Some anal or
soiling rage was present as seen in his reveling in dirt in early life, his favorite trick of wrapping feces in a package placed in the sidewalk for curious
passers-by to open, and in his technic of intercourse. Yet there was little
strength to this level of fixation. Rather his rage was of the biting "mad
dog" type, against which he defended by "sucking." His rage was bilateral
in that it was directed to the mother in its more superficial layer; largely,
however, displaced from its essential object, the father, in addition to the

primary oral rage of the child frustrated in the child-mother relationship. He could not escape the fright and reaction in relation to the father by retreat to a mother relationship since that only re-awakened oral hostility to her, and so re-emphasized his solitary position in a hostile family (first world).

C. Test and Clinical Findings in Perspective

An inner field of stress is the primary set of findings in this neurosis. This is the anxiety. The external stresses have been important; they have brought about the present organization of forces in the personality which now is Fisher. But their role has been historical. At present the balance of stresses pivots on three fulcra: inferiority feelings, passivity, violent discharge trends. Fisher encapsules these tensions within a well habituated attention to material success. At the root of the anxiety is a hopeless sense of loneliness. This is Fisher and his neurosis as described by the psychiatrist. It is Fisher as projected in his Rorschach test.

The inferiority feelings are a major dynamism, both structurally (p. 166); and in Fisher's undervaluing himself (p. 156). The test probes the intensity of these feelings, and correctly gauges them (p. 167). The accumulation of evidence in it, not adequately emphasized in my interpretation, is that the inferiority dynamism is serious enough to be of character structure. The clinical data sharply etch out the psychologic cause of these feelings: the strong father, the "king," one-time soccer player. Fisher has even tried soccer. He could not make it.

Fisher is passive. He must please, appease. He gets down on his knees for the therapist. The trait is mirrored in the test (a) structural data (p. 165); and (b) some nonscorable communications (p. 157). If anything, I have understated the Rorschach test data as to extent of the passivity. Three Y unmodulated by form is a very high quantity. The intensity implicit in the CF.Y should have been noted.

The violence of the exciting affects, the potential for rage, the temper tantrums, the compulsive agitation, clinically reported, are all developed out by the test's technic (p. 167). The psychiatrist's expression, "violent, volcanic" hostility is of especial interest in the light of my concern (above p. 171) about caution. I hold, nevertheless, to my position that in interpreting content for personal significance, caution is of the essence. The hysterical features mentioned by the psychiatrist did suggest themselves in interpreting the test findings from the emotional over-reaction indicated in the many pure color associations found in the framework of a neurosis in which the defenses are hardened. But so productive a record I have never yet found in a hysteric. The need for repression with which these patients are afflicted constricts their test productivity.

Anxiety is the essence of this man's personality, clinically. It is fully described in the test findings, (p. 171 ff.). One difference needs to be noted. The psychiatrist speaks of the findings as "free." The test result point against an all-or-none condition. They highlight the mixed quality. The test here in fact well reflects what are probably the real psychologic phenomena: ups and downs of this painful emotion; sometimes more free, at other times bound; eddies within a constant course.

Compulsions to certain acts recur in the clinical story (p. 183). They are reported by the test in various tactics, and in the armor-like defense (p. 160). The importance of this agreement is less in corroborating test technic, than it is for theory. My inference is: both sets of phenomena are expressions of the same psychologic need, namely of an inner command against which the ego is helpless. The patient *must* engage in certain acts; he must think certain thoughts. He must attend to certain elements in the ink blots and see certain forms in them.

The clinician notes "total absence of fantasy retreat" (p. 187). The Rorschach test language is "one kind of defense which this patient does not use is withdrawal into fantasy." (See also p. 162.) Neither method finds depression (p. 176, p. 187). The psychiatrist observes that there are only temporary deviations from reality (p. 186 ff.). The test findings evaluate the perceptual inaccuracies as of limited significance for the whole personality (p. 177). The correlation in these important operations, both of surface order, and in the inner living, are practically one for one.

Similarly the man's efficiency at his shrewd, practical level, even to the point of as a young apprentice cheating his employers. The Rorschach test language (p. 176): "makes the most of his abilities . . . success in the everyday world . . ." (see also p. 182 ff.). The test could not have indicated the peccadilloes. It is not yet that specific. It is to be reiterated that both clinical and Rorschach test reports were derived in total independence of each other.

The agreements are found also in that sphere more elusive to the test, i.e., personal dynamics as projected in the content themes. Leaving the sex interests for the moment and inspecting the others: oral topics, clinically (p. 187), and in the test (p. 180): aggression, clinically, in the character throughout; and in the test in the content (p. 180), as well as structurally (p. 175). Household topics in the test (p. 181) suggest the man interested in family, home and its comforts. The nearest corresponding clinical datum consists of Fisher's children, "his chief interest at home." The marital relation does not support indication of a strong pull toward the home. The test may, however, in this group of associations be uncovering interests that have not emerged clinically, even if they are compensatory for his ingrained inadequate sense: the mounted deer, the fire place. But at certain levels these can be utilized in treatment. Some may have more than surface value, e.g., the candles, a symbolism which the test is sectioning out and may not have emerged clinically. None of this amounts to disagreement between the two methods of investigating this person. Each complements the other, and contributes to the entire understanding of him, and to the therapeutic planning. Assuming my interpretation is correct (I do not yet know what this man's business is) the test is also tapping Fisher's vocational interests (p. 181). These are mostly at surface level.

The sexuality. The clinical facts show immature, primitive, needs. Fisher's desires are for prostitutes, especially dirty ones; and for various perversions. The Rorschach test does not uncover these needs specifically. The homosexual interest emerges once clearly (p. 179); once, inferentially and as leads to explore (p. 179; see also p. 173). With one (R 5) anal thinking also is manifest. In addition Fisher shows much toying with sexual imagery (p. 179). He can verbalize percept of the male genital. He persistently evades the female (p. 161). His ability to shut off crude sexual verbalizing is evidence of integration. It is in more disrupted conditions that such associations are liberated. The analytic sessions do, of course, tap these interests. The many evasions in the test are at the same time a positive finding. They serve to alert the therapist. The patient *is* hiding something. What that is he can, in the test, avoid exposing. That is one of the limitations on the instrument. The harder the defenses, the better the person encapsules the personally conflictual material. The examiner's problem is to assay all behaviors in the light of one another; and to know what the relations are to the unitary adjustment pattern.

The test's finding of pathological concern with health (p. 180) uncovers one of Fisher's especially virulent foci of anxiety: fear of syphilis, cancer, and of other diseases, including insanity. The persistent need for dirt in the clinical notes does not, however, appear in the test record.

An important clinical finding for which the test has only indirect equivalent is the guilt feeling. Its presence in Fisher, as in any patient, has to be deduced from the periods of rigid accuracy (p. 160). Neurotic persons with undeviating F+ are persons with clinically overactive superegos. This interpretation is more obvious in the depressed. The observation is based in logic, and I offer it as a hypothesis rather than as a rule. Another clue to guilt in Fisher's test record is the self-devaluating (p. 156). This is more direct evidence frequently found in persons who skirt directly accusing themselves by a depreciated attitude toward themselves.

Still one other line of evidence is the anxiety which the test so amply projects. Whether anxiety *ex hypothesi* always involves guilt is a theoretical problem, the consideration of which does not belong here. With reference to Fisher, the psychiatrist's notes do show an inextricable weave of the guilt in the anxiety. In fact, Fisher driven by his deeper anxiety engages in new acts which will generate guilt. His relation with the woman M is one example.

This deeper anxiety source is discerned by the test. The instrument must be content with a glimpse only. But this glimpse is a sharp one and accurate. I refer to the evidence for anxiety centering around the mother (p. 163 ff.), the father (p. 162) and to Fisher's consciousness of isolation (p. 165). The clinical picture (see the closing lines of the psychiatrist's notes) shows: rage (which must carry with it anxiety) towards the father; displaced on to the mother; from whom the patient is kept at a psychologic distance by his oral hostility to her. The Rorschach test findings differ from the psychiatric description only in emphasizing the mother as the prime well-spring of the anxiety. From the more obvious discomfort around the mother (p. 163) and the oppressive loneliness running through the record (the isolation themes), the test highlights the closing words of the psychiatrist, Fisher's "solitary position in a hostile family." Throughout his experience, man, boy, child, infant, that desperate state of mind had bred in him: aloneness.

CHAPTER V

AN ENGINEER AND MANY WOMEN

A. A TREATMENT STALEMATE, AND THE TEST

This man was referred in Boston by a woman psychiatrist after she had treated him for one year. The psychologic problem relative to Caine at the time he took the Rorschach test, and the reason for it are stated by the psychiatrist in her letter as follows:

Mr. Caine is in the early thirties, and is married to a woman nineteen years older. He has a deep-rooted anxiety neurosis and the wife has served as a defense against it. The defense worked well as long as his own mother lived. But after her death the anxiety over the possibility of losing his wife became overpowering and he went on a wild spree with women trying to find another woman whom he would have in addition to his wife. He seems to need two women. That acting out subsided after he was in therapy, for a while, possibly, by my becoming the second woman. However, he has been very fearful of the transference. This seems to deal with fear of my husband but more specifically, with my not being free to meet his demands as his mother and wife have. Both of them have hated just about everyone and centered their interest around the patient.

We have reached a stalemate in analysis which seems to resist interpretations to date. Actually, the dynamics of the anxiety neurosis seem pretty typical. It was my feeling that a Rorschach could help me in advising Mr. Caine as to the possible benefits from further analysis. He insists that he wants to be cured, to give up his present neurotic marriage, etc. but he does not seem much closer to doing so than when he entered therapy one year ago.

Mr. Caine is an engineer, very successful professionally. He has an excellent position with (a large firm), teaches in the . . . School of Engineering and at other institutes. His standards are very idealistic and I am sure he is one of the outstanding engineers in the city. His income is not commensurate to what it would be if he were on his own.

Mrs. Caine is a newspaperwoman (staff reporter) and from what Mr. Caine has told me, she is outstanding in her work. There are no children.

The test record, scoring summary and interpretation, follow:

RESPONSE RECORD

Figure I (4″)

1. W F+ A P
   1.0

'Looks like a bat to me (W);

2. W F+ Hd, My
   1.0

'a Janus-faced creature (W); two faces in opposite directions; with a long nose, like an old nose' (marked hand tremor was here observed).

192

3. Dds F— Ge — 'Looks also a great deal like a map, indentations of the Red Sea' (Dds 29 is Arabia; adjoining Dd is Red Sea).

4. Dd F— Hd, Anal — 'The dimple on the top looks like the part of a buttock (Dd 22).

5. D Y.M+ H P — 'Could be a figure dimly silhouetted in the middle' (D 3; of a nude female creature looking back, facing the other way; shading and form). (D 1; are birds in a nest; the mouths open for food). 'Arabia on the map.

6. D F— Ad — 'The two top figures look like parrots' heads (D 5).

7. D F— Im — 'And these two things could be crude Indian arrow heads (D 8).

8. Dds F Hd — 'I suppose everybody gets the idea these are eyes, these little white spots' (Dds on D 8).

Figure II

9. D C Bl — 'Well . . . they look like on the bloody side' (D 2, D 3; color only; from a patient in the operating room).

'Like paper folded in the middle, a duplicate picture.

10. D M+ H, My 5.5 — 'A couple of peculiar creatures (D 2) baring their fangs at each other; men from Mars or something like that, are not human; like in science fiction.

11. Ds F+ Art — 'And crude valentines we made in school by folding (Ds 5 with D 6).

12. D F+ Hd — 'A couple of faces with underslung jaw' (D 7; ape-like, terrific, underhung).

'And two more profiles on the bottom.

13. D FC— Na — 'This looks like coral formation' (D 3, because of the spikes; form and color).

14. Dds CF+ Hd, Sex — 'The diamond shaped structure is reminiscent of a woman's vagina in' (Dd 24, the white space; color and form).

194 RORSCHACH'S TEST

15. Dd C.Y An

'These spots have a leprous look' (the blotches in D 1; red on black; scaly, diseased).

Figure III (10")

16. D M+ H P
4.0

'More red. These figures have taken on ... human or (not animal, only human),

17. D F− A

'animal figures, facing each other; the head, the eyes, arms (not distinctly feminine ... but this could be the breast, Dd 27); also because of the small Adam's apple bent back, at the elbow; it looks static, a pose. I don't see any movement; no threatening gesture.

18. D F+ A

'A butterfly or moth (D 3).

19. D FC− An

'Something just removed from the heart or other organ, the artery leading away (D 2, form and color).

20. D F+ Ge

'A distinct resemblance to the map of Italy (D 5).

21. D YF+ An

'Torso of a human being (D 7); the lungs registering as dark on an x-ray plate ... as if pathological ... TB ... or something.

Figure IV (19")

22. W F+ A
2.0

>∨ 'Well here again ... hmm a bird shaped effect, (W), bird or bat; the wings going off in this direction' (form; has irregular pattern).

23. D YF+ A

'A tanned animal skin spread out on the floor ... used as a rug' (upper half; form and shading, with emphasis on the shading). ∨ ∧ ∨ ∧

'I don't see a heck of a lot here. I don't find it very inspiring to tell you the truth.'

Figure V (2")

24. W F+ A P
1.0

'A butterfly or moth again ... rather obvious (W).

25. D F+ A   > 'A bird with beak (D 9) insignia
                        of the Nazi army; bird with profile.

26. Ds F+ A   'Could be alligators, with mouth
                        open (D 10); and the aperture is the
                        mouth' (Dds).

Figure VI (5")

27. D FY+ A P   'The old animal skin rug again,' (D
                        1; shape, and mottled differences in
                        shading).

28. D F+ Ad   'Again the wing formation' (D 6;
                        sinister form).

29. D F− Na   'Stalagmites . . . stalactites . . .either
                        that or coral formation (D 6; form
                        only).

30. D F+ Ls   > 'Many of these have a craggy,
                        mountainous appearance . . . like pe-
                        culiar bad-land formation' (D 4, espe-
                        cially at edge; form only).

Figure VII (4")

31. D M+ H P   'Here we have the familiar two fig-
    3.0   ures looking at each other with a laugh
                        or snarl; a nice high hair-do; primitive
                        women (D 1).

32. D F+ Hd   'A clown-shaped head; same thing
                        on other side; a jester, cap and bells
                        (D 3; form only; static).

33. D F+ A   'The familiar butterfly or bat, seems
                        to appear on all these cards (D 4).

34. D F+ Ad   'These are figures of some kind . . .
                        as if there are tusks on them . . . small
                        ones, tiny' (D 8).

Figure VIII (10")

35. D F+ An P   'Well, well, ribs; could be a skeleton
                        (D 3).

36. D F+ A P   'And here two rodent-like creatures,
                        squirrels, or chipmunks (D 1)

37. D F+ Ls   'climbing on those rocks; they have
    3.0   long tails (D 2). > ∨

38. D FC+ Adx   'That wing effect again . . . in all these' (D 2; butterfly or moth; shape and color).

39. Dd F+ Ad   'Looks like the profile of a dog (Dd 26).

'Not much of anything out of this blue' (D 5; does not signify anything).

Figure IX (23″)

40. D F+ H P   'Here again we have the creatures with a peaked cap, long nose, eyes, protuberant tummy . . . like Snow White dwarfs' (D 3; as in the dime store).

41. D M− A   'A flat fish, flounder; malevolent looking profile (D 1; form only; blunt heads): an angry individual.

42. D F− Na   'Looks like he's blowing a gale out
2.5   of his mouth (D 3).

43. D FC+ Bt   ∨ 'This, is faintly like a large flower, could be a zinnia with flat blossoms; pale in color for a zinnia . . . the stem (D 9; form and color).

44. Dds F+ Ad   'The eyes of some creature' (Dds 23).

Figure X (9″)

45. D F+ A   'Well . . . seems to be, could be a lot of fish . . . creatures here, the octopus creature (D 1).

46. D F− An   'Here again the rib formation (D 5).

47. D F+ Im   'One of those controls on a machine; goes round and round, when it goes too fast . . . V-shaped, a governor (D 3).

48. D F− An   'Here again two lungs (D 6); form, bag-like.' (Patient tells of having a cough for last two weeks.) 'Whenever I have a cough I think of TB.

49. D F− A   'More examples of marine life, claws like a lobster . . . crab (D 7).

50. D CF− Ru   'A little like a wine-sack' (D 13; sac-like; with Dd as faucet; form and leathery tan color).

RESPONSE SUMMARY

R total 50

W	4	M	4 (1−)	H	5	F+ %	69
D	39 (s, 1)	Y.M	1	Hd	6	A %	38
Dd	7 (s, 5)	C	1	A	14	P	9
		C.Y	1	Ad	5 (x, 1)	s	6
	50	CF	2 (1−)	An	6	s %	12
Z	23.0	FC	4 (2−)	Art	1	T/IR	9.6
Ap	(W) D Dd!	YF	2	Bl	1	T/R	25.18
		FY	1	Bt	1	Af r	0.47
Seq	Methodical	F+	23	Ge	2	L	0.68
	with irregular	F−	10	Im	2		
	episodes	F	1	Ls	2		
				Na	3		
			50	Ru	2		
					50		

EB5/7

INTERPRETATION

The defenses. This patient faces his world with a composed outer mask; something of a "dead pan." But the shell has some easily penetrable spots. The guarding shows up in the sequence and in the approach. The sequence is the most correct possible in five of the six test cards in which the patient uses more than one variable (II, IV, V, VIII and IX). W always precedes D; D comes before Dd. The exception card is I, in which there is influence of strong initial shock. The inflexible method is even more apparent in the approach type (Ap) from Figure III through VII his preception selects only the most obvious; an unbroken drouth of D (the simple W of Figures IV and V are essentially D). The pattern persists, in fact, through Figure X since the one Dd in VIII and one in IX are only a small departure. All this makes for a too unchanging manner, a stiff pose. He shows this attitude too in the routine high production of F+ in Figures II through IX, with 100 per cent accuracy in five of these. The single F− in each of the three other figures is relatively slight relaxing of the guard. The two only material exceptions to his pattern are Figures I and X. In the one he is taken by surprise, in the other he is fatigued. For the most part, he obeys fixed habits which must reduce the man's psychologic suppleness, and must stand in the way of his enjoying himself. It all tells of the effort at close hold on the self and on reality. The low Z score is a serious price being paid by Caine in his defensive need. He is not seeing relations which he could. He is guarding against seeing them. There are connections he prefers not to see. This is the isolation defense. It is much more comfortable. The reasoning to the clinical behavior is that in his more conflicted moments, higher mental processes are much reduced.

Evasive qualifying, R 14, discloses the defensive attitude on perceiving the female genital. The tautology, "woman's vagina" I have observed only in persons sensitive on this topic at a very immature level. It is defensive avoidance which the double term only accents: the patient over-identifies that of which he is afraid; apologetic elaboration will be found in R 8. He denies either aggression or the fear of it in R 17, "no threatening gesture." In R 10, he either displaces, fully denies, or is in counterphobic flight; he attributes the hostility to something not human; as "men from Mars" they would be unreal. Evasive language will be noted also in R 9. Qualification for the record as a whole is not excessive. The qualifying and the avoidance, therefore, stand out; they are reflex reactions evoked by that particular association. The patient raises his arm, as it were, against the threatening blow. Obsessive attitudes appear in R 2 and R 5. In the latter the direction of the woman's activity is ambivalent. In the former the one creature is facing in both directions at once, a typically obsessive stance. Isolation of affect is betrayed in absence of color determinant in R 11; I have had this response content in affectively liberated persons, and they report color as a factor. A more stringent defense is the suppressing of an important response, following R 5, released in the inquiry.

Caine uses some phobias as defensive expedient. In the main these are only slightly more severe than usually found within normal range. See R 12 and R 28. In R 25 and R 26 he reproduces a frequent theme (threatening mouths); the phobic in it is something he shares with much of the population. Whether the "eyes" in R 44 has phobic significance to Caine would have to be established in him directly. To the extent that it is, the "some creature" motif accents the apprehension. Bound in with the man's anxiety are the anatomy responses. (p. 209). Their job is to shield the ego from more painful anxiety sources, too troubling to face. Especial interest attaches to R 41–42. Is the gale which this most innocuous animal is now producing a destruction fantasy? As such it is a counterphobic measure in which the individual is clearing out his fear by attacking the environment. R 41 also carries some projection thinking, as does also R 10. It will be noted in addition that the patient is structurally capable of fighting back; his white-space count is well above average. How he uses this trait is elucidated in certain other personality operations (p. 206 ff.). One other defense is affective withdrawal, moderate, discussed below (p. 200 ff.). For the counterattacks against a depressing stimulus, see p. 199.

The anxiety. Defense activity tells of need for defense. The person is alerted. The clue to this need in the present record is available in another set of findings. Caine suffers much mental pain. This must emanate either from conflict or from a guilt state. In either event, he wants something which he knows he must not want. It is ego against affect; the old fight, "higher" self against "lower"; spirit against flesh: in current psychologic phraseology, ego against id.

Anxiety shock is Caine's immediate reaction to the test. In Figure I, structure is worse than in any other of the test's cards. Sequence is essentially confused. Approach accents the small detail. This is an imbalance of the attention to the less essential which is also another defense tactic; it is avoidance of the major demand on the attention by pinning it down on the insignificant. In perceptual accuracy, the percentage is the lowest in the ten figures. The individual number of F— associations is greater than for any other of the figures, and approaches the number of F— in all the other cards combined. The number of Hd much outweighs the number of H, always a sign of obstructed mental life. The high productivity in this figure, more responses than in any other card, is only another defense activity, a reaction formation. The paradoxical increases of R in response to shock has been recently noted. An exposition of it appears in a paper by Bohm.[1] Caine has here been badly disconcerted. He is ready to sense threat. Figure I has set it going. The anxiety shock has been instant, sudden, and the ego's controls have failed him.

This very intensity of the reaction carries with it the reflex toward counter-measures. Caine attempts to bind the emotion. In Figures IV and V productivity sharply contracts. It only moderately expands in Figures VI and VII. For the four massive black figures (IV to VII) the number of associations is disproportionately low: 26 per cent of the total, in 40 percent of the test stimuli. In Figure IV card turning sets in for the first time, one way in which the ego's weakening is betrayed; there is motor evidence of inner agitation. The patient openly verbalizes the unrest: "I don't find it very inspiring"; in an expression of inability, in which there is also a rejecting defense, "I don't see a heck of a lot here." Other evidence is P failure. Time for first response is significantly slow.

In Figure V, the effect of the shock relaxes somewhat; Caine now produces one more association. There is a little relief from the stereotypy in the "insignia" of R 25, although this too is secondary to the principal association which is a simple animal content. In both IV and in V, Caine is undeviatingly accurate, which is a stiffening of the defenses. So also is the 100 per cent animal content, the stereotypy. In Figure V, time for first response is excessively fast, and this may have been another reaction formation.

In Figure VI the liberation goes further. Broadening content breaks down the stereotypy and the productivity even if only a little. Time for

---

[1] BOHM, E.: Der Rorschach-Test und seine Weiterentwicklung. Rorschachiana I. Bern: Huber, 1945, pp. 115–36.

first response continues rapid. Caine manifests thus a progressive ability
to free himself from the anxiety, and the F— in VI is, paradoxically, a
favorable finding. It softens the picture of unbending hold on the self.
In Figure VII he is able to maintain his productivity and his fast time for
first response. But the deadening effect of the anxiety is again evident in
the impoverished content. In all four of these shaded figures (IV to VII)
Ap has been inflexible, D! The patient grasps difficult relations (Z) at
minimal amount. This ability appears frozen. It is clear that the threat
stimuli inhibit this man. Once the defensive reaction has been mobilized,
it is hard and fast. The toxin antitoxin is functioning.

The anxiety starts out as a free one. The onset is acute in Figure I;
and again in Figure IV. But thereafter it subsides in the specific dynamic
imagery which each of the test cards activates (paternal, IV; maternal,
VII; phallic, VI). It is not a binding symptom, but a conscious hold on
reality by the ego.

The mood. Tones of discouragement and resignation with distress dominate. Five Y responses is a high score (adult mean is 1.96, SD 2.22). In the
majority of these, Caine is influenced more by the shading than by the
form element; the emotional factor is stronger than the intellectual. This
intensity is corroborated by the two blends, once with a fantasy, i.e., with
an internalized felt experience (Y.M in R 5); once with externalized emotion (C.Y.) in R 15. The inner unrest and disturbance in them are deeper,
more intense. A sensitivity to blue appears in Figure VIII (following R
39). Rorschach speculates over the greater responsiveness by the repressed to the cold colors.[2] Caine here screens the vulnerability by rejecting the stimulus, the defense by way of attack. The content in R 5 tells
one cause of the painful emotion, " a nude female," since as Y.M this is
also a fantasy structure and the wish is a deep one. Some dejection tied in
with longing at unconscious level for a woman is at present a factor. This
patient is reacting to strongly felt dysphoric needs within.

The lively emotions. Color-determined associations are few in the three
all color figures. But Caine's responses can be strongly saturated by color.
Two influences are therefore in evidence. One is the anxiety which commands him to be on guard at exciting temptations. It is an anxiety incident
to awakening of repressed gratifying wishes. This is the function of these
stimuli in the test; to arouse pleasurable emotions, permitted and taboo.
Oberholzer notes the point in relating color shocks to repression. In Caine
there has been contraction in the last three test figures insofar as he can
produce here only four color-toned associations. He responds with his other

------

[2] RORSCHACH, *op. cit.* pp. 37; 118–120.

form in the chiefly chromatic Figures II and III, with their single (red) hue. The total of eight color response is high enough to indicate sensitivity to these values. More such should appear in VIII to X. Hence, a defensive withdrawal before affect-toned events. This is a victory of the ego over feelings, but it is a Pyrrhic victory, gained at the price of capacity for adult emotional gratification. The sterile content in this superior man tells the same story, an inhibition such that he does not respond to the variety of stimuli in his environment. The affective ratio of 0.47 while within normal range, is at the low end of the normal (mean 0.60, SD 0.19). The bright toned figures evoke relatively few responses of any kind.

Secondly, the feelings that do come to expression can move Caine powerfully. Two of the color-dictated responses are pure color, and two are color-form, a high proportion out of a total of eight. The sharp, frequently disquieting red, of the second figure draws out fully half of the eight. The pure C reaction confirms the picture of vulnerability brought out in the anxiety inducing figures. It emphasizes the instability trait and the hectic, fidgety condition. The finding receives support in the one CF− and two FC−. In each of these the color factor is strong enough to break down the form accuracy. In the two FC− the ego's struggle against the affects is successful, but the strain is effectual. In the CF− response, emotional pressures are decidely in the ascendant, and the ego barely holds on to the reins. In the majority of instances Caine is irritable, hypersenstive, impulsive. But we have seen that he also contracts before affect-toned stimuli. Two contrary psychologic trends are thus in process in the one man at once; he must react with strong feelings; he must restrain or withdraw from them. The ego commands it. The net result of such opposition within one person is stress and psychologic pain.

There is one indication, barely perceptible, of potential for pleasurable mood experience. It is a touch only, the "zinnia" in R 43; Caine dwells on it long enough to indicate a moment of healthy reaching. Cogent also is the evidence provided by the varying nuances of the color responses, C, CF and FC, pointing against an unvarying emotional level or tone. In this there is the element of the springy, the resilient. It is the structure which can be converted into healthier emotional living.

A favorable finding usually, even if paradoxical, is color shock. There is ample evidence for it in the present record. Caine is sensitive to the world's exciting events. In a person in whom a dysphoric mood is prominent, color shock tells that he can be reached. The down swings are reactive. The structure is neurotic. Caine's color shock develops without delay. In Figure II, his perceptual interest turns to the very unusual detail (R 14, R 15); and two Dd in five responses is a high count, i.e., the Ap is out of line with normal expectancy. The first response to the figure is one of unmixed color, the affect rules. The P responses in a person who produces two such associations in Figure I, and a total of nine for the test are lacking in this test figure that provides three good P opportunities. At the other extreme, the content includes entirely individualized associations, all but one (R 13) of which are symptom-charged. In some the pathological thinking is grave, R 15 and R 9, 10. All this in a patient whose productions are soon to become so stereotyped. The conclusion is warranted that the shock has shaken up our patient badly. It has loosened agitating trends.

In Figure III Caine shows ability to recover but the effect of the shock persists. In his first reaction he is affect-shy, "more red," a sensitivity to color without using it in determining an association. Inaccurate perception alternates with accurate. Most serious is the content in R 19 and R 21, anatomy with hypochondriacal quality. Concerning the oppressive mood structure see p. 200. Yet the first response is the good M and P. Form perception is accurate in four out of the six associations. In contrast to Figure II, the patient now selects obvious details exclusively, in which we see his rigid approach setting in. Caine's ego can snap back out of the dysequilibrium into which it was thrown in Figure II, but the control is shaky.

The pattern in Figure VIII discloses modifiability of approach. A Dd, the first since Figure II, relieves the stringent D Ap. Emotionally, too, Caine is capable of adaptive rapport, the one color response is FC+. But the 100 per cent F+ for the figure is that pattern of inflexible control which he had followed in the immediately preceeding gray-black cards. In content there is a drouth, all the most trite associations for which this figure is known. The patient disposes of the figure with color rejection, he shuts the door to the opportunity to relate himself emotionally.

In Figure IX color shock is at its worst. Time for first response is the slowest, inaccurate perception reaches the level of distortion in R 42, and of regressive autistic fantasy in R 41. The latter is the more significant in the light of Caine's inability to produce the usual M in R 40. His fantasy capacity is impeded or it becomes entirely unfettered. The ego has relinquished control completely as in dream living, or goes to the other extremes of clamping down. In R 44, the possible phobic thinking has been noted (p. 198). The plowing up which this figure effects also yields fruit. Content, even if autistic, is exceptionally rich; and it is here that Caine permits himself the luxury of the "zinnia" with its healthy affective tone and structure. The Ap varies enough to include a Dd. The P response is present.

After severe color shock in Figure IX, the findings in Figure X yield critical information as to the ego's stamina under emotional stresses. Can the person recover his balance? In the present record color shock not only persists in Figure X, but provokes some of its worst results: inaccurate form perception in four out of the six associations; the very far departure from norm in R 49 is uncritical judgment; it speaks of attention flight. Ap is again fixed in the D. In R 50 the ego-affect balance, delicately maintained, goes against the ego (CF−). The P association again fails in the figure once more; paralleling the pattern in Figure II, anatomy thinking becomes prominent (R 46, R 48). In the oral interest in R 50, the ego is weakening sufficiently to expose what may be a very responsive need. This response is, however, very original and R 47 is moderately so. In these Caine discloses, therefore, differentiated breadth. This is of course an asset. The fast time for first response as compared with IX is the one other sign of recovery. But as a whole Figure X shows the patient very vulnerable. The persistent shocks from the three affect-exciting figures leaves him fatigued. The neurotic status is acute.

The content in the color associations lays emphasis on the individualized and the symptomatic. The feelings center around Caine's needs, rather than on those touching any broad sectors of the community. Such, signally, are the blood, disease, thinking of R 9 ("bloody... patient on operating table"); the "leprous look" of R 15; the surgery motif in R 19; and the redundant language in naming the sex percept in R 14. Of symptomatic quality also is the "wine sack" of R 50, with its self-satisfying connotations; and the possible oral symbolism, the "faucet."

In two of his other three color responses, R 38 and R 43, the association is more appropriate, judging by the responses which these stimuli normally draw. In R 13 he is moderately original and the suggested interest is in either nature or in travel. Emotional sensitivity to normal stimuli is thus available to Caine but the quantity is restricted. The heavy saturation of feelings is found around his own symptomatic needs.

The ego's functioning. It is to be expected that in this conflicted, anxious condition the ego will be taking some losses. Caine provides motor evidence of his shaky control in the tremor observed by the examiner at R 2. In a strict sense this is an extra-Rorschach finding, in not being a judgment on a perception. However, it is one of these behavioral notes, which when accurate, adds to the picture as drawn from the formal Rorschach test pattern. Another motor indication, entirely within the test technic, is that obtained from time for first response, and from the card turning. In four cards, I, V, VI, VII, initial response time is accelerated as compared with the norms set up by the average adult sample (the respective means are I, 22.39; V, 20.86; VI, 30.80; VII, 30.80). Slightly less so, but still very fast, are the first response times in III and X (means, III, 25.58; X, 34.20). Here is a too quick discharge disclosing an excessive alertness in marked contrast to the pattern of self-guarding; this is an inner nervousness beating against the outer shell. As to the card turning, the finding is a restriction on the motility, essentially no turning. This is a loss in flexibility. In IV alone, where the anxiety discomfort has been activated, the turning is notable.

In the perception, the probability is that in R 3, 6 and 49, the F— is impersonal. As such these are uncritical reactions due to attention disturbances. The ego's controls are momentarily lifted. But personal needs extensively shape Caine's perception: R 4, 19, 42, 48 and 50. Probably also R 7, 13, 17 and 46. The deviations from accuracy are thus more frequently personal. This is a less serious finding evident more in the neuroses. The impersonal F— is more distinctive of psychotics and helps identify patients with brain damage, and the feeble-minded. The personal F— too are Caine's furthest departures from accuracy, especially R 42 and R 46. It is need in him which sets going the irritability, confuses, develops erratic judgment, and in one instance, R 42, distortion.

Caine's attention can be diverted to the very minute, and in fact three of his Dd are among the unnumbered ones, R 8, 14, 15, i.e., very rarely selected statistically. These Dd do not, however, result from attention disorder. They are either evoked by personal needs, or are defensive activity. The only attention distractibility in this man is that indicated in the impersonal F—. The fact is, Caine concentrates well, too well, as the defenses show; and destructively so to his adaptive functioning. Such a finding is the nearly inviolate sequence, Rorschach's *straff*. Similar is the excess focusing on the obvious detail (D!). In consequence of this over-attention to D, Caine is taking a heavy loss in conceptual thinking (W), and in solution of difficult problems (Z). Internal evidence in the test itself so indicates, aside from what we should expect from a person at the professional level of an engineer. A man who spontaneously associates with "a Janus-faced creature" should, if liberated, produce for his 50 responses, 9 W. His Z score should be well above 40 or 50. Again the test projects the deleterious effect on the ego's accomplishment. The excess of Hd over H is a finding of the same order. The highly intelligent who is mentally free produces more whole human associations. It is one sign of the ego's freedom to be concerned about others. In the present patient the neurosis is hamstringing this trait.

The fantasy. If the ego under its pressures looks to Caine's fantasy to draw off some of this heat, it is looking to a scanty resource. The number of his fantasy associations is low for a bright person with 50 responses. It may be that he is not constitutionally an M person and, therefore, just not capable of more fantasy living. The relative roles of nature and of nurture in making for the ability that emerges as M requires investigation from the bottom up. It may be on the other hand that Caine has more ability and is taking a loss here too as the price of his neurosis. Is it hamstringing his fantasy living just as it does his solving of difficult problems, and his conceptual thinking? In either event, he is for practical purposes just as poorly off. If the limitation is due to the neurosis, Caine is travelling a vicious circle in his ego-fantasy operations. The ego cannot get relief in fantasy living; therefore the stress on the ego is more acute. Hence its increased defensive inhibition further curtails the fantasy, again diminishing sublimating activity and so on, in the circle. Yet five fantasy responses is far from full suppression. It exceeds the average normal (mean 3.50, SD 3.24). The test findings are a measure here of the degree of restriction. Some of the man's talents still free themselves and are functioning.

The fantasies which the patient does use accent the individualized in content, in the majority of instances. They are autistic activities. Structure is in the main sound. In one instance, R 41, 42, it is the regressive in the extreme, with the content a dream activity. In all, Caine does not use enough fantasy, nor is it regressive in enough instances to warrant concluding that he has gone into an introversive withdrawal. We see rather autistic flights such as are found within the normal range. The one instance of positive withdrawal is R 10. In this he does de-realize; the content is unique and a probable projection (proof of which would have to come, however, in exploring in the patient). One instance of probable repression is R 40. The reaction to the detail to which Caine is associating is very frequently M. It should be so in a person capable of five M. There is interference here.

The stance in the fantasy: Caine's humans either remain static or their movement is centripetal, with one notable exception. Or, each human engages in behavior which includes innerly opposed directions, the mutually cancelling ambivalences that stop their victim at dead center, achieving nothing. It is the obsessive's paralyzing pattern. Such is R 5. The lady is facing "the other way" but is "looking back." In R 17 the patient himself verbalizes the arrest of movement, "it looks static, a pose." He also tells the personal need behind this cancelling out defense, "no threatening gesture." The negative is the lead to the positive aggression he wards off. It is a thought which the patient stifles even as it is born. In R 31 the content is both friendly and hostile, "a laugh or snarl." The action here is minimal, and actually static. The centripetal fantasies are R 10, 16 and 31; of flector stance. The emphasis is on the search for the central support. Caine's fantasies do not project any supine submissive pose, nor the feminine sexuality patterned out in the deeply flector association by Rorschach. Rather they uncover the insecure individual's craving for something to which to cling. The one fantasy in which the action is centrifugal is also his most original and regressive, the dream M in R 41, 42. I return to this shortly.

The Levy Energy Scale. My estimate for the five responses follows:

R	Degree of Movement
5	2
10	4
16	2
31	4
41, 42	6

The energy is definitely low in two and at about the median in two. For these four the energy may be characterized as stirring, but weighed at or toward the low level. The high energy is that in the M— in R 41, 42. Here too the content is hostility in an animal actor, a displacement; with a question also of a paranoid projection. The thinking is quite archaic and the regression deep. The patient thus has wishes which he feels powerfully, but only when the deep unconscious is activated enough to become articulate—even though in disguise as here— can the existence of such energetic wish activity be known.

R 5 is the blend of Y with the M, and the Y the more weighty determinant. The blend indicates an intense affective charge, the quality of which as Y, would be painful (p. 200). Implicit in the sexual theme of the content is a disappointment, frustration experience.

Painful affect is prominent in the other fantasy associations. Thus R 10, hostile, aggressive, phobic. A disagreeable thought is suppressed in R 16. Also the patient here doubly rejects the female; explicitly, "not distincly feminine"; and in screening his thinking in animal association. Putting a breast on these usually male figures points to a homosexual component, not further confirmed in the test. The affective tone cannot be judged in R 31. The mingling of "laugh" and "snarl" suggests the sardonic, a blend of the pleasant-unpleasant. The caution needs to be emphasized that most judgments as to affective quality are subjective. In R 41, 42 the phobic and repugnant are explicit, "malevolent." But this complex of associations is much too regressive for interpretation except by the patient himself. He is reacting here to stimuli and imagery, more fearful than wishful, stemming from very old personal sources. Only the therapeutic exploratory sessions can clear up the significance which these thoughts have for him.

The opposition trait. Caine carries in him a need for contrariness. His six white spaces exceed the findings in the average adult (mean 1.90, SD 2.14). His per cent s, 12, compares with findings in the normal adult (see table 3) of mean 5.87; SD 4.70. It is very high by either criterion. The target of the opposition, in a person whose experience balance leans to the extratensive side, is the world outside himself. But the experience balance is close enough to ambiequality to warrant expecting that this person is opposing his own conscious needs.[3] Caine's resistance is, therefore, both to his outside world and to himself. Important influences concerning the dynamics of the neurosis follow. The contending against his desires results in his uncertainty, his self-distrust, and hence the obsessive doubting. The fight against the world is one way in which he stands up against his discomposing anxiety; with the aggression indicated in some of the content, it is the counterattack whereby he seeks to dispel his troubled state. But it is a conflict laden attack which generates fresh anxiety. The patient has to defend himself from himself, and hence his passive apprehensive mood, i.e., the fresh anxiety. And so on. It is the vicious circle from which the obsessives so suffer. The question is always how did the apprehension get there in the first place in any particular patient? Which was the chicken and which the egg? Did the resistance aggression set in first with the anxiety as defense? Or was he made anxious by his "biosphere," and he reacted with aggression?

The ego's total functioning. Caine is not utilizing in his daily functioning the abilities which he has. He is insufficient in conceptual thinking and in higher intellectual achievement. His low W and Z scores are inconsistent with expectancy from other evidence in the test, as for example, the promise in the very original R 2. He does not again equal this initial bright flash. But he does continue to show signs of broader interests and, therefore, of differentiated intelligence which must stem from a higher endowment than that represented in his actual W and Z scores. Such are the travel or geography associations of R 3, perseverated following R 5; the anthropology topic in "crude Indian arrowheads" (R 7); the nature topic in "coral formation" (R 13); found also in "stalagmites" (R 29). Original also is "jester, cap and bells" (R 32). Much of the language is that of the person who has been exposed to education. His big handicap is his intellectual stiffness (p. 197), failure to alter method with varying conditions, to "give" with changing environmental events, (stiff sequence and narrowed approach), deficient psychologic homeostasis. Another is the failure to recover, in Figure X, from the neurotic shock in Figure IX. He is not set to take the impacts of a busy and sometimes rude world. His psychologic shock absorbers are failing him.

The emotional aspect of this deficiency is the passivity (Y) as lackadaisical attitude or mental inertia related to moments of discouragement. These take the push out of his initiative. The effect intellectually appears in the rather high percentage of animal form (p. 208), one evidence of

---

[3] RORSCHACH, H. AND OBERHOLZER, E., *loc. cit.*, p. 210 ff.

anergy. However, Caine alternates this surrender attitude with its opposite. As he shows in his white space responses (p. 206) he does not take things just lying down. He also fights back.

The objective world receives Caine's attention at well within normal range. The lambda index is 68 per cent (adult mean, 70.17, SD 13.71). He construes reality within the normal range but with the neurotic's compromise between the demands of the affects and the commands of the ego. His F+ percentage of 69 accounts for the several instances of inaccurate living. At the same time we have seen him go through long stretches of undeviating accuracy, unbroken in Figures IV through VIII (and see also p. 197); his too fixed hold on himself is again an unadaptive way of life. His percentage of animal responses is also a compromise in recognizing familiar stimuli. The 38 per cent is high for his intelligence but it does not go to the point of sterility. It does reflect some withdrawal from the wider world since in stopping with the stereotype Caine is not reaching out with the originality of which he is capable. Again it tells of adjustment inferior to that promised by his abilities. The man is truncating his achievement just as he does in his lowered Z and W.

The man does show some capacity for emotional warmth, urge for friendly contact with others. The four FC responses so indicate. The weighted color sum of 7.0 and the fairly large absolute number of color-indicated associations are evidence of emotional reserve. The F+ in two of the FC strengthens this indication. However, the experience balance with total color overbalancing total of movement responses is evidence that Caine is more extratensive than he is composed. The M to be sure does absorb some of the C; he does introvert some of his feelings. But with two unmodulated color responses in this extratensive whole picture, an impetuous reaction pattern must be inferred. The five white spaces emphasize this finding; in one cluster with the pure C response they promise an impulsive response to his world's stimuli by our patient. The minus in one of the CF responses and in two of the FC also tell of instability. Maladaptive aggressive trends are to be anticipated. This is the man's neurosis. In the erotic sphere too, he will turn to maladjustive solutions, but internalizing his needs, and transforming them in the fantasy (see R 5 and R 16–17). For that matter, he internalizes the aggression, too (see R 10, R 41, 42).

The content. In R 4, the sexual interest is overt and the patient distorts his percept (personal F−) to see what so interests him. He follows with an unconscious wish (M in R 5) involving a nude woman. He mixes the sexes in R 16, 17; "breasts" on the usually male figures, and also "small Adam's apple"; but "not feminine." In seeing these figures as animals he is screening the homosexual interest projected in the blending of the sexes. But the degree of homosexuality in this whole test record is of secondary weight.

Assuming that R 4 is exposing a heterosexual wish, this imagery appears three times, in R 4, R 5 and R 14. In the one of these, R 5, of fantasy structure, the ambivalent behavior of the sexual is convincingly heterosexual. Caine articulates fine thought nuances with respect to this woman; the adverb "dimly" and her shadowy substance, she is "silhouetted." He does this with painful emotion (Y). One focus of his maladjustment is clearly the man's relations to women.

Another is projected in the anatomy associations. These are original. He reports them in very vivid language accenting thoughts of disease: "bloody . . . operating room" (R 9); "a leprous look" (R 15); "lungs . . . dark . . . pathological . . . TB" (R 21); and again "lungs . . . TB" (R 48). R 15 contains so much of the repellent as to indicate agitation. The "rib formation" (R 46) may also be screening a "lung" association. The patient is distorting the perceived form here as he does in R 48 and R 19. Content in the latter does not overtly refer to disease; but it is too original and the heart is too much a common cause of worry. It stresses in the pathological concern with health. Caine explicitly verbalizes this concern: "whenever I have a cough I think of TB." The "ribs . . . skeleton" of R 35 is, however, not evidence of this trait. The anatomy association to this detail is very frequent; one of the best authenticated P. The percept here is a function not of the patient but of the stimulus.

Phobic ideas are present in four responses and possibly in two others. The four are: "baring their fangs" in R 10 (p. 198); "insignia of the Nazi army" R 25 (the record was obtained while Nazi propaganda was a force); the "alligators . . . mouth open" R 26; the "wing formation . . . sinister" R 28. The two more questionable ones are R 12 and R 44 (see p. 198 concerning these associations). The diagnostic value of phobic content is two-fold: (a) as evidence of obsessive preoccupation, and hence a need for it, which therefore points to the fact that a deeper anxiety is being screened; (b) the specific content uncovers a vulnerable focus in the patient's thinking. It tells what he fixates on when trying to insulate off the more oppressive anxiety.

Caine caricatures twice: in R 2, "a long nose . . . an old nose" and in R 32, "the clown-shaped head . . . jester, with cap and bells." Whom he is ridiculing these responses do not tell. They disclose one of those hostilities in which he is attempting to clear out his own fear state by aggression upon the environment.

Oral themes. Caine verbalizes these and related ones with enough frequency to establish that much feeling centers around them. The specific emphasis varies: oral and phobic in R 25, R 26. It is very original in R 50 with drink intake motif. If the "breasts" of R 17 communicate the same oral need, a very primitive want is being recalled, a possible deprivation. It will require deep therapy to establish this, and also the meaning to the patient of the "blowing mouth" association in R 41, 42. Support of the intake surmise will be found in the unnumbered "birds in a nest . . . mouth open for food" following R 5. Caine did not report this until the inquiry; there is evidence that he was blocking it which in turn speaks of the strong feeling he experiences on this subject. The clinical history will in fact be seen confirming the indication of early deprivation which the patient shared with a sister. The "nest" in Caine's Rorschach test language is definitely "home." It is an association which with its symbolic value occurs with fair frequency in Rorschach test experience. The security motif usually also attaches.

Another childhood memory emerges in the "valentine we made in school," R 11. With its flavor of nostalgia it uncovers persistence of feelings around experiences when he was much younger.

The "Janus" creature is one of those originals that can be cleared up only by exploring in the patient. Is it the "double front" (Fenichel) of the obsessive-compulsive? Of similar order is "one of those controls on a machine; goes round and round, when it goes too fast . . . a governor," R 47. It is too individualized not to be significant.

Less convincing as projecting personal need are certain responses noted above as, nevertheless, evidence of interest breadth (p. 204). These are R 3, 7, 13, 29, 32. How charged these are with individualized emotional value one cannot say from the test alone. Some are F— which may only be impersonal. In any event, as breadth, they represent a personality reserve. To the extent that they are significant, they are assets. They provide leads as to the direction which some of the therapeutic effort may take.

How can we now answer the question raised by the psychiatrist in requesting this Rorschach test: will this patient benefit from further analysis? The neurosis is a well-set one. The intellectual contraction has been sharp. For a person of his endowment, Caine is functioning too narrowly. The defenses show signs of stiffness. Amenability to change at the intellectual level is therefore inadequate. A painful undertone courses beneath these adaptations of his to the problems which his life sets before him. This can, however, carry *double entente* for purposes of treatment. To the painful new facts which further analysis will bring to consciousness his ego will react by tightening the defenses. So far, the outlook is unfavorable. Yet a depressive reaction may be the first sign of a favorable turn in a treatment effort. Then too, Caine does have some malleability where it can be most effective; in those other sectors of his emotional life, the exciting, expressive feelings; and the fantasy activity. This is inner resilience. When found in a Rorschach test, it provides an affirmative answer to the question: can analysis be attempted? It tells of liberated emotions, and of willingness to communicate deeper wishes. Furthermore, Caine's ego is an integrated one. The intelligence is high; he should be able to see relations between the psychodynamic data that an analysis brings to conscious awareness. All these assets need still be considered in relation to the unfavorable ones. The whole person with whom the therapist must deal is structured out of all these many psychologic forces. The judgment as to further analyzability must, therefore, like Caine's neurosis be a compromise; the assets definitely warrant the effort, but the defenses may again set up the barriers, which would bring this neurosis once more to a stalemate. This Rorschach test can thus answer the questions as to immediate procedure. It cannot be unequivocal as to long time outlook.

B. FROM THE ANALYST'S NOTES

Caine married at 24 years of age. He came to therapy in the state of great anxiety: he wanted to leave his wife and could not. He had already set a date for the break-up about three weeks ahead, had made arrangements to take the apartment of a friend who was going on a vacation. At this time he had been seeing a young woman, single, about six years younger than himself. They have had dates but no sexual activities. He had once left his wife one year ago for a period of a few days. He could not stay away from her. He then went to one therapist who told him to "pull himself together," that he owed it to his wife to stay with her. The advice did not reassure him. One of his fears is that his wife will die and leave him alone. As he looks at her in bed he can see the unmistakable signs of age creeping upon her and he is frightened.

Caine met the present psychiatrist about two years previously when she saw his mother who at that time presented a picture of dementia. It appeared to be on an arteriosclerotic basis, but from what patient has told since his analysis began she had had a presenile dementia with paranoid trends, and accused her husband of infidelity for which there was no basis.

The patient is the second of two siblings; a sister is four years older. The family history is one of poverty, almost starvation at times and living in poor neighborhoods. The patient had been born in one of the small coastal towns of Massachusetts. The parents were of Scandinavian extraction. The family had moved to Boston when the children were small. The mother never broke away from old world customs. The father, a carpenter, not successful, is quite intelligent. He is active in a left-wing party, and organized the party in some neighboring towns. He and the mother first met at a party meeting.

The father did not believe in higher education for women. Therefore, the sister had to stop school at 16 years of age against her protests. She worked in an office. But she went to night high school and studied toward a diploma. She now does some lecturing. She has had some boy friends and one rather serious affair with a man younger than herself. The family, however, never approved of her male friends. She now lives with the father in quarters which Caine helped to fix up. The mother had died about six months before he came to therapy. For the last year or more before her death, he had cared for her in a boarding home where he paid $150 to $200 a month. His wife has not objected to the expenditures which he has made for his family.

Caine is a self-made man as far as his education is concerned. He is an engineer, has a very good standing, teaches and writes.

Mrs. Caine is very intelligent, well educated, a newspaper reporter. She was always impeccably groomed and made a fairly good appearance, but was obviously under a great deal of strain. She seemed willing to stay with her husband under any circumstances, even to closing her eyes to his running around with other women. She said that she and her husband had been lovers since marriage, until about two years ago at which time he started stepping out. She had asked little of him. He spent his money as he wished. She earns enough to support herself well. The couple eats out much of the time in very good restaurants, they drink quite a bit, entertain and just about use up most of their own money from month to month.

In the war the patient was diagnosed psychoneurotic. This did not bother him a bit.

Caine had had a love affair with a young woman about his own age just before he met his wife. His mother had raised such violent objections that he finally split off from the girl and soon after met his wife. He had had other girl friends and the mother had always objected. Soon after Caine met his wife, they had entered on a sexual relationship. He thought he should not settle down to an older woman, nor to any woman for that matter, before having more experience. Then he decided to break up but he became so panicky the next day that he decided he would just have to get married. He tried to call his wife-to-be, could not contact her, and when he did meet her she said that her phone had been out of order. Now he gets the same feelings of panic when he thinks of leaving her. He has had colitis for years; also a cardiac condition with EKG findings. But he does not limit his activities.

The analyst's first suggestion was that he delay his separation from his wife if he planned to go into therapy. Caine did not see how he could possibly do such a thing. He had decided upon a time and there would be no turning back. He has lined up two or three women for sexual relationships. He has thought of five different women as being a number with which a man should be pleased. Several years ago he had a short-lived episode with a girl about whom he cared little. This was clandestine.

When he left his wife last spring he went through another sexual episode, again short-lived. But when he was having an affair, he found it very difficult to stay away from his wife. It developed too, that when he was seeing his wife-to-be, he would get terribly upset and nauseated when he would think of going home after a week-end with her. The mother would always be angry but would prepare food for him. He devised a plan of complaining about the food. This would hurt his mother and she would start making apologies to him and they would make up.

Actually Caine was much too excited to treat, but the psychiatrist decided to make the attempt. After a few interviews she advised that Mrs. Caine also be treated but by someone else. Caine perpetually talked of how upset the wife was and how he did not want to hurt her. She resisted seeing a psychiatrist, but did so in the attempt to hold her husband.

Caine went into psychoanalysis. In the paragraphs that follow, I report the essence of the conflict and the dynamics in the anxiety as these emerged in the analytic sessions. I have condensed these from the very complete notes which the analyst so kindly made available to me.

At the core of Caine's neurosis is his need for his wife and his conflict over that need. His dreams tell this story which he confirms in his analytic sessions generally and in the timing of his somatic symptoms. In the first week of the analysis, he suffered attacks of colitis, diarrhea, migraine. They are related to thoughts of separating from the wife, which he is now planning for two weeks hence. Dream fragments which he reports at this time, disclose his anxiety over the projected separation. His talk is about the wife's having everything to lose by his going. The dream material shows him concerned with the loss which he himself will suffer. He now realizes what a psychologic haven the wife is to him.

A few days later, the session brings out that (a) he wants to leave his wife, and (b) he also does not want to. He is afraid of the dark and at night will touch his wife in order to reassure himself of her presence. He is planning an affair with another girl and he realizes that he likes her because she has traits similar to his wife's. She is intelligent, well read, enjoys music and the theatre. But in connection with her, Caine's inferiority feelings are stirred up. He fears that the girl's family will not accept him, think him not properly born. He now decides to broaden his acquaintanceship beyond the range of the intelligentsia so as to include more "average" persons.

He does leave his wife on the day set, and starts his new liaison. A month later, he reports an anxiety dream in which he is searching for his wife. His association to it: he used to go home for meals for about six months following his marriage. The analyst points out that now, in the dream, he is going back to his wife as formerly he used to go back to his mother.

The next session finds Caine reproaching himself for seeing the girl friend. He is now ruminating over returning to the wife. But he knows that if he does, he will wish that he had done the opposite. He rationalizes the benefits from the return. The new woman is a spendthrift; she will want babies; she is not interested in working. He is frequently haunted by two faces: his wife's, reproachful, sad; the girl's, smiling. Of her own accord, the girl decides to go on a vacation. Caine also goes on one to a resort where the wife is. His rationalizations: he needs the rest; the wife is clever, creative. The analyst, of course, sets him straight; Caine is anxious and cannot be alone. That is why he is going to see his wife. He had not resolved his conflictual problem.

Both analyst and patient now go on vacations. Following their return, Caine is in torture over thoughts of again leaving his wife. Whichever woman he rejects will be unhappy the rest of her life, he thinks. But if he breaks with both, he will end up in the city's "skid row" district. The analyst points out that this district has an attraction for him. He narrates that while his wife and girl friend were both away, he went drinking with some women, one of whom recited some very anal jingles. He decided such a woman could provide him with some interesting sex experiences.

At about this time he recalls that on returning to his wife he had dreamt of losing his teeth. He has, in reality, feared losing his teeth and his hair which would thus make him less attractive. He has much praise for his wife who has encouraged him, helped him to get where he is. She attended to many of the details for a book which he had written. There is only one love, and the wife is that. He does not believe in any hereafter, but when he fantasies one, he is there with his wife. When he thinks of leaving her, he sees her as lonely throughout eternity. When spending a weekend with her, he is usually all right until Sunday, i.e., when it draws to a close. But in instances he has become nauseated, his heart would beat fast; once he went into a terrible panic and recovered himself only by the thought that his wife would be with him throughout eternity.

The awful feelings of loneliness which come up when he thinks of leaving her remind him of a great fear he had when he first carried his lunch to school. He went into such a panic, that he ran home with his lunch. Thereafter for some time the mother would bring his lunch and stay with him in the hall while he ate.

Caine is clearly binding his anxiety in his wife. Doing so he screens the deeper anxiety centering in another person, which as the analysis brings out is the mother. In a dream the wife reproaches him. In reality she never does. It was the mother who had done so as the analyst points out to Caine. In fact the wife permits him to engage in his affairs and is always waiting for him. His free associations at this time disclose again the horror he experiences at the thought of leaving her.

He does not leave her, but he does maintain his liaison with the other woman. Actually, as the analyst points out, he is hostile to, and frustrates both. He feels his guilt, and to appease that, continues as the lover of each. In one of the sessions, he himself speaks of his anger toward both for making him so uncomfortable. At the same time, he continues to fall back on the wife in the "mother" role. He runs to her following "incidents" with the other girl. From the time of their marriage, and until recently, she has read to him, like a mother does to her little boy. His wife buys him something every time she goes into town. His mother was also always buying him something. At the same time he now has some complaints about the other girl. She is not as patient as she used to be. He feels as though he would like to give her up and stay with his wife. The latter is thus a haven to him as the mother used to be. The equation appears to be: the other woman is to the wife, as the wife was to the mother. About this time, luck treats him to some dramatic irony. He must order eviction of a mother and her son out of a house in which he has an interest. But he denies to the analyst that he is here recapitulating anything of his own story.

In another session it develops that the wife frequently remains inert to his wishes. She will not, for example, sit with him while he drinks his coffee after dinner. He reacts with much surprise to the analyst's pointing out that his mother was similarly unresponsive. "By Jupiter, she was."

Anxiety, centering around mother and wife emerges recurrently in the analysis. We read from the treatment notes:

The analyst: Your wife is very resistant. You have to spend so much time breaking her resistance down to reassure yourself that mother likes you. Now, why were you so uncertain, why were you so afraid that you would lose your mother?

Patient: She was always telling us that she was going to die. Mother was always talking of how unhappy she was. That gave me a terrible feeling, it meant that I did not mean a whole lot to her.

He adds at this point that the animus between his father and mother made him feel that they might separate.

The analyst here points out that all these anxieties made for intense feelings of insecurity in Caine. They involved also the fear of losing his father. This would stir up much guilt. The patient in fact says that he used to become much upset if the father did not come home on time. But with the wife, the analyst notes "you have not had all the fears that you had with your mother."

Recall of the father focuses the enquiry on that important person; on the other member of Caine's family, the sister; and on the unanswered questions concerning both. The sister is present in the first of many dreams which Caine brings in. She reappears in others. Early deprivations shared by the brother and sister and his sympathy for her are communicated in these dreams. They had been close as they grew up, and now, as he informs the analyst, she is maladjusted. She goes from job to job; has love affairs with younger men. The mother had inhibited both the patient and the daughter in their affairs. His sexual interest in the sister emerges in that first dream. It turns out to be related to curiosity which both the children had had concerning the parents. The precipitant to the dream: the wife had recently shown curiosity about the patient bearing on his relations to other women. This activated the older curiosity concerning his own parents, the one which he had shared with the sister.

The sister in fact appears time and again in the analysis; she is obviously an important character in the drama. Although her relation to the patient's anxiety remains obscure, her identification with the wife is established sharply. Thus, as Caine describes some of his wife's behavior when other people are present, it develops that she is hostile to them. He recalls too his wife's telling him that her mother did not like her.

Analyst: Does your sister feel that way too,?

Patient: Yes, she does.

Analyst: Could there be identification between your wife and your sister? You feel guilty over having been the preferred one?

Patient: I felt that way many times when a child.

The equation here appears to be: the wife was to her own mother as the sister was to hers (and to the patient's).

Two days after this identification is analyzed out, Caine has a dream exposing hostility to the father. He dreams of a prominent religious official. "His face was ghastly. He shouldn't make a public appearance. He is almost dead." He associates this person with his father; recalls that the father is reaching advanced old age; and that he wants the father "out of the way." Then he would be alone with the sister. In evaluating the therapy at one point, the analyst notes, in fact, that the patient suffers his greatest guilt in relation to his sister. He has been jealous of her because she gets love from the father.

The strong psychologic need for the father emerges at scattered points through the therapy. There was the fear of the parents' separation with attendant loss of

the father and interrelated guilt. Also, the apprehension when the father was late
in returning home. Another memory concerns the intense anxiety when the father
was in an automobile accident. The patient was then in his adolescence. He slept
with the father until puberty. His attachment to and trust in this parent is explicit
at one point in the therapy. While contemplating leaving his wife, he tells the analyst
that he will go live with his father after the separation. The analyst notes that he
had hesitated in pronouncing "father." The patient adds that he would receive much
support from the father, and this would offset some of the disadvantages incident to
the separation. To the analyst's question, how understanding would the father be if
the patient discussed the matter with him, Caine answered that he believed he would
be understanding. In evaluating the course of the therapy (about a month before the
patient had expressed this wish) the analyst notes "deepest longing in this man is for
good relationship with father."

The principal other personality structures brought to light in the analytic therapy
were (a) unconscious homosexual component and (b) serious feelings of inferiority.
The homosexual trend comes out first in an association concerning the mother who
had objected to all women in whom the patient was interested. She would do everything for the men whom he would bring into the house. She was, thus, encouraging
him into a homosexual reaction pattern. The dreams confirm this wish in him. It
was judged by the analyst as a passive homosexuality growing out of envy of the
sister and her relation with the father.

His feelings of inferiority emerge both in overt associations and in dreams. The
primary source of the feeling is sexual. In one dream he goes to a house of prostitu-
tion with another man who is prepared to have sexual relations nine times, the patient only three times. Another cause is the family background. This will impede
his success with one of his women friends. Her family, in one of his dreams, throws
a big party but does not invite him. When this girl receives the attention of another
man, Caine fantasies that he will crush him with his intellect. He uses it as his way
of winning in competition. He has always felt inadequate physically. He has always
depended on his high intelligence.

The foregoing is a representative sample of the material emerging in the
analysis; and of Caine's course while in it. The treatment continued for
slightly more than one and one-half years following the Rorschach test.
Meanwhile Caine had been progressing in his profession with outstanding
success. The psychiatrist began to prepare him for interruption or termina-
tion of the analysis. She comments, "Patient is upset, just as one might
expect." An anxiety dream preceded the final session. The analyst's note:

Analysis has been terminated for a trial time. The patient is a great deal improved.
The colitis has caused him almost no trouble for a year or more. The cardiac anxiety
is gone. He is making tremendous professional success, is doing a lot of teaching,
will be made a high executive officer of his firm in a year or so. Patient is much more
resigned to his marriage. He recognizes that he is too scared of younger women, and
at the same time has no real urge to change those feelings since he does not want to
make the sacrifices necessary to interest a younger wife, one who would make inroads
on patient's time which he wishes for professional pursuits; and one who would want
babies. Younger women represent his sister toward whom he has quite conscious sexual
wishes which stir up fears of the father who keeps the sister tied to him.

C. Test and Clinical Findings in Perspective

The two fields of stress that constitute this man and his neurosis are obvious. There are the needs related to the women that so dominate his course: mother, sister, wife, other woman, analyst. They are the principal forces in the outer field, the biosphere. Secondly is the conflict of needs within Caine himself, powerful urges and countering anxiety.

All these stresses and their effects are clear-cut in the test's whole pattern. A neurosis with little relief. The strain is unrelieved throughout the record. Shock leaves Caine in disruption. At the close we see him with balance not recovered (p. 203). The best he can do in the interest of integration is to contract. He does this at the cost of intellectual elasticity (p. 208). The anxiety and the painful affect saturate the treatment interviews; they are a major test finding (p. 199 ff.). From the rigidity so prominent in the test findings may be inferred the intensity of the conflict. It is a measure of the strength of the opposing intrapsychic forces. This affective quality stands out in his conflicted attitude around his wife. He must leave her and he cannot leave her.

Concerning the importance of women dynamically, the test is also explicit (p. 208 ff.). The question is even in order whether the shadowy woman in Caine's associations to Figure I can be directly correlated to the fear reported in the analytic session (p. 215). "She was always telling us she was going to die . . . that gave me a terrible feeling." Does the Rorschach test communicate the fear that the mother (wife) will fade out? Such specific interpretation of Rorschach test content can frequently be made. It is plausible. Yet it still carries too much risk of error that can seriously mislead the further clinical handling of the patient.

Caine's agitation, the deep set of his painful emotions projected in the blends, (C.Y, M.Y, p. 200) are the kind of intensities that go with the sense of abandonment which Caine communicates in this analytic interview. This same test technic communicates also the mixture of impulsivity and distress which describe him as he first came to therapy, and later, recurrently, at each thought of leaving his wife. The unsettling force of the neurosis, the sub-ego level to which Caine can have recourse, is evident in the nausea (p. 214) and the Rorschach test's severe color shock (p. 201) is entirely consistent.

Emotionally the analyst finds him at first too excited to treat. The affective structure in the test shows him out of hand, very labile (p. 201). The pure color responses are also a lead to Caine's urge for primitive gratification, an observation which I failed to make. My fault here was that of under-interpretation. The clinical manifestation is the drive for sexual experience, as a satisfaction in and for itself. As described in the clinical notes, it lacks the mature quality of an allocentric relation, one which satisfies the self by satisfying the partner. In Caine it is rather the infant's crying out to be surfeited. But Caine does reach for company and for social contacts in adult patterns. He goes out to dinner, theatres, he dances. This in Rorschach test language is FC (p. 201); it is projected also in the relatively high number of color determined responses (p. 201).

The likelihood that the patient will externalize his feelings (p. 213) is certainly the picture which also emerges from the analyst's note. So too is the outlook for aggression against the environment (p. 207). His hostility, as the psychiatrist shows him, is primarily directed against those individuals who make up so much of his field of stress, women.

The typical indecisions of the obsessive condition that run through so much of the clinical record will recall the similar Rorschach test observations at several points. The defense which principally emerged in the test, maximum effort to hold on to the self, I take also to be an obsessive phenomenon. As part of this pattern Caine again produces a specific association referable to the clinical datum: the "Janus-faced creature" (R 2 with its "two faces.") The identifying pattern of the obsessive is to look in opposite directions simultaneously. And in fact at one point in the clinical record Caine does try to follow two faces of different women leading in opposite directions simultaneously (p. 214).

Creativity, or imagination, is nowhere stressed clinically. Some may be inferred from his vocation and his progress in it. How much it suffers, is inhibited or blocked owing to the neurosis we do not know. The facts do appear to confirm the moderate amount of M found in the test. Similarly with respect to the man's intelligence. The test shows him functioning somewhat below the capacity which he must have and must be using in his profession. But certain test data dictate clear inference that he has more than he is using. The significant finding in the test is the potential, and the differential between that and the inhibiting influence of the neurosis. Given the favorable or necessary circumstances, a high intellectual achievement can be expected of Caine.

Among the more specific correlating findings there is the binding of the anxiety (p. 214; p. 200). The dysphoric mood moments of the test (p. 200) are the loneliness (p. 214) or the apprehensions (p. 214) clinically noted. A passive or resigned acceptance of his neurotic condition may be deduced from the analytic material: his reaction to being rejected by the military service (p. 212); more cogent, his final acceptance of the marriage, painfully conflicted though he was about it. Emotional passivity is one of the test's findings (p. 200). Another specific content equivalent is the birds (R 5) "mouths open for food." Two birds would be involved in the details to which he is reacting. His sister and himself and the poverty in which they were raised come to mind (p. 211). The oral content in the test (p. 209) may stem from the same source that manufactured the dream with the teeth (p. 214). My surmise in the interpretation as to the possible significance of this oral content is not confirmed by the interpretation of the dream in the analytic sessions. This means, of course, that the general lead which I followed is not always applicable. This points up again the need for establishing frames of reference by which to interpret Rorschach test content (p. 64).

Guilt consciousness appears in the clinical notes more frequently and more significantly than I report for the test. Again my fault is that of inadequately interpreting available test data. (But cf. p. 199.) The rigid reaction to the anxiety shock figures I have for some time recognized and reported as work of the overactive superego. Another source in the test from which guilt may be inferred is the dysphoric mood.

An important structural failure in this test record is the absence of vista responses. The clinical picture sharply etches out inferiority feelings. Self-devaluation behavior does appear but only periodically in instances of excessive qualifying. This is suggestive only of inadequacy consciousness. The fact is, however, that an important trait which contributes to the shaping of Caine's personality is not projected in his test record.

Two other weighty clinical findings cannot be extracted from this test protocol. They are the sister's and the father's roles in the neurosis. Both are very important; the sister, if anything, is slightly more. Still another is the homosexual need. The lead does emerge in the test vestigially. It is possibly a bit more accented in the analytic interviews. There is, however, essential agreement in respect to this trait.

In all, Caine is one of those persons of whom there are so many in our culture, one suffering from a probably never-ending neurosis. The man will get relief. Success will be his. But he is likely never to exploit his potential anywhere near its fullness. He spins around in too many circles. He is likely to maintain efficiency adequate for a high level of success. But the outlook is that he will be periodically returning for treatment.

Chapter VI

A BOY IN THE ORTHOGENIC SCHOOL

A. The First Test. A Growth Lag

This child was admitted to the Orthogenic School at the age of $5\frac{7}{12}$ years. The referral statement was: "a feeding problem from birth with regurgitation which has persisted through the years; extreme fears; poor muscular coordination."

Background history included the information that the parents own a small women's apparel shop and earn a satisfactory living. They had married young. Eddie was the second child. The first, a boy, died within eight months after birth. The parents describe him as "beautiful, well formed, alert," and contrast him with Eddie as "extremely ugly and ill." The mother, after eighteen years, still cannot talk of this first child without emotion. She shows guilt over her handling of Eddie.

Three Rorschach tests were administered to this boy in the school; the first, when he was $7\frac{9}{12}$ years old, or after he had been in the school 26 months. This test record, and the interpretation, follow.

RESPONSE RECORD

Figure I (5″)

1. DdW F− A — 'A picture of a fox (indicates Dd 22), cut to look like things.

2. Dds F+ Oj — 'and inside is a few holes . . . and

3. D F+ Ls — 'inside, the rock (details around Dds 26 and 29).
3.5

4. Dd F− Alph — 'A few dots . . . and one question mark (Dd 23) and three dots . . . five dots.'

Figure II (2″)

5. D C Fi — 'Fire . . . a few fires (D 2, D 3, fires are red) and some lights. Two points . . . one point cut in two (D4).

6. D F+ Ls — 'Some stones (D6), and here is a hole (Ds 5) . . . and there's sort of a little point . . . a round point on each side, and up here another point (Dd 22 and 23),

220

7. Dd F— Geom	'and one little circle on each side (Dd 22) and two little dots.'

Figure III (1″)

8. D C Fi	'A few fires (D 2, D 3) and sort of points.
9. Dd F— Ad	'Sort of a back of a chicken (outer edge of Dd 23).
10. D F— Ad	'Sort of feathers (Dd 22 ... I thought were feathers).
11. D FY— Ls	'Sort of a black rock (D 11) and this is a long stick, and this is a few points,
12. D F+ Oj	'and these two are broken sticks (D 5).'

Figure IV (2″)

13. W F+ Ls 2.0	'A whole rock there, a line going down,
14. Dds F— Geom	'and a circle ... up (D 4, and space inner to it) ... and a little point ... and another little point.
15. Dd YF Ls	'And up here still part of the rock ... and here sort of a whitish stone (Dd on D 3) ... and another round circle, and two more points ... inside is a piece of something ... some white stone (Dds around D 1).'

Figure V (2″)

16. D F— Ls Alph	'Here are two stones ... a stone that's cut like a V (D 8) ... and a line that's going down from the V ... and here's a point and here's a little point.
17. Dd F— Ls	'Here's a light piece of stone ... and a crooked piece of stone (Dd on outer edge of D 11). And that's all I can see ... two holes caved in (Dds in lower edge) and (patient continues to prate).'

Figure VI

18. D F+ Oj	'Here's a long post (D 5) ... a stone pole,

19. Dd F+ Ad

'and those are whiskers (Dd 26), and here's some crooked stone (and traces edge of D 1, then lateral of D 1) and it's caved in . . . and goes up and around, and makes a sort of a point.

'And here's a long circle . . . and the point comes up . . . and the stone goes to the circle . . . one hole (indentation near the bottom) and then caved in . . . (and continues this quality of talk).

20. Dd F+ Ad

'And sort of like feet (Dd 21, of a bird).'

Figure VII

21. Dd F− Ls

'Here are two points . . . two lines . . . and on each side (in area of D 6).

'And there's a cave-in (D 10, each) and after that there are crippled stones on each side (edge of D 10).

22. D F+ Ls

'And then there are some blocks (D 3, stone blocks) . . . you build a house with . . . (turns card). Two hands . . . and a block that's caved in . . . a circle caved in . . . then there's some things a point . . . something up and down.'

Figure VIII (15″)

23. D F+ A

'Is it up side down? . . . (E: no hold it as it is). Two tigers climbing

24. D F+ Bt
    3.0

'up a branch (D 4); and here's something dropped off . . . and here's sort of a point.

25. Dd M+ Hd

'Lines for hands (Dd 22). (E: Are they doing anything?) They're pulling something. (E: pulling what?)

26. D C Bt
    3.0

'Pulling a bush. (E: How do you know it is a bush?) On account it's green.

27. Dds F Oj

'Here are some holes (inner Dds); they are in the bush . . . (on E's question, P continued) A man cut the holes, so the tigers would fall through to the ground, (on further questioning) because he doesn't like tigers in his front yard (E questions) if the tigers fell to the ground ... they would die ... or hurt themselves much.

28. D C Fi

'A little light ... (because light is yellow and that is yellow, D 7).

Figure IX (3")

29. Dds YF— Hd

'Some orange. Some white teeth (Dd 21).

30. D C Bt

'On the tree and here's some leaves (because it's green) ... and there's a hole ... there's two holes ... and there's two other holes, two light lines.

31. D C Fi

'And here's some fire (D 3).

32. D M+ H
2.5

'Clowns doing funny tricks on the tree (D 1). (On E's question) leaves are always green.'

Figure X (5")

33. D M.CF— A

'Some blue monkeys (D 1, are holding on to the leaves) on each side.

34. D F+ Oj

'Here's a sort of pole.

35. D M+ H
4.0

'A man was pulling it ... two animals pulling it (D 11).

36. D C Bt

'And here's some sunflowers (D 2 and D 15) in the tree (because sunflowers are always yellow).

37. D F— Ad

'And part of an animal in the tree (D 3).

38. D F— Alph

'The letter A.

39. D C Bt

'And here's some green leaves (D 12).

40. D F— Cl

'And here's some clouds (D 9). And two blue things ...

41. Dds F Geom

'And two circles in the blue (Dds inner to D 6).

42. D F— Alph

'Sort of an A (D 10) except for the two points.

43. D F+ A

'Sort of an animal (same).'

RESPONSE SUMMARY

R total 43

W	1	M	3	H	2	F+ %	50
DdW	1	M.CF−	1	Hd	2	A %	21
D	27	C	8	A	4	P	0
Dd	14 (s,5)	YF	2 (1 −)	Ad	5	s	5
	$\overline{43}$	FY−	1	Alph	3	s %	11.6
		F+	13	Bt	5	T/IR	4.37
Z	18.0	F−	13	Cl	1		
Ap	D Ddll	F	2	Fi	4	Af r	0.95
Seq	Ir		$\overline{43}$	Geom	3	L	0.65
				Ls	9		
		EB	4/13	Oj	5		
					$\overline{43}$		

INTERPRETATION

A seriously underdeveloped ego is this boy's as it is etched out in this first of his three Rorschach tests. The intellectual life is immature, for a child of $7\frac{9}{12}$ years, essentially infantile. The test demonstrates this immaturity in Eddie's motor function and language, in his perception, attention failures, the thinking structure and the thought content.

In his language, Eddie uses a very childlike style. Such is the identification of the ink blot as "a picture" (R 1), the direct descriptive language, "cut to look like things," the objectivity with which he locates his percepts, "inside ears," etc.; and again, in Figure II, "a little point," "a round point," these "points," "lines," "circles," or just "things." Similar is his frequently identifying the white space as "a hole." Also, the enumeration formula, "three dots," "five dots," "one point cut in two." This description in simplest, basic terms is a pattern I have observed only in the very young child to about the fourth year of age and under. It is a concretistic way of seeing the world, one in which each object has its boundaries sharply defined from those of every other. It is a reduction of reality to its basic forms, or rather, to that phase of growth in reality perceiving before it changes under the effects of personal experience. This phase and perception pattern are neatly illustrated by the child in Hans Christian Andersen's story, "The Emperor's Clothes"; his Majesty's adult subjects, from old habits of obedience and loyalty, see their sovereign as he wants them to. The child, not yet habituated, sees his Majesty in his nude reality: "But he has nothing on."

Periodically, too, Eddie's verbal productions become especially childlike, successions of percepts unsynthesized. It is a question in these instances, how much of what Eddie sees is scorable response, and how much is sterile language, the jabber of the very young. Such are the reactions in Figures II, IV, V, VI and in part of IX.

In the structure, too, Eddie shows something of this concretistic mentality, namely in the Ap. He perceives essentially no wholes (W score:1). He rivets his attention on the D and the Dd. His vision embraces the individually defined object, each isolated off from the others. The components of reality are emerging, but not the larger view of reality. Thus, a structural finding in the test confirms the nonstructured, unscored observations. The unrich content, concerning which more will be said below, is essentially a structural finding. It is another index to concretistic thought processes.

At the motor level directly, the time for first response discloses the boy's nervous readiness to respond. Time was not recorded in two of the figures (VI, VII), reflecting the pressure on the examiner from Eddie's push to associate immediately. Again, this is a frequent experience in obtaining a Rorschach test record at the youngest age levels. For the eight test cards in which initial time was recorded, it was, in seven of them, at the very fast end of the range as obtained from the normal adult sample. The average computed for first responses in the eight cards, 4.37 seconds, is also very fast. The fluctuation of productivity is especially interesting in showing a failure so far to establish an even tempo of living. The average of all his nine fluctuations for the ten cards is 2.33, which is beyond the range of the third sigma above the mean for the 6 to 9 year sample (mean 0.92, SD 0.38). This is significantly above the average. The oscillation in his successive performances shows up more sharply as we inspect the response quantities from one test card to the next: productivity goes up from Figure II to Figure III; down from III to IV; then Eddie maintains a relatively even keel through the next three. But he now becomes very unsmooth, going up by four associations (from Figure VII to VIII), then down by two (from VIII to IX), and up by seven (from IX to X). We see him operating as most young children do, having moments of even absorption alternating with more vigorous expenditure of energy, and relaxing again into smoother sailing. The stabilized tempo which should be this person's when he has become adult, has not yet in his childhood stage been established.

The perception. F+ per cent for the record as a whole is .50. This is significantly low judged by findings in our 6 to 9 year olds (mean 67.17, SD 11.90). In his day-to-day living Eddie sees his world much less accurately than do most of his contemporaries. He fails to criticize himself. He also reiterates content without regard for change of stimulus, and so responds inaccurately under domination of a previous thought. This is perseveration to which I return below. Eddie here shows himself indifferent to, rather than distorting, reality. This inference is given also by the large number of F− which are impersonal: R 1, 4, 7, 9, 10, 14, 37, 38, 42. The "stones" do have some personal significance as appears in the "cave-in" theme and related ones, "crooked piece of stone" (R 17). The theme recurs (R 19, 21), even more meaningfully as "crippled stones." (See discussion of content p. 237.) Following this lead, I am judging the following F— as probably personal: R 11, 16, 17. Also, R 29. With regard to R 40 there is uncertainty; "cloud" has a personal (threat) significance to many people. But one cannot always argue from the general to the particular. R 40 may as well be impersonal, to Eddie, as personal. In any event, there are enough personal F— in the record to indicate that the boy does distort reality as his needs dictate.

The content in these personal F— provides a lead to the clinical investigation to be followed up. Does Eddie identify himself with the "crippled, caved-in" objects? If so, the test is here telling about that very important experience, the patient's perception of himself. It is in the present instance a self-devaluated one. It first emerges in R 12, "the broken sticks." The troubled mood which this attitude generates will also be seen structurally in the shading-determined responses (below, p. 229). One dynamic (a) may now be inferred: the boy is troubled over some disability in himself of which he is conscious. Another hypothesis: had he earlier in his development become unhappy, because he felt insecure, or deprived? Hence (b) he is settling into the retarded ego growth stage in order to obtain the support which he feels lacking. If so, the lag in growth is due more to psychologic needs than to inadequate endowment. It follows that appropriate psychologic treatment may reverse the process. Eddie is worth the effort at psychotherapy.

The attention suffers, as seen in both the unsteady focusing and in the limitation on scope. The unsteadiness is evident on the one hand in the very large number of Dd, which is distraction by the off-center, the unessential. In some instances, these are decidedly trivial Dd, and we see here one of the defense tactics (p. 234). Such are R 9, 14, 15, 17, 27, 41. The impersonal F— are another result of flighty concentration.

The limitation on the scope of the attention emerges structurally in the approach and in the content. The large number of Dd, aside from being evidence of scattering, also shows Eddie narrowing his vision excessively to this kind of stimulus. It is the minute or the most obvious (D), not the synthesized unit upon which his eye lights. The content highlights the narrow range of things to which he now responds. Essentially, all his responses group within one of three categories: animal forms, i.e., the most stereotyped; the geometrical forms and alphabet percepts; and the "caved-in" stone or related ideas. The latter, once they set in, take hold and become preoccupation with the one theme. He does this so much as to raise the question that—whether within the framework of an uncritical ego—he may not ultimately build delusional notions around this special topic. It is a suggestion which dictates against leaving Eddie untreated.

In his thinking Eddie shows lack of coherence, infrequent but clear-cut. Such is the long confabulation around the "man, tiger, hurt themselves" motif in Figure VIII. The DdW in the first response to the test is typical confabulation structurally (Rorschach). The "teeth . . . on the tree" (R 29, 30) are a bizarre juxtaposition. Similar ones, not so serious, will be found in R 36 and R 37. A contaminated association emerges in R 33, of an animal form and a color incompatible with it. The boundaries of the objects within his world still flow over one another in the thinking of this boy of seven years and nine months. Orderliness of thought processes is, however, not seriously impaired. The sequence is usually irregular, never confused. Sequence is a sensitive index, and this relatively favorable finding is another encouragement toward treatment.

Interference with the thought processes is, however, found in the almost entire absence of conceptual thinking (W) and in the pattern of his synthesizing activity (Z). In the latter, his total score 18.0 is more than adequate for a boy of Eddie's age (mean, ages 6 to 9 is 7.15, SD 7.40). One of his Z credits is, however, a gift made necessary by technic; this is the 3.5 for the "few holes . . . inside the rock," of R 2, 3. The organization activity here may be incidental to a flow of associations in which there is no real synthesizing. But it may also be the real thing. Whichever way one scores, there is risk of error. Here is an instance illustrating the subjectivity still in the test. Between Figures I and VIII he scores one Z, a weak one for Figure IV, as a whole, i.e., one of the lazy W's.

Judged by the synthesizing within the first seven figures, Eddie is anergic rather than alert in his thinking. He lacks abstracting ability, is intellectually stiff, has lost, or has always lacked, spontaneity. It is as though he is arteriosclerotic before he is 8 years old. The relation between the mood and this insufficiency, as also the role of the Dd in interfering with the attention to the larger configuration are separately discussed. Yet, beginning with Figure VIII Eddie's grasp of relations is truly vigorous; there are four good examples of organizing adjacent details, and these add up to a total of 12.5. He does, then, possess intellectual drive, a finding which again is a promising one in weighing plans for therapy. The apparent torpidity in the first seven figures is only appearance.

One other quantitative finding, total productivity, confirms the indication of intellectual drive. His score of 43 is well above the mean of the average adult (32.65) and hence even more significantly exceeds findings in children of his age (mean 21.93, SD 9.20). Productivity in the test is one of the manifestations of drive.

A serious deficiency in the ego's functioning shows up in the persistent perseveration. The boy does much of this with resulting impairment both in the attention and in the thinking. Examples are found in R 15, the "rock," perseverating from R 13 which may itself be a perseveration from

R 11. In fact, this percept has a hold on Eddie throughout the test record; it is seen in the unrelaxing grip which the related idea, "stones," has on him in R 6, 16, 17, 18, 22. Perseveration may also be present in the "holes" in connection with R 6 as stemming from the "holes" in R 2. But this is entirely surmise. Eddie may well be seeing the large inner white space within Figure II as a hole objectively, and in a child functioning at his undeveloped level, the inquiry in many instances cannot elicit the needed facts. We are here up against another limitation of the test. The probability of perseveration on the "hole" theme receives some support, however, from its occurrence again following R 30, the perseveration being apparently from the little story in R 27, the affect in which is heavy and would well carry into the following figure. In two other samples, the perseveration is of more limited scope. One is the "bush" of R 26, relating back to the "branch" of R 24 and also part of the affect-laden idea. The "in the tree" of R 36 persists into R 37 where the exact phrase immediately recurs and where the percept is totally inappropriate as judged from known experience with the details which the patient is selecting.

In fact, Eddie demonstrates, in this last example, one way in which the perseveration interferes with the thinking: it prevents a relevant association to the stimulus. Also, it is excessive and hamstringing, preoccupation with the perseverating topic. It is a reflection, too, of momentary low energy or drive in the patient's failure to shake off the association halo already affecting him, so impeding his grasping the new stimulus now in focus. The perseverating theme may then be disclosing a source of conflict or fear which, in fact, is explicit in Figure VIII; also in the stones damaged in one or another way.

Probably the most serious character weakness disclosed by the perseveration is an infirm will. The boy's thought processes remain channelized uncritically within an idea earlier activated. This is Bleuler's *aboulia*. It is suggestibility. The person is blown about, hither and yon, on the winds of circumstance, rather than judging values critically and determining his course accordingly. The findings here sharply point up a weak spot in the personality and, therefore, one on which the psychotherapy will need to concentrate.

Finally, the ego's retarded growth is evident in some of the content referring here not to its psychodynamic meaning (discussed below p. 234), but to its developmental quality. Such are the "question mark" of R 4, "circle" of R 7, 14, 41; of the same order also are the "holes" and "stones." Whether immaturities or peculiarities, the fact is that I have observed these as well as the alphabetical and the geometrical associations only in very young children and in schizophrenics. Regarding the psychologic cause for these percepts in the two clinical groups, I have no lead and, hence, no theory.

Eddie's mood is reflected structurally in the light-determined responses (Y) and in much of the content, especially in the perseverated themes. He gives primacy to the shading, YF, in two of his three Y associations. The child has given up emotionally. The inner state is one of void, unhappiness. In the setting of the excitability which is also a part of him, it is a fretful state. Some content projects painful themes stressing the sense of inner incompletion and possibly of decay. This motif sets in in Figure VI and becomes more prominent in Figure VII. In fact, more cheerless mood emerges in the content than in the structure. The two together raise warning of potential development into apathy. The restricted Z score supports this impression; the intellectual steam is shut off. However, a response total of 43 is high, especially for so young a child, and points against an anergic condition. Then, too, the large number of white space associations (p. 233) is one promise that Eddie will not have recourse to inertia. It is an aggressiveness which will be attacking the environment in the effort to dispel the inner disquiet.

This oppressed mood is always part and parcel of an anxiety condition. With this we should, in a Rorschach test response pattern, find anxiety shock. There is, however, none in this test. The intellectual structure is no worse in the test figures consisting of the large black masses than it is in the others. The pattern is, therefore, one in which Eddie always behaves as though in shock, a chronic anxiety. Is it a free or a bound anxiety? From its constancy throughout the test and from the absence of sudden onset I conclude that it is bound. What the topic is around which it is bound may emerge from other findings in the test, especially the content. So far, the pattern shows a child's mind weighed down to a degree found only in adults, and very troubled adults. Here may be one explanation of the ego's refusal to grow: the child so fights back against circumstances which are too painful, and which he cannot possibly master. The solution, to be sure, is one in which the ego cuts off the person's nose to spite his face.

All this dejection, passivity and resignation, are going on simultaneously with *readiness for excitement* and for outbursts. The sum of the color values, 13, is very high, whether compared with findings in young children or in adults. In our 155 normal Chicago school children, the mean of the sums of the color responses is 2.02, SD 2.11, median 1.30. For children in the 6 to 9 year range, mean is 1.98, SD 1.80, median 1.61. In adults, the mean is 3.11, SD 2.74. Even more telling is the concentration of these associations into the pure C group. Of the nine color determined responses, eight are scored C, one CF. Eddie's emotional set is a readiness for hair-trigger, undifferentiated discharge. At best, he is irritable, sensitive. But this latter in only too small a proportion, the one CF. This primitive emotional reaction level parallels the intellectual immaturity. With nearly all the color determined reactions of the same nuance, another conclusion is that a single, unvarying affect dominates. The patient has not yet learned those modulations of feeling that characterize the adult's and the older child's reactions to the varying stimuli of his world.

However, there are findings in this sphere on the credit side of the ledger. The affective ratio is 0.95, significantly above the average of Eddie's age mates; (mean 0.53, SD 0.23). The absolute number of color determined associations is high (statistics not available, but this empirical judgment is a safe one). Both of these findings are promise of affective fluidity. The boy will respond, even if unrestrainedly, to emotion toned stimuli. Appropriately oriented therapy can use this resource.

Sensitivity to exciting stimuli is also indicated in apparent color shock in Figure VIII. Also patient shows vulnerability to color influence in the greater fluctuation of productivity in the last three figures.

But the ego's dysfunction as we have seen is chronic in the test. The child's whole way of living is without consistent central control. Hence, we cannot speak of any appreciable color shock. But some slight additional promise that the boy does respond to affect-laden values is all we can here extract.

As to the themes around which his feelings play, "fire" appears in both R 5 and R 8. It is a thought related to destruction, and I have found it a phobic indicator in children. Concerning the "lights" with which he elaborates R 5, Eddie offers no clue. Its recurrence in R 28 does point to significance. The "bush" of R 26 and the "tree" of R 30 would ordinarily be grouped as nondifferentiating, a normally healthy reaction. But both are bound in with some odd thinking in which personal meaning appears present. The elaboration "leaves are always green . . . except in the fall" is suggestive only. In R 36 and in R 39, however, the interpretation would, on the basis of general experience and not from any direct indication in this record, be that the pleasurably toned objects do appropriately attract Eddie's attention.

The fantasy life. How much of all this feeling pressure can this boy introvert? For the first seven figures the answer appears to be none. It is not until R 25 in Figure VIII that Eddie produces his first M response. But from this point on, four of the associations are fantasy determined, M. This compares with the average per record in the adult years of 3.50, SD 3.24 and in children of Eddie's age, 0.87, SD 1.35. He *is* capable of an active imagination. Why did he not use the ability until so late in the test? Two possibilities are to be considered. One, conflict against his inner wishes is hard enough to repress them. But the test does not yield evidence of conflict. The current pattern is not that of a neurosis. The second line of reasoning is that the first seven test figures do not stir him into imaginative living. It takes the quickening effect of the color figures to set it going.

In the structure of his fantasy responses the boy shows immaturity once, regression once. In the M of R 25 he selected a rare detail and sees the action in a part human. M with Dd, or with Hd, is more characteristic of the less mature and of the simpler among the adult population. But Eddie *is* a child. The DdM or MHd structure is not inconsistent with expectancy in him.

More serious is the "blue monkey" in R 33. It is M—; the form is inaccurate, whether vaguely perceived or distorted. It is dream type of M. The critical work of the waking ego is lacking. The animal content is further indication of sub-ego fantasy activity—"sub-ego" with reference to the healthy adult as standard. The support for this conclusion is empirical; it is persons with insufficient ego functioning whose M associations are found in animal content. The insufficiency may be incident to an acute neurosis; to schizophrenia or to simply the developmental stage. Children are, to be sure, more at home with animal actors in their fantasies. Again, therefore, we would discount the seriousness of this unrealistic living were it not for additional evidence in it: *blue* monkeys are a reality acceptable only to the very infantile ego. Thirdly, this association is a blend of M with CF. Excitement intensifies the feelings which Eddie has converted into a fantasy. This helps explain the absence of criticism, and so the F— in the M.

Apparently sound in structure and grownup in content is the fantasy of R 34, 35, "a sort of a pole . . . like a man was pulling it." It is scored M, and the action projected on to a whole human, H. But within the moment the patient sees the same man as "animal," in which he is translating a similarity into an identity. That is, even while engaging in his good fantasy, he is perceiving in a way that characterizes the very young and that stage in the ego's development when it does not yet sharply discriminate the world's similar realities.

R 32 is, in itself, sound in structure and in content. But a person who can associate with M to D 1, the green mass at the middle, should be able to do so to the upper orange, D 3. In failing this Eddie is not using an ability which he has. It is an incomplete and uneven use of endowment. The test here sets a question. Is he regressing? Or, are we seeing the immature ego inadequately calling on its resources?

The stance in the fantasy activity is extensor, "pulling," in R 25 and R 35. It projects an urge in the unconscious to be free from the central support, to be independent. This is a most favorable finding. As wish in Eddie to grow up, it is in contradiction to his ego's conscious pattern. He is uncovering evidence here that he carries psychologic trends useful toward psychotherapy, a latency which may escape clinical observation, and for the detection of which the test is particularly suited. This finding is especially valuable since as M, it is at an effective layer of the personality.

But this unconscious desire to break away is not an unmixed one. R 33 projects out a flector, clinging stance. The dependency need is still on. Eddie has unconscious desires both to cling to his parents and to be free of them. The latter wish is now the stronger judging from the greater frequency of extensor M. In the other fantasy response, R 32, the stance is not clear either as extensor or flector.

By the energy scale (p. 55 ff.) I evaluate each of the fantasies as follows:

R	Degree of Movement
25	6
32	4
33	3
35	6

In two of these responses, the energy rating is at the high end of the scale. The total energy of 19 is, by empirical judgment, a high one for four associations. When Eddie does release his fantasy, he lives it strenuously. This is the very tentative interpretation, but resting also on significant content.

The experience in the fantasy appears to be a painful one because it is related to apprehension in R 25; uncertain, but the more likely surmise is that it is also painful in R 33 and R 35. My guess is it is clearly pleasurable in R 32. These are subjective judgments, all; they require confirmation in the therapeutic sessions. Similarly at surmise level is the personal meaning as to R 32, 33 and 35, to be clarified only by Eddie himself. The "holding on" theme has recurred in other patients as clinging motif. Concerning the "pulling" we have too little general precedent and its meaning to any one patient must be separately established. In R 25, however, together with the subsequent elaborations scored as R 26 and R 27, the content follows the pattern of a child's dream: the phobic and the related hostility with animal characters, the fearful "tigers." With true dream technic, the emotions are displaced on to this animal; they are also evaded through fixing on "a man" to achieve the counterphobic attack. Eddie is explicit concerning his aversion to this animal; the man "doesn't like tigers." The child also makes clear the sense of urgency in the animal's proximity: "in his front yard." But he dispatches the dangerous beast with the naive ease of primitive fantasy: "the holes . . . through which the tigers will fall . . . to their death, or at least their hurt." All this is manifest content. Insofar as such phobic-hostile thinking may, from the evidence in the psychoanalytic literature, be judged as having a constant meaning in all persons, Eddie's verbalizing here points to obvious personal attitudes. But Rorschach test technic still demands that any idiosyncratic meaning for any one person be adduced always directly from that person.

Returning to the question, how much of his vigorous and primitive discharge trends can Eddie convert into inner living? The answer: is not enough. The experience balance, Rorschach's *Erlebnistypus* is weighted much too heavily to the extratensive. This balance, and the unmodulated hair-trigger quality of the feeling charge, assume a special interest in the light of another finding, the opposition trait.

The white spaces. The count of five compares with an average white space score for children in the 6 to 9 year group of 0.75, SD 1.55; per cents, 2.8 mean, and SD 5.3 (Table 3). Eddie directs more attention to space details than enters into the scorings; as, for example, following R 6, 15, 17, 30, and in the elaboration of R 19. The immediate inference is that the boy's character includes a considerable trait of resistiveness. Inspection of his space details may throw some doubt on this conclusion. None of the scored s responses refers to a major s detail, statistically determined (Ds 5 of Figure II; Ds 7 of Figure VII; or Ds 8 of Figure IX). It follows that each is a Dds. However, interpretation of s as of weak force attaches to Dds only when it is perceived incidentally to a solid black selection as e.g., the eyes and grinning mouth of the cat's face or of the mask, Figure I; the similar facial details of the quarreling animals in Figure X (D 8); or the opening of the mouth of bird or alligator in Figure V (D 8 or D 10). In each of these, the s only fills out another primary association. In the present record, the s responses are all to white spaces selected out as such, out of the background of the blot. Eddie is, in fact, reversing figure and ground, the Rorschach test mark of the stubborn individual.

The very extratensive experience balance indicates that the attack, or trend to it, is directed against the environment. This only opens up a question of psychodynamics. Why has Eddie a need to fight his world? The possibilities are: (a) Eddie's ego, being ungrown, we see the total person in the infantile aggressive stage in which he unrestrainedly strikes out at anything. It is a personality arrest. The discharge is impersonal. Or, the cause may be (b) a defensive reaction against unsatisfying, frustrating living. Resenting an undesirable state of affairs and unable to do anything about an environment which manipulates him at its will, he fights back by fixating at the very infant's level which the environment establishes for him. He accepts its logic and follows through with a vengeance. It is his strategy for adjusting. Maladaptively but adjusting nevertheless. The trait is, therefore, very necessary to this boy if he is to be comfortable, an end toward which all organisms are always striving. Then, too, as equipment and tactic for attacking the environment, it is a countermeasure against the inner sense of void and the related discomfort.

The high white space count in its role of projecting stubbornness is also a promise—or a threat, depending on the whole personality course—that Eddie will obstinately stay within the personality configuration into which he settles. Should he, for example, develop delusions, a possibility not ruled out by this Rorschach test with its picture of immature ego and special preoccupations, he will hang on to them. But, it is a poor trait that can only serve ill. And stubbornness has a long world history of serving valuable ends. It will, therefore, in this boy add stamina to any constructive personality effort into which he is directed.

The defenses. These are symptomatic and such as to obstruct character growth. The principal finding is withdrawal manifest in the unique content, in the immature language, and in the other cited evidence of ungrown ego. But in the term "withdrawal" is also implicit the idea of arrival. One must withdraw *from* somewhere. Eddie's ego does not provide evidence of arrival; he has not yet made that much progress. His tactic is, in fact, a refusal. He elects *not* to make contact with reality. In this, the test sketches out danger of a fixation. This is, of course, the history of fixations; they start as defenses, the only possible defenses in the intolerable circumstances which some elders set up for the very young child. But Eddie not only refuses to come forward; he also wards off stimuli and hinders his own potential for larger perception. The narrowed-in content is his shutting out the world's varied stimuli. In the low synthesizing activity, he reflects the constraint on grasp of relations and so saves himself from painful understandings. These two habit patterns have forged an armor for the character. Either alone could do it. The two have reinforced each other. This character armor is reflected in some verbal mannerisms: total unqualified associating or introductory phrases that are monotonously similar. Among these are "a few . . . dots . . . a few fires . . . a few points." "Sort of a little point . . . sort of a back . . . sort of feathers . . . sort of a black rock . . . sort of like feet . . . sort of an animal . . . sort of an A." "Here's a hole . . . here's a point . . . here's a little point . . . here's a little piece of stone . . . here's a little crooked stone and here's something that dropped off . . . and here's leaves . . . and here's some fire . . . and here's a sort of a pole." "There's a little point . . . there's a long circle . . . there's a cave-in . . . and then there are some blocks . . . and there's a hole . . . and there are two holes . . . and there are two other holes." He does vary his words but only to go into another fixed formula: "Some lights . . . some stones . . . some oranges . . . some white teeth . . . some blue monkeys . . . some sunflowers."

Set habits, set to the point of being inflexible, and with the potential for becoming automatic phrases or actions are here operating. They are to their possessor assurance of an ever-ready response device. But, like all spinal behavior, they command the price of invariability. This can be costly, even to the failure of survival, when changed conditions demand new behavioral forms.

Eddie's excessive attention to Dd is another feature of this defense mechanism. By focusing on the minute he hampers his concentration on the major elements. This effectively separates them out from his vision. It is the isolation defense. The lowering of the Z and of the W scores are among the results of this separating out. Also, the relatively high productivity since the cluster consisting of high R with much Dd, is a frequent one in obsessive persons who utilize the isolation defense among others.

Phobic defense appears, and it is of obvious variety. This is the "tiger" fantasy of R 23 and those following. The boy is here projecting a real fear as well as the counter-phobic solution. The test's advice to the therapist is to explore for the extent to which this painful fantasy stems from: (a) sense of insecurity growing out of the patient's home living pattern; (b) expected punishment for wishes which he may be harboring; or (c) the sense of personal inadequacy. The entire little drama is developed with enough detail and abundant circumstances to indicate a deeply felt attitude. It is the kernel of what, untreated, will flower eventually into a pathologic phobia.

The three shading determined associations (Y) provide a measure of the painful quality in Eddie's defense activity. Three is not excessive for 43 responses, and so far, the boy has really only started on this road to unhappy mood. But the primacy of shading (YF) associations (see above, p. 229), dysphoric content, taken together with the accent on unmodulated color-determined associations, highlight the strong feeling experiences and the agitation which are constantly this boy's. He is anything but cheerful in his defensive retreat.

One other tactic which Eddie employs is the probable displacement, if not symbolism, in the "broken stick," "crippled stones" and other similar associations. Insofar as this is symbolism, it is a persistence of the young child's concretistic mode of perception (p. 224). But insofar as it also points to the use of the symbol for avoiding an unpleasant topic, it is an advance over the more primitive distortion, and equating by similarities, into which Fenichel[1] analyzes the symbol. The ego is here using the symbol with a purpose. This is growth as compared with Eddie's otherwise retarded stage. And even though the present personality stage as a whole is still an insufficiency, it is a promise that the child can progress.

The total picture. The boy's overall use of his abilities is grossly inadequate. The limited interest horizon (content), the restriction of his attention (Ap), the deficit in conceptual thinking (W) and the uneven achieving of difficult intellectual solutions (Z) are all a forecast of what is ahead: a very inferior adaptation unless treatment tailored to the need alters the course. He does show flashes or originality in the alphabetical and the geometry associations, and in some of the symbolism. But it is a poor

---

[1] FENICHEL, O., *op. cit.*, p. 27 and 48 ff.

originality, not any true breadth. It is a result not of a differentiated perception, but of his immaturity and the limited interests into which he has channelized himself.

In this narrowness he also manifests an inadequate reaching to the realities which normally interest a boy in his year. The essential sterility of the thought content betrays this deficit, a limited aspiration. The stereotypy in this record is not measured by the per cent of animal content alone. The recurring "stones," "rocks" with the related "holes" are another such simple category. These, together with the animal associations amount to 46.5 per cent of the total; and with the five alphabet or geometry forms, oddities that these are, the percentage of straitened thinking rises to 60.5. The correlate to this sterility is the low total of whole human associations. The truly original individuals see many.

In one other finding this patient measures as inadequately responding to external stimuli. His lambda index is 65 per cent. Mean for the 6 to 9 year olds is 78.40, SD 12.25. Eddie's score, therefore, is more than one standard deviation below his group's mean. He is, to this extent, failing to focus on the objective world. It means that he is more than normally responding to inner stimuli. A glance at the response summary tells what these are: those tapped by the test in C, M, and Y.

Finally, stereotyped though Eddie's thinking is, it is not conventional. On the contrary. The zero P score indicates that he has not even begun to concern himself with conformity to social canons. In these contradictory trait indications offered by two sets of findings within the same individual, the test discloses its multidimensionality. Nor is this contradiction inconsistent with the known facts concerning human nature. "The elements so mixed in him." Even for so ungrown a personality as is Eddie's, these words describing the complicated Brutus, still apply.

A low P score speaks for intellectual offishness, in this boy to the point of estrangement. The P finding is, thus, another facet of the trait structured out in the high white space count. In his face-to-face relations with his world Eddie is unwilling to take things lying down or on the "say-so" of an elder. However, a question of suggestibility is raised by the perseverations and by the stereotypy within certain content categories. Can the same person possess the contradictory traits of both egocentric autonomy and suggestibility? Can he be easily led, and at the same time be as resistive to change as would have to be inferred from his world-excluding defense? *A priori* the answer is "yes." The elements can be that mixed. Such, in any event, are this Rorschach test's indications. Confirmation must, of course, still be forthcoming from the clinical facts.

All this is unadaptive handling of reality. It accents the finding in that other important measure: F+ per cent, low. It is an ego insufficiency which becomes the more significant in the light of the inner unrest. The lack of FC warrants the additional conclusion that emotional understanding of others is now lacking. Infantile discharges are his sole emotional trends. The final conclusion is that, in his dealing with others, Eddie is in danger of externalizing his aggressive impulses.

Erotic and sexual desires do not now interest him as judged from the content; but unless the personality structure changes, his handling of these, too, will, when they emerge inevitably in adolescence, be maladaptive.

The content. A principal lead is that the consciousness of being personally damaged, inadequate, eats into this child. It first appears in the "broken stick" (R 12). Does the patient refer to himself? The test will not give proof positive. But the *leitmotiv* so much punctuates the record as to reflect a preoccupation. Thus, the "crooked piece of stone . . . caved in" (R 17); "some crooked stone . . . it's caved in" (following R 19); "there is a cave-in, and after that there are crippled stones on each side" (R 21); "a branch, and here is something that dropped off the branch" (R 24). So much absorption in this kind of thinking must mean something, and the hypothesis passed on to the therapist is: a concern with personal disability. Entirely at the hunch level is the question whether the perseveration with the "holes" theme stems from sense of personal incompletion. Eddie may never have heard of Omar Khayyam, but the spirit of his associations is akin to one note of complaint in the Persian bard's poem:

> "After a momentary silence spake
> Some Vessel of a more ungainly Make;
> 'They sneer at me for leaning all awry:
> What! did the Hand then of the Potter shake?' "

Eddie suffers this sense of inadequacy on a background of insecurity feelings that center around his home as a whole. This is the hint to be followed up in the "some blocks, that you build a house with" (R 22); substantiated by "a few fires" (R 5) recurring in R 8. Children anxious about the very foundations of their security do respond with "fire." The heavy load of fear which weighs down on Eddie is clearly projected in the fantasy around the "tigers" (p. 232). Content significance in fantasy and in affect-dictated associations has been discussed in exposition of these factors (pp. 230 and 231 ff.).

Treatment. The findings in this record provide some answer to the two major questions that need always to be asked in relation to therapy. One, what is the need? Two, what are the patient's resources? From the answers to these two, the corollary usually follows as to the kind of treatment to be attempted.

The need is clearly great. The ego's lag is severe. The potential for a more serious turn into possible delusional notions (p. 226) was noted. The fantasy of dream structure (p. 231) alerts also to danger of autistic living. Suggestibility points to another weakness (p. 228).

Against these deficits, there are assets. In at least one index, the ego is relatively firm (sequence, p. 227). Drive is available to Eddie as Z and as R (p. 227); the four M are added evidence of it. In the important sphere of the emotions he does respond (p. 229). The fantasy includes the favorable extensor associations (p. 231). Possibly, most important is the reasoning that the whole pattern is a reaction to a situation and, therefore, reversible.

There are, then, assets. Treatment effort is, therefore, dictated since there is need. In fact, the severity of needs is a measure of the strenuous efforts to be exerted.

But what is the outlook? Will Eddie respond to the efforts invested in him? The outlook is not encouraging. The affective response is egocentric. He reaches to the world only to gratify his momentary impulses. The intellectual pattern is a defensive stiffness. It does not readily yield to to influences for change. Against these psychologic barriers the modest assets provide only a small hope. It is under such handicap that the school and therapist continued.

B. The Second Test, and Disappointment

If the student, turning to Eddie's second Rorschach test, looks for evidence in it that the personality has grown, he will be disappointed. This test was administered 38 months after the first. Eddie was now $10\frac{11}{12}$ years old. He had resided in the school just short of 64 months. For the behavior course, at this point, see the clinical notes (p. 278).

RESPONSE RECORD

Figure I (25″)

1. D F+ Ad   'This could be a design of an eagle (D 7; D 5 is head, and D 8 are wings).
2. D FV+ Ls   'A design of a hill (plays with card at odd angles) (D 2; going up, looks like it, the shape and how little it is, the hill is small—not far away). That's all I can think of . . . a design of a mountain (fingers card in odd way).
3. D F+ A   'A design of a crow (D 7, with Dd 22 as part of the head).'

Figure II (7″)

4. D F+ A   'A design of a butterfly (W excluding D 2; the shape, the way it looks).

A design of a moth (is not attentive to card).

5. Dd F— Ad   'A fly (in each D 2; put together; just Dd of D 2 are the feelers).

6. D F— A   'A small robin (D 6 ... by looks of the beak, D 4). That's all I can think of ... a little chicken (same as robin); a small crow.'

Figure III (15″)

7. D F+ A   'A duck (D 11, one duck put on the other). A duckling ... (deep sigh) ... a blue jay ... a bluebird ... a crow ... an eagle ... that's all I can think of.'

Figure IV (7″)

8. D F+ A   'A frog (W, excluding D 4; because of D 2 as feet).

9. D F+ A   'A butterfly (W, excluding D 2).

10. D F— A   'A tadpole (W, excluding D 4; it's littler, smaller, looks like it); a moth ... a crow (same as butterfly). A robin ... a blue jay ... a bluebird... a swallow.'

Figure V (5″)

11. W F+ A P   'A moth (W) a butterfly.
    1.0

12. DW F+ Ad   'An eagle (in the wings ... the wings look like it ... just the wings) a crow ... a blue jay.

13. W F— A   'And a bird ... a robin. That's all I can think of.'

Figure VI (15″)

14. D F+ A   'A butterfly, (D 1 the shape) a moth ... a swallow. A bluebird ... a blue jay

15. D F— A   ∨ 'a robin ... a swallow ... a crow (D 12). That's all I can think of.'

Figure VII (11″)

16. D F— A   'A horse ∨ (each D 2 put together they have to fit together, put one on the other).

17. D F+ A   'A dog (D 2) a cat ∨ a cat . . . a
                                kitten . . . a puppy (you put each one
                                on the other). That's all I can think of.'

                          Figure VIII (15″)

18. D CF− A   'A peacock (D 2 and D 1 colors and
                                shape).

19. D FC− A   'A parrot (W excluding D 2; shape
                                and some of the colors); a swallow . . .
                                a robin . . . a blue jay . . . a bluebird
                                (plays with socks; inattentive). That's
                                all I can think of.'

                          Figure IX (10″)

20. D F− A   'A butterfly (D 11; shape, with D 5
                                as feelers).

21. D F− A   'A swallow (D 3, looks like it). A
                                moth (D 11) . . . and eagle . . . (D 3) a
                                robin . . . a swallow . . . that's all I can
                                think of.'

                          Figure X (10″)

22. D F− A   'A butterfly (D 15; if they were put
                                together, the way it's shaped; points
                                indiscriminately).

23. D F− A   'An eagle (D 9 and D 6; if it were
                                folded; D 9 are the wings; D 6 is the
                                body . . . the way the wings are folded
                                and shaped).

24. D F− A   'A woodpecker (D 10 with D 5 as the
                                beak; it looks like one and stands like
                                one; the shape).

25. D F− A   'A robin (D 7; they way it looks).
                                'A swallow (D 15), the beak.'

RESPONSE SUMMARY
R total 25

W	2	CF−	1	A	21	F+ %	46
DW	1	FC−	1	Ad	3	A %	96
D	21	FV	1	Ls	1	P	1
Dd	1	F+	10		25	s	0
	25	F−	12			T/IR	12.0
			25			T/R	49.8
Z	1.0						
Ap	(W) D! Dd	EB	0/1.5			Af r	0.47
Seq	Not enough					L	0.88
	variation						

INTERPRETATION

The quantitative summary of the scoring is a picture of unrelieved mental poverty: animal percentage nearly one hundred, and hence the converse, differentiated interest and breadth, essentially at zero; the inner world (EB) at a very low ebb (0/1.5) and so in a torpid state; the intellectual life, narrowed in and sluggish.

A retreat from a better endowed to a more sterile mental life is not uncommonly found in a patient's second Rorschach test. The explanation may be hazarded that as the ego, growing in the understanding of reality, is coming to grips with its affects, with the meanings of the fantasies, it defensively restrains them. Hence the personality loses some of the flashes, creative and emotional, which make these children the ever lively, if at times vexing, problems that they are. Where formerly there was "never a dull moment," the patient now chokes off his self-gratifying emotional experiences, his wishful living. It is a victory for the ego; but again, a Pyrrhic victory.

In fact, this self-conquest is one of appearances only. The person succeeds in eliminating response to inner stimuli. But in so doing he emerges much the worse for wear. In the sphere of the ego, Eddie is taking exceptionally heavy losses.

In the motor sphere, specifically language, a very immature pattern persists. Associating is unqualified throughout the record. His arbitrary pronouncements are characteristic of children under about age 6 in mental development. It is their egocentric handling of life's issues, the infantile self-assurance which belongs only to primitive youth before the hard world dents this confidence and breeds self-doubt. As we read these associations we are impressed, too, with an unending sameness in the formulation, stereotypy of manner, something which belongs to restricted personalities. For a brief period, in Figures I and II, Eddie also makes use of a particular fixed formula: "a design of a hill," "a design of an eagle," "a design of a butterfly" and others. As another mannerism, he uses diminutives, the small child's way of describing his percepts. It bespeaks an infantile view of his perceived world. The content in these responses has a personal significance (p. 248). They are found in R 2 and three times in R 6, "small robin," "little chicken," "small crow." In R 7; following R 9 (tadpole); and following R 17.

Stiff, too, is Eddie's language style describing the structure of what he sees. Each is "put together, just the feelers," (R 5); "they have to fit it together," (R 16); and following the "puppy" of R 17, "you put each one on the other"; and in the inquiry, R 22. Significance of this language and mode of associating is not clear. The occurrence is rare and, hence, the opportunity to study it is limited. My present surmise is that it is an undeveloped mode of handling one's objective data. The patient attends to the stimulus as such, rather than enter on to the play world, the opportunity for which the test offers. Support of this surmise is available in the above-noted qualified language form which Eddie uses much. Principally this is found at age levels at which thought manipulates the concrete, and I look on it as primitive form of thinking and communicating.

Another motor indication of ego insufficiency is the average fluctuation in speed of first responses. In Eddie this average is 6.55. For his age group the mean is 32.11, SD 17.45. His is notably less than normal fluctuation; it is inflexibility, tending toward fixity. Average time for all the responses is slow, 49.8 seconds. This judgment is empirical; satisfactory means are not available. He does not possess that free swing and plastic "give" belonging to most children his age.

In a single instance (Figure I), the examiner notes "odd angles" in which he holds the test cards; this a possible representative of odd stances or grimaces of the clinical sphere. But more work needs to be done toward establishing the clinical correlate of this Rorschach test behavior.

The ego's deficit is severe in the perceptual inaccuracies. The F− is very far from the norm in numerous responses, e. g., R 5, 6, 10, 15, 16, 18, 19, 21, 23. The great majority of all the errors appear to be impersonal, the result of an indifferent focusing on the stimulus. Attention is weak. Behavioral evidence of flighty attention is specifically noted by the examiner in Figures II and VIII. An asthenic ego, it lacks the stamina wherewith to attend to, inspect and judge the picture developing in the perceptual apparatus. Rorschach's third criterion for F+ is missing:[2] "The ability to maintain the attention stable during the entire test procedure, a certain capacity for concentration. Only then are the really clear-cut perceptions possible. When the attention grip loosens—as owing to flightiness, fatigue, manic state, delirium, organic brain disease—then perception of form will become unclear in at least portions of the test." The critical hold is infirm. Result: perception is erratic.

A personal determinant of the inaccuracies needs to be considered in R 10, 16, 23. The "eagle" is traditionally a power bird and the "horse" a power animal. The "tadpole" involves a relation to the theme of the newborn. Conclusive internal evidence within the test record is lacking, and these judgments as to "personal-impersonal" F− are necessarily subjective.

Inadequate ego functioning is evident in the x reactions. These are found only in the inquiry but in it they are numerous: "feelers" (of the fly); "wings" (of the crow); "head" (looks like eagle); "but not the neck" (of a duck); and others. The boy is here narrowing in his perceptual horizon, attending to a portion of the animal where his healthier fellow sees it in its entirety. The inadequacy consists in a limitation on the attention with

---

[2] RORSCHACH, H., op. cit., p. 61.

resulting restriction of the field. It is as though Eddie has greatly reduced the aperture in the diaphragm on his lens, admitting only a minimal portion of the presented image. This finding is confirmed by others in the structure, the manner of approach (Ap): (W) D! Dd. The accent on D is a cramped intellectual posture, a selective perception of only the most palpable.

Attitude to, and perception of, the self: Eddie shows a trace of resignation (Figure I only) as is found in passive submission, in self-devaluating persons. His much visualizing in terms of the small or the very young (p. 248) suggests that he is living still the experience of being a smaller child, seeing himself as ungrown, and of less maturity value than his chronological age demands. More of this is reflected in the mood tone (p. 246). On the other hand, there is the immature lack of self-criticism (p. 241). It is not yet overevaluation. But continued into adult life it becomes an unrealistic, arbitrary self-reference by which he acts.

The thinking is being tangled up in perseverations, both of the stimulus and probably of content. Stimulus perseveration: in Figure I, in "mountain," he reacts to the same detail as in "hill"; Figure II, the "robin, chicken, crow," all to the same blot area; similarly throughout Figure III; in Figure IV, the "tadpole" and the "frog" in reaction to the entire excluding D 4; also the "moth, crow, robin," and the others, following the "butterfly" for the whole figure excluding D 4; in Figure V the "wings" of the several birds, all in reaction to D 4; in Figure VI D 1 holds him for five associations; then he selects D 12 and adheres to it for three more associations. In Figure VII, it is D 2; in Figure VIII, the entire excepting D 2; in Figure IX, D 11. Only Figure X, with its multitude of details, of differing valences, finally breaks up this sticky intellectual pattern.

The perseveration, into different blot figures, of the same content is inferred, it cannot always be proven, from the monotonous repeating of the bird forms, viz., crow, eagle, blue jay, frog and tadpole (in the same figure); robin, swallow. Also perseverative dog-puppy, cat-kitten, puppy (Figure VII).

The essence of perseveration, behaviorally, is not that the patient dictates the element of his environment which he is to select, or what he is to see (p. 27). A previous percept, a former stimulus, performs this important directive task. He can hardly, in these moments, declaim

> I am the master of my fate:
> I am the captain of my soul,

He is anything but. The ego, in other words, is being manipulated by forces outer to itself.

This is decided weakness. It describes a suggestible, easily yielding person.

The most destructive effect of perseveration is that it prevents appropriate reaction to new stimuli. It prevents adaptive thinking. The individual is not coping with his environment by adequately employing the mental equipment which he has, or using it with the efficiency of which he is capable.

The cause of the perseveration is an anergic condition. It may be due to weariness, sleepiness, drugs, or insufficient ego-states. The patient lacks the energy necessary toward freeing himself from an old impression. This, it may be guessed, is what produces perseveration of the stimulus. When content perseverates, it may be because the theme has personal significance to the patient. If not, it is again uncovering the slowed-up ego.

A personal theme, in turn, is a lead to a critical psychologic dynamism. Such, though found more rarely, is perseveration of the stimulus in certain blot details having personal meaning, especially sexual, as, for example, one of the projecting details in the test figures for the penis; or D 3 in Figure II, D 7 in Figure III, D 3 in Figure IV, Dd 28 in Figure VIII, for the female genital. When the perseveration stems from such personal cause, the impairment may be apparent in the lower number of P associations. It prevents the patient's becoming aware of normal community percepts. He has inadequate regard for social canons. In Eddie's present Rorschach test, the P score is one.

The defenses. The pattern is a withdrawal but not into autistic fantasy and with some psychologic pain.

The defense strategy is most apparent in the cramped intellectual attitudes. Eddie is hardening his psychologic skin. Let these habits persist for any time, especially now in his formative years, and they become fixed. He enters on adolescence, and later adulthood, with an inflexible set of reactions. Behavior will lack the fine appropriate adjustments that go with differentiating cortical perception. Drawing out the fires that make for spontaneity and for satisfying living his ego will choke off pleasurable moments before they can gain momentum. It will effectively halt intellectual reaching and opportunity to learn and to grow. Defense operations are thus crippling the whole psyche. They are projected in Eddie in several Rorschach test variables, and in the quantitative shifts in these, in the second as compared with the first test. It is the *shifts* that are the thing, disclosing the differential functioning, and the contraction, which the ego is effecting.

The variables and the courses in them: productivity (R) lowered; grasp of relationships, synthesizing (Z), shrunk to essentially zero; selective perception concentrated almost entirely on the obvious (Ap: D!); now undeviatingly orderly in logical method (Seq); reacts almost exclusively to external stimuli (lambda); with concommitant shutting off of the inner (M, C, quantities very low) and, hence, nearly complete binding of the inner life (EB, narrowed); impoverishing of the thought content, in an extreme degree (A per cent nearly 100, and lack of other content). In all these, the scoring is in the direction of a lowered psychologic tonus. This is character armor as fashioned in the Rorschach test arsenal. The patient has grown a psychologic integument hardened as that of the ancient dinosaur, and has rendered himself just as sluggish and unimaginative. The full freezing of the Z activity is one drastic expedient. The extreme to which Eddie goes in it is a measure of his need. It is dangerous for him to see connections, certain ones; and, if need be for comfort, better to see none. But he eliminates the useful together with the distressing ones.

The precision alternative is an obsessive phenomenon in R 4 and R 10, e.g., "moth" for "butterfly." The P count of one is indifference to proprieties, one aspect of withdrawal. Eddie had already manifested this in his first test. Also a carryover from that earlier period, are the fixed formulas. They forecast the cramping of the personality to set in. His minimizing of the hill (R 2), "how little it is; the hill is small" requires exploring. Is it "small" because of great distance? If so, he is accenting the inferiority feelings. Or, is he counteracting the size of the large object? "It is also a mountain." If so, he is undoing that with which he compares to his disadvantage. So, he would be defending against the inferiority feelings. The test cannot answer these questions. Only Eddie can do so in therapeutic sessions.

He does counteract the distance motif, "not far away." But in so doing, he adds new questions. Is he dissipating the distance thinking? It can be very painful. Or, is he reassuring himself that the hill is really small?

In denying this unpalatable motif, he is, of course, bearing witness to it. He gives other evidence that the withdrawal is not without distress in anxious affect (p. 246) and irritability (p. 246). A favorable finding this, as in a person loath to quit the pleasant sun of social contact, and "the warm precincts of the cheerful day."

The net effect to the personality of this defense is a severe loss in intellectual efficiency and achievement, and in emotional resilience. The patient's armor protects him, but immures him. It shuts out the world's wealth of quickening sights and sounds. Sunshine and air are kept without. Like Sir Launfal's castle:

> Summer besieged it on every side,
> But the churlish stone her assaults defied;
> She could not scale the chilly wall, . . .
> The castle alone in the landscape lay,
> Like an outpost of winter, dull and gray.

It is a picture of Eddie shut in. He is, in fact, now mentally brittle, a turn of events the significance of which an alert therapist will not miss.

The anxiety. This emotion is not now an active dynamism. The reaction pattern is not more disturbed in the massive black figures than in those with colors. Perceptual accuracy is, in fact, better. In Figure I, time for first response is slowest for the test. He may, therefore, suffer some initial shock. The one other vestige of shading shock is the patient's disliking Figure IV most. After the test he said it was "dull," a counterphobic gesture. The slow time (in I) is a gauge measuring the sudden rise in the anxiety. To this extent there is free anxiety in Eddie. But for the most part he binds it. His defense measures are forestalling any disintegrative effects.

Though overtly at peace, Eddie does not deceive himself as to his spirits. The devaluated perception of the self (above, p. 243) always goes with a disheartened mood. In this vein is the resignation formula, "that's all I can think of." Depressed individuals regularly use it. Eddie outdoes the resignation of most such persons. It appears three to five times in a record, even in the severely depressed. He uses it seven times in II, III, V, VI, VII, VIII, IX. The prevailing mood is a discouraged one.

The lively emotions are stirring but not extensively. Eddie is neither bland nor affectless. He achieves emotional contact immediately on exposure to all-color figures. In Figure VIII his first two responses are both color-determined. In both, the content is of healthy affective quality; more so in a child to whom "peacock" and "parrot" seen in colors are likely to be pleasure-awakening responses. He prefers Figure VIII, because there are colors in it. This adds up to assets, spontaneity in the emotional sphere.

But his spontaneity is of modest quantity. In limiting himself to only two color determined responses he is not permitting the feelings to participate much in his percepts. The personality aborts the spontaneity before it materializes. Pressure of feelings nevertheless persist. Structure in the two color determined associations includes F−. One is FC−, effort at mastery over the feelings unsuccessful, tending to instability. The other, CF−, instability heading toward impulsivity. The boy is restive, skittish. On the background of the cheerless mood, it would be a painful restiveness, overflow from unhappy tension. His prevailing mood inevitably blends with and alters the total composition of the emotional life. The affective ratio is low, 0.47 for the 10 to 13 year olds, mean is 0.59, SD 0.21. Together with the small total of the color associations, it tells that liberated emotion is at a low ebb, such as results from discouragement or apathy. Cross currents in the affective stream are the indication from this Rorschach test. Yet, in this intellectually arid picture the fidgety inner condition may be a promising symptom. It is a mark of life, a straw for the therapy team to grasp.

The question of color shock provides some difficulties. The overall appearances of intellectual impoverishment and impairment gives a first impression of chronic ego weakness. This would point against color shock and make for a more unfavorable prognosis. But inspection of these scorings in the ten cards highlights the complete absence of any F+ in Figures VIII, IX, X. Of the 12 F− associations, 8 are produced by Figures IX and X together with Figure II which is conspicuous for inducing color shock. Perceptual accuracy persistently fails in the presence of color stimuli. The patient is vulnerable. There is potential for development into a neurotic reaction pattern with the implicit conflict state. This forecasts agitation. But it is always a more hopeful finding than no reaction.

The fantasy life. M, zero. Retreat *from* autistic solutions. In his first Rorschach test Eddie produced four M, a high quantity for an 8 year old. He has now reversed his course. His withdrawal is not into daydreaming. But the M failure is a recession also of that inner liveliness which would emerge as wish fulfilling imagination. This activity has been stilled.

The experience balance (*Erlebnistypus*, EB). M totally lacking, and sum of color values very low make for an extremely coarcted experience balance. This is inactive mental life. It is a cutting down of the inner world. This morbid picture is one result of the stiff hold on the self. It thus reflects again Eddie's current mood. "All depressive conditions group toward zero M, zero C; among the *koartierten* and *koartativen*," Rorschach notes.[3] Again, "a narrowing of the *Erlebnistypus* goes with depressive mood."[4] But, the pitfall is that other clinical pictures manifest a narrowed experience balance. Rorschach points to the "emotionally dull, the anergic, dementia simplex."[5] The differentiation is worked out, as always, from the total configuration.

The white spaces. Whatever this whole picture to be developed, Eddie's fighting spirit is now low. This is the meaning in a white space count of zero. This, too, is consistent with findings in cheerless states. Morale is low. Treatment does this to patients. And, paradoxically, it may be a salutary finding, the ego's awakening to superego proddings. "Whom the Gods would destroy, they first make mad," observed the Greeks. Modern psychotherapeutic philosophy modifies the adage: "Whom the Gods would make whole, they first make sad." Nor were the Greeks unaware of the relation between psychosis and subsequent reconstructing the personality to a stronger integration. In the Agamemnon trilogy, Orestes must go through the sufferings inflicted by the Furies, madness, before Apollo, light, is permitted to restore him.[6]

---

[3] *Ibid.*, p. 100.

[4] *Ibid.*

[5] *Ibid.*

[6] Under the moral code of Orestes' society, a son must avenge his father's murder by slaying the murderer. In Orestes' case this was Clytemnestra, his mother. Such is the revolting compulsion and conflict in which this son finds himself. The code is

Returning to Eddie, he uses the vista determinant only once. As shading-toned associations, it represents a distasteful psychologic pill. Does it un-cover a sense of dissatisfaction with himself as small? If so, it reinforces the downhearted mood tone. The content is the "hill," equated to "mountain" (R 2). It involves the sense of smallness. But as we have seen (p. 245) Eddie here opens up several questions, all unanswered. The structuring is the essential thing. As feeling of inferiority it involves comparing himself with a standard. This is ego work, which is the raw ore to be refashioned into stronger character. And so, for all the barren mental picture, there are here and there, rare enough, findings which may be promises of more construc-tive development.

Summarizing the *present total functioning*, Eddie's adaptation is now clearly an inferior one. In fact, he looks anergic, in lack of the richer mental productions. Actually, he is not anergic as he shows in his total productivity and in a flash here and there of originality. He does withdraw from social participation; he withdraws both intellectually and emotionally. Interest in the world, in its variety of sights and sounds, is reduced to a degree seen in many a mentally deficient.

Eddie does maintain a kind of a contact with his world. But it is a dull and stolid attention that he gives to it. In fact, he mundanely overattends to it with great loss in both range of feelings over which his spirit plays, and of imaginative fancy. Yet his hold on accuracy is weak, critical judg-ment poor. One can be all worldly in his perceptual interests and yet fail to concentrate on objects enough to see them clearly. Then, too, Eddie is quite indifferent to the most social conventions. Depleted of inner living resources, stiff and unbending intellectually, he is without that pliability which makes him amenable to influence for change. At the same time, he also shows signs of that contrary weakness, suggestibility. That is, he goes to the extremes of (a) brittleness or (b) passive yielding. When he does activate any inner living, he externalizes rather than introverts the feelings. These emerge as a moderate instability, unrest. But he does show a glimmer of effort—difficult for him to maintain—toward affective contact with his environment. Such aggressive or erotic leanings as he experiences, he will externalize, and maladaptively so. But these leanings are now few.

The content, and possible dynamics therein projected. The need to see the small, the young animal, recurs with great frequency: a small robin, a little chicken, a duckling, a kitten, a puppy. One of his animals is a develop-mental form, "tadpole." It follows next but one after a "frog," with which

---

inexorable. He kills his mother. The psychologic strain follows its logical course. As Sophocles' *Antigone*, the second play in the trilogy, closes, the Erinyes (the Greek proper name for the Furies, a word which also means "madness"), are taking pos-session of Orestes.

he appears to make the comparison, "littler, smaller." The "kitten" and the "puppy" also follow on the full grown of these animals.

The lead to be investigated is Eddie's identification with the ungrown. Displacing this thought on to animals, he is screening the perception of the self as small. And in the fact that he uses it as defense his ego states that being small is an undesirable condition. Yet, the emphasis on the motif is also the Rorschach test clue to the thought, and so to the wish. Assuming that this conjecture is clinically validated the test is here projecting Eddie's need to cling to the smallness status. It is a comfortable status, since it leaves to others the burden of caring for one, with the worries attendant thereon. The obtained comfort is destructive to the personality. It can be the beginning of fixation.

Eddie's many perseverated birds require investigating owing to sheer weight of quantity. Thus, the "robin" in Figures II, IV, V, VI, VIII, IX, X. The "crow" in Figures II, III, IV, V, VI. The "bluebird" in Figures III, IV, VI, VIII. The "blue jay" in Figures III, IV, V, VI, VIII. The "eagle" in Figures I, III, V, IX, X. The "swallow," Figures IV, VI, VIII, IX, X. The test record provides no internal evidence that any or all these bird associations derive from some need in this patient. Certain symbolic values do attach to some: the bluebird, the crow, the eagle. But significance in any one person needs to be shown case by case. Another perseveration is the "butterfly-moth" percept in Figures II, IV, V, VI, IX. But the likelihood of these being significant is even smaller. They are too much the stock forms perceived in the test, and not personally meaningful.

In all, the content in this second Rorschach test of Eddie's does not throw light on present personal dynamics. A record with nearly 100 per cent animal forms is one of nearly 100 per cent stereotyped content. As such, it is the very opposite of the original or unique productions which, for good or for ill, differentiate one person from another. Eddie, at the time of this Rorschach, was mentally most undifferentiated.

The report of findings in this second test was not, therefore, an encouraging one to the administration of the Orthogenic School. Treatment outlook in the second test is extremely unpromising. The rigidity, which is also fragility, provides little cheer to a therapist. A little restlessness such as might bespeak a salutary depression trend; possible dissatisfaction with the self in the modicum of inferiority feeling; enough color shock to indicate reactive structure; and a not-too-brightly burning spark of affective reaching. This is what Eddie was providing the school staff to work with.

C. THE THIRD TEST. DIFFERENTIAL MEASURES

Just prior to Eddie's discharge from the Orthogenic School, its Director requested another Rorschach test. The boy was then $13\frac{5}{12}$ years old. Table 7 provides a synoptic view of the ages at which the tests were taken;

the intervals between each and the date of admission, and between one another.

TABLE 7.—*Eddie's Ages at the Three Tests. Time Intervals for Tests*

AGE IN YEARS	BETWEEN ↓ AND →	INTERVAL IN MONTHS		
		Admission	First Test	Second Test
$5\frac{7}{12}$...............	Admission		26	64
$7\frac{9}{12}$...............	First Test	26		38
$10\frac{11}{12}$...............	Second Test	64	38	
$13\frac{5}{12}$...............	Third Test	94	68	30

The protocol for the third test, with scorings, and summary of scorings, follow.

RESPONSE RECORD

Figure I (10″)

1. W F+ A P
   1.0
   'What I think this could be ... a big butterfly (W; without the holes).

2. Ds F— Bt
   3.5
   'Two leaves with pieces cut out (each D 2 with Dds 29).

3. W F+ Art
   1.0
   'Could be meant to be a design (W; patient shows some tension; is slow).

4. Ds F+ Rc
   'Pumpkin face (D 4 with inner white spaces). That's all I can get ... nothing at all.'

Figure II (15″)

5. Ds F— Fd
   'This one could be a pattern of a beet (Ds 5).

6. D CF— Bt
   '∨ Also it might be a leaf in fall (D 1; the color of it, the red; also the shape, and the black).

7. D F+ A
   'This could be meant to be a butterfly (one big butterfly; D 6; form only).

8. D F— Rc
   'This could be meant to be a puzzle (D 6; the shape ... not made yet).
   '∨ Could be meant to be a map (D 6; any country ... one map). ∧∨ Can't think of anything else ... nothing ...

9. D FC— Bt
   3.0
   'A leaf with cocoons on it (D 2; looks like silk, the threads, the color and the

way it's made; accents the form). I'm
going to think for a while (very slow).'

Figure III (15″)

10. D F— An
3.0

'This could be meant to be an animal
skeleton (D 9; the way it's made; D 10
is the hand and D 5 could be attached).
'> A design (talks to self; points to
D 2, D 7; question of description only).

11. D F— Bt

'∧∨ This could represent two trees
(D 11; form),

12. D F+ Oj

'With sticks on the ground nearby
(D 5; legs chopped off).

13. D F+ A
3.0

'And then a butterfly (D 3; fluttering up near the trees). ∧∨∧< Ink
blotches . . . (deep sigh) ∧∨∧∨∧∨
> I can't seem to find anything else.'

Figure IV (12″)

14. W F+ A
2.0

'This could be a big butterfly (W;
the artist made it).

15. D F+ Bt

'A leaf (upper third; rubs card hard;
D 4 made me not want to say it; I have
no idea about it).

16. D F+ Ge

'A map made by a little kid (D 6;
Italy).
'A design (D 1 . . . nothing special
. . .). Did I say it might be a butterfly?
A leaf if I didn't say it . . . ink blotches.

17. DW F+ A

'∨ A make believe animal (W, because of the feet). ∨∧<∧∨ (Aimless
turning).'

Figure V (6″)

18. W F+ A P
1.0

'∨ This might very well be a butterfly (W, excluding Dd 22). And might
be a small bird . . . and might be a big
moth. Might be a design of ink blotches
(any kind, W excluding D 2 and D 3).

19. W F— A
1.0

'∨ Could be a picture of a make
believe fly (W; a big fly because none
are that big).

20. W F+ Rc
1.0

'∨ Could be a kite (W; I just thought of a Chinese kite of a bird dragon . . . and, this, a bird).

21. W F− Ge

'∨∧ Could be a little kid's map (W).

22. W YF+ A P

'∧ < ∧ Could be a bat (W; the black and wing look; shading and form). ∨∧ No . . . nothing else.'

Figure VI (7″)

23. D F+ Rc A

'∨∧ This could be a pattern (D 1; a folding turtle; a cardboard turtle; unfolded; head and legs).

24. D F+ Bt

'Might be two leaves (D 4 part of their shape). Could be a make believe animal. ∨ Might be a turtle when you fold it. ∧ Could be some ink blotches.

25. D Y.T Ls

'∨ Could be a swamp land (D 1; soggy dirt, the color and the way it's made).

26. D F+ H, A

'∨ Two twins (D 4; did I say that for this one? Animals, any kind; twins are identical).

27. D F+ Ge

'∧∨ A small kid's map (D 1).'

Figure VII (12″)

28. W FV+ Ls
2.5

'∨ This could be a rocky hill (W, each half; jagged things).

29. W F+ A

'∨ Two twin elephants, holding (D 2; the trunks and head),

30. D FY+ Ls
3.5

'the rocks (D 4; form and shading).

31. D F+ Ge

'∨ Could be a map (D 2; a young kid's). ∨ A design; could be some ink blotches (traces and feels D 4).

31a. D VF+ Ls

'∧∨Two animals inside a cave (D 4 is the top of the cave . . . a real tall cave and real small elephants; a round shape; and elephants under it).

32. D F+ A
1.0

'A butterfly with two animals (a butterfly flying right over head). ∨∧ There doesn't seem to be anything more.'

Figure VIII (10″)

33. D F− A

34. D F− Bt

35. D F+ A
3.0

36. D F+ A P

37. D F+ A
3.0

38. D C Bt

'<∧ Two frogs (D 1, faces of frogs),
'climbing a leaf (D 5; irregular outside),
'with a butterfly holding on to the leaf (D 2; form only and touching at Dd 29; not a single bit did color help; he had spoken of this "green" part).
'> Two animals and a butterfly holding on to a leaf (D 1; gophers, almost the same except for the animals).
'Or else two butterflies resting on a leaf and the animals holding on to the butterflies (D 4, D 2; just thought of it as one, at the time, as if they wanted the butterflies to give them a ride— then they had a good grip on the leaf).
'Might be two under-water animals holding on to leaves or moss (D 5; "messy"; C only; Dd of D 1 is a fish's tail). Might be a picture of two twin animals (D 1; exactly identical). ∨∧ >∨ That's the only thing I can get out of it.'

Figure IX (4″)

39. W CF+ Art
5.5

40. D F+ Ge

41. D F− A

42. D F− Bt
2.5

'∨ This could be a design, a young kid's drawing (rubs over D 1 and D 3; just putting down anything; an older person wouldn't make the colors run).
'∧ Or else a young kid's map (both D 1; it didn't look like any country or state).
'>∧ Two twin birds (D 1),
'on a leaf (D 6; the claws are holding on to the leaf—it's design; shape only; the color almost made me decide against it). ∧ It might be a bunch of designs (D 3 and D 7; two things the same; D 5 is a geyser but I decided against it). ∧ A finger painting design (W; looked exactly like one—all the colors mixed in). ∧∨ As far as I can see, nothing else.'

Figure X (25″)

43. D M+ A

'∨ Two birds on each side (D 6; the way the heads are together),

44. D FV+ Ls
    4.0

'of the cliff talking to each other (D 9; it would be hard for animals to climb up the cliff and birds could just fly up). That could be a mountain with animals holding on (holding on for dear life; D 2 are birds, D 7 are insects and D 6 the bird). Could be a design (W, excluding D 6 and D 5; all the things).

45. D CF+ Art

'<∨ Could be blotches of paint, could be two pictures of the same sort of thing.

46. D M+ H, A

'∧>∨ Could be a parachute jumper and some birds (D 5; he is holding on to green strings, and this is rest of the parachute).

47. W FV+ Ls
    5.5

'And a mountain scene (W; D 9 is the mountain and all the animals and birds are on the mountain). ∧>∨ Could be a young kid's picture (mountains aren't red; the way it's made, it should have more right colors . . . these are wrong). That's all. Now for the questions, right?'

RESPONSE SUMMARY

R total 48

W	12	M	2	H	2	F+ %	68
DW	1	C	1	A	16	A%	33
D	35 (s, 3)	CF	3 (1−)	An	1	P	4
	48	FC−	1	Art	3	s	3
		YF	1	Bt	9	s%	6.2
Z	49.5	FY	1	Fd	1	T/IR	11.6
Ap	W! D	Y.T	1	Ge	5	T/R	44.2
Seq	Methodical	VF	1	Ls	6		
		FV	3	Oj	1	Af r	0.45
		F+	23	Rc	4	L	0.71
		F−	11		48		
			48				

EB   2/5

SOME QUANTITATIVE COMPARISONS

Certain measures of his psychologic progress in the interim since the second Rorschach test can now be directly read in a comparison of the quantitative summaries for the three tests. These trace the direction of this child's psychologic life over the period covered by the tests. Since he was residing in the School throughout this period, the score differentials are measures also of changes that developed in a child such as this in this School.

R 48. This compares with R 25 in the second Rorschach test. Eddie is now liberating his mental energies. In fact, the swing is over-sharp using his present age group (10 to 13 year olds) as frame of reference. Their mean productivity is 27.40, SD 14.35. The productivity is thus now well within the second standard deviation above the mean. In his second Rorschach test, he was staying close to his age group's center (still the 10 to 13 year group). However, the productivity of 43 in the first Rorschach test leads to the conclusion that Eddie is now only returning to a level customary for him. His 43 was also significantly above his then group's average, mean 21.93, SD 9.20 (the 6 to 9 year olds). He was, in fact, within the third standard deviation above their mean. How much of this is symptomatic explosion, overflow of emotions undisciplined by the ego? How much of it is Eddie's healthy display of constitutional drive that much above average, something he can convert into constructive effort? The snap back in the third test to the first level of productivity suggests that that was the truer gauge.

W. In percentage terms, this is 25. It compares with 15.3, SD 18.9, in the 10 to 13 year group. In his second Rorschach test, W score was 8 per cent; in his first 2.32 per cent. For the 6 to 9 year olds, mean is 13 per cent, SD 12.4. The arresting fact is Eddie is now going far beyond all his previous showings in intellectual reaching out. He is extending himself. The ego is taking the offensive.

He confirms this in his Z rating. His score of 48.5 is far above not only the expectancy for age 10 to 13 (their mean 8.45, SD 10.10), but also for that of the adolescent children (mean 28.90, SD 23.0). It is higher than the achievement of the normal adult group (mean 22.48, SD 14.91). It comes close to the standard set by a superior adult group. It contrasts sharply with his Z of 18.0 in the first test, and the complete freezing of the ability, score 1.0, in the second. The skepticism is in order, therefore, that the present high Z score is spurious, blown up by the many W's, and as ego-extension, may be more symptomatic than genuine intellectual level of operation. This doubt is dispelled by adding up the Z total, minus that contributed by W. This is 26.0, still very high. Z is index to more fluid intellectual process than is W. By this index, Eddie gives evidence of quite superior achievement. Again, the first test gave a truer measure than did the second (when his condition was so lethal to his intellectual life).

Especially striking is the course of the Ap in the three tests. The expectancies and findings are reported in tables 8 and 9.

The course is from excess Dd in the first test, to accent, in the second, on D at the expense of W and Dd, but not with severe loss in these two scorings. It then goes to total disregard in the third test of Dd, while overaccenting W, with D at expectancy. The progression is constant from accent on Dd to that on W. In psychologic terms it is from undirected scattering

TABLE 8.—*Ap According to Adult Norms*

	R	EXPECT	ACTUAL	AP
First Test........	43	W,8 D,31 Dd,4	W, 1 D,27 (DdW,1) Dd,14	D Dd!!
Second Test......	25	W,5 D,18 Dd,2	W, 2 D,21 (DW,1) Dd,1	(W) D! Dd
Third Test.......	48	W,9 D,35 Dd,4	W,12 D,35 (DW,1)	W! D

TABLE 9.—*Ap According to Children's Norms*

	R	EXPECT	ACTUAL	AP
First Test....	43	W,6 D,31 Dd,6	W, 1 D,27 (DdW,1) Dd,14	D Dd!!*
Second Test..	25	W,2.6 D,18 Dd,4.4	W, 2 D,21 (DW,1) Dd,1	W D! (Dd)†
Third Test...	48	W,5 D,35 Dd,8	W,12 D,35 (DW,1)	W! D†

* According to norms for ages 6–9.
† According to norms for ages 10–13.

The Ap's in table 8 were obtained by using the aduld Ap as a standard. But Eddie is a child, and he has been changing in the time covered by the three tests. Since Ap formulas are now available for three growth stages in children, I also calculated Ap by these norms. They are reported in tables 9. The Ap's are essentially the same as those obtained by the adult norms. It therefore appears that children, while giving on the average fewer responses, maintain normally the proportion of W, D, Dd, found in adults. Stated the other way around, the Ap formula used in adults is applicable also to children. It has the value of a universal rule.

of attention among the minor and the unessential stimuli, through a condition in which the patient binds the perception in the obvious, and finally to domination by the larger, inclusive stimulus. The course is from least integration to most intellectual drive and need to impress by achievement. He uses a DW in each test. The alogical method stays with him.

Sequence is principally methodical, although variation is small. In the second test, not enough variation. In the first test, irregular with trend to confusion. In this trait, Eddie moves from disorderliness to essential rigidity. He is least orderly and borders on confusion in his first test. His accent on D in the second (only three out of the 25 responses are scored other than D) leaves him with little opportunity to show himself either orderly or disorderly. In the one figure in which he does use Dd, his Seq is irregular. In his third test the Seq is rigidly W − D in any test card in which he uses both of these variables. The apparent exceptions in Figures I and X are only apparent. In Figure I, R 2, both D 2 with the Dds add up to W. In Figure X the W for the "mountain scene" of R 47 is so scored as a technical necessity. It is essentially identical with R 43 and 44, the first two associations in this figure; these amount to a W. So, in his Seq, Eddie is demonstrating a fixity which was already seen in the second test, but there disclosed rather in the D! Ap. In both these sets of findings (Ap and Seq) in both tests (the second and the third), there is the dead weight of constraint set by his ego as it developed its defenses. Here is one price of the therapy.

The inner living is undergoing some important changes.

M. Eddie is again producing M associations. The course for the three Rorschach tests: 4, 0, 2. The present quantity is thus small but the level is intermediate between those of the first two tests. He is still not as free with his daydreaming as in the first phase. But he does once more show some release. The course is one which patients frequently follow in relation to therapy.

C. In expressing his feelings, Eddie engages in his most extensive and critical swings. Outstanding is the quantitative variation of unmixed C: 8 in the first test, 0 in the second, 1 at present. The measures in the normal school children in the 6 to 9 year olds, Eddie's age group when taking his first: mean is 0.43, SD 0.79. The range is 0 to 4. For the 10 to 13 year group, mean is 0.27, SD .74. Range is 0 to 5. For the adolescents, mean is 0.33 SD 0.62. Range is 0 to 2. For 155 normal school children, mean C score is 0.35, SD 0.75. Range is 0 to 5. Eddie in his first test discharges well beyond all findings in normal school children. In the second test he reflexes back to total lack of excitability. In the third, he shifts again, this time into the range for his age group. Feelings can now again move him strongly. But he is no longer the infant, responding so much at sub-ego level. It is a clear retreat of feelings with growth; undifferentiated id gives way, in the face of ego.

CF. In the present test, this score is CF 3 (1−). In the first test, he scores M.CF− 1; in the second test CF− 1. In this immature but partially ego-restrained emotional nuance the course shows least variation. A common factor in all three is the minus in the F. The pull is always toward the impulsive, infantile. An important difference between the first and the second tests is the blend with M in the first. It is combining excitement pressure with feeling internalized as fantasy. This is a richer, more full-bodied, emotional experience than any of which he is capable in the second when he was in his most constrained state. The increase to 3 CF in the third test is consistent with the direction the personality has been taking toward liberation. Eddie is now more at ease in giving vent to his feeling pressures. His present CF 3 score compares with the findings for the 10 to 13 year olds of 0.47, SD 0.77.

FC—, 1. In this one trait Eddie continues as in his intermediate phase. It is an effort at mastery as against the initial condition. In the third test he is maintaining the progress achieved by the time of the second, doing no better, but no worse. But there is a minus sign both times. The ego's struggle at harnessing the feelings is unsuccessful. However, the FC finding has an important value in itself. It promises effort at emotional contact with the environment, at reaching out socially. This is character growth.

The sum C. The present color total score is the one from which the therapist will perhaps derive most comfort. It tells of real freedom, as compared with Eddie's constricted reaction pattern in the second test; it also tells of relatively mature restraint as contrasted with the first. The total now of 5.0 is still much above the mean of 1.62, SD 1.87 for 10 to 13 year olds. It also surpasses, but is nearer to the showing by the adolescents, mean 3.03, SD 3.02. The quantitative facts are that Eddie has shifted, as he is about to leave the School, toward a socially more desirable responsivity and to more adjustive distribution of the nuances of the emotional life.

The affective ratio remains essentially unchanged in his present test as compared with that in the second: now 0.45, as against 0.47, and close to the mean for 10 to 13 year olds, 0.59, SD 0.21. Eddie's responsivity to exciting stimuli continues unchanged and adequate. The big swing in this ratio takes place between the first and second tests, from the very high 0.95, to 0.47. This retreat from response is a gain which he is holding in the third test. There is a big difference in the third and second test in the way he uses the emotional sensitivity represented by the two nearly identical findings of 0.47 and 0.45. The differential is projected in the color sums and in the total number of color determined associations. The feelings are now finding expression.

A conspicuous shift has taken place in Eddie's experiencing of painful emotions. Of the self-consciousness projected in the V trait, he shows progressively more with each of his three tests: 0, 1, 4. His present count of 4 is well above not only the 1.06 (V total) mean for his age group (SD, 1.50), but it is also above that of the adolescents, mean 1.92, SD 1.60.

Eddie is returning to about where he was in his first test in apprehensive mood reactions, total Y. Score is 3, both times. It, too, exceeds the average for his age group, 0.58, SD 0.99. A slight deepening of the experience is also apparent in the one pure Y. In his first test, all the light determined responses were either YF or FY. The inference is that growth and the treatment are reactivating depressive mood moments, a sign of super-ego activity. Eddie has been introjecting standards and feels their proddings. At the time of his second Rorschach test he had no need of conscience.

Texture. The texture response, T, is found only in the third test. Whether progress or not, it is different; it means liquescence in the personality. Eddie now permits the test to tap an emotional experience in a new modality, one related to the touch sense. Its psychologic significance is anything but satis- factorily established. The hunch, which continues consistent with clinical data, is that it projects a contact yearning, one that stems from early child- hood. As erotic desire, this can be the forerunner of biologic urges soon to flower in a 13 year old.

Experience balance is now 2/5.0. In Rorschach's language, extratensive "dilatiert." The shift is significant in the inner living as compared with that in the second test, where it showed up as essentially frozen. EB was 0/1.5. Eddie is now expansive and reaching out. It is a real swelling out of the feelings. But it still does not compare with the 4/13 expansion which, in his earliest stage, he had permitted himself.

In the third, or content column of the summary, the H score again ap- pears. Eddie had excluded the human form in his second test. He had seen it in the first. The quantity, 2, is small both in the first and third. He is not removing the blinders that shut humans out from his vision. But one quali- tative improvement now appears. He does not restrict his perception to parts of humans. The constriction and the anxiety he formerly manifested in the Hd variable are lacking.

Animal content. The per cent of 33 is a critical change. Gone is the un- relieved drought of the almost 100 per cent animal forms of the second test. This had itself been a recoil from the 21 per cent in the first test which, for his age, was less than normal recognizing of familiar forms. The mean for 6 to 9 year olds is 45.86 per cent, SD 16.50. His 21 per cent puts him a good 1.5 SD below the mean. In his present test his score is below the mean of his new age group by just about 1 SD. For the 10 to 13 year olds, animal per cent mean is 51.68, SD 16.35. He has thus moved nearer to center for those of his years; but still below the mean as he is, measures a trend to see the unusual, which may mean the original.

This clear improvement toward a variegated perception is further mani- fest in the non-animal content. In the first, these are either characteristically immature ("question mark," "circle," "holes"); or a concentration in one perseverated topic ("stones"), stereotyped adhesion to some one form. Ed- die's low animal per cent in the first test did not result from any large store- house of impressions and ideas. On the contrary, it uncovers a very limited repertory, a growth stage long ago left behind by Eddie's age mates. Its only originality is as departures from the expected norm, an unfruitful originality. At present Eddie is not altogether free from some personalized divergences. But the totally immature percepts are lacking. And the content does now have some breadth, even if not as much as is to be wished in a healthy boy of 13.

There remain three items in the summary that need to be considered together. They are F+ per cent, P and lambda. They are indexes to the patient's way of dealing with the world outer to himself.

Eddie's ability to see the world accurately is now where we should expect it for a 13 year old. His F+ per cent of 68 compares with the mean in his age group of 73.69, SD 12.40. More important, it has risen from the weak 46 per cent of his second Rorschach test and 50 per cent in the first. (Mean for the 6 to 9 year olds is 67.17, SD 11.90.) From the essentially unchanged and low F+ per cent it follows that the sharp contraction in personality found in the second test was not due to any rigid hold on the self or on reality such as would improve accuracy. The contraction was a reaction to stresses which had not abated. But in the interim between the second and the third tests Eddie had learned to attend to his stimuli and to criticize his percepts. He now does this at a level to be expected at his age.

Of even more import is his present P count of 4. In his first test he was capable of none, and he scored only a single P in his second. But by now he is progressing toward recognizing social canons, toward making them part of his thought repertory. The findings for 10 to 13 year olds is mean 5.23, SD 2.33. Again Eddie is moving toward center in his adjustment.

Lambda's value is as a gauge of the patient's ability to attend to outside stimuli in their competition with the ever-demanding inner ones. The healthy 13 year old maintains a lambda balance around the mean point of 83.35, SD 12.15. In the 6 to 9 range, the mean is 78.40, SD 12.25. The illuminating findings in Eddie's lambda scores are in the directions and the violence of the two shifts between the three tests. Behind these shifts are the ups and downs in the mental resilience that permit response to emotion-toned stimuli and liberating the fantasy. The scoring is from 0.65 in the first test, to 0.88 in the second test, and back to 0.71 in the third. On the first occasion, he drops to well within the second SD below his age group's mean. On the second, he has swung upward, moderately above his group's lambda average. The third phase finds him seeking the normal level for his years. Thus he grows from an excessive response to inner stimuli, to an unhealthy loss of resilience, and then to its regaining. His lambda is now his healthiest.

The opposition trait. The s counts are 5, 0, 3. The group findings are for 6 to 9 year olds, mean 0.75, SD 1.55; for 10 to 13 years, mean 1.19, SD 1.41. Eddie appears now *not* significantly above average in obstinacy. The percentages (s/R) are about as significant (see p. 233). They are 12, 6.2. See table 3 for s percentages in children.

The psychologic course so judged has been from high average resistance to the contraction that so completely shapes the second picture, and a rebound to just about average.

Average speed of first response remains unchanged in the two latest Rorschach tests: 12.0″ and 11.6″ respectively. However, both sharply differ from this score in the first test: 4.37″ (this average was obtained for only eight figures; the time was not recorded in Figures VI and VII). The fast time in this earlier Rorschach test is the result of immaturity. The younger children have not yet built in the mechanisms that delay their discharges. The growth reflected in the ability to delay was, therefore, already operative in the second test.

Average time for all responses is moderately faster in the third test, 44.2″; with that in the second, 49.8″. These time observations had not been recorded in the first test. Nor are those time data available for our groups of normal school children. How meaningful this slightly faster average time in the third Rorschach test cannot, therefore, be judged. The general significance of such a change is that a patient does less halting or blocking between responses. His mental productions are that much smoother, less impeded by the undergrowth which the emotions place in the way of efficient intellectual going.

In fact the going looks too smooth for our patient's good as his very small fluctuation in initial response time shows, 5.4″. (Mean, 6 to 9 year olds is 27.0, SD 15.35.) This is even a lessening of this fluctuation as compared with the 6.55‴ in the second test. His tempo is monotonous, even more when judged by that of the 10 to 13 year olds. Their mean is 32.11, SD 17.45.

Fluctuation is also somewhat narrow in productivity from test card to card: 0.77 in the third Rorschach test compares with an average for his present age group of 1.21, SD 0.54. He rates, therefore, well below average. This 0.77 just equals his fluctuation rate of 0.77 in the second test. This fluctuation in the first Rorschach test highlights a striking difference. It was then 2.33, or 3.72 SD above the mean for the 6 to 9 year age group, an abnormally high rate of mental ebb and flow. One factor in the earlier volatility was the younger age. Another, accounting for the changes in the interim, is the environment in which Eddie has been living. The Orthogenic School was set up and is being directed with a view to achieve this very stabilizing effect.

D. The Progress and the Implications

Such has been the course, as traced within the quantitative findings, which Eddie has followed in the five years and eight months spanned within the dates of his three Rorschach tests. It is a span which, too, sees the boy progressing from about the middle of the latency period, at the age of $7\frac{9}{12}$ years, to the early stages of adolescence when he was $13\frac{5}{12}$ years old. In having these three sections of this personality's growth available, the therapist has at hand two sets of data critically important for understanding the human being whom he is attempting to treat. One is the information as to the interim developments, and so of the latencies within the personality and their trends in these intervening periods. Any one test by itself tells principally where the personality has arrived on that date. It is a picture of its psychologic structures, their functioning, organization, integration, and the present status of the whole. It makes possible certain inferences as to potential and warrants certain predictions. It tells all this as inherent in a condition at any one moment. It is as though one arrests a life for a moment, much as when in a moving picture the operator stops the film to enable the more deliberate examining of some one pose taken by the actor. But life is never still, and it is in a series of tests—whatever the technic, provided it is valid—with their differential measures that we see the movement of that life, its advance toward maturation, or its retrogression. At the same time, and especially in dealing with a problem of treatment, the therapist must know the patient's condition, his mental status as of the time when he is carrying on the treatment. For this purpose, the latest test findings are his governing body of data. They are his topographical map by which he plans his next action course. Eddie's personality as projected in his third Rorschach test, taken by itself, therefore becomes now the especial and immediate object of scrutiny. Our interest centers not only on the quantitative compass points and the major directions which they set, but also in those finer nuances of functioning and adaptive effort which emerge in the test behavior.

The defenses. These are developing an illuminative pattern in the third test. They are forecast of what may not only be the patient's next personality phase, but his life long personality structure. Eddie is fashioning an obsessive structure. Should this eventuate it will insulate him against the schizophrenia which threatened in his first test. It is the organism developing its protective outer skin. This cautious behavior includes a precision delimiting or correcting, or explaining. Samples: R 1, he corrects his butterfly, "without the holes"; in R 10 the arm detail of the skeleton "could be attached"; in R 14 the butterfly is "the way the artist made it." In R 18, two precision alternatives. Hesitation over a percept and trend to reject it, owing to his doubt, in R 15; but "this (D 4) made me not want to say it." Similar dissatisfaction is voiced in R 40. In one instance, Eddie fully rejects an association and we know about it only from the inquiry, the "geyser" following R 42. In "a puzzle . . . not made yet" (R 8), the boy sees the stimulus as not complete, an offensive-defensive tactic. In criticizing the outer object, he is scattering his own apprehension. We see more of this in his use of the term "design," a sometimes scorable, at times simply descriptive response. More tellingly, they are "ink blotches," "paint blotches," five times (in Figures III, IV, V, VII, X). This is the most realistic and accurate description of these stimuli. It sidesteps the issue, that of identifying the stimulus for what it means to the patient, i.e., for its threatening value. The mechanism is that of aggressive counteroffensive against the insecurity, and therefore threat, set up by the test. It is one way of rejection; it is defense by way of attack. In this, again, the test nicely provides a cross-section of a person's behavior in life. Eddie is not afraid of the blots as such, as no patient is. But they set going an apprehension which must be in the character structure to be set going at all, a readiness to be afraid. To react to fear by counter-attack is a sample of his reaction to fear-inducing stimuli in the great world beyond the ink blots.

Eddie is impressed repeatedly by the identity in the bilateral details resulting from the symmetry of the test (see R 26, following R 38, R 41 and the comments that follow R 41). His use of the term "twin" can be deceptive since it can refer to a critical motif. But he rejects such dynamic meaning by the description "things are the same." In R 26, he questions explicitly with surprise in the inquiry that he had said "twins," and he corrects to "any animals" except that twins "are identical." The need to attend to the symmetrical aspects in the test figures is one mechanism whereby obsessive individuals attempt fullness, motivated by their thirst for security.

Of the nature of ego-extension is the boy's several times tagging his "maps" percepts as "made by a little kid" (R 16, 21, 27, 31, following R 39, R 40, and following R 47). The lead is to his warding off the painful possibility that he is himself still "a little kid." In his second Rorschach test Eddie identifies with the young (p. 248). The motif is persisting but he now maintains his psychologic distance from it. Eddie is also conducting a campaign of undoing. He repeats the topic over and over, a mechanism the ego uses to divest an unpalatable idea of its value.

In three instances he de-realizes the perceived object: in R 17, 19, and the elaboration of R 23; in the comments following R 24 the animals are "make believe." In saying, R 19, that "none are that big," he is providing a clue to what he is fending off, the insect theme as threat. The "make believe" is an undoing and, speculatively, may have in it an element of depersonalizing. In any event, a counter-phobic move. Still another device is that of displacing ideas concerning which he is personally sensitive. This is also a screening device. (See R 31a; 33–4; 35; 43–4). The core meaning in these associations is insecurity.

Eddie has already beaten a path toward an obsessive structure as manifest in certain character hardening phenomena. These appear in three of the test's operations. The 100 per cent F+ scoring in Figures IV, VI, VII is a stringent control over reality. The patient is stiffening his defenses as he senses threat. Second is the Ap. Eddie is limiting his selections to W and

D, ever-accenting W. To accomplish this he completely excludes Dd. This in a patient who, in one Rorschach test, selected 14 Dd! His handling of life's problems, as indicated in the present Ap, is inelastic. He does not adequately vary approach with changing conditions. Too much caution produces an excessively controlled intellectual method. Third is the very even tempo of productivity. As the quantitative comparisons have shown (p. 261) it is persistence of a defensive rigidity which had been a most destructive condition in the second test. It has relaxed some as we can see from the present pattern as a whole. But the habit lingers and continues its strait-jacketing. It is behavior always predictable and, to that extent, safe. But it is safety purchased at a heavy price. It parches off the resilience and makes for brittleness under stress. The human personality being the tough material that it is it will take a very individualized psychotherapy, one blueprinted *ad hoc*, and of long duration, to soften these defenses.

Eddie is capable of fantasy associations since he produces two. But none in the first nine figures. The inference is that there is repression. He is defending himself from his unconscious wishes. The ego finds it more salutary for the whole personality's well-being to keep these wishes altogether incommunicado. The needs projected in the fantasies that do come to light offer some clue to the urgency for holding them under censorship (see below, p. 267).

The anxiety. The story is in part told in the quantitative evidence (p. 258). The qualitative observations: in Figure IV, Eddie betrays his pained state by the measures he takes to master it. Essentially every response which this figure elicits, scored or unscored, is such a reaction. There is the uncertainty about himself: "Did I say it might be a butterfly?" "A leaf, if I didn't say it." All the forms are scored plus, an over-reaction. The control is not fully successful as the DW attests. A motor manifestation of unsettlement is much and aimless card turning. It is a bound anxiety and Eddie continues the binding, using a variety of artifices. In Figure V, he scores only W's in five responses. This results from two traits, either or both: (a) unvarying and consequent inability to break up the stimulus into its component elements; (b) the five W's are symptomatic ego-extension. It offsets the apprehension.

But he is only delaying the shock effect; the inaccuracies in Figure V betray the uneasiness. In Figure VI the Ap is again fixed, though in all D; and all the forms are plus, rigidity again. He responds, too, exclusively to inner stimuli once, R 25, a mood determined, blending with a tactile need.

In Figure VII the binding persists in the unadaptive approach (the W's technically so scored are virtually D's) and the rigid plus perception. But there are important differences in comparison with Figures IV, V, VI. Three of the associations are structured in V or Y; they are dysphoric in tone.

The content is essentially all personal, significant. The patient liberates much energy which he converts into difficult intellectual operations, Z. Productivity is his highest in the test so far, equalled only in Figure VIII. All this in the "mother" figure. The stimulus which activates that important person's image is, therefore, awakening some deeply felt painful thoughts. It also animates him into using latent abilities. It does all this while he maintains his control ever accurately. The test is thus highlighting, as a dominating condition, an attitude to the mother, one in which there is potential for useful exploiting, or for aggravating the neurosis.

Mood. The quantitative summary rubrics a moderate amount of passive-apprehensive mood. The patient verbalizes a resignation trend in Figures I, VII, VIII. Of like temper, are his expressions of inability, the source of which is self-depreciation (below, p. 269). This is a depressing experience always. Eddie is not comfortable with himself. It is one result and phase of the therapeutic process.

The lively emotions. The prevailing affective tone is, however, being called out by the exciting and the pleasure-awakening stimuli of the test, the colors. As the quantitative findings show Eddie is reacting both with more freedom and with more control than heretofore in this sphere. He is attempting, even if ever so little and unsuccessfully, to make an affective rapport of socialized quality. Yet, his are a mixed set of emotional experiences. He reacts restively, peevishly. In Figure VIII, for example, he is more than commonly positive in excluding color as determinant: "not a single bit did color help" (R 35). He fights the colors more explicitly in R 41, 42, "the color almost made me decide against it"; and once again following R 47, "the colors, these are wrong."

Discomfort and fidgety behavior in the test figures with colors tell of unsettlements produced by emotion-arousing events in the real world. It is one sign of color shock, an unstabilized ego-affect balance. But as evidence of a fighting ego resisting the affects it is a good sign. As compared with the dulled ego state in the second Rorschach test any color shock is progress.

The shock is very effective in Figure II. It diverts Eddie's attention from the usual major details to a white space as the first association, and a reversal of figure and ground. F+ per cent drops to 33 as compared with the 68 per cent for the test as a whole. The feelings break down the form control within the two color-dictated associations, a total of four inaccuracies in five responses. This is a high degree of inaccuracy. The ego takes another loss in not recognizing any P form. The content in three of the associations (R 5, 6, 9) is concerned with symptomatic conflictual needs.

His first association in Figure III is a borderline F−. Some students would score the "skeleton" F+ ; perhaps not "animal skeleton." This would raise his F+ per cent in Figure III to 75. To this weak extent the ego is attempting a comeback from its set-back in Figure II. But this is the limit of Eddie's recovery. The content in these first associations is of sick quality and probably symptomatic in R 11, 12. The P responses are still missing.

In Figure VIII and in IX the emotions are again throwing the ego off balance. Figure VIII opens up with two erratic perceptions of which one (R 33) is very far from norm. The thinking in his organizations is quite unrealistic, uncritical (R 33–35 and R 37). All the motifs in this figure stem from very disturbing ideas. Yet Eddie snaps back. His perception becomes realistically controlled in three F+, including one P. The test is uncovering here a constant give and take between intellect and affect, between ego and id forces. As Eddie finishes with this test card the emotions dominate; he is reacting to undiluted color. Sub-surface contaminatory thinking is also present in the inquiry, R 37. But the F+ per cent of 60 indicates that the feelings have not seriously broken down his control. In Figure IX, however, F+ per cent drops to 33 and once more he liberates a deeply significant theme. The P associations again fail. Yet structural findings are otherwise favorable; he achieves a W, a difficult feat in this figure; he does more organizing (R 41, 42). Striking is the high speed of initial response, Eddie's fastest for the ten figures. The ego has been needled. The speed is a reflex reaction. These expedients are evidence of the need for them, i.e., of shock against which the ego reacts; hence, its inability to maintain its grip on the rudder.

In Figure X speed of initial response is Eddie's slowest for the test; this is sharp fluctuation in contrast to Figure IX. It is a departure from the unhealthily oversmooth pattern up to this point. Attributed to the color stimulation it is the patient's sensitivity to affect-toned values. For the three intervals, Figures VII–VIII, VIII–IX, and IX–X, the sum of the differences in initial response time is 29 seconds; total fluctuation between all the test cards is 49 seconds; or a percentage of 59 for only a third of the intervals. The undoubted shock disclosed in the slow initial response time in Figure X does not demoralize or even upset Eddie. The only additional effect is the resistance to the colors. Not one of the associations, however, can be scored unmixed F. Eddie is now responding much to stimuli from within; fantasies, feeling pressures, inferiority consciousness (M, C, and V). While the personal values can still stem from unsatisfying sources the quality is now the richest for all three Rorschach test protocols. Eddie has been liberated by the color figures. Continued exposure to affect-toned events has been bringing results.

He supports this conclusion partially in the content in the three color determined associations. "Leaves, or moss" (R 38); "a design . . . a drawing . . . the colors run" (R 39); "paint" (R 45). None of these is a sick or strictly immature motif. Each is a theme which, in a maturely developed personality, projects a usually satisfying activity. In Eddie who as yet has much personality progress to achieve only the makings are present. The net conclusion in this sphere is that Eddie has emotional reserves which can be drawn out in the treatment effort. The objective is to channelize them into a contact with his environment so that he will feel with and know his world emotionally. In a word, to make him a social-minded human being.

The fantasy. The quantitative findings showed that by the time of the third test, Eddie regained some of the ground which he had so completely lost between the first and the second. But qualitatively he is showing little gain. His fantasy life is immature, autistic, sometimes with archaic processes including some under the surface. The articulate regressions are found in R 43 and in the unscored "birds" of R 46. I estimate the energy investment (Levy scale) in them as follows:

R	Degree of Movement
43	3 to 4
46	5 to 6

The range is medium to high. The tentative interpretation is that Eddie fantasies with moderate to high intensity. This can be a favorable finding. It discloses wishful living which can be converted healthfully. The centripetal movement in R 43 uncovers the clinging or dependent attitude. How acute the themes is made clear in R 43 and in R 46. The insecurity is painful in the extreme. Eddie is living and suffering J. B. Watson's loss of support, one of the "unlearned" causes of fear which the father of behaviorism discovered in infants. Both carry the nucleus for a panic development in the motifs of "hanging on for dear life," and in the "parachute jumper . . . and birds, holding on."

Of similar, either painful or repressed archaic quality, are the fantasies approaching expression and not quite making it. They are the "elephants . . . holding the rocks," elaborated in two "real small elephants . . . inside a real tall cave" (R 29 and 31a); the "two frogs climbing . . . holding on to the leaf" R 33; and the "animals holding on to the butterfly . . . as if they wanted the butterfles to give them a ride" (R 37); "a bird . . . claws holding on to the leaf" (R 41). In R 31a, Eddie moves from a grandiose theme to the opposite, in which the animals' small size contrasts with the "tall" cave, a probable fear theme. In R 33–35, and R 41–42, the pangs of insecurity. In R 37, the ego is disregarding reality altogether. But this dereistic thinking is entirely latent, emerging only in the inquiry, strongly suppressed.

Evidence that Eddie is repressing fantasy is his not using this activity at all in the first nine figures. In those liberated, he tells that his buried ideas are too trying. Here the test confronts the therapist with the need for making an important decision. Is Eddie better off in repressing these aggravating thoughts? And ought he be aided in strengthening the ego's defenses against them? Or will it be healthier to ventilate these, at present, unconscious ideas?

The decisive fact is that, at the core of the boy's unconscious, there is a frightening feeling of being in jeopardy. He repeatedly stirs up pictures of support giving way. He is either falling or in imminent danger of it. This fear has eaten deeply into the psyche and can only adversely affect the character. Does the test give any clue as to personal needs in which this unhappy state of mind is rooted? Not enough to be satisfactory. The "mother" imagery does stimulate uneasy feelings. But that anxiety is not so acute as to indicate that she is so devastating a dynamic. The reaction to the "father" figure points to even less sense of threat at that source. Are the parents, then, and the need for them, not critical in breeding his anxiety? Or is this Rorschach test not adequately projecting the psychodynamics? The clinical data will need to clear this question up. But the well equipped clinical psychologist will here turn to some other of his tools, another projective test that can short-cut the labor of uncovering. Murray's TAT would be this writer's next instrument.

The inferiority consciousness. This feeds on the sense of the difficult and on the insecurity feelings which appear to cause especially much suffering. The tie of one to a fantasy (R 43, 44) is direct; both recall the loss of support that is so alarming in Eddie's unconscious. R 28 calls for exploring both for the sense of smallness and the difficult; R 47, smallness. Eddie is explicit concerning a difficulty in R 43, 44, "it would be hard for animals to climb." The content in R 31a has the sharp flavor of symbolism, "animals inside the cave." But we need to know more concerning the meaning of caves.

The dynamic relation between the inferiority feeling structure and the acute sense of insecurity is not clear. Which is cause and which effect? Did (a) destructive developmental experiences breed the insecurity feelings which became a character structure, and (b) did the ego later fashion the inferiority fiction in order to rationalize the frightening insecurity? Or (c) was the inferiority consciousness imposed on the then helpless infant? Did he never get over his sense of helplessness? And (d) did he perpetuate the attendant emotion of unsureness? These questions remain unanswered in the Rorschach test material in this case.

The one *texture* association, R 25, appears in its content to be vividly recalling an early tactual experience, one in which the substance is soft and undifferentiated as to form, "soggy dirt." The writings of the psychoanalysts necessarily come to mind, as to the relation between feces, smearing, the prohibitions on this topic, and the formation of the anal character. If this lead is confirmed, it is projection of an emotional reaction belonging to earliest growth levels, presumably repressed, yet not so dormant but that the ink blots quicken it into life. An anal need may, therefore, be here being established as still active, under repression, and a focus of conflict.

The *opposition trait* has been noted as of medium strength (p. 260). The direction of the resistiveness is against the environment as it is in a cluster with C>M. Externalized aggressiveness, show of resentment, testiness, are to be expected out of Eddie in about normal amount for a growing boy.

The ego. The signs of deficit functioning are many. But Eddie has made progress as compared with his conditions in the earlier tests. The thinking weaknesses are striking. The very inaccurate "trees" of R 11 appears to be a happenstance suggested by the accurate "legs" of R 12. Eddie verbalized the legs only in the inquiry, but this does not contradict the conjecture. Not infrequently the earlier percept is communicated later, or only in the inquiry which thus elucidates the free association.

A perseveration is obvious in Figure VI; he continues talking about the "turtle" of R 23 after one intervening association although he is now holding the card in a new orientation. The question is in order whether all the "maps" are perseverations. The absence in them of any detectable personal significance so points. Perseverations impede appropriate reaction to the stimulus on hand. They are a heavy drag on the thinking.

The boy expresses a queer idea in "a folding turtle" (R 23); and even worse (R 37) in the "animals holding on to the butterfly ... as if they wanted the butterfly to give them a ride." This is severe thinking regression. Eddie can still be very immature. The odd reasoning is found also in some of his organizations: R 32; R 33–35; in addition to the one in R 37 which is also contaminated thinking. Uncritical elaboration and trends to it appear in Figure X and in the inquiry at various points.

In his perception Eddie is rarely so immature. Only once does he go to extremes, in R 11. The principal impairment is in the probably impersonal character of some form deviations (R 19, 21, 33). The significance of the impersonal F− is in indicating unsteady attention. Eddie's ego suffers lapsing moments. When personal investment misshapes the percept, the diagnostic value of the F− is less serious as product of wish and of conflict, and these are amenable to treatment. The possibly personal F− are R 5, 6, 9, 11, 34, 41, 42.

Perception of the self. Devaluation is prominent. Qualifications around responses are numerous. Figure II is heavy with unsureness. Eddie articulates his hesitation (following R 15) and his self-uncertainty (following R 16). His sensitivity over "kid" maps may be an apprehensive statement about himself as ungrown (p. 263, p. 272). The patient overtly states his inability (following R 8, and following R 13). Self-depreciation is not an unmixed deficit. It can, paradoxically, mean progress as stemming from a sense of guilt. The treatment has reached the patient's super ego. Or the treatment and the setting in which it is being carried on are building one in Eddie.

Language findings. These include the childlike descriptions (p. 262); a stereotyped formula, "could be," "could represent"; an aside which is odd behavior, talk by the patient to himself, at close of Figure II: "I am going to think for a while."

His card turning is without aim or visible control. In all this Eddie's ego is halting in its growth.

The total functioning. Yet, he is growing. His language and grammar now frequently follow mature forms; reflecting both capacity for learning and the desire to do so. Among his expressions are: "also it might be a leaf in the fall" (R 6); "a butterfly fluttering up near the trees" (R 13); "this might very well be a butterfly" (R 18). Correlative with the maturer diction are the originals, broadening scope and achievement. Samples are numerous: R 2; R 9; the "fluttering" in R 13; the "Italy" association in R 16; R 20, which is a superior original; essentially all the ideas excited out of the patient by Figure VIII; and much in Figure X. Much of this originality is, to be sure, unique and the perception in it is too frequently F−, inaccurate. But original. A differentiated intelligence is here operating. Contrast this with the interminable animal forms in the second Rorschach test. Eddie's ego is now launching out along wider horizons.

The liberated mental life makes itself known in conceptual thinking, in grasping difficult relations, the new distribution of attention between part and whole, orderliness, and those important traits constituting the behavior vis-a-vis the objective world F+, A, P, L. These have been discussed as the quantitative data (pp. 259–260).

Eddie's regard for social canons is unpredictable. His P responses fluctuate widely. He sees one such form in Figure I; none again until Figure V when he sees two; then none until Figure VIII, his final one. The total of 4 is close to his group's mean, 5.23, SD 2.33. He can recognize the conventionalities of life. But much is yet to be achieved. He leaves it uncertain as to whether and when, he will or will not know and do the appropriate.

He leaves room for improvement also in his approach. The defects are two. First, at times he restricts himself to a part of the stimulus in associations which usually attach to a larger area or to the whole ink blot. In the "pumpkin face" of R 4 he is reacting, in Figure I, to D 4 together with the white spaces, on the order of what Klopfer has identified as the "cut-off W." The percept "pumpkin face" or similar "faces" or "masks" are nearly always W. Eddie's limiting himself to a portion of the stimulus is not the same as the x response (Rorschach's Do). But the psychologic behavior behind it is similar, a restriction on the perceptual field. The second defect is in overweighting of one element, W, with total ignoring of another, Dd. He is thus insensitive to the smaller niceties of his perceived world. In Figure V, in which he goes through one long stretch of attending to the same thing exclusively, (five responses, five W's), the insufficiency is an inadequate suppleness intellectually. It handicaps Eddie in his adapting to change. Carried to an extreme he will be intractable to therapeutic effort.

But in his emotional life Eddie does show resilience. The experience balance is fluid. He is expressing his feelings and he has released some fantasies while more are knocking at the censor's door. Given a total character structure in which the intellectual habits show fixity while the inner forces are in flux, the latter provide the more critical evidence as to changeability. In its depth strata the personality is elastic. The color determined responses as evidence of emotional reaching out are, in the Rorschach test's technic, the principal psychologic material out of which is fused the transference. The one FC means that Eddie actually achieves emotional warmth toward others. Yet, the F in the FC remains an F−, as it does in one of the CF. The ego is in a taxing struggle as against the feelings. But it does struggle. It does perceive forms. The outer world has cut into Eddie's id. The ego has taken the initiative. It is on the march.

In his experience balance, this boy is more extratensive than he is introversive. Taken by itself this most weighty of Rorschach's indexes is forecast that the emotions will press outwardly; behavior will impinge on the external world. Irrespective of whether in symptomatic or constructive ways, then, since the emotionality is still more infantile and of the child's level than it is grown up, Eddie is still ready to be impulsive, easily irritable. He will need to watch his aggresive urges and the erotic ones that he will soon be noticing. They can take maladjustive behavior form. To prevent such untoward events, the ego has built its defenses, turns passive, sometimes has recourse to fantasy.

All these activities go to make up a total personality. All must be measured and the relations between them understood. These inter-relations and the integrating them into a purposeful unit of action is the work of that important agent in the personality, its central directive, the ego.

The content as personal dynamics. Much of this has already been reported in relation to the determinants. Outstanding is the motif of insecurity, lethal to Eddie's well being. "Holding on for dear life" (R 44) appears to be the *leitmotif* of this personality. Throughout Figure VIII he is gripped by this need to "hold on." He speaks it also in Figure IX (R 41, 42). The thought becomes most traumatic in Figure X.

The fear in these associations must have some roots in a sense of being small. The "kid" themes and the effort at undoing these thoughts will be recalled, (p. 263). The notion of the "big" appears with reference to three animals in R 14, 18, 19. Implicit is the contrast with the small and this contrast is explicit in R 18. If Eddie is talking about himself in one of these animals, he is using the defense of displacement. Such are the exploratory directions which the test opens up. The smallness theme was a forceful one in the second test. Its trace is thus still emerging, still alive.

Dysphoric motifs support the structural evidence for passivity-apprehension. The "leaf in fall" (R 6); the "animal skeleton" (R 10); and the "tree" from which some sticks have been "chopped off" (R 11, 12) require exploring for such significance. The latter is of a kind frequently found in aging persons, a displacing of their discomfort over the sense of decline.

The "swamp" (R 25) is a desolate landscape. Depressed adults produce this variety. The psychologic source is the sense of isolation. It is rare in children, and a bad sign when found in them. When the "bat" (as in R 22) is "black" the phobic undercurrent is inferred.

The "cocoon" (R 9) involves the reproduction process. This and similar themes frequently appear in the Rorschach tests of children. Eddie's numerous "leaves" must arouse our curiosity; they do not satisfy it. The percept has affective loading in R 6 and it is organized in with the personally significant "cocoon" of R 9. The presumptive evidence is for a personal value in the numerous recurrences of the percept (R 2, 15, 24, 34). Nothing else in the test supports the surmise, of a lead. The therapist becomes alerted for a meaning if and when it should emerge. The "beet" of R 5 is an original and a possible food interest.

Eddie also provides leads to assets than can be directly exploited in the treatment effort. The "kite" of R 20 is an active child's recreational interest and probably the "pumpkin face" of R 4, the "puzzle" of R 8. Whether the several "designs" stem from any artistic preferences, the "maps" from an interest in geography or a travel wish, must be tested out directly in the patient. To the extent that these and the recreation motifs prove valid, they are media to which the therapy can turn at once. Unlike the deeper unconscious reserves these assets are immediate.

Treatment implications. The findings are informative, both as to what must be the specific aim, and the available psychologic resources. Eddie is heading toward an obsessive structure. This would mean an impermeable outer character armor, and a stiffness which can be crippling. Therapy now has to soften defenses which had been needed but developed beyond the optimum. Eddie must not only be tough but also supple. It is, of course, easier to state an objective than to design the plan for reaching it. How much, for example, ought Eddie's fantasy living to be encouraged? It liberates and it communicates, but it also arouses the frightening and oppressing. The test can only bring to light the opposing possibilities. The decision is a technical one in therapy, to be made by the therapist.

The test does inform that Eddie has the strength now with which to come to grips with the unpalatable. His ego can take it. He also has the personality resources. They are drawn out at certain layers (e.g. mother imagery). Depressing moments are seismographic record of a rumbling superego. Again, a big help, if it stays at the optimum rather than be activated at the maximum. He is vulnerable, too, to the excitements of life. These activate some rich psychologic resources. He possesses emotional reserves, such as capacity for warmth, still to be exploited. He possesses, also, intellectual resources. Drive is high; intelligence above average. He is disclosing specific interests; some at deeper, some at more surface levels.

The net evaluation at this third test is that Eddie now needs psychotherapy critically. He will need skilled directing for a long time. The final product, the adult human personality will be scarred; never as innerly smooth, and as adaptively efficient, as would have been its functioning under more satisfying life's viscissitudes in his first years. But, the outlook is now much the best for any point within the span of years covered by his three Rorschach tests. The therapy can be continued with the knowledge that the therapist will be smiling with the satisfaction of efforts bearing fruit.

E. From the School's Notes, Psychiatric and Social Work

The history raises a question of early delivery by several weeks; it was an instrumental delivery. Eddie did not walk until he was between $2\frac{1}{2}$ and 3 years old. He was slow in talking. His health is reported as "never good." He developed trench mouth within the first few days after birth, and had to be fed by means of an eye-dropper for six months. Thus he was a feeding problem; and regurgitation "through the years" for which he was referred was no doubt related. Frequent constipation is reported. He has been underweight. Physical history: german measles at age $2\frac{1}{2}$; chicken pox at $4\frac{1}{2}$; influenza, mild, at 3; tonsils and adenoids removed at 4; a question of allergies, at $3\frac{1}{2}$. The family pediatrician raised the question of poor coordination. On his advice the family consulted a psychiatrist who referred Eddie to the Orthogenic School.

The symptoms meanwhile had included his poor eating habits. Also, he did not get along with other children. His mother throughout this time has been having difficulty in handling him. She is described as "unstable." It will be recalled that she has not recovered from the shock following the death of her first child with whom she compared Eddie so unfavorably (p. 220). In her handling of Eddie she first smothered him with love. She saw that this was making him dependent. Thereupon she went to work, leaving Eddie to the care of someone else.

Personality symptoms at the time of referral to the Orthogenic School included excessive attachment to one person and violent fears of (a) stairs; (b) torn paper. The latter fear is not explained. Regarding the former, he had fallen on some stairs when he was $2\frac{1}{2}$ years old, had had a clothes pin in his hand, and this had penetrated the roof of his mouth. The treatment required nine stitches. The note soon after his admission to the School includes the following traits: coordination, very poor, of spastic quality. Eddie is slow in dressing and in eating. He is shy, repressed, fears aggressive boys in games, and is used by them as the weak member in their play. He daydreams; masturbates much and openly. In the classes, however, he enjoys discussion groups and is especially alert in history and related studies.

Parental history. The father had a very unhappy childhood. His parents were divorced when he was 13, and he lived with each of them. His relations were most satisfying with a grandmother who had sent him to school after the grandfather refused to do so. The relations between his parents had always been a source of concern to the father. There had been many divorces in the family, and he had always wanted "a real family of my own . . . a real family." Further, the father describes much neurotic illness in himself; extensive medical examinations had found him negative, and the physicians had given him "pills for his nerves." He reads Freud much, is "a perfectionist." He feels he is being pushed to make Eddie do well. Among his own symptoms are becoming ill whenever Eddie does and ending up in bed. He too had found the first child an easy baby to handle. But Eddie frightens him. He speaks of Eddie as not a happy child, but one who looks sad and does not laugh.

The mother reports that she had a very happy childhood. Her own parents were always happy together. There was however much illness in her family. She was raised in a small college town. Family ties were close. Her own mother was protective of her father, and the children were taught to control their emotion in order to spare him. Eddie's father and mother married young, and they described their life together as one of mutual understanding. "We have grown more or less inseparable. We are together constantly, in business and at home." They own and operate their women's apparel shop. The father appears dependent on his wife, although he tries to show how dependent she is on him.

The first child had died at the age of 8 months from a streptococcus infection. He had had convulsions with projectile vomiting and death came within three days. Affect is very strong in both parents concerning this first child. They describe him as a beautiful, well formed and alert baby.

Quoting the mother, "he was a different type than Eddie and that was what affected our relationship. Eddie was extremely ugly and ill besides." After the first child's death the parents went South but could not ease their pain. They returned to Chicago and had their friends move their furniture out of the apartment; they then busied themselves in their shop, working long hours. The mother had cared for the first child herself; but on the father's insistence, she hired nurses to take care of Eddie so that she could be in the shop with the father. She expresses guilt over her handling of Eddie.

Eddie's attitude to his parents: he displays affection to them, but, "there is a cloud." He does not answer them unless he is in the mood. His attitude has at times been aggressive, dictatorial. He did not want both parents to go away at the same time; they were to be within a radius of about a block "in case something happened to both of us at one time." Some of these attitudes are reported as of more recent date, i.e., after Eddie had already been resident in the School. The mother is tense whenever Eddie is home (on visit). The parents go where he wants them to even though they do not so prefer and he so senses. When he is at home life for them is not real. The mother stays at home. "We don't eat out; and since he is only there for a short time we can't assume parental roles."

The feeding history: since the dropper was used the first six months of Eddie's life (owing to his trench mouth) it was very difficult to change him to normal habits. He always remained a slow eater. The vomiting persisted and the constipation coincided with periods when he vomited. When bowel movements were satisfactory, he would also retain his food. Sleeping: he shared a room with a nurse until he was 8 months old; then with a maid until he was $3\frac{1}{2}$. After that he had his own room. But he did not use it. He slept in his parents' room.

In the Orthogenic School, on admission Eddie rated an intelligence quotient of 113; a year later, in the low 90's; a third rating, fifteen months later, is 115. All examinations were by Stanford-Binet. The fluctuation in the measurements was attributed in part to changes in counselors, and the related changes of influence on Eddie.

Eddie's personality course is traced in the following excerpts taken from the School's very complete records. I am reproducing them in chronological order beginning just about six months prior to the first Rorschach test, and continuing until six weeks before the final one. During most of this time Eddie was under study by a woman psychiatrist. The majority of the excerpts are taken from this psychiatrist's notes, and are not otherwise identified. Those marked "staff" were culled from conferences. They may represent the opinion of the School's Director, any member of his staff, or the psychiatrist. Those marked "SW" were set down by the social worker. Each of my paragraphs represents a separate date.

(SW) Other boys take away the blocks and toys with which Eddie is playing. They hit him, without objection by him.

(SW) His voice is weak, high-pitched.

(SW) Eddie hits his counselor with his pajamas. Meanwhile food had been playing an important role in several of her notes. Eddie plays the game of what there would be to eat at the next meal. He frequently asks the counselor whether they would eat and where. While at the Aquarium he complains about being hungry. He will take the counselor to his house, and she can have anything to eat, corn on the cob, lamb chops, orange juice, ice cream, cake.

(SW) Eddie shows much pleasure in finger painting.

(SW) "When Daddy comes, I'll give him a big hug... I'm going to hug him almost to death."

(SW; nearly three months later) Eddie has shown aggression toward this counselor recently, both verbal and physical. "I am going to hurt you." "I am going to push you." He always says this playfully. He wants to take her away from her room-mate, and she is to sleep in the boys' dormitory.

(SW) He tells the counselor she can paint anything, except a girl. Counselor: "Don't you like them?" The boy grins.

(Staff; the date is exactly one month prior to that of the first Rorschach test.) The medication in his mouth is stressed; he has no taste in it. The parents' considerable dependency on each other is noted. Eddie is evaluated as in contact; he emphasizes eating, rivalry and the need to be resistive and aggressive. His regurgitation and slow eating are aggression. The psychiatrist advises more regression in the patient when he is alone with the therapist but when in a group, his growing-up behavior must be encouraged.

(SW) Eddie shows firm opposition to another boy. He refuses to give in to the demands, and to the begging of the other in trading sticks. His own stick is the bigger, and he wants to keep it.

(SW) He will hug his father so as to hurt him (on an impending visit of the latter), and he will not see the father's face when hugging him. Actually, at the visit, the father did most of the hugging.

(SW; the date is that of the first Rorschach test.) Attitude and mood about going for the test are pleasant. He had expected to go with the parents, but when told that "Jim" from the School would take him, patient said: "Oh, I'm so glad." Talking about the test on the preceding day, he had hoped it would not take a whole hour.

(Two and a half months after this first Rorschach test.) I found him very much improved, despite the ominous Rorschach. The psychiatrist reports further that Eddie says he likes his group, to share things, to talk about his friends. He cut up some pieces of paper; no longer fears scraps of paper.

(Staff) Evaluation: Eddie had been overwhelmed in the feeding situation. He has the impulse to fight, but is convinced of his helplessness. The stronger the impulse, the greater the sense of helplessness. He has rage in him; much hostility because unable to carry it out.

(Staff; nearly nine months later.) The patient knows he can throw his parents. This gives him power over them.

(Staff) Eddie's problem is one of self-regulating of his primitive drives, establishing his own control, as against that of his parents. There is a problem also in his relation to male adults. The father is much dependent on the mother; and essentially a sibling relation exists between father and son. The father's rivalry for the mother is seen in his own vomiting. The patient's behavior is characterized as infantile at this time.

(Staff; about six months later.) The counselor has been treating the patient by expecting more of him. But he reacts by being more helpless, more poorly coordinated, and more messy than he needs to be.

(About this time, psychiatrist notes.) Seems rather remote and withdrawn today. He picks toys, certain guns, the top with which he is doomed to failure. Behaves with some of the old omnipotence. Gets depressed when defeated. Withdraws to pick up stick playing. Today shows distinct evidence of spite, e.g., rattling the table at my turn. However, every interference of his kind is followed by extreme clumsiness: defeatism on his side, and is never able to pick up any sticks after such interference on his side. Or else he chooses the most inaccessible one and fails. This is pointed out to him: "I want it that way. Did you see Tommy on Friday?" (No.) "That's better, let's play." Later: "Why did you change my appointment?" Toward the end of the interview he asks me to put the nipple back on the bottle; he had removed it earlier. He is sad, aloof.

He is in much better shape; talks with pleasure about going home for three days; is reluctant to leave the psychiatrist.

He is in much better shape. Continues work at the airplane with insight and independence, i.e., shows ability to see limitations of technics, materials and his own skills. He engages my help and utilizes it well without any of the previous exaggeration or self-depreciation. There is no reference to school, home, or to a friend.

(Less than a week later) At beginning of interview, speech and coordination are extremely poor. He puts himself the difficult task of finishing the chair. Makes it more difficult by speeding himself up. I suggest he finish plane instead, since he is obviously torturing himself. To that he agrees. While working at the boat he talks very poorly about going to mother. His mother is a child too. But she remains the same grown-up. (Differences between grown-ups and children?) Grown-ups smoke and have a business, otherwise are the same. (What do grown-ups do for children?) They give them plenty of fresh air and play games with them. (What games?) Who can do it faster, that's how we dress and eat, that's what I play here, before I go home. (So what do you do?) I am slow. Grown-ups breast-feed children. (How do you know?) I read it in mother's cookbook. It is good for them. I think my mother did it too. In the cookbook is a picture of it, the baby but I don't remember. My mother does not make the cake so good.

A week later the note reports Eddie very competitive. Two weeks later, which is exactly one week before Christmas, "in excellent spirits."

However, the first interview following the New Year reports him withdrawn, poor in his speech, and aimless in activity. A week later he is late for his appointment. Speech is poor. He coughs, seems nauseated at various points.

(Staff, at about this same date.) Eddie has been gagging at meals, he does not vomit; "but he acts as if he is going to." He now defends himself better against assaults by other boys. He has been using very little fantasy in his play session with the psychiatrist, and he is repressing because he knows he cannot compete aggressively. The boy is now in a depression. In his school work, he is poor, slow; sometimes does well, but only for a short time.

In appearance, manner of speech, and independent attitude, much improved. But the disjointed, autistic evaluation, by the people around him, is now much more obvious. In the interviews, he hardly plays, pays no attention to the bottle, food, and lends himself to conversation in which he is not spontaneous. One has the feeling that he tries to come to terms with people and events but fails to do so.

(One month later.) He looks very disheveled, pants unbuttoned, face dirty, and when I just look at him he replies, "I know, I know." He buttons up and washes his face with relative speed. He has stopped calling me by name as he used to previously, which may be in line with increasing detachment from me also.

(Staff; four months later.) Eddie is better. He cannot hold his own in motor competition with other children. He does try to stand up to other new children, but not as formerly, to be superior. His rage at his disappointments is seen as equivalent to his oral frustration. His being slow, dirty, are symptoms. He has need to achieve in nonmotor spheres, since he will never compete where coordination is required. He wants to do things that are impossible, owing to the parents' hostility to him.

(Two months later.) Throughout this interview, he gives the impression of much greater contentment than I have ever observed in him. He hums and sings. His coordination, especially of his fingers is slightly spastic at the beginning of the interview. But it becomes very good as he builds with the interlocking bricks, which actually requires rather minute coordination. Throughout he builds in a very concentrated way and learns how to make a window. Tries it out, but after he can do it decides against using it. Points to difficulties in building, as he overcomes them. Makes "joke" and is very pleased with his joke.

(Staff; four months later.) Eddie has been talking about his plan for a trip; and this is seen as developing independence. It is noted that he has made progress in one area, taken losses in another. Thus his school work is now sloppier. Also he is manifesting random movements.

(Five months later, and ten days before the second Rorschach test.) Throughout the interview he is stiff motorically, has an expression of aloof disdain, chin thrust forward. While he is quite clean himself, he smears chocolate on desk. This stiffness is interrupted by periods of hyperactivity during which he clears his throat incessantly. At other times his hands are in constant motion, twisting and turning the paper wrappers of the chocolate bars. He repeatedly directs a piercing look at me; is resistively compliant. The idea of story is agreeable, but discontinued when he starts out about Mark Twain. "A story in which I did not invent anything." Later he wants to follow up his idea of last time, story of his life. But he remains mute and resistive and abides silently to my comment that he does not have to. When I point out his anger in expression, silence, meaningless compliance and throat clearing, he neither admits nor denies, stops coughing; after a while, motor hyperactivity with paper, which then stops also and ends in rigidity, sitting stiffly upright with arms at his side. This sequence characterizes the motor pattern during this session throughout.

It was about this time that the School had discontinued home visits which he had been making. The reason for the discontinuance, as Eddie understood, was that he thought of home too much. The two days before the second Rorschach test, the psychiatrist reports an empty interview, with suspicious looking compliance on Eddie's part. He talks about his school activities, about shop. But his conversation peters out to recurrent generalities. Five days following the test, he wants to tell about what has been going on but the effort peters out with much throat clearing and gagging. A week later, more of this behavior: throat clearing, grimacing, much motor activity, including kicking the desk, and kicking the psychiatrist's legs.

(Three months later.) Neat, clean, well coordinated but aloof and arrogant. He has nothing to say. While free from all mannerism (does not eat either), his hostile isolation is marked. Finally there is some activity on his side to forestall all communication. After stating categorically that everything is well, he is silent and stares at me provocatively rather than in his previous mournful and reproachful way. After some staring we discuss his coming here. He comes only because the counselor tells him to, he does not know why, nor does he wish to come at all. I make the suggestion that the coming here will now be left to his initiative. He'll not be sent by counselor; someone will be ready to bring him if he indicates it. He agrees aloofly. In the office he fidgets with a torn sleeve, no button, exhibits and hides his extremely dirty hands. He admits that he has not washed them this morning or last night; pauses expectantly to wait for a comment from me. Fidgets, masturbates while talking about the arrival of a new boy which was delayed because the new boy got a cold. He may become a friend. That is if he is "nice." Nice and someone you like. He likes Sammy, enumerates activities in which they join. Puts much stress on stamps. Sammy has more stamps though. "One really can't say though, because I have more stamps at home." "Maybe he is more interested in stamps."

(Fully six months later.) He is particularly dirty and disheveled today. His fly is open and he does not manage to button it in spite of several attempts. One shoe is just slipped on and dragged. His mouth is crusted with food and he drools saliva in big bubbles as he talks in nasal intonation and very indistinctly. He sits down next to me and displays marked motor hyperactivity, rubbing the chair, dropping his shoe. When I point out the various forms of disarray, he admits them with a bland nod.

(A month and one-half later.) Looks disheveled, drools, motor stereotypies during interview, rubs hand against chair. When this is pointed out, sits on his hands for a while then starts again. Speech is rather poor; walk is loose-jointed. He bumps against furniture: loses shoe laces, does not tie them. Avoids looking at me. In the schoolroom, where I call for him, his isolation from the group is marked. The rest of the children stand around the table while he sits forlornly at his desk not working.

Not for another six months is this course reversed. Then an improvement sets in, which Eddie appears to be maintaining. The psychiatrist's notes:

There is considerable change. He seems more mature, with more tonus in movements, speech, approach to others. He looks neat, walks uprightly, and when recurrent movements occur, they are energetic, rhythmical. He clasps his fist on the palm of the other hand to accent his conversation.

When I watch him on the play field he seems free and relaxed. Throws a ball from a sitting position with good coordination. Follows me without objection but is quite

unapproachable insisting that "everything is just the same" and being so obviously
pained by the interview—with the intent to make me quite uncomfortable—that I
leave it to him to leave or stay. He leaves quickly.

He is better put together than I have ever seen him. Only one unlaced shoe reminds
of former sloppiness and his comment when I point to his shoe: "one is all-right, I
can always fix it," and he proceeds to do so. His posture and gait are much better
coordinated, and the dirt on his face does not give the impression of the previous
partly helpless, partly actively helpless drooling. There are no mannerisms of fingers
and his whole appearance is one of steadiness and adequate motor control. When I
call for him he runs toward me and takes two steps at the same time. He is very eager
to describe to me in detail the program his class is going to put on today. The topic
of the program is "School. Just like we really have School." This program is however
much better and quite different from the programs they used to have before. He likes
this kind better: "Because I am older. I can do more things. I get more parts and I
want to do them."

He is in good shape, talks clearly though somewhat more nasally than he used to
and is one of the few children without a cold. There is a recurrent flicking of his fingers
of both hands throughout the interview. He is in good contact. Starts out mentioning
proudly that he is able to swim two half-lengths in the pool. Then discusses the
various strokes. Then grades himself in homework. He is "excellent I should say in
reading," "good" in arithmetic and "only fair" in spelling. Recently he advanced
from fifth to sixth grade speller, but finding it too hard, Miss L. gave him another
speller. Probably an in-between one. He'll catch up. His writing is poor and does
not improve. (Flicking becomes more intense.) Then he grades himself more thor-
oughly and comes to the conclusion that he is third best in both reading and arithmetic. He gets along with most boys, sometimes, with a few most of the time. He
minimizes his pride in going out to spend his allowance by himself, admits as the only
advantage that it is faster. Then he talks about his home visit. The funniest thing
was the night he slept with his boy friend John. He really could not sleep, since John
took all the blankets. Once he called his father, who gave blankets back, but in the
morning it was the same thing. On Saturday his grandparents came to stay overnight.
They slept in parent's room, mother on studio couch, father "in my bed." He radiated
when he tells that. It was very nice, cozy, he had blankets, so had father. He looks
forward to go home Christmas. "Doesn't everybody?" And while nobody has said
anything about the visit yet he is sure that he'll go.

Just exactly one year from the date of this last note, the third Rorschach
was administered. Eddie was about to be discharged. The psychiatric treatment had been interrupted but was to be resumed after the discharge.
Summaries written by the social worker at this time provide a clear-cut
picture of the person that Eddie is after his long stay in the School. Somewhat condensed these follow:

Academically Eddie has made good progress but this has been hampered by the
tendency to daydream. His poor muscular coordination prevents his writing with any
ease or mastering the typewriter. His grade placement at $7\frac{3}{12}$ years was 2.4 and
at not quite 13 years, his grade was 7.3. He enjoys discussion groups and shows
alertness in his favorite subjects, history and other social studies. He resists doing
arithmetic in an orthodox fashion, but arrives at the answer by a devious method.
Eddie has been seen by me since he was 10 years old. At first he permitted himself to

play with the modelling clay and experiment with the nursing bottle, but he was able to mess more freely under conditions set up by himself by the use of a beginner's chemistry set. Even there he had to change the instructions and pretend that the results were just what he wanted.

A toy to which he frequently turns for motor expression is the Bang-a-Ball. Often when he is angry he will reach for this toy before telling why he is angry. Many times he is not able to talk about his anger but will express a wish that he could.

After the period of some experimentation in messing Eddie used much of his time with me in gaining some ability in throwing a ball and in catching. Later the ball was used as a resistance to talking to me. At such time he would bounce the ball against the wall and obviously was fantasying himself the member of some big league team.

When I acquainted Eddie with some of the facts of his history his response was, "I don't want to hear it." Even as recently as a few months ago when he happened to pinch the cheek of a rubber didy-doll and some milk another child had "fed" it came out of its mouth, Eddie gagged and was on the verge of vomiting. Eddie does not permit himself much freedom in the room with me as he did. I think the change came about the time that I insisted on his at least attempting to talk to me instead of just bouncing the ball. It is interesting too that Eddie was the only child who could not permit himself the pleasure of eating during the session. Twice lately he got up courage to ask me for something special and when I brought it for him he would turn it down.

Eddie was told of his having had a brother that died. This information was given him by his mother on his visit this summer. His mother offered to show him a picture of the brother but Eddie said he was not ready to see it. He was not able to tell me about this until I asked him if he had not gained some more facts about his family. He looked blank at first as though he had deeply repressed the information. He talked about it without emotion but then had to change the subject suddenly.

Present status in the group: Eddie is in the Rough Riders group where he is more tolerated than enjoyed. He has learned to play baseball and to compete in this game with the younger members of the group. He frequently associates with the less physically adequate children or lends himself to the dictation of a younger more aggressive child.

When building things or doing any kind of handwork he meets with great frustration. He did not learn to swim until he was nearly 11 years old. It was at this age too that he mastered throwing a ball as well as catching it.

Eddie's eating habits are still exceptionally poor. He often daydreams at the table. He is also very untidy about eating. He is frequently very dirty in his personal appearance. He usually collects a great amount of dirt around his mouth. He has trouble with saliva and the effect is that of drooling. Mucus frequently gathers in his nose and he makes little effort to take care of it.

Eddie may well sense that plans are on foot for him to leave us, but he has not indicated this directly. However, when he was telling me with great enthusiasm that he ate breakfast out with C, I said, "Eddie, you must get pretty tired of eating at Orthogenic School." This small amount of permission to criticise the School released many of his feelings about having been here so long. Previously Eddie has needed to praise the school and compare the two administrations. He even gained courage during another session to ask how come he had to stay so long. He was able to be realistic about this. In fact, this ability to face his apparent difficulties has been more notable lately. It has been a long slow process from "I don't want to hear about it" to asking "How come?"

He seems more relaxed with me since then and freer to express more of his opinions. He permits play with the soldiers and in this I have noticed the opposing army is always of the same strength almost to a man. The Americans won and on this side he always chose a "sweating" Indian which I have the feeling is somehow associated with himself. This Indian can crawl around the enemy camp and learn its secrets, he explained.

Though we have more frequently than not been discouraged with Eddie this is one of the times we feel encouraged with his efforts to try to overcome some of his handicaps. It may be too rosy a picture due to his new enthusiasm about something new happening in his life but on the whole I believe there has been some slight movement in a more healthy direction.

F. Test and Clinical Findings in Perspective

How now do these two portrayals, the one by means of the test, the other clinically drawn, look when held up for simultaneous inspection, and comparison?

The major, and overall story which both tell is that Eddie's adjustment has been a reaction. We saw it in the test (p. 234). The condition is a painful withdrawal, at its worst in the second Rorschach test. Clinically the dynamism requiring such withdrawal is only too clear in the mother's sudden shift from much show of love, and protection to abandonment (p. 273 ff.). The parents' hostility is the ever constant field of stress. What could Eddie do but withdraw? The defensive pattern is apparent in other phases of his life. He does not stand up to other boys, does not permit himself freedom with the social worker. He is not ready for his brother's picture. Here is a defensive anxiety since this is the topic around which his own severely disadvantageous position centers. Thoughts of the brother can only lead to thoughts of the parents, the deal he has received from them, and the resentment this must breed. His inability to talk about his anger (p. 278) is a clear-cut example of defensive anxiety. The cloud in the relation to the parents (p. 275) is, of course, his withdrawal from them.

The adjustment is a maladaptive one at an immature ego level; this is the Rorschach test conclusion. Sub-ego standards of behavior are disclosed throughout the clinical findings. Eddie does not care about his personal appearance. In school he can do well, but does so for short periods of time only. He masturbates openly. He makes himself more helpless than necessary, and the eating habits can be of archaic developmental level. The ego insufficiency of the Rorschach test has its full counterparts in the School's observations. His self-devaluation (p. 269) would be a result from the health history, which was never good. It would also follow from the ego-destructive attitude of the parents toward him.

The anxiety is of the bound variety. Eddie is shy, repressed, does not permit himself freedom as the psychiatrist's notes especially show. The mood is dysphoric, with passivity as the School notes show, since he is not happy, sometimes depressed, or symptomatically compliant. Yet there is also evidence, in depressed findings, of unused affective reserve which is potential for pleasurable mood reaction. This becomes especially evident in the School notes covering the final year of Eddie's residence there.

The emotional picture otherwise: rage and hostility are detected by the staff. Eddie's first test, with its many pure color responses, is a pull to undisciplined discharge. Then he goes through a period of essential immobility. See especially the psychiatrist's note, "throughout the interview he is stiff motorically" (p. 278). It is essentially the equivalent of the behavior projected in the second Rorschach test. He can be warm, reaching (p. 279), when not defensively contracting. He can engage in fantasies, daydreams and we have seen that the test makes manifest some quite regressive fantasying. The test also shows the fantasies to be more flector than extensor; and it will still require some rearching in the patient to ascertain whether he is more passive and clinging, than seeking to make himself independent of his parents. Is he more extratensive than introversive clinically? There is evidence that he can, although he does not now, daydream more than he does, and more than he reaches outwardly emotionally. If so, there is here an important discrepancy between the two personality patterns.

The progress cautiously noted by the social worker as Eddie is about to be discharged, is apparent in the third test. The test is, in fact, more optimistic than the social worker. Future events will, of course, offer the critical check. But even now there are observations that Eddie can be alert; his school work is at times better than others. He does have unused resources.

Other correlating findings: clinically, poor speech; in the Rorschach test he uses the infantile language forms. Temperamental sleep; inner unrest. Egocentric conditions imposed by the patient on others, especially on the parents; this was his primitive emotional structure and general infantile adjustment pattern, in the first two tests. Aggressive, resistive, toward the parents, hostile generally, but all unevenly; the opposition trait in the test.

The content. The "tigers" in the man's "front yard" now assume very important significance as a probable defensive phobia, binding the anxiety in his attitude toward his parents. The "crooked ... crippled" objects have relevance in view of the clinical evidence of physical disability. The hunch about the "house" and the "fires" (p. 237) receives confirmation in the insecurity in which Eddie can justifiably feel about his own home as haven of security. The many young animals of the second Rorschach test become more ominous in the light of the severe regression to which he can have recourse. The insecurity, depressive ideas, which the test projects (p. 272) is, of course, confirmed by the unhappy state which characterizes this boy.

Certain discrepancies must still be noted. The clinical group reports the patient as in contact. The test uncovers perceptual deviations, at times thinking incoherence. Both sets of data are correct. The test shows a potential for erratic perception and disturbed thinking which it is important to measure. Findings as to ego losses in the Rorschach test are never all-or-none findings. They are the latencies. Given the appropriate conditions, this is how the person may function. The clinical observers must miss this, excepting in those moments when they happen to catch the patient in upset.

The attachment by Eddie to some one person (p. 274) is a trait which Eddie's Rorschach tests do not mirror. One should expect such a trait from an introversive, rather than extratensive person (p. 271). The mouth and the alimentary symptoms are, of course, very important. I am not able to deduce these from the Rorschach test patterns excepting by reasoning and inferences too many steps removed from the test data themselves.

Of especial interest are the psychiatrist's notes reporting an episode of regression in Eddie. I refer to "he is particularly dirty and disheveled today' (p. 279). These post-date the second Rorschach test by some nine months. The very discouraging report in that test thus foreshadowed the personality development. The course in the three tests appears to parallel the personality course. In both pictures are projected an immature ego with latent resources, withdrawing maladaptively from very painful life's events. The clinical evidence accents more the neurotic conflict with immature solutions. In the Rorschach test the picture of neurosis is more screened by the immature adjustment. But the third test uncovers a promise which, in the final clinical note, Eddie shows signs of making good.

CHAPTER VII

SYNOPSIS AND COMMENT—CRITICAL
AND SPECULATIVE

Four patients and seven Rorschach test records are demonstrated on the pages preceding. The two boys spread over an age range of from $5\frac{7}{12}$ years to $13\frac{5}{12}$ years in Eddie; and from $15\frac{11}{12}$ to $18\frac{3}{12}$ years in Duncan. The two thus cover the years from young childhood through adolescence. The two men are in the prime of adulthood, the thirties.

Eddie, in his first test is more infant than child. Whether only limited brain tissue is available to him —the Jacksonian "organ of mind"—or whether he is inhibiting the functioning of tissue available to him—the Freudian hypothesis—the total output is the same. The second phase finds him worse than the first. Has he lost brain potential or is he inhibiting it more? In the third phase he is again nearer to that in the first. The second was therefore a tightening up. Eddie was sensitive and contracting. His ego was reacting. By the time of the third test he is reacting in a healthier direction. His mental potential is now more kinetic. The Jacksonian equipment must have been available. The Freudian inhibition has eased. In this interim he has been living in the benign environment of the Orthogenic School. This has been an especial set of field forces. Eddie's new total behavior is the result of operations of the new total field of stress (Lewin) or life Gestalt (Angyal) in which he is one unit. An unknown quantity in this change has been the factor of growth itself as such. To what extent does the personality in the third Rorschach test represent a normal reorganizing of Eddie's abilities? an integration as freer activity of his neopallium (Sherrington), looking toward a goal more consistent with his age. The personal dynamics which have set this course consisted of the parents' shock and their long, essentially pathological mourning over the death of their first child, also a boy. Their anxiety in reaction to that event has propelled itself into, and malformed the personality of the second child, Eddie. Such is the clinical story. The three Rorschach tests trace the course of Eddie's growth under the therapeutic conditions in which he was living. At the close he is responding with favorable outlook. What will the final product, the adult in his society, be? The question so far as our study brings this boy is an open one.

When Duncan comes for his first test, his intellectual equipment is already matured. His character is organized at the level of adolescence. But he is not a well adolescent. An abiding unhappiness is gnawing. His ego must deal with something which his ego cannot accept. The nucleus in the Duncan psychologic picture is repression. Freud's hypothesis explains him.

The effect can, however, be described by Jackson's reasoning: a functioning at less than the "highest level of evolution." So entangled is Duncan's mental living that he is less free or achieving than he needs to be—if his brain, his "organ of mind," were not impeded by his troubling emotions. To be sure, the Jacksonian logic does not provide for the emotional expression, painful or otherwise. But dissolution there is in Duncan as he starts his treatment, and as is shown by his improvement at the close. The psychotherapy has been the principal, critical force altering Duncan's personality structure. One may think of the therapy as introducing psychologic enzymes; catalysts that set his organ of mind into motion and help him to perceive facts, events and other connections which until now he has been missing. The therapy was thus one of the stresses in the Lewinian sense. Another was the . . . Institute to which he went to live as escape from his more essential field of stress. Thus again the parents set the stage and generate the mood with which this boy reacts and which so permeates him—his oppressive anxiety. As his therapy draws to a close at the same time as his second Rorschach test he is clearly a stronger person. The underlying pain is still gnawing, although he does take it better. But it is still there, with the likelihood that it will continue.

Fisher presents that personality picture not at all uncommon among adult males in our culture: beautifully sufficient in pursuit of a well-defined goal, and this in the setting of a character crippling. His success in business is the measure of his efficient use of a practical intelligence. His ego is very ably integrating his ability. He earns wordly success and thereby compensates for ravaging inferiority feelings. His sexual life is, throughout all this, rank persistence of very early personality practices out of sub-ego (by adult criteria) levels. In this behavior sector he is in dissolution, or, he has never evolved. The ego has either not solidified adult sexual values, or it is insufficient to restrain the primitive urges when some sexual object stimulates them out of repression. Perhaps Fisher is even an argument in support of Allport's functional autonomy. The sexual aberrations flourish in independence of the otherwise sufficiently knit personality structure. However, the lines of communication between the several sectors in Fisher's personality are at the time of his Rorschach test still to become clear. The psychoanalysis is in its relatively early stages. The insight into his fears and into the dynamics behind his drive is only beginning to develop.

The core of his psychologic condition consists of a deep set inferiority sense and of an anxiety which can produce moments that are insufferable. Each parent has played his appropriate role in breeding these states of mind. So far as the therapy has gone it has helped Fisher dissipate some of his self-depreciation. It has relieved some of the anxiety. It has not yet removed the effects of the old stresses, those which have formed his life Gestalt, and so malformed his character.

In Caine too, certain psychologic forces are effecting a "dissolution." Possessing an intelligence well superior to Fisher's his ego is less sufficient in its struggles against his emotions. It is engaged in a constant running battle with them. Caine makes decisions which he cannot execute. He sets goals from which he is turned aside. Thus a checkered behavior picture, as of one operating unevenly and at once, at more than one of Jackson's levels of evolution.What the repressed needs that are obtruding, the psychoanalyst has been helping Caine to see. It is her help here that eases the stresses of the conflict and so permits a more sufficient functioning by his ego with the attendant success obtained by Caine in his profession. The stress sources are again and only too clearly the parents. The mother is the leading "dramatis personae." A sister is prominent in the cast. The anxiety at the close of the drama is little relieved.

The extent to which the two sets of findings, clinical and test, parallel each other, has been discussed for each patient, (pp. 145, 188, 217, 282). The validations are, therefore, whole person for whole person. This is one task which I set for myself in this volume. It is as I stated at the outset, the only concept of personality that interests me, behavior *in toto*. But questions as to the validity of the individual Rorschach test assumptions are currently being raised. Numerous experiments are being carried on to test them out. This is, of course, essential. It can only work to the test's weal and make it a more soundly based instrument. But I have my criticisms of the experimental temper with which so much of the investigating is being carried out.

One is the matter of constancy of test technic. It is a first principle in experimental method, learned in the earlier weeks of elementary science courses, that if results are to be compared they must have been obtained by technic that duplicate one another. In Rorschach test procedures this first principle is being honored, so far as I can see, entirely in the breach. There is little constancy in administering. The associations obtained in deviating ways are processed and scored by technics that vary not only among the "schools," but also from one experimenter to the other. The original technic as published by Rorschach in the *Psychodiagnostik*, that to which the Swiss refer as the classical procedure is still generally followed in Europe. In the United States only a very few do so: Oberholzer, of course, and Levy, principally. My own procedure has departed in some features from the "classical." It does follow Rorschach's in its fundamental structure and the major details. Klopfer's alterations have been the most extensive. Hertz, Piotrowski and Rapaport have altered this alteration. Yet reports of experiments are published using one or the other of these differing methods. From such findings the investigator draws conclusions purporting to refute or support Rorschach's hypotheses. I realize that I am here speaking polemically. It is an impatience which should be understandable as reaction to a practice by psychologists who have traditionally accented and prided themselves on scientific method as American psychologists have. Here then is one basic fault in a number of investigations testing out the test.

Secondly is the logic underlying statistical method whereby the test variables are being tried out. They just are not appropriate to the problem which the Rorschach test sets up. They were devised in the first instance to isolate and measure separate behavior variables. How does any item, x, distribute in a given population irrespective for the moment of the incidence of the other items? The Rorschach test asks as its directive questions: how do the many observed behavior items distribute and recombine within any one individual? The procedure must differ to meet this problem. This is the more significant problem for a science of personality. Any one person acts always not as a splintering of behavior items in a population but as a structuring of behaviors within him as one unit. The method of inspecting the single variable has rendered great service in the study of personality and will continue to do so. It fails to answer the essential question, of what psychologic operation is the individual whole personality constituted?

The method that has so far attempted to cope with this task is Stephenson's Q technic. It does this while using the usual statistical procedures, factor analysis; analysis of variance; and the related ones. I am applying the Q technic currently in two researches on schizophrenia being conducted under the National Institute of Mental Health Grants.[1] Reports of these are now in preparation.

The core of the whole personality logic is that no personality variable has any meaning in isolation from others. The patients in this volume and their Rorschach tests so demonstrate this. Interpretation of any one test finding is always with reference to others and to the personality as a whole. The inter-relations and the behavior of the unit tell the story. It is the essence of the human personality. Overt behavior, the ego facing the outer world, has meaning only with reference to deeper motivation, the ego in reaction to its always emotion-toned values, whether these are conscious or unconscious. To return to my argument of pp. 11 ff. and 14 ff. the whole human cortex is a complex of many activities. The final product of any one personality consists of these inter-reactions and the coordinating of them toward that person's goal. Thus many behavior variables are simultaneously contributing. A scientific logic and method focusing on only one operation, or even a cluster of operations, is not applicable.

---

[1] At the Institute for Psychosomatic and Psychiatric Research and Training in Michael Reese Hospital, Chicago.

Perception is an operation of two universes, the perceiver and the object perceived. When two such universes intersect there is a percept. This is the theory of perception with which I have been using the Rorschach test. I think it is applicable to all perception. Experiments in perception which focus on stimulus only are disregarding one of two universes that go into the percept.

But the perceiver in whom we are interested, a human being, is constituted not only of intellectual reactions. He is also a great reservoir of emotions.

Now in their raw structure the emotions are a non-ego factor. This brings us to still another proposition relative to personality generally, and one which I see in the workings of the Rorschach test. It relates to the role of the emotions in knowing. Intellectual knowledge alone is not adequate as adaptive instrument. That three dimensional comprehension we call insight cannot be obtained by a simple intellectual perceiving of various facts or grasp of the relations between any number of them. Emotional experience is essential to knowing. It is an ingredient *sine qua non* in understanding in that broader sense which is wisdom. It is a critical medium for the knowledge which the person must have and which he must integrate if he is to adapt most efficiently to his total situation. The schizophrenic for example lacks such emotional wisdom.

Thus again it requires a personality test which will cut across both kinds of mental operations and will pattern out their interactings. Whether it is the Rorschach or any other test, this is the assignment. The Rorschach test does now undertake the job and claims a measure of success. I should add that I never look on any Rorschach test interpretation as other than hypothesis. The findings are never an absolute prediction. They are a statement as to a personality structure and the implicit latencies. The interpretation is a hypothesis to the effect that given certain conditions, the patient will manifest such and such behavior. Given a certain kind and degree of outside stress, strain on the ego, and this type of person may break down into psychosis. Another, under the same strain, will not. Eddie, but for the good fortune and benign and well directed psychologic climate, would have settled into schizophrenia. Duncan as we know him could not have so done. The difference is in the quality of the two boys' egos.

Here caution must be stated concerning the test's weaknesses and present limitations. A measure of success is all that I claim for it above. This is to say also that we encounter in using it a measure of failure. More rarely, but in instances, actual error, an inaccurate diagnostic description. The weaknesses result from incomplete objectivity in identifying the scoring categories. The amount of objectivity varies for the several categories. In D, Dd, P, Z, the statistical basis is as adequate as for most if not all the tools in psychometric science. The W factor is identifiable *a priori*.

Similarly, content is either animal or not animal, human or not human. Whether it is anatomy or should be classified as part human (Hd) is a matter of definition, and easily settled. The white space has provided some difficulties, now ironed out. A statistical rule is available for measuring distribution of W, D and Dd, (Ap). In respect to Seq we still have recourse to inspection, although the error here is relatively light. It is in the variables in the middle column of the summary that room for subjectivity is greatest. This can be more critical because in this column are set the scoring categories most interpreted as representing emotional operations; M and its blends; C and its nuances and blends; Y, V, T and their nuances and blends.

It includes also something that is to me very important, F+, F− judgments. Now, operational definitions can be formulated for each of these. Criteria for F+, F− can be set up. Yet I am not deceiving myself that these we now have meet the needs for frames of reference. They do provide a working tool. The errors in personality description that are still found I assume to result from errors in recognizing the scoring categories. This in turn is due to the crudity of our methods for recognizing them. Which is to say that the experiments reporting failures of Rorschach test can only mean at present that the experiment's technic in identifying scoring categories has been faulty. My present position is that pure C responses correctly so scored really mean undisciplined emotional reaction. An M response correctly so labeled indicates some wish experience more or less vivid and personal. So on for the other variables.

The test is then not now any complete instrument calibrated to measure the human personality either in its larger structure or in its fine nuances. But these are weaknesses which can be corrected. To do so requires strictly controlled scientific effort. More and more sharp frames of reference by which to identify all the at present more subjectively judged categories (C, M, Y, V, T) are necessary. The obligation for developing this rests as much on Rorschach test investigators as it does on the laboratory workers.

The test's limitations are principally two. Of these one is inherent in the test itself. That is, its present technic is not set up to overcome this limitation. I refer to the inability to identify specifically the symptoms in which the structure as a whole, the person's conflict expresses itself. For example, we can say that the neurosis is following a psychosomatic course. We cannot except very rarely say from the test which body organ is involved. The findings tell with assurance that a patient will attack his environment or that he has uncontrollable impulses to do so, that these are in reaction to painful psychologic experiences. They do not disclose whether the attack will issue as a delinquency involving money matters, a sexual assault, or a destructive attack on property or person. The reaction pattern may be one of those inflexible ones which in political behavior issues as adhesion to a fixed blueprint. It still is not known whether the bell-wether which this citizen is following herds him to one or the other of the orthodoxies that happen to have currency at the moment. To be sure even with regard to some specific behavior certain accurate inferences can be made from structure in a small per cent of patients. But when confirming content is lacking the inferences are that much less safe; many test protocols just do not include the necessary content. This is a limitation which research cannot correct. To the extent that the patient does not communicate we cannot know what ails him. The test can only use the data which it extracts.

The other limitation is one which is subject to correction by research. This is our understanding of significances of relations between test variables, the meaning of such relations in terms of whole personality behavior, and of the psychologic equilibria that issue as the different clinical pictures. We know the main structural outline in the test for the several nosological groups. One inference from the test patterns is that the descriptions can be understood as belonging on a continuum in terms of quantitative relations between the major test or corresponding psychologic operations. The balance of processes in one disease as compared with others shifts to a point such that a difference in degree becomes a difference in kind. This is one hypothesis which would fit the balances being obtained in the test. Whether the several varieties within the two broad groupings, neuroses and psychoses, each represents a quantitative balance differing from that of the others, is another question to be explored. Can we establish a series of numerically stated relations dependably corresponding to a conversion hysteria and differentiating it from a psychosomatic neurosis? Similarly, can we distinguish some character disorders from latent schizophrenia? the relative contribution of an affective structure to a personality disruption: is the breakdown on a hypomanic basis? or a schizophrenia?

Research in the test will, however, alone never arm any one investigator to answer these questions. I will put it this way: a major limitation on the test is set by the limited equipment, in their knowledge of personality and psychopathology particularly, by persons using the test. No instrument is better than the man or woman applying it. The significance of Rorschach test findings will be understood to the extent that the examiner understands personality. This is a function of his (a) experience; and (b) ability to learn. This rule holds not only for the Rorschach, but for all tests, including psychometrics in the usual sense of that term.

An illustrative incident comes to mind. I recall watching Tredgold doing a psychologic test in the University College Hospital in London in 1934. The patient was a male of 17 of about medium degree of mental deficiency.

Tredgold was using some very simple performance test: the Mare and Foal, among others. But what he obtained from that dull boy, in terms of significant data, went far beyond the significance in the strictly numerical findings. The reason clearly was Tredgold, and what he knew about mental deficiency.

As for the Rorschach test, it is still the instrument whereby its user obtains the data which his understanding translates into clinical behavior data. An accurate interpretation of a Rorschach test protocol is an operation of two universes: the protocol and the interpreter. Which is to say that this test, or any test, cannot be used by however good a clinician "intuitively." Its working principles must be understood and applied.

The question of the "blind" use of the test deserves a word of comment. When the psychologist is carrying on research, no other method is permissible. Findings must be derived strictly from test data and from significances in their inter-relations. In practical clinical use, the "blind" technic can be carried to limits which defeat the sole purpose of asking for the test: illuminating the clinical condition. I still prefer to work "blind" as I evaluate each record. But I find I can be more helpful to the psychiatrists or other therapists by applying my findings to the clinical problem. I prefer, therefore, to have available a note stating something of the problem. I do not read it until after I have evaluated the record and have drawn my conclusions from the test data alone.

The test and treatment. In appraising treatability, test results need to be inspected from the following three principal points of reference: (a) What, in the given patient, are his personality resources and reserves? (b) What in the patient are his ego's integrative and directive sufficiencies? (c) How flexible and resilient is his personality?

In answer to the first question, the focus is first on the C and the M responses. Assuming other findings are not unfavorable the patient with both M and C is better than one without either. If the therapist can choose a patient with either M or C, with one but not with the other, the patient with C alone will be more responsive than one with M alone. The choice is that between the extratensive and the introversive personality. The latter is habitually withdrawn. He can even evade the therapist and his own ego when the going gets too rough, i.e., when he can not endure the painful news about himself which the therapy is bringing to light. But if the patient responds with C alone, or overwhelmingly, it is not to be all pure C or even much pure C with CF−. His reactions are in this instance too primitive and seeking gratification. They can be handled only by an ego much firmer than is likely to be possessed by a person who has need for psychologic therapy.

Should the patient produce M alone he is not by that fact shut off from treatment. He will be more difficult. But he can be treated depending on the quality of the M, both in structure and in content, and on the stamina of the personality as a whole. For the logic behind the psychologic course, the reader can do no better than to read Rorschach's exposition of the *Erlebnistypus*.[2]

The principle of the gap between maxima and optima must always be kept in mind. This holds not only for the experience balance but also for all the test factors. The maximum finding is never the optimum. Or, let us say "hardly ever." A person with a very expanded EB, say a superior adult with an EB of 16/16, or one of average intelligence with 7/7, is too responsive to inner world. He is too much at the mercy of his emotions.

Aside from the quantity, important qualitative differentiations need to be made in regard to the M and to the C associations. The range of qualities will be found described in Chapter II. It need hardly be added that the better the quality of the M and C responses, the better treatable material is the patient.

The treatment resources emerge in R, content, F+, Ap, Seq, W-Z, P, A. This is the approximate order of their usefulness in indicating treatment assets. What the maxima: and what the optima, will be deduced from the exposition in Chapter II A and Chapter I B. A neat illustration of the differential between maxima and optima is provided by R. The too productive may be as mentally ill in degree as the underproductive. Content is a more important index to the person's differential interests, his achievement potential (Chapter II M), and so to his adaptive flexibility. The asset value of W-Z as personality reserve or their expression of a character deficiency is indicated in Chapter II B. Similarly, A percepts and the P responses. In all these, the maxima are never the optima. Parenthetically it is to be noted that neither does the minimum correspond with the optimum.

The optimum varies according to two sets of conditions. One is the standard set by the patient's peers, his age group and the social and economic levels into which fortune and he himself have channelized him. This ranking in his group can readily be found by the statistics that are available for the test variables. The other is the amount of any one trait relative to the others in that individual. It is necessary to measure each person against himself. An R of 40 is low in a professionally trained person; it is high in an average adult habituated to a modest occupation. The implication for treatment from the same R of 40 will be different in the two patients. Similarly from an F+ per cent of 85; W, 10; Z, 20; and the others. Again it is a question of balance. In the balances, and what is more significant, the imbalances which may be indicated are implicit to diagnostic description, and from these in turn, the kind and amount of therapy.

---

[2] RORSCHACH, H., *op. cit.*, pp. 78–127.

It is in answer to the second questions concerning treatment outlook
that F+ and Seq are especially useful. F+ is chief manifestation of the ego
as critic and as sufficient to maintain that control which is needful in the
individual if he is to keep to a directed life course. The full F+ per cent is
really a function of three variables: the person's growth stage; his emotional
stresses; and the ability to master those stresses. The reasoning concerning
F+ will be found in Chapter I B, also at various points in Chapter II;
that concerning Seq is in Chapter II B and C. It must be clear that F+
per cent is very important in judging treatability. This, and sequence. An
important qualification here is that the insufficiency disclosed in an F+
per cent too low for the individual when measured against his own personality structure is not necessarily an indication that the patient will not
respond to therapy. This, provided the break is not below the statistical
range for his peers, so low as to indicate a break with reality. Barring such,
a very disturbed personality may actually be in a return to better mental
health. More of this in a moment.

The third question is answered by the evidence as to the defenses. Two
sets of data need to be interpreted. One is in the intellectual sphere and
the other in the inner living. The Ap here becomes of especial importance.
How fixedly does the individual adhere to one reaction mode? The more
onesided the approach the less responsive is the patient to change, the
less he can learn the new. This unfavorable treatment outlook will be
accentuated when there are found also the other signs of maximum defense
efforts (Chapter II C). The inner resilience is principally projected in the
M and C factors (above pp. 49 ff., 42 ff.). For the EB as such, the rule is that
the more coarctated the EB the more difficult the treatment, if it can be
done at all. A 0/0 EB means that the person's inner resources, his ability
to respond to the therapist, is meager or lacking. He cannot feel with others
whether through overt emotional reaching (C) or through imaginative living
and understanding (M). His inner life is cold, whether by reason of original defect, or as an acquired reaction pattern. Treatment potential is limited or nil.

Certain test behaviors, only recently identified, still require study for
their values in treatability. They are the affective ratio (p. 46 ff.), the
lambda index (pp. 31, 44), and the fluctuation phenomena (p. 25 ff.). The
treatment hunches concerning these are noted in the pages referred to. I
look on the lambda index and small fluctuation as adding to the evidence
for a brittle structure. These persons do not change.

The painful emotion indicators can be important signs of the patient's
readiness for treatment. That is, they are, when found, favorable findings.
The clinical logic for this is clear from consideration of color shock. This
tells that the patient is vulnerable to emotion toned events. He reacts.
In this he differentiates from the person who does not react; from the

torpid, the indifferent, the mentally deficient, the organic in whom deterioration has gone far. The empirical side of the evidence is that it is the characteristically neurotic who suffers color shock. The neurotic is in conflict. His ego is staying in the fight. It is when the ego has given up, that the condition is the more malignant one.

The reasoning is parallel with regard to anxiety shock. That tells of guilt. This is further evidence of a consciousness of standards and of a differential between behavior and standards, assuming again that the reactions do not go to the maxima, whether in color shock or anxiety shock; that the ego is not overwhelmed by the sudden flood of feeling, "What have I done!" or "What am I thinking of doing!" On the same grounds, test evidence of depression, provided it does not go to an invalidizing degree, favors treatment effort. This holds especially for reactive depressions.

When test findings indicate schizophrenia they can still contribute information as to assets which are to be exploited. Is there latent any affectivity which can be fanned? Ego structure which can be built up? Guilt moments which can be needled further? The most ticklish problems in this connection are those presented by adolescents. Many tests obtained in this age period show the disruptive patterns that look like schizophrenia. Discount for the growth phase must be made. The differential as between schizophrenia and a less malignant condition is likely to be available less in the structure than in the individual signs of regression. $M-$, autistic, and regressive; $F-$, peculiar and perplexing; highly unique content. The structure can be deceptively disorganized. Finding of color shock is a critical sign for a more benign condition. Its absence is not unquestionable proof of malignancy. The dysfunctions may be so great as to obscure shock.

The worst disruptions, the sickest Rorschach test records, but which still dictate keeping fingers crossed, are found in my experience in about the 16 to 22 year range. When the patient is older the indications in the test for schizophrenia is likely to mean schizophrenia. Similarly at the younger ages the test findings of schizophrenia are ominous. This is true also for the earlier years. I am referring to findings of a kind which in an adult would be construed as indicating schizophrenia. That is, as Rorschach test findings go, the manifestations of schizophrenia are constant whether in children or adults. The purported resemblance between normal childhood thinking, and that of adult schizophrenia is not borne out by the test findings in the two groups. A healthy and even very young child will respond with associations and a pattern that are different from those of adults or even of older healthy children. But they are not like those in schizophrenics, children or adults.

In conclusion, I refer back to the four patients whose test records constitute the body of this volume. It will not have escaped the student that they resemble one another in the following respects. One, anxiety is the destructive dynamism in all. Two, the condition producing the anxiety, malforming or crippling the personalities, are in the four instances the parents. In three of these four the mother is the critical person. In the fourth she plays a role not much less important than does the father.

Now the fact is that so far as the psychologic structures in these patients is concerned, they were a random selection. The determining factors in my picking these from the number that were available to me were two: (a) they were to exemplify an overall sampling of Rorschach test data and (b) very full clinical material was to be available. It was not until the book was well under way that the fact of the patients being all males struck me. I had originally planned an even number from both sexes. Considerations of economy prevented my increasing the present number. But the most striking fact was that which stood out with completing the interpretations. The consistency in all four of the major personality force was anxiety; and of the field of stresses behind that, i.e., the life conditions set up for each patient by his parents.

I am assuming that these four persons offer a representative sampling of the more severe stress states lived by persons in our culture. Also, that in varying degree these tensions are approximated by those of the population at large in our times. The result is to add to the mounting evidence—it is the subject of much current publication—as to the determining fact which anxiety is, in our time. The statistics for mental disease to be sure accent schizophrenia as taking more hospital beds than do so many other diseases. But schizophrenia is an end result. It is a way out. Anxiety is the painful stress from which these persons have sought relief. This makes schizophrenia a symptom, not the disease. It follows, therefore, that if a goodly portion of the beds now being filled by schizophrenics are to be emptied, the world scene will have first to be relieved of anxiety. This is the problem with first priority in the interest of a more general national health. Whether the world's statesmen and the people who are maintaining them in political power can see the relations between the conditions they are fashioning and the new anxieties that result, the destructive defenses against these, and so on, in an ever vicious downward spiral, only a later historian will tell.

BIBLIOGRAPHY

ALLPORT, G. W.: Personality: a psychological interpretation. New York: Holt, 1937.

ANGYAL, A.: Foundations for a science of personality. New York: Commonwealth Fund, 1941.

BECK, S. J.: Error, symbol, and method in the Rorschach test. J. Abnormal & Social Psychol. **37**: 83–103, 1942.

———: Rorschach's test. Vol. II. A variety of personality pictures. New York: Grune & Stratton, 1945.

———: Rorschach F plus and the ego in treatment. Am. J. Orthopsychiat. **18**: 395–401, 1948.

———, Rabin, A. I., Thiessen, W. G., Molish, H. B. and Thetford, W. N.: The normal personality as projected in the Rorschach test. J. Psychol. **30**: 241–298, 1950.

BEHRMAN, S. N.: Profiles. The days of Duveen. New Yorker. **27**: 36 ff. in No. 36, Oct. 20, 1951.

BLEULER, E. P.: Textbook of psychiatry. Transl. by Brill, A. A., New York: Dover, 1951.

BOHM, E.: Der Rorschach-Test und seine Weiterentwicklung. Rorschachiana I, Huber, 1945, pp. 115–136.

CAMPBELL, C. M.: Human personality and the environment. New York: Macmillan, 1934.

FENICHEL, O.: The psychoanalytic theory of neurosis. New York: Norton, 1945.

FRANK, L. K.: Projective methods. Springfield (Ill.) Thomas, 1948.

FREUD, A.: The ego and the mechanisms of defense. Transl. by Baines, C. New York: International Universities Press, 1946.

FREUD, S.: Collected papers. Transl. by Riviere, J. Vol. III, pp. 149–289. London: Hogarth, 1934.

FROMM, E. O. AND ELONEN, A. S.: The use of projective techniques in the study of a case of female homosexuality. J. Proj. Techniques. **15**: 185–230, 1951.

FÜRRER, A.: Über die Bedeutung der "B" in Rorschachschen Versuch. Imago **11**: 362–365, 1925.

GRINKER, R. R.: A comparison of psychological "repression" and neurological "inhibition." J. Nerv. & Ment. Dis. **89**: 765–781, 1939.

HERTZ, M. R.: Current problems in Rorschach theory and technique. J. Proj. Techniques. **15**: 307–338, 1951.

IRWIN, F. W.: Motivation. In: Theoretical foundations of psychology. Edited by H. Helson. New York: Van Nostrand, 1951. Chapter 5, pp. 200–253.

JACKSON, H.: Selected writings. London: Hodder, 1932.

KLOPFER, B. AND KELLEY, D. M.: The Rorschach technique. New York: World Book Co., 1942.

LEWIN, K.: Field theory in social science. Selected theoretical papers. Edited by Dorwin Cartwright. New York: Harper, 1951.

LINDER, R. M.: The content analysis of the Rorschach protocol. In: Projective psychology. Clinical approaches to the total personality. Edited by Abt, L. E. and Bellak, L., New York: Knopf, 1950, pp. 75–90.

McCLELLAND, D. C.: Personality. New York: William Sloane Associates, 1951.

MOLISH, H. B.: The popular response in Rorschach records of normals, neurotics and schizophrenics. Am. J. Orthopsychiat. **21**: 523–531, 1951.

——, MOLISH, E. E., AND THOMAS, C. B.: A Rorschach study of a group of medical students. Psychiat. Quarterly. **24**: 744–774, 1950.

MURPHY, G.: Personality. A biosocial approach to origins and structure. New York: Harper, 1947.

MURRAY, H. A., et al.: Explorations in personality. New York and London: Oxford, 1938.

OBERHOLZER, E. in DuBois, C.: The people of Alor. Minneapolis: Univ. Minnesota Press, 1944, Chap. 22, pp. 588–640.

RORSCHACH, H.: Psychodiagnostik: Methodik und Ergebnisse eines wahrnehmungsdiagnostischen Experiments (ed. 2). Bern and Berlin: Huber, 1932. Transl. by Lemkau, P. and Kronenberg, B. New York: Grune & Stratton (distr.), 1942.

——, AND OBERHOLZER, E.: Zur. Auswertung des Formdeutversuchs. Ztschr. f. d. ges. Neurol. u. Psychiat. **82**: 240–274, 1923. Transl., J. Nerv. & Ment. Dis. **60**: 225–248, 359–379, 1924; in Rorschach, H.: Psychodiagnostik, pp. 193–227 (transl., pp. 184–216).

SHERRINGTON, C. S.: Brain. Encyclopedia Britannica. Chicago: University of Chicago, 1946. **4**: 1–8.

SIIPOLA, E., KUHNS, F. AND TAYLOR, V.: Measurement of the individual's reactions to color in ink blots. J. Personality. **30**: 153–171, 1950.

THETFORD, W. N., MOLISH, H. B. AND BECK, S. J.: Developmental aspects of personality structure in normal children. J. Proj. Techniques. **15**: 58–78, 1951.

TITCHENER, E. B.: A text-book of psychology. New York: Macmillan, 1924.

WITTENBORN, J. R.: Level of mental health as a factor in the implications of Rorschach scores. J. Consult. Psychol. **14**: 469–472, 1950.

ZUBIN, J. and YOUNG, K. M.: Manual of projective and cognate techniques. Madison: College Typing Co., 1948.

INDEX

A. Authors and Subjects

Abt, L. E. (ed), 67
Adolescents, 26, 53, 81, 295
Aggression, 35, 53, 65
Allport, G. W., 1, 2, 8, 286
Angyal, A., 1, 9, 11, 12, 285
Attention, 22, 27, 28, 90, 91

Beck, S. J., 12, 16, 69, 105, 110, 160
Behrman, S. N., 54
Bellak, L. (ed), 67
Berenson, B., 54
Bleuler, E. P., 7, 23, 28, 66, 158, 228
Blocking, 25, 37
Bohm, E., 199

Campbell, C. M., 64 f., 90
Cartwright, D., 10
Character armor, 29 f.
Children, 26 f., 47, 60, 119, 224, 237, 261, 295
Confabulation, 23

De-animating, 41
Delusions, 63
Depersonalizing, 41
Depression, 5 f., 24, 26, 29, 32, 40, 46, 48, 51 f., 58 f., 295
Displacing, 35 f., 37, 41, 53
Du Bois, C., 75

Ego, 15, 58 f., 63, 66, 158, 271 294 f.
Elonen, A. S., 67

Fenichel, O., 9, 19, 29, 30, 32, 39, 40, 53, 86, 169, 210, 235
Frank, L. K., 53
Freud, A., 29, 85
Freud, S., 5, 8, 9, 12, 285
Fromm, E. O., 67
Fürrer, A., 119

Grinker, R. R., 8 f.

Hallucinations, 63
Hertz, M. R., 50, 287

Homosexuality, 25, 51, 67 f., 84, 95
Hypomanic, 7, 32, 45 f.
Hysteria, 28, 39, 41, 47, 59, 65, 188

Intelligence, 23 f., 28, 62
Interpretation, concept of, 13, 94, 284
Introversion, 50, 60
Irwin, F. W., 3
Isolation defense, 36, 54, 63

Jackson, H., 3, 7 f., 12, 158, 285 f.
James, W., 14

Kamman, G. R., 27
Kelley, D. M., 22
Klopfer, B., 22, 156, 174, 270, 287
Kuhns, F., 43

Levy, D. M., 55, 287
Lewin, K., 4, 9 f., 285, 286
Lindner, R. M., 67

Mental deficiency, 24 f., 33, 295
McClelland, D. C., 3, 9
Molish, E. E., 50
Molish, H. B., 22, 50, 110, 160, 163
Mood, 45, 59, 75
Murphy, G., 3
Murray, H. A., 12, 64, 268

Oberholzer, E., 75, 119, 170 f., 200, 207, 287
Obsessive neurotic, 5, 22, 27, 30 f., 32, 36, 39 f., 58 f., 61, 164, 207

Paranoid pattern, 22, 34 f., 37, 51, 61, 63, 67
Passivity, 47 f., 59, 61
Piotrowski, Z. A., 287
Postponement, 37
Projection, 33 f., 50
Psychosomatic illness, 39, 41, 59, 65

Rabin, A. I., 160
Rapaport, D., 287

B. RORSCHACH TEST TOPICS

Date Due

9-7-79			
8-25-83			
	PRINTED IN U. S. A.		